W9-BRS-077

the
FRAZZLED
FEMALE

A DEVOTIONAL JOURNAL

ISBN: 978-0-8054-4743-9
B&H Publishing Group
Nashville, Tennessee
www.BHPublishingGroup.com

Dewey Decimal Classification: 248.843
Women \ Christian Life \ Stress (Psychology)

Printed in Malaysia

2 3 4 5   14 13 12 11

the
A DEVOTIONAL JOURNAL
FRAZZLED FEMALE

30 DAYS TO FINDING GOD'S PEACE
IN YOUR DAILY CHAOS

cindi wood

B&H
PUBLISHING GROUP
NASHVILLE, TENNESSEE

A DEDICATION TO . . .

The Frazzled Female Prayer Warriors, twenty-five amazing women who consistently lay this ministry before the Throne.

You girls are not only my sisters and friends, but valiant soldiers who have marched alongside me to and from every event and through every mile of travel. From your knees, you've paved the way through prayer for me to share Jesus on planes, in hotel lobbies, and restaurant booths. Together, we've embraced the goal of our ministry: bringing people to Christ!

You've also prayed unwaveringly for frazzled female study groups throughout the country—and beyond. Your prayers have sustained me as I connect with stressed-out women, helping them realize the peace, joy, and victory available through a personal relationship with Jesus Christ.

As I think of the many times I've called and emailed you requesting prayers for spiritual and physical stamina, I'm nearly overcome with emotion picturing you tossing me to Jesus—over and over and over again.

May our Frazzled Female Devotional Journal be a divine tool, bringing hope and encouragement to our stressed-out sisters. And may they discover new purpose for living, as Jesus becomes the joy of their strength!

Keep comfortable on your knees—lots more praying to do!

More than ever, Cindi

"We are confident of all this because of our
great trust in God through Christ."
(2 Corinthians 3:4 NLT)

TABLE OF CONTENTS

Introduction 1

WEEK ONE: Mary Chose the One Thing Needed, So Will I 5
    Day 1: He Loves Me 9
    Day 2: The Journey of Intimacy 14
    Day 3: Hearing When God Speaks 21
    Day 4: My Heart's Longing 28
    Day 5: Something More 36

WEEK TWO: A Less Than Positive Attitude 45
    Day 6: A Positive Beginning 48
    Day 7: You Become What You Think 54
    Day 8: The Power of God 61
    Day 9: The Gift of His Power 67
    Day 10: Being Positive in Negative Circumstances 74

WEEK THREE: I Don't Have Enough Time! 85
    Day 11: God Is in Control 87
    Day 12: More 93
    Day 13: The Core of the Problem 99
    Day 14: Blessed by God 106
    Day 15: Making God Priority 111

WEEK FOUR: People Are Getting on My Nerves!......................119

Day 16: Living Peacefully..121

Day 17: It Depends on Me!..127

Day 18: This Is My Part...132

Day 19: Loving Others...138

Day 20: When I'm Angry..144

WEEK FIVE: Feeling Frazzled.......................................153

Day 21: My House..156

Day 22: Seeking God's Guidance....................................163

Day 23: The Stress of Sin...170

Day 24: My Identity..177

Day 25: Yoked with Jesus..184

WEEK SIX: Near to the Heart of God..........................191

Day 26: The Faith Test..194

Day 27: More Than a Case of the Blues.........................201

Day 28: Help Is Available..207

Day 29: Jesus Is Praying for You.....................................214

Day 30: The Frazzled Female Complete.........................221

How to Become a Christian...228

Notes...230

 # INTRODUCTION

Frazzled Female (fra-zeld fee-male) n
1: a woman of the twenty-first century who is stressed, frayed, challenged, frenetic . . . and totally dependent on God to keep all the segments of her life together;
2: YOU?

I remember clearly when I first accepted the fact that I had joined the ranks of women who classified themselves as "frazzled." They didn't call it that, of course, but they wore the look, walked the walk, and talked the talk.

I saw no one sporting "Frazzled" tees or wearing "Frazzled" designer jeans, but yet most women I knew had the invisible insignia FRAZZLED embossed on their foreheads.

You *do* know what I mean, don't you?

Here's what *frazzled* looks like, sounds like, and walks like.

THE LOOK

- A "wannabe" fresh radiant face that can't quite make it
- A not-so-put-together outfit that used to be in style

- Signs of wear and tear on a body that was once in pretty good shape
- Traces of twitching caused by an overloaded central nervous system

THE SOUND

- Less than positive words reflecting a "what-the-heck" attitude
- Strange noises caused by gastric juices jumping around in the stomach area
- A tone of voice that more often reflects misery, disgust, and "I've had all I can take" instead of joy

THE WALK

- A heavy gait giving one the appearance of carrying an oversized dirty laundry bag as opposed to a light, springy step
- A body that doesn't move like it used to, after too many days of "I don't have time to exercise"
- Hunched shoulders from carrying too many burdens for too many people

Whether married or divorced, single, with kids or without, working on the home front or out in the work world (or both), you may qualify for membership in the Frazzled Female Club!

The Frazzled Female Ministry is a ministry reaching out to all females who long for more peace and sanity in daily living. Women gathering for luncheons, seminars, or weekend retreats all share the same goal: seeking a life that's less stressful and more fulfilling every day, not just occasionally. It's my joy to share with women from all walks of life how to begin and then continue to live a victorious life—one that is not free from stress but one that is lived with the confidence, power, and peace that an intimate relationship with Jesus Christ offers!

One thing's for sure: living life on the twenty-first century fast track is not easy. But, girls, there's hope. *And hope's name is Jesus Christ!*

I'm excited for you to work your way through *The Frazzled Female Devotional Journal.* After reading a brief chapter for each day, you'll find a Scripture verse to meditate on, a simple prayer to pray, and then some practical ideas for placing all the cares of your day before the Lord—in very deliberate, very liberating ways. There's also a specific area for you to turn over the details of your day to the Lord. This will help you recognize His Lordship throughout each busy day.

In addition, you'll find pages at the end of each section to record how the Lord has spoken to you throughout that week. In this daily love relationship with Jesus, you will discover peace and joy, not to mention sanity. And this peace and joy will begin to affect the way you walk, the way you talk, and the way you look.

Read on, sister, and dare to imagine that a frazzled life can also be a joyful and saner one than you've ever imagined. That's the promise and assurance that a life lived day in and day out with Jesus offers.

WEEK ONE

Mary Chose the One Thing Needed, So Will I

Seek first the kingdom of God and His righteousness,
and all these things will be provided for you.
Matthew 6:33

Do I sleep for five more minutes? What am I going to fix for supper tonight? Do I really need to stay for that meeting after work? So . . . do I exercise now or put it off until tomorrow?

Oh my, so many choices! Have you ever considered how many choices you make in any given day? Whether it's choosing your attitude or your clothing, those choices you make can critically impact your day (and the day of those around you)! The choices you make will determine how your day goes.

I remember as a young mother when I chose to put my two-year-old son Brandon on a leash at the shopping mall. I ditched my pride along with my concern about what others might think of me strapping a leash to my son as if he were an animal. And I can tell you, for me, securing that leash was a good choice, a sound choice, and a choice that brought freedom for me to enjoy being out with my little guy and not having to spend all that time racing around after him. (Besides, if I had not made that choice, we would have never left the house!)

Every day as a busy woman you make countless choices, choices that have to do with everything from household duties to self-improvement to professional development. So it's truly important that you consider your options carefully.

No matter how many choices I make during any given day, I have discovered that the most important one for me and the one that has the greatest impact on how my day goes is to *choose* to spend time with Jesus at the beginning of my day.

Now most of the time that means getting up earlier than I would if I just hopped out of bed and jumped on my to-do list. But I've realized that my day is not half as good (or productive) if I don't have that quiet time with Jesus. Without choosing to be with Him first, before I tackle anything else, I'm pretty agitated, strung out, and soon run out of energy. So the most important choice I make every day, the choice that determines the flow of the rest of my day, is to be with Jesus right when I wake up and before I do anything else.

Now, before you think I'm endowed with some sort of special equipment that enables me to tune into Jesus when my eyes pop open in the morning, let me rush to tell you that I haven't always been this way. Choosing Him first has not always been my practice. Making this choice is a process, just like choosing to exercise or eat right or invest money into a savings account. You choose to spend time with Him one day at a time until that choice becomes your lifestyle.

One of the things I've done that has helped transition my daily choice into a lifestyle was to create a rendezvous place for my quiet time with God. There's a special place each morning where I sit with Him, reading some Scripture and talking to Him. "My spot" is at my kitchen bar. Before I go to bed, I create an inviting place to spend time with Him the following morning. Sometimes I place a candle or a small lamp close by, as well as my Bible and notepad to record my thoughts. When I walk into my kitchen the following morning, I just ease into enjoying this time with Jesus. Other women have shared with me that they enjoy their devotional time in a corner of a guest bedroom, or a deck in warm weather, or even a section of a big closet.

There's nothing magical about having a special location. It's just a comfortable spot you set aside for your time with Him.

You see, the practice of creating a warm and inviting place to meet Jesus is to help you move forward into choosing a lifestyle that gets you rollin' with Him as soon as your eyes open! And when you make it a practice to spend time with Him each morning, you will find that gradually your days begin to be filled with more peace and joy and less frustration and irritation.

You'll also learn other strategies in this journal that will help you connect with God throughout your day whether you're in heavy traffic or stuck in a line at the grocery store.

The foundation of this devotional journal is the encounter between Jesus, Mary, and Martha as found in Luke 10 of the New Testament. We'll explore it a little more deeply later, but for now let's just say that in this passage Mary made the choice of being with Jesus, while her sister Martha busied herself with the day's tasks.

The Scriptures allow us to step into one of Mary's quiet encounters with Him. And this quiet time was at a very unlikely time; it was a quiet encounter during the very moments that her sister Martha was "[overly occupied and too busy] . . . distracted with much serving" (Luke 10:40 AMP).

In this passage, Jesus uses the individual choices Mary and Martha made to point us toward a vibrant, living, and powerful relationship with Him—a relationship that greatly impacts every moment of your every day, if you choose to enter into it!

Day 1: He Loves Me

I will be the same until your old age, and I will bear you up when you turn gray. I have made you, and I will carry you; I will bear and save you.

Isaiah 46:4

The movie was ending. Although Anna enjoyed the film, watching the sappy love story on TV made her feel she was missing out on something in life. Ed and Sally were caught up in a passionate romance. They had no children, jobs that left them with plenty of time to be together, and plenty of energy to take care of each other's needs. They spent hours talking and enjoying each other's company. Every part of their lives was absolutely wonderful because of the intimacy of their love!

"I'll never experience that kind of love" was the thought that played over and over in Anna's mind.

We perceive love in all sorts of ways. Whether we connect love with someone helping us around the house, sending flowers, complimenting the way we dress, or writing a mushy note, women crave LOVE!

Depending on our age, circumstances, and immediate needs, our definition of "love" varies. To my grandmother, for instance, love meant sitting and talking eyeball-to-eyeball with her. My niece Kyra experiences love when I spend the day shopping with her, while my daughter-in-law Bonnie loves it when we take a hike up the mountain together. Whatever form love takes, when we experience it, it meets our basic needs for security and significance.

In Dr. Gary Chapman's book *The Five Love Languages*, he addresses the significance of feeling loved. "I am significant. Life has meaning. There is a higher purpose. I want to believe it, but I may not feel significant until someone expresses love to me. Without love, I may spend a lifetime in search of significance, self-worth, and security. When I experience love, it impacts all of those needs positively. I am now freed to develop my potential."[1]

Now let me tell you about love, about *true* love. The true love story of every believer is the journey of her heart. The One who loves you the most calls out to your heart every moment. Jesus longs for you to spend time in His presence, listening to His voice. In the middle of your daily stresses, He wants to have a relationship with you. He wants you to step back from all the good things you are doing to experience the *best* thing, an intimate relationship with Him! He wants to say about you what He said about Mary . . .

"One thing is necessary. Mary has made the right choice, and it will not be taken away from her" (Luke 10:42).

Many women work hard doing so many good things for so many people that they bypass the one thing in life that's most important, and that's an intimate love relationship with Jesus. God wants us to minister to and meet the needs of others; however, our time with Him is more important to Him than anything we can do for Him. Out of this love relationship, a lifestyle of doing things for others will naturally flow.

If you have already accepted Jesus Christ as your personal Lord and Savior, then He is longing for you to experience a deep and satisfying love relationship with Him on a daily basis. He wants to give your life deeper meaning, filling each area of your life with His peace and His joy. And He wants to do this right in the middle of your daily stress!

Now if you haven't invited Jesus to live in your heart but you are yearning to experience an out-of-this-world love relationship, then the good news for you is the same good news that countless women have experienced as they have chosen to invite Jesus Christ to be the Lord of their lives. I invite you to turn to "How to Become a Christian" on page 228 to learn how to begin your personal relationship with Jesus Christ.

Date: _____

> Seek first the kingdom of God and His righteous-
> ness, and all these things will be provided for you.
> – *Matthew 6:33*

Today, Lord, I praise You for these things: _____

_____

_____

_____

_____

_____

_____

Think About This

Personal contact with Jesus changes everything. What
changes have you recently noticed in your life because of
spending more time with Jesus? Are there areas in your life
where you need the transforming power of God to change
you? _____

_____

_____

_____

_____

_____

_____

Today, I give You these details:

_____
_____
_____
_____
_____
_____
_____
_____
_____
_____
_____
_____
_____
_____
_____
_____
_____
_____

Today's Prayer

Father, Your Word says if I seek Your Face and put You first in my life, then You will provide for all of my needs. I'm needy, Lord. I long for You to come into my heart and into the details of my life and make me a new creation in You. Help me to be aware of You and give You every detail of this day. I love You!

Day 2: The Journey of Intimacy

Martha was distracted by her many tasks, and she came up
and asked, "Lord, don't You care that my sister has left me to
serve alone? So tell her to give me a hand."
Luke 10:40

Micki had heard about Mary and Martha for as long as she could remember. Pastors, teachers, and Christian speakers all pointed to Mary as the ultimate example of the devoted follower of God. Micki also recalled the picture her fourth-grade Sunday school teacher painted of Martha being too busy even to notice Jesus while Mary did nothing but sit and listen as He talked. Even as a child, Micki remembered thinking, "How could anybody just sit and listen when there were so many things to do?" As an adult, she realized her feelings were much the same.

We live in a world constantly screaming to get our attention! Women tell me they don't have time to exercise and eat right. No time to clean their houses or spend quality time with their family and friends, and certainly no time even to consider doing something special for themselves.

How then can we possibly think it's realistic to enter into a personal and growing relationship with Jesus Christ? That takes time! To have the proper view of Mary, we must understand the nature of "sitting at His feet." For me it's being preoccupied with God. Each day I pull back from all other responsibilities and sit quietly with Him. Most of the time this is early in the morning when I begin my day. I read my Bible, sing softly to Him, talk to Him about what's in store for me that day, and pray for my needs and the needs of others.

Now there's another way I "sit at His feet." I call it *emotionally and mentally sitting at the feet of Jesus.* It's simply thinking about Him throughout my day. I ask Him to go to the bank with me, help me as I get my groceries, be my companion as I drive across town, and give me the words I need before I make a telephone call. I invite Him to become involved in every detail of my life.

To be honest with you, some days I'm much better at this than others. Some days I'm like Mary, longing to be with Jesus and being aware of Him throughout the entire day. And then there are those other days, the days I'm like Martha—inviting Him in but immediately going about my daily duties, neglecting His presence and never asking for His help, or forgetting that I even *did* ask for His help.

Let's look at this well-known passage from Luke 10. Perhaps you can identify with one (or both) of these sisters as you think about your typical day.

Now while they were on their way, it occurred that Jesus entered a certain village, and a woman named Martha received and welcomed Him into her house. And she had a sister named Mary, who seated herself at the Lord's feet and was listening to His teaching. But Martha [overly occupied and too busy] was distracted with much serving; and she came up to Him and said, Lord, is it nothing to You that my sister has left me to serve alone? Tell her then to help me [to lend a hand and do her part along with me]! But the Lord replied to her by saying, Martha, Martha, you are anxious and troubled about many things; there is need of only one or but a few things. Mary has chosen the good portion [that which is to her advantage], which shall not be taken away from her. (Luke 10:38–42, AMP)

On the days I'm like Martha, as described in this passage, I welcome Jesus into my day when I first get up in the morning, but then I become "overly occupied and too busy" with everything I have to do, forgetting to acknowledge His presence and forgetting to ask Him for His help.

I'm most like Mary when I spend time with Him first thing in the morning and then continue to think about Him throughout the day as I run though my never ending to-do list, inviting Him to be a part of each and every thing that occupies my mind, my energy, and my time!

You see, your Heavenly Father longs for you to think about

Him as you go about your daily activities. Can you believe it? Honestly, it amazes me when I really think about that fact. It's just so hard to believe that Jesus would want to spend time with *me*, in all the little "nothing kind of things" that fill most of my days. Truth is, He wants to be part of every detail of my life and yours too, whether you're planning dinner or cleaning your desk at the office or scrubbing your messy bathroom.

In desiring to spend time with you, your Heavenly Father is longing to fill your life with wonderful blessings.

In the Amplified version of the Bible, we capture the full meaning behind the original Greek text. In verse 42, Jesus responds to Martha, "Mary has chosen the good portion [that which is to her advantage], which shall not be taken away from her." An "advantage" is a favorable circumstance, a benefit. As we grow in intimacy with our Lord, we will notice many benefits. Here are some that women say they have experienced as they grow closer to God:

"I am much calmer than usual."

"I'm laughing more and enjoying life."

"Things don't get to me like they used to."

"My children and I are getting along better."

"I'm not as short-tempered as I used to be."

"My life seems to have more meaning."

"The more time I spend with Jesus, the more I love Him."

Of all the benefits mentioned, the last one seems to sum up this love relationship! I spend time with Jesus because *I love Him!* And the more my love grows, the more I long to spend time with Him. Then out of this love relationship, I experience many benefits, and so do the people around me!

My friend, if you're longing for more joy, peace, and—yes— excitement in your life, a growing relationship with Jesus will help you discover all of these qualities. If you're longing to have a close friend and a renewed reason for living, ask your Heavenly Father to help you grow your relationship with Him. If you ask Him, He will give you the desire to become more aware of Him throughout your day as He begins to fill your life with His peace in the midst of your frazzledness.

Date: _____

My soul, praise the Lord, and all that is within me, praise His holy name. My soul, praise the Lord, and do not forget all His benefits. – *Psalm 103:1–2*

Today, Lord, I praise You for these things: _____

_____

_____

_____

_____

_____

_____

Think About This

Mary chose "that which was to her advantage" by sitting at the feet of Jesus. Like Mary, we need the advantages that a deep relationship with Jesus will bring. By seeking the Lord and spending time with Him every day, what benefits would you like to experience in your daily routine? _____

_____

_____

_____

_____

_____

_____

Today, I give You these details:

_____

_____

_____

_____

_____

_____

_____

_____

_____

_____

_____

_____

_____

_____

_____

_____

Today's Prayer

Lord, it excites me to know that when I spend time with You, I become more like You. I want to be like You, and when I'm like You, my family also reaps the benefits! Help me to learn Your ways and take on Your gentleness and patience as I continue to spend some time each day sitting at Your feet. Thank You, and I love You.

Day 3: Hearing When God Speaks

He said to them, "Come away by yourselves
to a remote place and rest a while."
For many people were coming and going,
and they did not even have time to eat.
Mark 6:31

One of the exciting benefits I notice as I continue to grow my love relationship with Jesus is the inner peace He gives to me. Going to that quiet place enables me to rest my mind and tone down my emotions.

It's an ongoing, gradual process. I still remember the excitement I felt as a small child, as I inched upward on the measuring stick my mom kept tucked away beside the washer.

The same principle applies when measuring your "growth" with the Lord. A wonderful love relationship doesn't just happen overnight, and the beauty of the process is the joy that you feel as you grow closer and closer to Him.

Unlike any other love relationship you experience, this quest for intimacy is divinely propelled. God loves for you to desire to grow close to Him, and He longs to delight your heart with His love!

If you've thought of "intimacy with God" as a goal that could never be reached, I hope you'll reconsider. "Intimate" means "deep and personal." So it's not like you ever totally arrive. You just keep growing deeper and more personal with Him, and the whole process of growing in your intimacy with Him can be a beautifully satisfying journey.

In our relationship with Jesus, intimacy becomes a goal that is ever before us, one that we can celebrate each step of the way.

In the period of the Old Testament, God sometimes spoke audibly. Scripture records the experience of Samuel, a young boy who had been taken to the tabernacle to be raised by Eli the priest. Samuel had not yet begun an intimate relationship with God, and he had never heard His voice. But after hearing Him speak three times, Samuel finally recognized the voice to be the voice of God.

> The boy Samuel served the LORD in Eli's presence. In those days the word of the LORD was rare and prophetic visions were not widespread. One day Eli, whose eyesight was failing, was lying in his room. Before the lamp of God had gone out, Samuel was lying down in the tabernacle of the LORD where the ark of God was located. Then the LORD called Samuel, and he answered, "Here I am." He ran to Eli and said, "Here I am; you called me."

"I didn't call," Eli replied. "Go and lie down." So he went and lay down.

Once again the LORD called, "Samuel!" Samuel got up, went to Eli, and said, "Here I am; you called me."

"I didn't call, my son," he replied. "Go and lie down."

Now Samuel had not yet experienced the LORD, because the word of the LORD had not yet been revealed to him. Once again, for the third time, the LORD called Samuel. He got up, went to Eli, and said, "Here I am; you called me."

Then Eli understood that the LORD was calling the boy. He told Samuel, "Go and lie down. If He calls you, say, 'Speak, LORD, for Your servant is listening.'" So Samuel went and lay down in his place.

The LORD came, stood there, and called as before, "Samuel, Samuel!" Samuel responded, "Speak, for Your servant is listening." (1 Sam. 3:1–10)

Samuel thought it was the priest Eli speaking to him. He was quick to respond when he heard his name called but did not recognize the voice of the Lord. Three times God called out to him. Each time Samuel rushed to the elder priest and answered, "Here I am." After the third time, Eli perceived that it was the Lord calling the boy.

As I think about my growing relationship with God, I'm aware that He speaks to me in many ways. I often sense Him speaking to me as I read my Bible. Sometimes I'm particularly close to Him and sense His voice when I'm surrounded by nature. There are times when a friend calls me and I'm sure that what she says is straight from God. At other times He sings straight to my heart through beautiful music.

When I'm thinking about God or at least aware of His presence, it's easier for me to "hear" Him. If my mind is preoccupied with all I have to do, or if some negative thought keeps creeping in, it's harder for me to discern His voice. It's natural to be preoccupied with life. Great demands are placed upon you in all the roles you play. You may be much like Samuel, simply preoccupied with your duties and not recognizing God's voice.

But God keeps calling your name. He is so persistent with His love! He wants to enter into your busy schedule, minister to you, and soothe you with His peace and His joy. Through spending time with Him and thinking about Him throughout your day, you *will* begin to recognize His voice. And recognizing His voice means experiencing Him. Experiencing God means being aware of His presence, His love, His joy, and His peace.

Someone may say something to you in conversation, and you just know it is a word from God. Sometimes you may become acutely aware of beauty in nature and hear God speaking. You may recall a Scripture passage during the day that speaks to a certain need, issue, or circumstance. These are all examples of God speaking to you!

The fourth time the Lord spoke to Samuel, the boy answered, "Speak, for Your servant is listening." This passage reveals the consistency of God! He's unchanging in His love for us. Just as He continued to call Samuel, He continues to speak to us and pursue us wherever we are and whatever we are doing.

When I think about little Samuel, I can just imagine how excited he was when he finally realized it was God who was calling him. Excitement and joy are always present when you hear from God. When you desire to know God and begin to seek Him with all your heart, you'll begin to experience Him in ways you never thought possible.

I always want the response of my heart to be, "Speak to me, Father. I'm listening!"

Date: _____

> I pray that the eyes of your heart may be enlightened
> so you may know what is the hope of His calling,
> and what are the glorious riches of His inheritance
> among the saints. – *Ephesians 1:18*

Today, Lord, I praise You for these things: _____

_____

_____

_____

_____

_____

Think About This

God speaks to us in many ways: through nature, music,
conversation with others, Scripture, and even random circumstances. The trouble is, we often get so preoccupied
with the cares of life that we miss His voice. And yet, He continues to call our name, inviting us to that quiet place of rest.
What are some ways you've experienced God speaking to
you? How has this awareness affected your walk with Him?

_____

_____

_____

_____

Today, I give You these details:

_____

_____

_____

_____

_____

_____

_____

_____

_____

_____

_____

_____

_____

_____

_____

_____

_____

_____

_____

Today's Prayer

Lord, I long to hear You speak. Give me ears to hear You and eyes to see Your involvement in every moment of my day. This day, I will be alert and excited to receive all You have for me. I love You for loving me like You do.

Day 4: My Heart's Longing

The Lord is near the brokenhearted;
He saves those crushed in spirit.
Psalm 34:18

Women are programmed with intense emotions and the capacity to yearn for life's best for themselves, their families, and their friends. God has equipped us with desires so deep that when those desires go unmet, we often experience pain—physical, emotional, and mental! Women in Frazzled Female sessions have told me that the longings they experience are often so intense that they consume their every thought.

My friend Kaye and I were friends long before she married in her forties. I remember the deeply emotional conversations we had about the longing of her heart to be married and to be a mom. Kaye had a relationship with Jesus Christ, and she gave this burden to Him, but on many days she still felt unfulfilled.

I know other Christian women who, because of preoccupation with the intense longings of their heart, often experience sleepless nights, lack of energy, and extreme weariness.

If you, like me—and like scores of other women—have ever experienced those unfulfilled longings, then let me assure you, *God knows the longing of your heart!* And furthermore, He cares about your deep desires and He longs to fulfill your deepest needs.

I have listened to women pour out their heartaches to our loving God. The longings are as varied as the women themselves. While some women long for children, others long for Christian husbands. Some yearn to serve God in ministry, and others are preoccupied with desires for their children. Whatever the deep desire of your life at this time, be assured that God knows, He understands, and He truly longs to be the answer to your need.

We read about little Samuel in the last chapter. Before his birth, his mother Hannah experienced the heart-wrenching turbulence of a longing unfulfilled. For a wife in ancient Hebrew society, to have no children was a terrible trial. She not only felt lonely and unfulfilled as a woman, but she also carried the burden of feeling she had displeased God. Since children were viewed as gifts from God, Hannah experienced a deep sense of guilt as well as the reproach of others.

The following Scripture takes place upon her visit to the temple where she was pouring out the longing of her heart to God. Eli the priest was there, observing her display of intense emotions.

Deeply hurt, Hannah prayed to the LORD and wept with many tears. Making a vow, she pleaded, "LORD of Hosts, if You will take notice of Your servant's affliction, remember and not forget me, and give Your servant a son, I will give him to the LORD all the days of his life, and his hair will never be cut."

While she was praying in the LORD's presence, Eli watched her lips. Hannah was speaking to herself, and although her lips were moving, her voice could not be heard. Eli thought she was drunk and scolded her, "How long are you going to be drunk? Get rid of your wine!"

"No, my lord," Hannah replied. "I am a woman with a broken heart. I haven't had any wine or beer; I've been pouring out my heart before the LORD. Don't think of me as a wicked woman; I've been praying from the depth of my anguish and resentment." (1 Sam. 1:10–16)

This passage almost makes me laugh. While I identify with the way Hannah poured out her deep longing to the Lord, it amuses me that Eli thought she was drunk! I wonder if she knew he was looking. I tend to be quite theatrical when I'm alone with the Lord, laying my deepest needs before Him, and it makes me sheepishly smile to think of someone looking in on those private and personal moments!

God wants you to lay it all out before Him. He wants you to turn your soul inside out to Him. Whatever you are experiencing on the inside, He wants you to bring every bit of it to Him—anger, frustration, helplessness, fatigue, whatever.

First Samuel 1:10 in the New International Version reads, "In bitterness of soul Hannah wept much and prayed to the LORD." Now if you identify with Hannah in the intensity of her longing, then you most likely identify with her bitterness. Hannah may have felt that she had reason to feel bitter about life and even about God. Circumstances in life can lead us to bitterness and may even cause us to question God's love for us.

God wants us to bring such thoughts to Him. He longs for us to bring our sorrow, our bitterness, and our heartbreak to Him so He can comfort us and ultimately give us the desires of our hearts.

Yes, Hannah did exactly what God wants us to do. Instead of allowing her distress to get the best of her, she took her sorrow to the Lord. Prayer is the only way to gain strength to overcome both your emotions and your circumstances.

Dear friend, when I continue to run to Him with my burden, my focus gradually shifts from my burden to my God. As I spend more time talking to Him about my deep desires, I begin to realize that He is reaching into my soul and is saturating my inner being with a desire for Him. Sticking with God when my prayers seem unanswered is only possible with the Lord's help.

Romans 8:26–27 tells us, "In the same way the Spirit also joins to help in our weakness, because we do not know what to pray for as we should, but the Spirit Himself intercedes for us with unspoken groanings. And He who searches the hearts knows the Spirit's mind-set, because He intercedes for the saints according to the will of God."

Persistent praying is the realization, based on faith, that He sees my need and longs to help me. This kind of praying takes me deeper into intimacy with the Almighty Father. If we allow Him, God uses our longing as a divine tool to bring us deeper into a relationship with Him.

As you turn your desires over to God, you invite Him to bless you by giving you His answer to your particular need. If God denies your request, He has something better planned for your life. I have come to the place in my life that I choose to give my yearnings to the Lord, following them with the prayer, "But Father, if you have something better in mind, cancel my request." This kind of prayer can only come from an intimate relationship based in faith and the knowledge that God's will for my life is always best!

God always answers prayers. "In my distress I called to the Lord, and He answered me" (Ps. 120:1). We must realize that His answer may not be in our way or in our timing, but He always answers!

I pray that you are beginning to birth a willing spirit, offering Him the longing of your heart so that He may bring you closer into His love and meet your deepest need. In asking Him to give you what He knows is best for your life, you are placing your trust in the One who has every need of your heart covered. In turning to Him, you can be absolutely confident that what He has in mind for you is better than anything you could ever imagine. And remember, total faith and reliance on Him will not happen overnight but will gradually grow as you spend time with Him, pouring out your heart and trusting Him to give you His best!

Date: _____

> I pour out my complaint before Him; I reveal my trouble to Him. Although my spirit is weak within me, You know my way. – *Psalm 142:2–3*

Today, Lord, I praise You for these things: _____

_____

_____

_____

_____

_____

Think About This

God wants you to bring your bitterness of soul and unfulfilled longings to Him. He wants you to give Him all of your confusion and heartache. If you don't, you'll begin to experience a distance in your relationship with Him. But as you offer Him your deepest desires, you will gradually come to know His complete fulfillment. Record your feelings about one deep desire that you need to give to God. _____

_____

_____

_____

_____

_____

Today, I give You these details:

_____

_____

_____

_____

_____

_____

_____

_____

_____

_____

_____

_____

_____

_____

_____

_____

_____

_____

Today's Prayer

O Lord, my life hurts when my dreams are unfulfilled and my hopes dashed. Even though there are times I can't imagine getting beyond this yearning, I know that the deep longings of my heart can truly be met in You. Keep my heart focused on You, Jesus. Thank You for loving me.

Day 5: Something More

You will seek Me and find Me when you
search for Me with all your heart.
Jeremiah 29:13

Patti had been a Christian for many years. She loved the Lord and enjoyed being involved in church. That's why it surprised her to realize she was becoming dissatisfied with life. It wasn't anything she could put her finger on. She just didn't feel like spending time with God the way she used to, and she wasn't enjoying the time she did spend with Him. She was busy doing many good things, God's things. All of her free time was spent doing things that revolved around her love for the Lord.

But she wondered what was happening in her walk with God. Why did she feel so blah?

There may be many times during your Christian walk when "life with God" seems less than exciting. This experience seems to become painfully obvious if you have ever once experienced a vibrant relationship with Jesus Christ. It's easy to get discouraged when you don't feel that excitement and joy.

Consider the following reasons that may contribute to the loss of zeal in your relationship with Him:

- Unconfessed sin
- Problems with people
- Difficulty focusing on God
- Being preoccupied with other things
- Not taking time to sit still in His presence
- God creating the dissatisfaction

When I go through these times of spiritual dissatisfaction, I am learning to cry out with the words of the psalmist, "Search me, God, and know my heart; test me and know my concerns. See if there is any offensive way in me; lead me in the everlasting way" (Ps. 139:23–24).

When I pray this prayer, He gives me a sense of what's wrong. It may be that I am caught up in concerns of my own, distracting my focus, or I may just be so busy that I'm not slowing down enough to talk quietly with Him.

I've also discovered that willful and/or unconfessed sin in my heart will create a barrier between God and me. These may be obvious sins that I'm aware of and am just refusing to turn away from. I'm not wanting to turn my heart to Him in repentance. Or they may be sins that I'm unconsciously harboring in my thought life. That's why praying the prayer of Psalm 139 brings unconscious sins to light. As I pray this prayer, God either reveals an area of sin in my life so that I can confess it, or He gives me peace knowing that sin is not the reason for the distance I am experiencing.

In the book of Colossians, Paul wrote to struggling Christians. He encouraged them to be strengthened and comforted, having their roots firmly planted in Jesus, filled with thanksgiving. "As you have received Christ Jesus the Lord, walk in Him, rooted and built up in Him and established in the faith, just as you were taught, and overflowing with thankfulness" (Col. 2:6–7).

You need plenty of faith to be joyful when you don't feel the joy. Life on earth is like that. Sometimes you just don't feel happy. But Paul encourages us to remember what we were taught and to continue to overflow with thanksgiving.

When I experience a void in my spiritual life, it usually leads me to want more of God, to thirst after Him. In one of the greatest invitations ever offered, Jesus stood up in the middle of the crowds in Jerusalem and said, "If anyone is thirsty, he should come to Me and drink!" (John 7:37).

Thinking about it, the reason I first came to Jesus was because of my thirst for Him and my longing to experience His love and salvation. And the longer I live with Him, the more I desire to grow closer and closer to Him! So when I feel a distance in our relationship, I'm driven to keep searching and praying until I figure out why the distance is there.

Paul viewed intimacy with Christ as the supreme goal in life. His goal for all believers, as recorded in Colossians 2:2, is that they "be encouraged and joined together in love, so that they may have all the riches of assured understanding, and have the knowledge of God's mystery—Christ."

Speaking of that "distance" thing, when we get too busy with too many things—even *good* things—our focus moves from the Lord to whatever we are doing. It's also easy for us to become distracted because of our emotions, or people, or the feeling that we just don't have time.

I encourage you to push through those times when you are less than excited about your love relationship with Jesus. Just talk to Him about it. Be honest. Tell Him about your dissatisfaction in your relationship and ask Him to create a desire in you that will bring you closer to Him.

I know for certain, based on the authority of God's Word, that He will never turn His back on a heart that seeks Him. Feeling distant from God is not geographical. It's personal! If Jesus Christ lives in your heart, then you are always in His presence. There may be times when you do not feel this closeness, but He's there, and He's not going anywhere. According to Hebrews 13:5, His promise to us is, "I will never leave you or forsake you."

As we move into next week, we'll be exploring how a positive attitude can help you in deepening your relationship with Jesus. He longs for you to enjoy His presence, and He's all about equipping you with everything you need to experience life at its fullest!

Date: _____

> Why am I so depressed? Why this turmoil within me?
> Put your hope in God, for I will still praise Him, my
> Savior and my God. – *Psalm 42:5*

Today, Lord, I praise You for these things: _____

_____

_____

_____

_____

_____

_____

Think About This

It's normal in the Christian walk to experience times of feeling distant from God. But as you grow your love relationship
with Him daily, these times will become fewer and farther
between. It's important to talk with Him about it. Acknowledge your lack of joy, asking Him to stir your heart again, to
refresh your yearning for His presence. _____

_____

_____

_____

_____

_____

Today, I give You these details:

_____

_____

_____

_____

_____

_____

_____

_____

_____

_____

_____

_____

_____

_____

_____

_____

_____

_____

Today's Prayer

Father, help me remember that You never change. When I feel less than excited about being with You, You are still there—loving me and longing for me to spend time alone with You. Reveal anything in my thoughts and behavior that may be interfering with our love relationship. I love You.

WEEK TWO

A Less Than Positive Attitude

Pleasant words are a honeycomb:
sweet to the taste and health to the body.
Proverbs 16:24

A positive attitude does not take care of all your problems, but it sure will help you have at least a little bit of your sanity left by the end of the day!

I was headed home after a three-day Frazzled Female event not long ago. Feeling rather exhausted, I was looking forward to sleeping during the hour-and-a-half flight. As soon as I snuggled up in my little cubby next to the window, I heard the piercing cry of a baby somewhere behind me. "Oh no!" I sighed, as my thoughts of slumber quickly drowned in the chaos that was happening several rows back.

If that poor mother was feeling stressed out and exasperated, it wasn't half as much as the passengers in rows one through twenty were feeling! The screaming continued through the instructions on safety belts, oxygen masks, flotation devices, and emergency exiting (which I was strongly considering).

Just when I had convinced myself that I could stand anything for an hour and a half, the captain's voice came over the speaker, "Ladies and gentlemen, I'm sorry to inform you that due to weather conditions, we are having to delay our flight. Since we are next in line for takeoff, we'll just sit tight until we're cleared to go. I apologize for this inconvenience. Try to relax and enjoy yourselves during the wait."

And I did try to relax as Baby X surpassed any previous attempts I had heard at being number one in the Loud-Screaming-With-No-Breathing category.

I knew very well this was a test! God was checking me out to see if I really believed everything I had spoken about just hours ago about choosing a positive attitude in the midst of stressful circumstances. Just as I was considering whether or not I would pass the positivity test, I looked across the aisle and noticed the pain-plastered look on the face of the woman seated there. She was clenching her teeth and holding her head. I touched her on the arm as I said, "Do you have *grown* children?" A mere nod told me that she did, to which I exclaimed, "Aren't you glad!"

That halfhearted attempt to make a little stab at humor, when I felt anything but joyful, paid off. My new support sister and I spent time talking, laughing, and swapping tales of crying babies and depleted moms.

When you choose a positive attitude, you're choosing an attitude with muscle! A positive attitude strengthens you and equips you with hope and endurance to deal with whatever the circumstance may be.

You know what? That ol' plane did finally take off forty-five minutes later; and approximately one hour and a half after that, we landed, screaming baby and all, safely at home. Home never seemed sweeter (or quieter).

Day 6: A Positive Beginning

Rejoice always! Pray constantly. Give thanks in everything,
for this is God's will for you in Christ Jesus.
1 Thessalonians 5:16–18

Sometimes it takes sheer determination to choose to be positive. Being positive in the words we speak, the facial expressions we make, and the thoughts we think are opportunities of choice throughout any day. When I have a recurring negative thought—you know, one that just won't go away—I often choose to take a twenty-four-hour fast on negative thinking!

Here's how it works: when a negative thought keeps interrupting what I am supposed to be thinking about, I just ZAP it, and I keep zapping it for the entire day. Now according to the laws of zapping, when you zap a thought, you have to put another thought in its place, or it won't stay zapped!

Let's say, for example, you walk into the kitchen early in the morning to find a mess left by your daughter and her friends the night before. Instead of allowing your angry feelings to take over and ruin your morning, you immediately toss—no, *throw*—the negative feeling out of your mind, determining to focus on a positive one. For me, the best positive thoughts are Scriptures. For this situation, how about: "Be glad in the LORD, you righteous ones, and praise His holy name" (Ps. 97:12).

You have to train yourself to apply this approach, as well as keeping your arsenal of Scriptures close by. Believe me, thinking positively doesn't come naturally. Being upset and thinking negatively does! But when you respond to a situation in this way, you're better equipped to address the situation later—like when your daughter gets up! Since you've made the choice to react positively instead of negatively, you are better equipped to deal with the problem rationally.

Also with this approach, I know I can deal with some issues tomorrow if I still need to—even though I often find that "tomorrow" takes care of the problem on its own, and I don't even have to revisit it. Choosing to think positively fuels my energy, keeps me focused, and saves time!

One of my positive heroes in the Old Testament is Abraham. When God told Abraham to set out for a new land, Abraham chose to listen. He also chose to be positive about God's direction for his life. Abraham's obedience in his attitude and behavior caused him to be uprooted from his familiar way of life yet led him to discover God's greatness. He chose to trust even when God's promises seemed impossible to believe. Abraham sometimes strayed from the path by trying to work things out his way, but he continued to listen and be obedient as God called for his trust.

The LORD said to Abram: Go out from your land, your relatives, and your father's house to the land that I will show you. I will make you into a great nation, I will bless you, I will make your name great, and you will be a blessing. I will bless those who bless you, I will curse those who treat you with contempt, and all the peoples on earth will be blessed through you.

So Abram went, as the LORD had told him, and Lot went with him. Abram was 75 years old when he left Haran. He took his wife Sarai, his nephew Lot, all the possessions they had accumulated, and the people he had acquired in Haran, and they set out for the land of Canaan. When they came to the land of Canaan. (Gen 12:1–5)

God called Abraham to leave his home and family and go to a foreign country. I'm sure Abraham must have experienced some intense emotions. Perhaps he was not really pleased that God had asked him to do such an exciting thing. Maybe he even doubted what he thought God had said. He could have been afraid about what people might think of him, doing something so seemingly crazy. But even though he didn't understand God's plan, he chose to trust Him nonetheless.

Any time you move in obedience to God's call, it's a positive choice. Any time you listen to God and obey His words, you are moving in a positive direction. Sometimes God will ask you to step out of your comfort zone and do something you're not naturally inclined to do. But if you follow in obedience, any discomfort you experience will eventually lead you to God's blessings.

As Abraham continued in his journey of obedience one small positive step at a time, the Lord continued to reveal Himself and His plan. Abraham, in turn, worshiped God. As you grow in your walk with the Lord and gradually develop a lifestyle of listening to Him and obeying Him, remember to worship Him along the way. Worship is an integral part of developing a positive lifestyle. You can rejoice that your Heavenly Father is leading you and that you are following Him in obedience.

Being positive involves more than what we think about. For the Christian, a positive attitude encompasses our whole being. We become positive by listening to God, obediently following His directions, continually worshiping Him, and seeking His presence.

Date: _____

My heart is confident, God; I will sing; I will sing praises with the whole of my being. – *Psalm 108:1*

Today, Lord, I praise You for these things: _____

_____

_____

_____

_____

_____

_____

Think About This

It takes sheer determination to remain positive day in and day out. The real test comes on those days when you don't feel your best or when others are simply annoying you. It helps me remember that I have a positive God who will help me keep my focus. List some areas where it's difficult for you to have a positive attitude. _____

_____

_____

_____

_____

_____

_____

Today, I give You these details:

_____
_____
_____
_____
_____
_____
_____
_____
_____
_____
_____
_____
_____
_____
_____
_____
_____
_____

Today's Prayer

Dear Lord, give me Your positive outlook today. With Your help, I can face the negative things about today with a genuine positive spirit, because You are God and I am safe in You. Thank You for loving me.

Day 7: You Become What You Think

Lord, I turn my hope to You.
Psalm 25:1

Maybe you are beginning to identify areas in your life where you could grow a more positive attitude by listening to God a little more closely. Maybe He's impressing you about some specific circumstances where a positive attitude would be helpful.

When my sons were teenagers, I knew God was telling me to be a more positive mother. He was telling me to *look*, *speak*, and *act* in more positive ways. I soon discovered that being positive did not come naturally, but being negative did! As I shared with you earlier, I realized that it was no easy thing to get rid of negative thinking. I frequently had to trash the negative thoughts. I can tell you, this created plenty of room to store the positive ones. And if I didn't hurry and put the positive ones in, the negative ones would rush back in to fill the space! Our minds cannot hold a void. *Something* has to be in there! So after various attempts with little success, I learned the best way to stop the negative flow was by plugging it with Scripture.

When you spend time meditating on the Word of God, you are taking hold of His supernatural power! There's not a self-help book anywhere that can equip you with the divinely supernatural power of God. That's why I choose to speak Scripture often throughout the day. The benefits I gain are totally indescribable. (The people around me greatly benefit too!)

"Finally brothers, whatever is true, whatever is honorable, whatever is just, whatever is pure, whatever is lovely, whatever is commendable—if there is any moral excellence and if there is any praise—dwell on these things" (Phil. 4:8).

Reflecting on this powerful, supernaturally propelled verse from Philippians helped me a lot, and I believe it will help guide you toward a positive lifestyle. If you begin to think about what you're thinking about and determine to place a positive thought in your mind when the negative one jumps up, then you're making progress.

If you dwell on your messy house, for instance, are you following the guidelines of this Scripture? No! If, however, you think about how much you love your family who made that mess, you're on track!

Come on, friend, trash the negative thought that you can't be positive, and join with me as we tackle a more positive lifestyle together. It's an ongoing process, and some days are easier than others, but the benefits of choosing to at least try to be positive greatly pay off. Truth is, your positive or your negative lifestyle will indeed affect every function of your body. If you dwell on negative things, you will spout negative words and have negative facial expressions and body gestures. Being negative keeps you unproductive and focusing on self. When you think negatively, you simply do not accomplish as much in a day as when you think positively.

Dr. Charles Stanley writes about sowing to the flesh (catering to your negative thoughts) and sowing to the Spirit (choosing to think positively):

> Every morning when you and I awaken, we begin sowing. In our minds, we sow thoughts—positive or negative, good or evil. In our actions, our attitudes, our habits all day long, we sow either to the flesh or to the Spirit. The things you sow in the Spirit are life-producing and have the potential for eternal reward. The very nature of the Holy Spirit is life, and the things you sow to the Spirit produce a zest for living. They have an ability to produce, multiply, and flourish into an abundant harvest. The more you sow to the Spirit, the greater the harvest of things that result in your ability to achieve the goals that God has helped you set.[2]

Sowing to the Spirit by being positive will help you accomplish all God wants you to accomplish! So are you ready to take on a more positive lifestyle? Becoming the positive person God wants you to be begins with examining your negative thinking.

Here's a sampling of negative thoughts I've collected from "wannabe" positive thinkers:

- "I can't stand going home to a messy house after I work hard all day at the office."

- "Thinking about cooking tonight makes me sick."

- "If only my husband would help out with the kids."

- "Washing, cleaning, cooking, running—I never get any thanks."

- "This job stinks. I wish I could do something I like."

- "Life's just one chore after another."

- "There's never enough time for me."

- "If she weren't such a busybody, she'd get more done."

Could you add a few (or ten or twenty) thoughts yourself? It's easy to think negatively. It's also the natural thing to do. Truth is, every one of these negative thoughts may be reality for you. You may feel that many situations in your life have created your bad attitude. A lot of people feel that way. But take a look at what

Paul (who was in prison at the time) said in divinely breathed Scripture. "Rejoice in the Lord always. I will say it again: Rejoice!" (Phil. 4:4).

So you see, my friend, according to Scripture, rejoicing in the midst of all things is not a suggestion but a command. It won't happen overnight, but with determination you will gradually become more positive. And if you've had more positive thoughts than negative ones at the end of today, then you're making progress! With that movement of obedience comes God's grace, His blessing, and a positive attitude!

Date: _____

> Your heart will rejoice like one who walks to the
> music of a flute, going up to the mountain of the
> Lord, to the Rock of Israel. – *Isaiah 30:29*

Today, Lord, I praise You for these things: _____

_____

_____

_____

_____

_____

Think About This

Being negative comes a lot easier than being positive on
most days. With a life full of stress, including schedules, time
constraints, and people . . . a cynical spirit brews quite easily.
What are some areas in your typical day that seem to pull
you towards negative thinking? _____

_____

_____

_____

_____

_____

Today, I give You these details:

_____

_____

_____

_____

_____

_____

_____

_____

_____

_____

_____

_____

_____

_____

_____

_____

_____

_____

_____

_____

Today's Prayer

Dear Father, I need Your supernatural power to make my day ahead a positive one. Right now, I turn my thoughts to You and my heart to You. Give me Your positive direction for everything I have to deal with today. Thank You for helping me. I love You.

Day 8: The Power of God

For in Him we live and move and exist.
Acts 17:28

All week Debbie had been looking forward to sleeping in on Saturday. Every day she had gotten up at her usual early time just to get things done. Her week was filled with putting out fires—everybody else's. People were always wanting her to do something but were never satisfied with anything she did. Every time she made a little progress with her work, she had to add another item to her to-do list.

Early in the week, Debbie promised God she would really try to have a more positive attitude. She told Him she wanted to spend more time with Him to soak in His goodness and joy. She had an aging parent, however, who took much of her time, and a family that didn't help with housework. By the end of the week she was exhausted and grumpy. The only thing she looked forward to was sleeping late on Saturday morning.

On Friday night, Debbie's friend Erin called telling her that her husband, Jeff, had to report to work at 7:00 the next morning.

Erin was sick and wondered if Debbie could keep two-year-old Carly on Saturday. Jeff could drop her off on his way to work.

It is so easy for those good intentions for a positive attitude to be annihilated when a week soars high on the stress scale! I don't know about you, but if I were Debbie at the end of that particular week, I would be so tempted to pretend the phone lines were botched up and I couldn't hear a thing that Erin said!

Oh, my! Life can be so frustrating! It's such a challenge to react positively when stressors are continually thrown your way. I have found that many times we women can handle the big things in life that produce stress. Maybe it's because we've planned in advance for them and realize they are coming. It's the accumulation of common daily hassles that seem to sneak up on us and rob our joy and positive attitude.

What's a woman to do? Well, you can try to do better, but trying in your own strength results in major frustration! Instead of relying on my own ability, I'm getting better at recognizing God's power in my life! He can put that positive attitude back where it belongs and keep me from getting helplessly frustrated when the little (and big) things pile up.

We believers forget that it is the power of Jesus Christ living within us that enables us to become more Christlike in having a positive attitude! Paul talks about it in Ephesians:

> I pray that the God of our Lord Jesus Christ, the glori-
> ous Father, would give you a spirit of wisdom and revela-

tion in the knowledge of Him. I pray that the eyes of your heart may be enlightened so you may know what is the hope of His calling, what are the glorious riches of His inheritance among the saints, and what is the immeasurable greatness of His power to us who believe, according to the working of His vast strength. (Eph. 1:17–19)

Now perk up your ears! Paul's about to tell you what kind of glorious power is available to you for having a positive attitude toward cleaning bathrooms, cooking meals, shopping for groceries, making a speech, taking care of family and friends, and for anything in your life that calls you to exert mental, emotional, and physical strength!

He demonstrated this power in the Messiah by raising Him from the dead and seating Him at His right hand in the heavens. (Eph. 1:20)

I want you to grab hold of this. The Word of God says that, with Jesus Christ living in me, I have power to do anything—and it's the same power that God used when He raised Jesus from the dead! This includes having power for a positive attitude!

I remember when this reality first sank in with me years ago. I was teaching about the power of God, using the Ephesians text. All of a sudden, the Holy Spirit seemed to whoosh over me (as only the Holy Spirit can) with the truth that I didn't have to dread cleaning the week's worth of mess in my house because I had the power of God to get me through it, and I could still smile when I finished! Right during the middle of my speech that day, God spoke to my heart saying, "I'm all you need to have the positive attitude I want you to have. And this positive attitude is available right in the middle of all the negative things filling your life!"

Friend, what is in your life that the power of the living God cannot handle?

I pray that you will be filled with a fresh new insight about how your Heavenly Father longs to help you and get you through the rough moments of your day. He especially wants to be a part of all the areas you've never considered giving to Him—areas like laundry, garbage, telephone calls, cleaning your desk at the office, and attending those long meetings!

God in all His practical and positive power longs to share it with His children. I took Him up on His offer years ago, and for me, cleaning the bathroom in my own strength is a thing of the past!

Date: _____

> Position yourselves, stand still, and see the salvation of the Lord. . . . Do not be afraid or discouraged. Tomorrow, go out to face them, for the Lord is with you. *– 2 Chronicles 20:17*

Today, Lord, I praise You for these things: _____

_____

_____

_____

_____

_____

Think About This

Life has a way of interrupting your plans! I take much care in planning my days so that I can accomplish as much as I possibly can. So when interruptions to my schedule come crashing in, I don't always remember that they have been filtered by God. How do you react to those "unplanned opportunities" that interrupt your day? _____

_____

_____

_____

_____

_____

Today, I give You these details:

_____

_____

_____

_____

_____

_____

_____

_____

_____

_____

_____

_____

_____

_____

_____

_____

_____

Today's Prayer

Father, help me to remember Paul's words—that it's in You that I move, breathe, and have my being. Teach me to immediately talk with You about the interruptions that come my way. Help me to remember that each one of them is an additional opportunity to share Your love. Amen.

Day 9: The Gift of His Power

I pray that the eyes of your heart may be enlightened so you
may know . . . the immeasurable greatness of His power to us
who believe, according to the working of His vast strength.
Ephesians 1:18–19

You've been reading about the availability of God's power. As
His children we have the gift of accessing His power in every situation we face, including our daily attitudes! The power available
for you to have a positive attitude is the same power God used
when He raised Christ from the dead. How powerful is that?

And what's your part in accessing this mighty power? The "us
who believe" phrase in the Ephesians verse above refers to those
of us who have trusted Jesus Christ to be our Lord and Savior. We
believe in the resurrected Son of God who died for our sins, dying
a substitutionary death for our sins so that we will not be separated from God. We believe He is now sitting at the right hand of
God waiting for us to live with Him throughout all eternity.

It's almost mind-boggling to think that all we have to do to
tap into God's power to give us a positive attitude is to believe.

But you see, dear friend, Jesus already did the hard part. That's why our part is only to believe. And because I have trusted Him as my Savior, I can also trust Him to help me find a positive attitude.

It still thrills me to know that God not only saved me for eternal life with Him after I die, but He saved me for *now*—while I'm here living this life. I don't have to wait until eternity to experience His tremendous power, joy, and love. I can experience it now, right here on earth, while I'm living and breathing and being frazzled on many days. His presence in me is what I need to have a positive attitude. I certainly can't experience it through my own effort.

This means I can believe God for a positive attitude in my relationships with my family, as well as believing Him for a positive attitude at work, in running errands, and even while trying to finish up everything before I go to bed at night. I have the positive attitude of Jesus Christ living inside of me to make me positive about everything!

Remember, though, the first step to being positive is to determine to think positively! It's a matter of choice, an act of will.

Without believing that I have access to this power, I tend to fall prey to whining and complaining. We live in a much less than perfect world. In fact, as stated earlier, it's more natural to behave in negative ways than in positive ones. We are born with a sinful nature, and not until we invite Jesus into our hearts do we have the opportunity of His positive spirit guiding us. The opportunity and challenge come in *choosing* to be positive in a negative world. Only God can provide that positive attitude when daily living is filled with so much stress. He provides it, but He allows us the opportunity to choose it!

At times I intellectually grasp a concept, but I can't quite plug it in to my way of doing things. I find it so frustrating to understand what God is saying when I am uncertain how to put it to work in my life. I mean, I know that He wants me to have a positive attitude, but in some areas it's just hard to understand how to be positive.

Again, that's when I turn to Scripture and pray! "Help me understand Your instruction, and I will obey it and follow it with all my heart" (Ps. 119:34).

When I pray that prayer, God gradually—or sometimes immediately—begins to show me how to be more positive. You can be assured that God will always answer when you call out to Him. He will impress upon your heart what words to say or which way to go. As you seek Him and long to hear from Him, remember He longs to speak to you and fill you with His presence.

When you're anxious about something, it's difficult to feel positive. Anxious feelings can multiply rapidly, causing you to become focused on them, then preoccupied with them, unless you keep them in check. Anxiety and worry can lead to an extremely negative attitude. Before I chose to put positive thinking on my daily to-do list, I remember often waking up in the morning and becoming so absorbed in all that I had to accomplish that day that I was worn out from running before I ever got out of bed! The enemy used worry to make me become self-absorbed, keeping me distracted about the positive power of God. The devil doesn't want me to have a positive outlook and a life that glorifies God, so he tempts me to focus on me!

Years ago, after praying about the worries that were occupying my mind and stealing my peace, the Lord gave me this strategy. I found a small box and named it my Worry Box. Then I wrote on slips of paper the worries that were occupying my mind and robbing me of His peace and joy. I placed each slip of paper in the box, committing not to worry about them for an entire week. I was instantly amazed at the freedom I experienced. It was proof to me that by worrying I was not resolving the situations, only increasing the emotional turmoil inside of me.

As I continued this practice of creating worry-free weeks, a wonderful benefit became apparent. Often by the end of the week, the worry had taken care of itself, or at least didn't seem nearly as harassing. And for the big issues, even though I had to continue dealing with them, I experienced a break from the worry that was attached to them.

His positive power is also available for those little tasks that irritate you. A lot of times this irritation spills over to the people behind them. Many women experience major frustration (that's mildly said) at the end of the day when they are already tired and worn out and have to clean a dirty house. When that happens to me, I choose once again to focus on Scripture! "And whatever you do, in word or in deed, do everything in the name of the Lord Jesus, giving thanks to God the Father through Him" (Col. 3:17).

Honestly, sometimes as I'm praying that prayer, I begin laughing. The intensity of my irritation determines the number of times I speak, sigh, or shout this Scripture. If you are truly determined to get God's positive attitude to burst within you, then you won't stop until you become positive!

I smile when I think about the young mother of three little boys who came up to me after a recent Frazzled Female session. I had been teaching about how God wants us to talk to Him about everything in our lives, especially about those many irritations that fill our days. She said, "God doesn't want me to talk to Him about the underwear my little boys scatter through the house, does He?"

My reply: "Oh, yes, He does!"

Dear friend, does God want you to experience peace of mind? Does He want you to have a positive outlook on life, one that leaves you feeling energized with His power living inside of you? Does He want you to be free from the worry and negativity that is robbing your joy? Oh, yes, He does!

Feel encouraged as you take the tiny baby steps of growing a more positive attitude. Life's hard, and being positive requires desire and persistence. But remember, you have a loving Heavenly Father who is taking notice of you and is cheering you on as you turn your heart and thoughts toward Him.

Date: _____

Can any of you add a cubit to his height by worrying? If then you're not able to do even a little thing, why worry about the rest? – *Luke 12:25–26*

Today, Lord, I praise You for these things: _____

_____

_____

_____

_____

_____

Think About This

Why should I be positive? Because I have a positive God! And if Jesus lives in my heart, then I have all the positive I need. I can choose positive thoughts and actions throughout my day. It's up to me. What are some possible situations in your day ahead where you need to practice positive thinking and behaving? _____

_____

_____

_____

_____

_____

Today, I give You these details:

_____

_____

_____

_____

_____

_____

_____

_____

_____

_____

_____

_____

_____

_____

_____

_____

_____

Today's Prayer

Dear Lord, keep me mindful of Your powerful and positive presence during the day ahead. Before I react, nudge me to pray. And when negative thinking creeps in, help remind me to replace it with positive Scripture. I trust You to keep me positive this day. Amen.

Day 10: Being Positive in Negative Circumstances

Search for the Lord and for His strength; seek His face always.
Psalm 105:4

"No way!" Glenda thought as she read her devotion about being positive in the midst of trials. The author challenged her at the very point of her vulnerability. She had been engaged a year ago to a man she desperately loved and longed to spend her life with. But three weeks before the wedding, he walked away, pledging his love to another. Glenda had experienced a wide range of intense emotions, and none of them were positive! From shock to anger to confusion and finally rejection, she had sunk as low as anyone could sink. How could she possibly see anything positive about this horrible situation that left her extremely cynical and negative!

During the writing of this book, I received a phone call from a friend who was also experiencing difficulty with the concept of being positive when her world was falling apart. "It doesn't seem humanly possible," she said, "to be positive when so many bad things are happening to me. It doesn't seem realistic," were her words.

God understands our inability and even our resistance to being positive when everything inside us feels negative. He knows that in our weakness we are not able to overlook all of life's negatives and immediately jump into a positive lifestyle. He doesn't want us to ignore the facts of the negative situation, but He does want us to rely on His power to get us through, one step at a time.

Again, I remind you that sometimes you have to fight to be victorious with that positive attitude. It's a choice you make. Remember positive Abraham from Genesis 12? His arsenal was filled with exactly what you and I have: God and the ability to choose.

Against hope, with hope he believed, so that he became "the father of many nations," according to what had been spoken: "So will your descendants be." He considered his own body to be already dead (since he was about a hundred years old), and the deadness of Sarah's womb, without weakening in the faith. He did not waver in unbelief at God's promise, but was strengthened in his faith and gave glory to God, because he was fully convinced that what He had promised He was also able to perform. (Rom. 4:18–21)

Abraham believed God, not because things made sense but because he knew God would and could do what He said, even though Abraham had reason not to believe. But I imagine, considering the condition of his and Sarah's bodies, this was not an easy choice. I'm sure that Abraham had fighting moments at times, where he had to strengthen his resolve and *determine* to believe that God would do what He said He would do. And, you know, God continued to bless Abraham for his hope and positive attitude.

God will continue to bless you, too, for hoping in Him and for striving to keep your attitude positive. And by the way, being positive doesn't necessarily mean that you're happy. *Life does not always make us happy!* And being a Christian does not make you immune to the trials and troubles of life.

I want you to realize that being happy and being positive are not the same thing. Even when we are not happy, we can be positively confident that God is in control of our lives and that we have the ultimate victory over all of life's negatives in Jesus Christ!

As Christians we have a reason to be positive. We have a positive God! And sometimes God may ask you to be positive and hopeful about a situation simply because He is God and He is in charge of your life. The world says, "Seeing is believing." But the Bible says for us to "(trust in, adhere to, and rely on) God" (Rom. 4:24 AMP). And many times that's when we don't "see" the outcome.

In thinking about positive versus negative attitudes, maybe you've heard someone say (or you've thought this yourself): "I'm not being negative; I'm just being realistic." Some people think being positive is not being realistic. That line of thinking is contrary to Scripture. Just like Abraham, you can face each situation by choosing to place your faith and hope in God. As you practice this, you will develop a mind-set that is open to the will of God, whatever that may be.

Consider Glenda, whose fiancé ran out on her. By adopting a negative attitude, Glenda might say, "My life is over. No one will ever want me again. I'm going to be miserable the rest of my life." But by being positive and realistic, Glenda could say, "I hate that this happened, and I hurt so much. I know it's going to take time to get through this, but I trust God to restore me. He may send someone else my way if that's His will for me. God knows what's best for my life now and in the future."

Whether you realize it or not, messages are being encoded day by day in your mind. You carry on conversations with yourself, interpret situations, and cast judgments. This self-talk can either be explosive and filled with doubt and criticism or positive and filled with hope. Here are some examples of self-talk:

- "Why don't I just give up?"

- "God is in control. Things will work out somehow."

- "I don't understand, but I trust Him."

- "God must really be disappointed in me."

- "I'm never going to make it through this."

- "Father, I turn this over to You. I choose to believe You will take care of me."

Along with self-talk, there's also the talk of others influencing you. You may have grown up in an environment filled with negativity. There may be those in your life who are continuing to fill you with criticism and gloom. Remember, you are responsible to God in your relationship with Him. To be successful in your attitude and in your life, you must not take on the negative spirit of those around you. This is all about you and God! If you ask Him, He will help you lay the negative comments of others to rest.

I am now training myself to focus on my Heavenly Father right in the middle of negative talk and circumstances. It's a continual choice, and sometimes it's difficult. But God in His love and grace is helping me along the way and blessing me by offering His continual energy, forgiveness, and power to turn the hopelessly negative into powerful and positive moments with Him!

The same can be true of you. So keep goin', girl! Your little steps are leading you closer to the heart of God!

Date: _____

Rejoice. Be restored, be encouraged, be of the same mind, be at peace, and the God of love and peace will be with you. – *2 Corinthians 13:11*

Today, Lord, I praise You for these things: _____

_____

_____

_____

_____

_____

_____

Think About This

There are many situations when it doesn't seem possible or realistic to have a positive attitude. And yet God calls us—just like Abraham—to trust Him and remain positive because He is God! Are there areas in your life where You need God to transform your thinking into His thinking?

_____

_____

_____

_____

_____

_____

Today, I give You these details:

_____

_____

_____

_____

_____

_____

_____

_____

_____

_____

_____

_____

_____

_____

_____

_____

Today's Prayer

Father, there are times I just don't have it in me. There seems to be no positive thinking for some situations in life. And yet, Lord, I know You and I trust You. In humble obedience and with a seeking heart, I bow before You. Please fill me with the joy of a positive mind-set. I need Your thinking to get me through this day. I love You.

WEEK THREE

I Don't Have Enough Time!

Be still and know that I am God.
Psalm 46:10 NIV

With tons of time management programs, tips, and strategies available to help us more effectively use our precious minutes, why is it at the end of the day we still throw up our hands and cry out, "I just don't have enough time!"

God spoke to me about this particular issue in a really specific way when I was putting together a seminar on time management. What He revealed to me seemed so simple that I couldn't believe I had missed this truth for so long. After consistently trying out my "new plan" from Him, I have not only become more time-efficient but more peaceful instead of running consistently at a breakneck speed to get everything done and marked off my daily to-do list.

He revealed His time management plan with this Scripture: "'Bring the full 10 percent into the storehouse so that there may be food in My house. Test Me in this way,' says the Lord of Hosts. 'See if I will not open the floodgates of heaven and pour out a blessing for you without measure'" (Mal. 3:10).

I sensed Him telling me that this verse applies not only to the money I give to Him but also to the way I give Him my time! I got so excited as I realized He was saying that if I spent time with Him every single day, then He would open the floodgates of Heaven and pour out His blessings on my life.

The principle is this: God desires a relationship with you. He desires daily communication that includes worship, prayer, and Scripture study. And when you give Him your time, He showers His love and peace and joy throughout your day. The things you do become more God-centered and less frenetic. He takes your time and multiplies it with His blessings. You don't actually have more time, but it seems like you do.

Begin to imagine a lifestyle of less huffing and puffing and more calmness and fulfillment. When you recognize that God is in control of your time, you actually get the things done in a day that you need to get done! It can happen—and will happen—if you put God's time before your time.

Day 11: God Is in Control

He must increase, but I must decrease.
John 3:30

God had given Jochebed, the mother of Moses, the gift of a beautiful baby boy, yet Pharaoh had ordered the death of every Hebrew male baby. How overwhelming her circumstances must have seemed! The mother of Moses knew God. Knowing Him led her to trust Him to take care of her child. Hebrews 11:23 tells us she disobeyed the king by hiding Moses for three months. What a courageous act of faith to place her baby in the bulrushes at the river's edge. As a woman who loved God and understood the yearning of her own heart, Jochebed trusted Him completely with the welfare of her child. Her faith was rewarded as God inclined the heart of Pharaoh's daughter to save the child, making his mother his nursemaid.

Now a man from the family of Levi married a Levite woman. The woman became pregnant and gave birth to a son; when she saw that he was beautiful, she hid him for three months. But when she could no longer hide him, she got a papyrus basket for him and coated it with asphalt and pitch. She placed the child in it and set it among the reeds by the bank of the Nile. Then his sister stood at a distance in order to see what would happen to him.

Pharaoh's daughter went down to bathe at the Nile while her servant girls walked along the riverbank. Seeing the basket among the reeds, she sent her slave girl to get it. When she opened it, she saw the child—a little boy, crying. She felt sorry for him and said, "This is one of the Hebrew boys."

Then his sister said to Pharaoh's daughter, "Should I go and call a woman from the Hebrews to nurse the boy for you?"

"Go." Pharaoh's daughter told her. So the girl went and called the boy's mother. Then Pharaoh's daughter said to her, "Take this child and nurse him for me, and I will pay your wages." So the woman took the boy and nursed him. When the child grew older, she brought him to Pharaoh's daughter, and he became her son. She named him Moses, "Because," she said, "I drew him out of the water." (Exod. 2:1–10)

Just imagine the intense emotions Jochebed must have felt as she lowered her baby boy into the water! She certainly was in the middle of an unsettling circumstance, yet she trusted that God was in control.

It takes sheer discipline to trust God in the midst of unsettling circumstances. Feeling like you don't have enough time to get everything done that needs to get done is definitely unsettling and can leave you feeling extremely anxious about life in general. It's frustrating and even exhausting just trying to plan how to get meals fixed, the house cleaned, groceries bought, people taken care of, not to mention the endless meetings, phone calls, and appointments that fill our days.

I'm sure Jochebed drew from her maternal instincts in designing a plan she hoped would protect her baby. More importantly, she drew strength from her God who led her to protect and preserve not only the life of her young child but an entire nation of God's children. How the Hebrew people would be blessed through the faithful leadership of Moses!

Through Jochebed's example we can learn two important principles of time management. First, Jochebed relied on God. Second, she was persistent. Her firm faith gave her the strength she needed to do what God had called her to do.

Do you need more time in your life to exercise or plan nutritious meals? What about more time to build family relationships or show kindness to neighbors? Maybe you just need a little more relaxation time—time to do something just for you!

It takes tremendous faith, discipline, and persistence to manage your time God's way. Perhaps it's time for you to seek His counsel about what you do with the time He has given you. I bet if you put Him first, He'll do for you just as He did for Jochebed and what He's doing for me—reward you with His strength, His joy, and His provision. In fact, I'm sure He will!

Date: _____

> The Lord your God is among you, a warrior who saves. He will rejoice over you with gladness. He will bring you quietness with His love. He will delight in you with shouts of joy. – *Zephaniah 3:17*

Today, Lord, I praise You for these things: _____

_____

_____

_____

_____

_____

_____

Think About This

Feeling like you don't have time to get everything done during the day can leave you feeling anxious and exhausted. But spending time with the Lord each morning and talking with Him about your day will help you experience His peace. Where do you need God's peace in your life this day?

_____

_____

_____

_____

_____

Today, I give You these details:

_____

_____

_____

_____

_____

_____

_____

_____

_____

_____

_____

_____

_____

_____

_____

_____

_____

_____

_____

_____

Today's Prayer

Lord, I need You to settle me, because my nerves are raw and my spirit anxious with everything I have to do. I come to You in faith right now, knowing that Your peace lives inside of me. I'm trusting You to settle my soul. Thank You!

Day 12: More

God, create a clean heart for me and renew
a steadfast spirit within me.
Psalm 51:10

Betty read in the Sunday church bulletin that a ladies' Bible study would begin next week. Her heart jumped with excitement as she anticipated gathering with Christian women to study and talk about Scripture. She longed to grow in her relationship with the Lord. She wanted to experience His peace and joy in her life on a daily basis.

By Thursday night, though, Betty was exhausted from working at her daily job and coming home to begin "second shift" (the title she gave her responsibilities at home). Once again, she shelved the idea of the Bible study, feeling she didn't have enough time. She would attend when life wasn't so busy.

Oh my! Can't we all identify with Betty—longing to grow in our relationship with the Lord so we can experience His joy and peace, but just not having enough time to do so?

Having a quiet time with our Heavenly Father and growing

that love relationship doesn't scream at us the way daily life does. It's so easy to put off our time with Him, convincing ourselves that it will be easier to spend time with Him when life isn't so hectic.

Women often ask me if it's okay to have their daily quiet time while driving to work or getting ready in the morning or while doing a number of other things throughout the day, focusing on God while they're busy doing these things.

My answer: Yes, but first . . .

Yes, God so longs for you to invite Him into the midst of all your busyness. He wants you to have a lifestyle of being aware of Him and consulting Him during every part of your day.

But first, it is my strong belief based on personal experience that I cannot tune into God and be totally aware of Him as I go through my day unless I have first had my quiet and personal time with Him. This is a time when I focus *exclusively* on my love for Him, worshiping Him, seeking His guidance, and reading and meditating on Scripture. Sure I can do these things while driving or cooking meals or getting ready for work, but I can't do them without being somewhat distracted.

God longs for your undivided attention. Multitasking with God is not the same as focusing exclusively on Him! He honors your effort and blesses you beyond imagination when you dedicate time just for Him while doing nothing else. I'm reminded of the time when my boys were little. If I tried to do something else when I was sitting on the floor playing with them, they would grab my face to get my attention, look me straight in the eyes, and say, "Play, Mommy, play!"

Now God is not going to grab you and make you stop everything to spend time with Him, *but He wants you to.* He's allowing you to make that choice. Maybe you don't have a lot of time to do this each day, but don't you have *some* time?

The benefit, you see, is that in offering God some of your time exclusively each day, He will bless you beyond measure. By sitting still with Him and becoming comfortable in what "still" feels like, you will be better able to still yourself in Him when troubling times hit. If you've never been still with God, then how will you be still with Him when the rug is pulled out from under you, when you desperately need to feel His still calmness invading your circumstances and saturating you with His peace?

I have learned to take Him from this still, quiet place into the noise of life. After my early morning quiet time, yes, I do worship Him as I drive, as I get ready for work, and as I move throughout my day. But in order to experience Him in those other places, I have to go to the quiet place first. Honestly, for me, it just won't work any other way.

Liza shared this experience with her Frazzled Female Bible study group: "When I walked into my kitchen at 6:00 a.m., I looked at the dirty dishes in the sink and then at my Bible. For a moment I was torn about what to do. Doing the dishes would give me a head start on my day, but I wouldn't have time for Bible study. I decided to read my Bible, and I had the most wonderful experience with God. The rest of my day went smoothly because I was filled with His peace."

That's exactly what God wants to show you. Remember what He said in that Malachi verse? "Test Me in this way. . . . See if I will not open the floodgates of heaven and pour out a blessing for you without measure" (Mal. 3:10).

He's calling me. He's calling you. He's calling all of His children to a quiet, loving, and deeply personal relationship with Him. He wants you to test Him in this so that He can show you all the blessings He longs to shower upon your life as you gradually learn to love Him more and more.

No, you will not have more time, but the time you have will be more! I can't explain it, but I know it's true! And so do many other women who have taken on this challenge of giving God their time and attention first thing in the morning before tackling the chores of the day.

Perhaps this is a testing ground for you. God is longing for you to "test Him in this" so that He may "open the floodgates and pour out a blessing for you without measure."

Date: _____

Therefore let everyone who is faithful pray to You at a
time that You may be found. When great floodwaters
come, they will not reach him. – *Psalm 32:6*

Today, Lord, I praise You for these things: _____

_____

_____

_____

_____

_____

_____

Think About This

God is calling you to a deeply personal love relationship with
Him. The trouble is, the world often shouts louder! I encourage you to grasp the reality of God! If you determine to draw
away with Him—even for a short time—your life will take on
new meaning. Commit your desire for Him in writing.

_____

_____

_____

_____

_____

Today, I give You these details:

_____

_____

_____

_____

_____

_____

_____

_____

_____

_____

_____

_____

_____

_____

_____

_____

_____

_____

Today's Prayer

Lord, it's hard for me to let everything go and sit quietly with You. But I know this is where you're calling me. Help me to trust You this day and determine to spend time alone with You. Thank You for rocking my world! I love You.

Day 13: The Core of the Problem

Turn my eyes from looking at what is worthless;
give me life in Your ways.
Psalm 119:37

Emily had managed to get away from her family to attend a women's retreat for the weekend. As she sat in a crowded auditorium with other women who shared the same frustrations of having too much to do and too little time, she heard these words: "God will not bless you in doing the things He has not called you to do—even if they're good things." Emily was stunned. Her life was full of good things. Could it be that God didn't want her to do all these things?

Take a look at the following list of "good" things:

• Teaching Sunday school
• Serving on a committee
• Volunteering in school
• Singing in the choir
• Tutoring

- Belonging to a civic club
- Visiting the elderly

Oh, such a small sampling, but you get the idea. And you could add a lot of other examples from your own life, I'm sure. In fact, I know many women who have filled their lives with way too many good things!

Many Christian women, swallowed up in an endless array of duties, responsibilities, and service, miss out on God's best for them. This plethora of activity often steals their creativity, their playtime, their joy, and leaves them physically, emotionally, mentally, and spiritually depleted.

God has a beautiful invitation to all who find themselves caught up in the lifestyle of too many things to do with not enough time to do them. Through Isaiah, God issues an invitation to all who are thirsty, to all who are not satisfied with life, to all who are too busy to enjoy His peace and joy.

> Come, everyone who is thirsty, come to the waters. . . . Seek the Lord while He may be found; call to Him while He is near. . . . "For My thoughts are not your thoughts, and your ways are not My ways." This is the LORD's declaration. "For as heaven is higher than earth, so My ways are higher than your ways, and My thoughts than your thoughts." (Isa. 55:1a, 6, 8–9)

I assure you, if you are anxious, pressured, and depleted by the demands placed on your life right now, God has something better in mind for you. Too little time is not actually the problem. The core of the problem may be having too much to do! And through accepting the invitation of the Lord to come to Him, He will give you His thoughts about the scheduling of your time!

God does not want you to do every good thing. I can't tell you which things you should be doing, but He can. That's why you must check His thinking and seek His counsel in everything you do. Isaiah admonishes us to seek the Lord and consider His thoughts and ways. He alone can tell you what you need to be involved in during this time in your life.

I know it may sound a bit cut and dried at first, this notion of just asking God what you should be doing and waiting for Him to tell you, but, friend, it's true! If you offer your heart, mind, and emotions to your Heavenly Father, He will direct you about all the things He wants you to be involved in during your daily schedule.

For me, the revelation about what should occupy my days comes in my quiet, alone time with Him. Part of what I do during this time is to go over my plans for the day, praying over each item and asking His take on what fills my day. More than once He has impressed me to strike something off my list.

I've learned not to assume that just because something is good, this doesn't mean that God wants me doing it at this particular time in my life. After all, just about everything I do could be classified as "good"—from visiting in the nursing home to serving on committees at church to checking in on neighbors. I can't, however, do *all* of those good things *all the time.*

When I seek God's counsel, asking Him to be in control of my to-do list, He truly impresses on me what should be on it in the first place. Sometimes I'm impressed to strike off "little things." There have been other times when He has called me specifically to drop out of an activity for a while so that I can have more time to be with my family and grow our relationships.

After the birth of my second child, for instance, I was seeking God's guidance about being the mom He wanted me to be. He clearly impressed on me to refrain from night meetings during the first year of my baby's life. I have to tell you, now, it's rare that the Lord has been so specific about "what to do" down to the time element. But that particular event was one of those occasions. I was obedient to what I knew He had told me to do and stepped away from all activities that caused me to be away from home at night for the first year after Lane's birth.

That "baby" is all grown up now, but I can look back on the situation and know that it was a blessing to move in the direction of my Father's leadership. I still don't know fully why God gave such a clear admonition in this. He did not lead that particular way when my older son was born, and does not lead many other women in the same way. But for me, He knew that this was best. I trusted Him then, and I trust Him now to be in control of what fills my days.

I believe God wants us to learn to enjoy His fellowship at a more relaxed pace. For some reason, we busy women equate being busy for God as being productive for Him. But He is showing me that I'm more productive when I'm less busy and more relaxed.

It's my prayer that you will begin to check areas in your life where you might be overcommitted. Take some time with the Lord, seeking His direction. Making sure you are less busy will help you have more time for sitting at His feet, and that's to your advantage!

Date: _____

> There is need of only one or but a few things. Mary has chosen the good portion [that which is to her advantage]. – *Luke 10:42* AMP

Today, Lord, I praise You for these things: _____

_____

_____

_____

_____

_____

_____

Think About This

Too many good women doing too many good things! Do you fall under that umbrella? It's so easy to get caught up in doing good things because . . . well, they need to be done! Free yourself from the anxiety of trying to do it all, by realizing that God never intended for you to do it all in the first place. Talk to Him about it. Where do you think He's telling you to cut back? _____

_____

_____

_____

_____

Today, I give You these details:

_____

_____

_____

_____

_____

_____

_____

_____

_____

_____

_____

_____

_____

_____

_____

_____

_____

_____

Today's Prayer

Oh Lord, I so want to be blessed in doing things for You. But doing so much often keeps me feeling distant from You. Help me realize that more than "doing for You", You want me to "be with You" and to get to know Your heart. I love You.

Day 14: Blessed by God

Charm is deceptive and beauty is fleeting,
but a woman who fears the Lord will be praised.
Proverbs 31:30

Sue's heart sank as she considered the description of the virtuous woman in Proverbs 31. She had recommitted her life to God, asking Him to show her how to be the woman He wanted her to be. She also asked Him to show her how to get everything done on a daily basis, glorifying Him in the process. She was flooded with feelings of guilt and self-doubt as she read through the qualities of God's ideal woman.

Do you ever compare yourself to other women? At times God may give you an example in another woman. He may speak to you through her words or lifestyle, drawing you to His character through what you see in her. At other times, however, *you* are the one initiating the comparison, and the focus becomes jealousy and self-pity because you can't seem to measure up.

Let's take a look at that virtuous woman of Proverbs 31. Here's my paraphrase:

She was up before dawn.
She had her own garden.
She made clothes for herself and her family.
She owned and ran her own business.
She was a wonderful homemaker.
Her husband praised her.
Her children adored her.
She was intelligent.
She took care of the physical needs of her family.
She spoke with wisdom.
She helped others.
She was in shape—physically, emotionally, spiritually.
She feared God.

Well, what do you think? Any possibility of your getting a close comparison? Now before you toss out this chapter, let me answer for you with a resounding *yes!* You can become the ideal woman. Not because of what *you* can do but because of who God is!

When I scan this list of descriptives, one quality towers head and shoulders above the rest. Do you know which one? *She feared God.*

The phrase in Proverbs from the Amplified Bible reads, "She worshipfully feared the Lord." In other words, she worshiped God and put Him at the top of her priority list. Only one thing is mentioned in Proverbs 31:10 (KJV) as making her value "far above rubies," and that's her spiritual life. It all goes back to sitting at the feet of Jesus!

As you worship Him, read His Word, and seek His counsel, God will tell you what things should be part of your life. "Planting your garden" may be sowing seeds of kindness through a volunteer project or maybe showing particular interest in a family member's activities. "Being a wonderful homemaker" may be offering daily encouragement to your husband or listening to your child pour out frustrations about friendships. It's accomplishing *many* things by first doing the *one* thing, and that's making time with God top priority, which will strengthen you in every way—mentally, emotionally, and physically.

Be affirmed and encouraged, dear sister. God longs for you to experience peace in your daily activities. He wants your life to be filled with joy, not turmoil and panic. And to that end He is inviting you to the place of ultimate comfort, rest, fulfillment, and excitement—His presence!

Are you catching the point of what all of this has to do with your time management issues? There's simply no better way to take control of your time than by choosing to give your time to God! In seeking His direction about your daily schedule and all the things that take up your day, you are inviting Him to be part of every element that makes up how you spend your time. Taking time to do this will result in blessings on your life that you simply can't experience any other way!

Date: _____

Lord my God, You have done many things—Your
wonderful works and Your plans for us; none can
compare with You. If I were to report and speak of
them, they are more than can be told. – *Psalm 40:5*

Today, Lord, I praise You for these things: _____

_____

_____

_____

_____

_____

_____

Think About This

Do you often compare yourself to other women who seem
to have it all together? Usually when you do that, you are not
living in this reality: that God created you uniquely for a designer relationship with Him. There's none other who comes
close to you in God's eyes. Record some unique qualities
about you below. _____ _____

_____

_____

_____

_____

Today, I give You these details:

_____
_____
_____
_____
_____
_____
_____
_____
_____
_____
_____
_____
_____
_____
_____
_____
_____
_____
_____
_____

Today's Prayer

Father, help me never to forget that You created me with a divine purpose in mind. You made me just like I am and love me because I'm Your designer creation. I turn my heart to You right now, asking You to reveal Your love to me and help me to love myself.

Day 15: Making God Priority

By His own choice, He gave us a new birth by the message of truth so that we would be the firstfruits of His creatures.
James 1:18

My friend Janet and I were talking about the difficulty of scheduling our time with God on a daily basis. Janet is a woman dedicated to the Lord, her husband, her children and grandchildren, and the children in her elementary classroom. She is on a mission to serve the Lord throughout her busy day as a wife, mom, grandmom, and teacher. But being a late-night person, she is not inclined or dispositioned to have her quiet time in the wee morning hours. Getting up early to prepare for her school day ahead is about as much "early" as she can handle.

While going back and forth about the busyness of life and how it's so difficult to even think about setting the clock half an hour earlier, she remarked: "But you know, offering God the firstfruits of my day is what it's all about. I know that even when I don't feel like getting up any earlier than I already do, I honor Him when I give Him this part of my day."

You may be like Janet, a late-night person who loves the Lord but struggles with early morning times with Him. When you go to bed so late, it's just hard to get revved-up for any early morning commitment—especially for one you don't have to keep!

Think with me about the first part of your day and how offering God this "firstfruit time of the day" becomes an act of worship. During Old Testament times, the firstfruit was the first gathered fruit of a harvest, and it was offered to God in gratitude. God instructed the Israelites to bring their first and their best to Him.

By offering God the firstfruit of *anything*, I'm acknowledging His priority in my life. I can do this by spending time with Him at the first part of my day, or by giving Him the first money before I pay for other things, or by choosing to voice Scripture with the first words I speak each day.

Firstfruits are also the first results of an undertaking. Let's say God has given you a day of feeling really good and energetic. You may choose to worship Him by setting aside time to take a walk, letting this be a "walk of thankfulness" for the energy He has given you. Or maybe you complete an assignment at work, and before you email it, post it, or announce it, you take it before the Lord, thanking Him for His clear insight and instruction, then commit this project to Him before others get involved.

This is "priority with God" kind of living—thinking about Him, praising Him, worshiping Him as the minutes and hours unfold. These thoughts and behaviors keep you centered on Jesus throughout the busyness of your day.

I understand that I should make Jesus the priority of my life, and indeed that's my goal because I love Him so much. But more difficult for me to grasp is the reality that I am the priority of Jesus Christ! Did you catch what you just read? You, dear frazzled sister, are the priority of Jesus!

James 1:18 tells us that we are the "firstfruits of His creatures." In other words, out of all creation, *we* are first and foremost in His mind! I'm finally getting this as I study the words of Jesus in John 17. Look how He forms His thoughts as He prays for us—His priority—starting in verse 15 and moving on from there to the end:

- "I am praying . . . that You protect them."

- "Sanctify them by the truth."

- "I have given them the glory You have given Me."

- "May they be one as We are one."

- "I desire those You have given Me to be with Me where I am."

- "I made Your name known to them and will make it known, so the love You have loved Me with may be in them and I may be in them."

I cannot read these words without my heart overflowing with love for Jesus! He loves me so much, and He longs for me to love Him back. We get caught up so often in doing things for our loved ones, and the emphasis becomes entirely placed upon doing the things that need to be done for them instead of growing our love relationship with them. I so understand how this happens. Life is busy and full, and there's much to do with little time to accomplish it.

The truth remains, however, that more than anything I can do for my family, it's spending time with them that reveals the depth of my love. I know it's difficult in the age in which we live to focus on the love relationship within the family and with the Lord. It's the desire of His heart, however, that our focus for Him and others remain the greater priority of our days.

Date: _____

> I'd rather for you to be faithful and to know me than to offer sacrifices. – *Hosea 6:6 CEV*

Today, Lord, I praise You for these things: _____

_____

_____

_____

_____

_____

_____

Think About This

First thing in the morning, your body, mind, and emotions are (hopefully) rested from a good night's sleep. By turning your attention to the Lord during these first moments of your day, you are honoring God by making Him the priority of the day ahead. It's your "firstfruit" offering. How does having quiet time with the Lord affect your day? _____

_____

_____

_____

_____

_____

_____

Today, I give You these details:

_____
_____
_____
_____
_____
_____
_____
_____
_____
_____
_____
_____
_____
_____
_____
_____
_____
_____
_____
_____
_____

Today's Prayer

Lord, I want to offer you the firstfruit of my day. I know that loving You will be my motivation. Please show me how to love You with all my heart and soul and strength. I commit to spending the first moments of my day with You. I love You.

WEEK FOUR

People Are Getting on My Nerves!

*Thanks be to God, who gives us the victory
through our Lord Jesus Christ!*
1 Corinthians 15:57

Okay, let's bring it down to gut-level honesty here. Can't people just drive you crazy?

Years ago I was in the mountains of North Carolina, leading the administrative staff and congregation of a small church through a team-building session. We were exploring the strengths and weaknesses of various behavior styles, highlighting the differences of each. Volunteers from the audience represented each style of behavior. It surprised us all when one mild-mannered deacon erupted on the spot, "I just can't stand people like that!"

Truth is, there are just days when people can get on your last nerve! But since we will be living alongside others as long as we

breathe on this earth, it's important to examine spiritual strategies to help us deal with all the people Jesus loves, including the
ones who rub us the wrong way.

> Be in agreement with one another. Do not be proud;
> instead, associate with the humble. Do not be wise in
> your own estimation. Do not repay anyone evil for evil.
> Try to do what is honorable in everyone's eyes. If possible,
> on your part, live at peace with everyone. Friends, do not
> avenge yourselves; instead, leave room for His wrath. For
> it is written: "'Vengeance belongs to Me; I will repay,' says
> the Lord." (Rom. 12:16–19)

Day 16: Living Peacefully

Lord, set up a guard for my mouth;
keep watch at the door of my lips.
Psalm 141:3

A few words spoken by another can throw you off track and disrupt your peace. Jesus' words had this effect on His disciples as He prepared them for His Heavenly departure.

"Your heart must not be troubled. Believe in God; believe also in Me. In My Father's house are many dwelling places; if not, I would have told you. I am going away to prepare a place for you. If I go away and prepare a place for you, I will come back and receive you to Myself, so that where I am you may be also. You know the way where I am going."

"Lord," Thomas said, "we don't know where You're going. How can we know the way?" Jesus told him, "I am the way, the truth, and the life. No one comes to the Father except through Me." (John 14:1–6)

Can you imagine the surprise, confusion, and fear the disciples must have experienced at these words of Jesus? They had left everything to follow Him, and now He told them He was going away—actually leaving them! I believe they desperately wanted to understand, but more than that, they wanted the answer to the question that lodged in their pounding hearts: "What about us?"

Self lies at the heart of many problems we face in dealing with people. We want to know . . .

- "Why are you telling me this?"
- "What am I supposed to do?"
- "How should I feel?"
- "Who is going to help me?"
- "Why don't you understand me?"
- "Don't you care about me?"
- "What's going to happen to me?"

Consider Sharon, who works in an office with five other people. They often eat lunch together and chat during breaks. Sharon recently realized that Alesa is acting differently toward her. She seldom speaks, and when she does, it's in a condescending tone. Alesa's unfriendly attitude is beginning to bother Sharon. She wonders, "Why are you treating me this way? What happened to our friendship? What can I do to make everything okay?"

I'm like Sharon. My style of behavior is one that enjoys interacting with people. So when people say things and behave in ways I don't understand, I can be easily hurt, confused, and offended! It's an ongoing challenge for me to accept and apply the peace of Jesus when I encounter difficulty with what others say and how they behave.

John 14:27 is a comforting verse that is often quoted during funerals and memorial services. It has also given me great insight into experiencing the peace and comfort of Jesus in "people" situations. He said, "Peace I leave with you. My peace I give to you. I do not give to you as the world gives. Your heart must not be troubled or fearful."

I often allow the words and behaviors of others to confuse and unsettle me. I believe Jesus is saying to me through this verse that I don't have to be troubled, afraid, agitated, intimidated, or unsettled in any area of my life. He has given me His peace!

It's a good thing to recognize unsettled feelings, but it's not productive to get self-absorbed in the process, to get caught up in the "me" aspect of it. It is only by shifting your focus from yourself to the peace of Jesus—getting self out of the way—that you can open the door to understanding.

The good news is, you don't have to shift this focus in your own strength and by your own efforts. You have a personal trainer who will pick up that heavy weight of self, set it aside, and reposition your focus. In fact, He's waiting for you to ask for His help! If you have invited Jesus to live in your heart, then your Helper—the Holy Spirit—dwells within you, ready to energize you with the peace of Jesus!

For me, His peace rushes in to settle my whirling and random thoughts. Then I'm energized with a new focus. It's a focus not on self but on the ways of Jesus. I'm training myself mentally to step back from the negative feelings, asking the Holy Spirit to take over my mind and emotions. My "people problems" are gradually providing more and more opportunities to experience the peace of Jesus! And you know what? That's a pretty exciting thing!

Date: _____

> I will ask the Father, and He will give you another
> Counselor to be with you forever. – *John 14:16*

Today, Lord, I praise You for these things: _____

_____

_____

_____

_____

_____

_____

Think About This

As women, we often allow our emotions to interfere with
making rational assessments of a situation. Think of a time
when you were hurt by someone's tone of voice or behavior
towards you. How could you have dealt with this in a more
positive way by shifting your focus to the peace of Jesus
instead of self? _____

_____

_____

_____

_____

_____

_____

Today, I give You these details:

_____

_____

_____

_____

_____

_____

_____

_____

_____

_____

_____

_____

_____

_____

_____

_____

_____

_____

_____

_____

Today's Prayer

Lord, I don't want my emotions to rule me. Help me to know that You are my comfort and peace when I feel attacked by the words of others. Teach me how to respond in Your way, not mine. Amen.

Day 17: It Depends on Me!

Now as we have many parts in one body, and all the parts do not have the same function, in the same way we who are many are one body in Christ and individually members of one another.
Romans 12:4–5

These words are part of a personal letter from Paul to the church in Rome. I enjoy Paul's writings immensely. He just has a way of laying things out, doesn't he? People are different, and he addresses those differences. We may have different spiritual gifts, different behavioral styles, and different points of emphasis and priority. But Paul encourages believers in Jesus to reach out aggressively to others through Christ's love, regardless of the differences.

Reaching out with the love of Christ can sometimes be challenging because differences often breed conflict. I was in earshot recently of a verbal conflict where tensions and heart rates were escalating. The disagreement was over the best way to handle a memo that had come into that particular office. To me, an innocent bystander (and happy to be one), this conflict was a perfect example of how two people with two points of view can each be right, but each one thinks her way is the only way!

Truly, many conflicts could be avoided if we simply stepped back, took a deep breath (or three or four), and conceded our right to be right. I realize that conceding our right to be right and getting rid of self is a slow and ongoing process. But for me, there's peace in even taking little baby steps in this direction. I know that when I become preoccupied with my way, my feelings, and my rights, then my energy is drained and my peace slips away. But when I make a conscious and deliberate choice to put *me* out of the way, then I can more easily turn the situation over to Jesus and let Him handle it.

And that's basically how I do it. I slow down and say aloud, if the circumstance permits, "I'm moving self out of the way. Jesus, please take over this situation!"

As simple as this sounds, that's just what you do. You *choose* to stop focusing on your feelings and your rights, and force yourself to put the other person's viewpoint above your own. This is often a difficult thing for me to do. But with persistence and determination, it's becoming an easier choice!

It's particularly difficult when your "self feelings" are justified. You may have been treated unfairly or unkindly. Getting rid of self depends on your degree of hurt. It may help you to remember this: By giving up self, you are in no way justifying the other person's behavior. You are simply following the commands given in Scripture to "bless those who persecute you; bless and do not curse. . . . Do not repay anyone evil for evil. Try to do what is honorable in everyone's eyes. If possible, on your part, live at peace with everyone" (Rom. 12:14, 17–18).

I remember years ago being so frustrated about trash that was left lying around in our yard after the cans had been emptied on trash pickup day. Week after week I had carefully secured each bag, hoping all the contents would make it to the trash bin instead of being scattered throughout the yard. Finally it occurred to me to show a little appreciation for the trash service instead of being concerned with the remnants. I mean, *most* of it was making it to the truck! With great care, I painted a sign and plastered it on the outside of our two backyard garbage cans. It read, "I appreciate you for carrying off my trash." That was the last time trash was scattered across our yard.

I learned a valuable lesson that day. That incident helped me learn how to deal with people in my life who frustrate me. A little appreciation and kindness go a long way. And since that time, I've considered frustrating circumstances as opportunities to put self aside, practice God's love, and experience His peace.

Date: _____

Be devoted to one another in brotherly love. Honor one another above yourselves. – *Romans 12:10 NIV*

Today, Lord, I praise You for these things: _____

_____

_____

_____

_____

_____

_____

Think About This

When I shift my focus from self to the other person, I begin to view them differently. Think of a recent experience which provided an opportunity to show the kindness of Jesus in the middle of a trying circumstance. What can you do today to spread His love? _____

_____

_____

_____

_____

_____

_____

Today, I give You these details:

_____
_____
_____
_____
_____
_____
_____
_____
_____
_____
_____
_____
_____
_____
_____
_____
_____
_____

Today's Prayer

Lord, continue to help me think like You think when others offend me. Help me to see them through Your eyes, and then offer them the compassion that You would extend to them. With Your help, I will spread Your love and joy today to all around me. Amen.

Day 18: This Is My Part

Do not conform any longer to the pattern of this world, but be transformed by the renewing of your mind.
Romans 12:2 NIV

Several weeks ago I was eating lunch with a friend. When the server brought a basket with three rolls in it, my friend remarked, "Why would she bring three rolls for two people? Does she want us to have it out over the third one?"

Now I can tell you straight up that the world's way would be to fight it out! You know, stand up for yourself and take care of number one. But according to Colossians 3, that's not God's way. "Set your minds on what is above, not on what is on the earth" (v. 2).

In Paul's letter to the Colossians, he gives encouragement and something for the reader to hang on to. Then he fills this letter with practical applications for how we should live.

Therefore, God's chosen ones, holy and loved, put on heartfelt compassion, kindness, humility, gentleness, and patience, accepting one another and forgiving one another if anyone has a complaint against another. Just as the Lord has forgiven you, so also you must forgive. Above all, put on love—the perfect bond of unity. And let the peace of the Messiah, to which you were also called in one body, control your hearts. Be thankful. Let the message about the Messiah dwell richly among you, teaching and admonishing one another in all wisdom, and singing psalms, hymns, and spiritual songs, with gratitude in your hearts to God. And whatever you do, in word or in deed, do everything in the name of the Lord Jesus, giving thanks to God the Father through Him. (Col. 3:12–17)

There's a distinct connection between getting along with others and focusing on Heaven. It's difficult, however, to set your mind on things above if you are being mistreated on earth, isn't it? Oh, my, when those human emotions are aroused, it takes all the self-restraint we can muster to focus on Heaven and behave with a Heavenly mind-set!

For years I taught school. The years I spent in the middle school classroom led to my belief that teenage girls have the market cornered on volatile relationships. "High Voltage" was the invisible sign hanging on my classroom door. Those girls just seemed wired to experience emotional pain, as well as dishing it out. I loved them, and I loved teaching this age. But it was a real challenge to dig through the layers of raging hormones and help them learn how to deal with the pressures of life (as well as learn some academics along the way).

Many walks to and from lunch and talks after school were spent on helping them understand that emotions can drive you nutty, and that trying to figure out why people did things and said things was often wasted energy. I instructed them to write positive comments on a small tablet. They were to keep this tablet close by and refer to it often, rehearsing these lines so they could get used to saying them. Then when their feelings were hurt or they were treated unkindly, they were to retaliate with a kind and positive reaction instead of giving in to self-absorbed feelings that caused them to focus on how they had been hurt.

This strategy didn't always work, but it was a start at helping them redirect their thoughts from the immediate pain they were experiencing. They began to learn that they *did* have a choice to focus on something other than their hurt. And in the long run, there were less emotionally charged events to deal with on a daily basis.

Do you see how this strategy applies to focusing on "things above" when things on earth are getting you down? That tablet of positive comments is the Word of God. When people get you down by something they say or do, pull a positive thought from God's Word and place it in your mind. Talk to the Lord about it. Say the Scripture along with your thoughts to Him.

Like, "Lord, I'm trying to set my mind on what is above right now, not on what is going on here on earth. Help me to focus on

You! Help me not to be absorbed with my own feelings but to focus on Your peace and Your love for this person. I know You want to help me. And I know You want me to be filled with Your peace. By faith I'm choosing to focus on Your love for this person instead of on my hurt."

Oh friend, don't you just long for the peace of Jesus to rule in your heart? I long for His peace in a mighty way. When I get ruffled or agitated, I'm determined I'm not going to stay that way. I keep going to the Lord with it, talking to Him about the situation, and keeping it before Him until I experience His peace.

As you become more intimate with the Savior, you will begin to experience His peace in indescribable ways. As you set aside a time each day to worship Him, to thank Him, to recognize Him as the Lord of your thoughts, emotions, behavior, and your life, you will gradually move into a peaceful state of living. You'll find that as stress hits, your reaction will be softened and seasoned with God's grace. You'll begin to experience freedom from self. It's the gift of being in His presence. It's the gentleness of Jesus.

Date: _____

> Now the Lord is the Spirit; and where the Spirit of the Lord is, there is freedom. *– 2 Corinthians 3:17*

Today, Lord, I praise You for these things: _____

_____

_____

_____

_____

_____

_____

Think About This

You can choose to let the hurtful words of others bounce off instead of letting your emotions suck them in. When you mix others' harsh words with your volatile emotions, you end up with an explosive mess! Write a few sentences of determination about your Godly response the next time someone hurts you. _____

_____

_____

_____

_____

_____

_____

Today, I give You these details:

_____
_____
_____
_____
_____
_____
_____
_____
_____
_____
_____
_____
_____
_____
_____
_____

Today's Prayer

Father, it's all about You, not me. Help me remember that. Remind me that Your Spirit lives inside of me, helping me to respond with Your love—even when I don't feel like it! I know that retaliating with love brings You honor. I love You and will honor You today. Amen.

Day 19: Loving Others

Be strong and courageous; don't be terrified or afraid of them.
For it is the Lord your God who goes with you;
He will not leave you or forsake you.
Deuteronomy 31:6

A friend recently shared with me about how she and her husband regularly meet with a group of friends for an evening meal. On one particular occasion, their friends engaged in conversation with everyone at the table except them. Ouch! Remembering times that I, too, have felt left out, I hurt for my friend. And then I remembered Jesus' words to His disciples. "I am going away to prepare a place for you" (John 14:2).

These words were not meant just for the disciples but for us too! He's preparing a special place for us where there will be no loneliness, no people competing with one another, no hurt feelings, just harmony and acceptance in Jesus.

With Jesus living in your heart, you can look forward to a grand celebration where you will be honored right alongside Him. Just imagine it! When you enter the marriage feast of the Lamb,

Jesus will be there. He is saving a place for you. John was instructed to write these words recorded in the book of Revelation:

> Then I heard something like the voice of a vast multitude, like the sound of cascading waters, and like the rumbling of loud thunder, saying: "Hallelujah—because our Lord God, the Almighty, has begun to reign! Let us be glad, rejoice, and give Him the glory, because the marriage of the Lamb has come, and His wife has prepared herself. She was permitted to wear fine linen, bright and pure." For the fine linen represents the righteous acts of the saints. Then he said to me, "Write: Blessed are those invited to the marriage feast of the Lamb!" (Rev. 19:6–9)

I imagine there will be much laughter and music and many conversations going on, but the King of kings and Lord of lords will offer you a special seat, as if you were the only one there. According to Revelation 2:17, Christ will give you a new name written on a white stone—a name known only to you and Him! In other words, you and Jesus will be perfectly at home together enjoying each other's company. Isn't that tremendously exciting and comforting?

You will never again feel left out, unwanted, or overlooked, because Jesus Himself will bring you into His presence and surround you with His love. Honestly, my friend, just focusing on this Heavenly scene, knowing that it will last for eternity, helps me deal with the stress I face until then. When I look at "people problems" in this light, I can get through the difficult times because of Christ's love and the promise of spending forever with Him.

Meanwhile, during the wait, here are some strategies that help me keep my focus. Perhaps you'll find them helpful too:

• *Make it not matter.* Sometimes people do things that hurt us. When this happens to me, I pray, "Lord, just make it not matter to me." I have a tendency to get my feelings hurt easily. So when I am consumed with my self-pity, I pray this prayer and trust the Lord to lift the burden of self. And He gradually (sometimes immediately) does.

• *Walk away before you blow up.* If you feel your emotions soaring and your fuse lighting, remove yourself from the situation. This could mean ending a phone conversation or physically walking away from someone. This takes determination but is well worth the effort. When you calm down, you can think more clearly. You'll have time to talk to the Lord about it before you speak.

• *Breathe deeply.* If you begin to feel uncomfortable in a situation, take several deep breaths. This will help your blood and oxygen flow more freely to your brain and will help you think more clearly. It also helps you think before you speak.

• *Deal with your negative attitude quickly.* Don't allow negative thinking to find a home in your heart and mind. These disruptive thoughts can cause brain drain. Replace them with something positive, like a Scripture verse or pleasant thought.

• *If you are wrong, admit it quickly.* Admitting that you're wrong shows your willingness to behave in a Christlike way. You model His compassion and His forgiving nature as well.

John 15:3 states, "You are already clean because of the word I have spoken to you." In other words, you are clean with Jesus living inside of you. You are Jesus-clean even though there may be times when you feel covered in dirt because of how others are affecting you. I'm reminded of how I used to love to clean up my little boys after they had been outside playing. It never bothered me when they got covered in dirt from head to toe. I knew that dirt was temporary, and pretty soon those little bodies would shine after I scrubbed them clean. And to tell you the truth, I enjoyed the process. It was fun to see them all squeaky clean after they had gotten so dirty.

When Jesus Christ came to live in your heart, He cleaned you up and filled you with His righteousness. He knows your personality, and He knows the problems you experience. If you focus on Him by worshiping Him, loving Him, and seeking His guidance, He will empower you to get along with others, no matter how difficult the process may be.

Date: _____

No one has ever seen God. If we love one another, God remains in us and His love is perfected in us.
– 1 John 4:12

Today, Lord, I praise You for these things: _____

_____

_____

_____

_____

_____

_____

Think About This

One day, the King of kings will honor you at a feast held in your honor! That reality fills my heart with such wonder! Just think, it's all about you and Jesus, together forever in eternity. Determine to focus on this thought today. In a few sentences, express your love to Him for loving you so completely! _____

_____

_____

_____

_____

_____

Today, I give You these details:

_____
_____
_____
_____
_____
_____
_____
_____
_____
_____
_____
_____
_____
_____
_____
_____
_____
_____

Today's Prayer

Father, I know that what You have in store for me for all eternity should keep me singing all day long! Help me today to keep that reality freshly before me. As the day unfolds with its various complications, bring me back to the reality of Heaven. I love You!

Day 20: When I'm Angry

Be angry and do not sin.
Don't let the sun go down on your anger.
Ephesians 4:26

Anger is a powerful emotion. And if left unchecked, it can grow disproportionately to the initial cause of the anger itself. Unbridled, it doesn't sit still but gets bigger, affecting everyone within the path of the angered person.

When you're in the middle of a tense situation and you realize you're rapidly heating towards your boiling point, it's good to pull away and assess the situation at hand. For me, this usually means getting away from others and alone with God. I realize that when I become angry and I'm around others, communication with them shuts down. Now, I didn't say that there's a shortage of words; rather, communicating those words in a Christian way is next to impossible when tempers are flaring and voices are raised.

There's a place for anger—righteous anger. I get angry, for example, when I'm around parents who verbally abuse their children. Having spent many years in the classroom, I've seen the negative effects of this abuse, and it just angers me when children are treated that way. I also get angry while watching the news. Killing, stealing, lying, cheating—they all make me angry. I get angry at sin! There are plenty of justifiable reasons for anger in a world ravaged by sin.

Recognizing this fact and realizing that we are wired with emotions that can easily be swayed by people, circumstances, and hormones, it's imperative that we as Christians learn to appropriately deal with anger issues.

Honestly, at this time of my life, my biggest challenges involving anger are private. It's unusual for me to blow up at someone and lose control. (This may be because my children have now left the home front.) But when someone or something makes me angry, I can scream and go ballistic on the inside, with a tempestuous storm of flailing emotions and elevated blood pressure. I'm thinking particularly of occasions when someone disagrees or challenges me in areas that are dear to my heart.

So now as I write, I'm wondering: Is this any less displeasing to God, just because nobody's looking? The reality is, He's there watching and listening and giving me opportunity to respond His way *any time* I'm angry. Whether our anger is righteous and justified, or spawned by emotions gone haywire, there are measures we can take to avoid the negative consequences of uncontrolled anger.

First, *recognize anger as an enemy.* When anger moves in and hunkers down, you're in for a rough ride if you don't identify and take control of it. Even if your anger is biblically justified, you can morph into a woman possessed if you don't deal with your anger properly. By recognizing and accepting your anger issues, you can then move forward to work through them with God's help and not in your own strength.

Secondly, *ask yourself, "Why am I angry?"* Am I overreacting because of personal issues? What does this outrage in me have to do with *me?*

And finally, *detach and attach!* Emotionally step back from the situation and cling to God. Talk to Him about it. "Lord, give me Your insight. Teach me something through this situation."

Recently, I had the opportunity to apply these principles myself. (Notice the word "opportunity." These situations are indeed opportunities to grow us spiritually.) A ministry associate and I were discussing a mutual project. His words came across to me as being critical and unsupportive of my work. Since we were not working face to face, it was easy for me to retreat to the anger zone in private. For the next few hours, I fumed inside before realizing the tremendous opportunity at hand to learn deep spiritual truths from this experience.

After recognizing and owning up to this, I realized the source of my anger. It was "all about me" thinking. I felt disapproved of, ignorant, and unworthy. I wasn't any of those things, of course, but the enemy strategically put together a package of defeat, tailor-made for me. He knows exactly how to do that, and he pulls this off many times when we are distracted by unsettled emotions.

After these insights, I immediately moved into dialogue with the Lord: "I see something spiritual here, Lord. I know there are times when I feel disapproved of and unworthy of Your love. I'm seeing that these are lies sown by the enemy and that Your love is strong and constant even when I mess up. You love me no more on my most perfect day than on those days when I seem to fail miserably on the scale of holiness."

Friend, this kind of dialogue with your Heavenly Father is so freeing. Because anger is such a volatile emotion, the corresponding spiritual teaching is rich and powerful. You give Him all the glory when you offer your anger to Him by recognizing it, searching within, then *detaching* while *attaching* to God Himself!

Date: _____

A fool gives full vent to his anger, but a wise man holds it in check. – *Proverbs 29:11*

Today, Lord, I praise You for these things: _____

_____

_____

_____

_____

_____

Think About This

Anger, even when it's justified, can wreak havoc both emotionally and physically. Take some time to assess your anger temperament. Talk to the Lord about it. What is a spiritual strategy you can apply next time you're tempted to lose it?

_____

_____

_____

_____

_____

_____

_____

_____

Today, I give You these details:

_____

_____

_____

_____

_____

_____

_____

_____

_____

_____

_____

_____

_____

_____

_____

_____

_____

_____

_____

_____

Today's Prayer

Lord, there are times when my anger "feels right." Help me to examine each anger episode in light of Your truth. Keep me focused on You before I speak—especially when I'm angry. You are my peace, and You alone can help me know how to respond in any situation. I trust You. I love You.

WEEK FIVE

Feeling Frazzled

The Lord is near the brokenhearted;
He saves those crushed in spirit.
Psalm 34:18

Sometimes, living just takes the life out of you, doesn't it? At best it seems that life is full of too many things to do, too many places to go, and too many people to take care of. It takes constant prodding and perseverance to keep things, situations, and people in some sort of orderly fashion. Well, this gal has noticed: ducks do not come in a row! And I can sure frazzle myself trying to get them to line up.

My friend Debbie called me one afternoon. It was Friday, her day off. She works in an orthodontist's office Monday through Thursday, and has the typical schedule of today's busy woman with a family to take care of, a job to work, and night meetings to attend. So Friday, her off-work day, is usually filled with more work than the other days. This is the catch-all day, the day that fills up with car repairs, doctors' appointments, housecleaning, bill paying—you get the picture.

Yesterday I caught the laughter in her voice as she said, "I took a nap this morning, right in the middle of everything I had to do, and it was wonderful!"

"You go, girl!"

That was my reaction to my friend's confession. The time has come for all frazzled females to boldly take back what has been taken from them—*life!*

And friend, you have to determine to take care of yourself—to take time for you. It *does* not and *will* not come without effort, because daily living is filled with too many pressures and things to do. I find that "taking time for self" is on the bottom of the list for most women I know.

But taking care of yourself and spending some time just enjoying life is preventive maintenance. It's a way of helping you become less frazzled and frenetic. It's also a wonderful gift to your family, because you're nicer when you do something just for you!

Go ahead. Dream of something you love to do but never seem to have time for. Need a jump-start? How about: take a relaxing bath, get a manicure, go for a leisurely walk, go to a movie with the girls, cuddle up with a good book, eat out, go shopping, hike a trail, run a race, climb a mountain, or just soar on wings of eagles with ideas of learning something new and exploring life in new ways. It's like finding the child within you who used to love to romp and play, anticipating snow and springtime and barefoot weather and birthday presents.

I strongly believe that life would be so much more enjoyable if we would just chill a little. We would not be as stressed out if we'd take more time to relax, exercise, eat properly, and enjoy God's gifts of celebration.

Now I know you're probably thinking, "How am I supposed to find the time to do this?" It starts in the mind. Just entertain the notion that possibly you could come up with one or two ways to take better care of yourself . . . and read on!

Day 21: My House

Therefore strengthen your tired hands and weakened knees,
and make straight paths for your feet, so that what is lame may
not be dislocated, but healed instead.
Hebrews 12:12–13

It's only 8:00 a.m., but it already feels like afternoon to Janet! Before leaving for work at 6:30 this morning, she washed a load of clothes and got things ready to cook dinner for her family that evening. Now at work, the list of things she needs to accomplish seems endless. Just thinking about the day ahead makes her exhausted. She can't imagine how she will accomplish everything that needs to be done before the end of the day, much less by the weekend.

Janet's been plagued lately by physical problems. Her exhausted body cries out through headaches, backaches, shoulder and neck tension, not to mention sheer depletion. Her family has noticed she's not taking care of herself and has encouraged her to get some rest and relaxation. But Janet feels there's simply not time to take care of her physical needs in her hectic schedule.

Whew! I can relate to Janet. How about you? Read over the following list of physical symptoms brought on by a stretched-to-the-max lifestyle.

- stomach cramps
- headaches
- shortness of breath
- fatigue
- neck pain
- racing pulse
- muscle twitches
- blurred vision
- shakiness
- unexplained rashes
- jaw pain

Can you throw in some others? Truth is, the aches and pains you experience are tailored for the weak spots in your body. Stress will find its way to the vulnerable places in your particular physical makeup and then settle in for the long haul, producing pain and debilitation if you don't do something about it!

My friend, your body belongs to God, but He has housed you in it while on this earth. And if it is going to be taken care of while you're here, you'll be the one to do it! It's your choice to honor God with what He has given you, and part of what He has given you is a physical body that needs proper rest, proper exercise, and proper nutrition. "Do you not know that your body is a sanctuary of the Holy Spirit who is in you, whom you have from God? You are not your own, for you were bought at a price; therefore glorify God in your body" (1 Cor. 6:19–20).

When I really grasp the reality that my body is God's temple, then it becomes my personal goal to take care of this temple—for Him. I love God. I love His Holy Spirit. I can honor Him and show Him my love by taking care of my body. When I go through periods of not getting enough sleep, exercise, or the right kinds of food, then I am dishonoring God by not taking care of His earthly home.

This reality grieves me because I so long to honor Him in everything I do and with everything He has given me. Perhaps if we could always view taking care of ourselves as doing something for the Lord, then we would be more inclined to do so. It's just so easy, however, to get caught up in the daily-ness of life and use all of our energy addressing the more pressing needs of family and work. Too much to do often steals our goals of taking care of our body, mind, and emotions.

This is what happened to Libby. It was all she could do to keep up with the demands at work and manage her household. Because of her busy lifestyle, she viewed an exercise program as a luxury. It required all her energy to fix an evening meal after a hard day at work, let alone exercise. She was already missing sleep by staying up late, taking care of things around the house.

During lunch break she usually grabbed fast food while she

was running errands. Sometimes she stopped at these same fast-food restaurants after work to buy supper for her family. She often resented that some women seemed to have time to exercise regularly and fix nutritious meals at night. She decided those women just weren't as busy as she was! Libby felt that she didn't have time to eat right, exercise, and get enough rest.

Many women feel like they just don't have time to take care of themselves! In the Frazzled Female seminars, when I ask, "What keeps you from exercising, eating properly, and getting enough rest?" the response in unison is, "I don't have enough time!"

If you're running on that treadmill of too much to do and not enough time to do it, then it seems almost impossible to get off. You simply *must* make the choice—and follow through with it—to take care of your physical needs!

After years of excruciating pain in my jaws and neck brought on by a hectic lifestyle that took precedence over taking care of myself physically, I can speak from personal experience. I ended up having two surgeries with months of recovery before I learned to slow down and take better care of my body! If you don't take care of your physical needs by choice, then you will eventually be forced to deal (not by choice) with a body that succumbs to the daily stress and strain which you're placing on it.

Eating. Sleeping. Exercising. Relaxing. Ignoring any one of these areas can make you tense, irritable, and unable to tackle even little things. Plus, the longer these areas go unattended, the more your body, your emotions, and your mind will suffer. "Glorify God in your body" (1 Cor. 6:20). This not a suggestion but a command straight from Scripture to take care of your physical house. And I don't see the phrase, "when you have time," dangling on the end of that command.

Now for the good part. Feel encouraged! (We'll work through this together in the days ahead.) Women who exercise regularly, eat nutritiously, and get enough sleep are better equipped to deal with stress on a daily basis.

I know you're a proactive woman, one who is interested in climbing above the frazzledness of your life. Making it this far in this book is evidence of that! I pray that you will explore ways to get better at taking care of *you* and that you'll set some goals, asking your Father to show you ways you can honor Him with your body.

Date: _____

> My eager expectation and hope is that I will not be ashamed about anything, but that now as always, with all boldness, Christ will be highly honored in my body, whether by life or by death. – *Philippians 1:20*

Today, Lord, I praise You for these things: _____

_____

_____

_____

_____

_____

_____

Think About This

The demands of living often exceed our ability to give! With everything that has to be done for everybody else, it seems next to impossible to take care of ourselves, doesn't it? When you realize that you will eventually be forced to pay attention to your physical needs, you'll become more proactive in fighting the stress-attacks on your body. What are some small steps you can take today to combat physical stress?

_____

_____

_____

Today, I give You these details:

_____
_____
_____
_____
_____
_____
_____
_____
_____
_____
_____
_____
_____
_____
_____
_____
_____

Today's Prayer

Father, help me! I know that my body is suffering because of all the stress in my life. I know that You created me, that You love my body and want me to take care of it. Help me to honor You—starting right now—by taking care of the body You gave me.

Day 22: Seeking God's Guidance

*Make Your ways known to me, Lord; teach me Your paths.
Guide me in Your truth and teach me, for You are the God
of my salvation; I wait for You all day long.*
Psalm 25:4–5

Diane is exasperated. It's early evening, and she has just gotten home from work. Much of what she wanted to accomplish during her day at the office is still undone. She is tired and her body is beginning to ache.

Diane's doctor recently told her that her physical discomfort and emotional depletion were direct results of stress. He encouraged her to find a hobby and get regular exercise—anything to keep her mind off work when she wasn't there. He gave her a pamphlet about the benefits of a regular exercise program and suggested she get started right away. "It will take a time commitment and may even interrupt your schedule, but the benefits you will experience will be well worth the inconvenience," he said. Then came the sobering words, "If you don't start taking care of yourself now, you'll pay for it later."

Sometimes we just don't consider the amount of stress we heap on our bodies. We must understand that stress has physical consequences. For example, if I allow stress to keep me from eating right, I may run out of steam and lose concentration. It's important that I accept responsibility for the choices I make. I do have control over my eating patterns. When I take ownership and realize that getting the proper nutrients can affect the way I feel, look, and behave, then I'm more motivated to eat properly.

Perhaps you are beginning to realize that something must be done to ward off physical and emotional problems that are likely headed your way because you are not taking care of your physical needs. Many times, when faced with the gloom of reality, we shift to panic mode. I encourage you to know that your God is not confused or even ruffled in the least about your schedule, your time limitations, and the fact that you need to devote time to taking care of yourself. He understands this and has the solution all planned out for you. His promise offers you hope that He is in control of your schedule and your body.

"'For I know the plans I have for you'—this is the LORD's declaration—'plans for your welfare, not for disaster, to give you a future and a hope'" (Jer. 29:11). And furthermore, He longs for you to come to Him and talk with Him about all your concerns. He promises to listen to you, and He wants to help you with your goals of self-improvement. "You will call to Me and come and pray to Me, and I will listen to you. You will seek Me and find Me when you search for Me with all your heart" (Jer. 29:12–13).

Carole Lewis, best-selling author of the *First Place* weight-loss program, puts it this way:

It has been said that our perception of reality is our reality. If we think we are in a fog, we are in a fog. I'm glad that my God is never in a fog. Even when the darkness of my present circumstances prevents me from seeing clearly, my darkness is not dark to God. God knows where we are this very minute. He knows where we're sitting, what we're thinking, and what we might be eating; and He knows how we feel. Jesus said in Luke 12:7, "Indeed, the very hairs of your head are all numbered." Yes, God knows where we are.[3]

Dear friend, be encouraged and full of hope. God does know, He does care, and He will help you begin a lifestyle to honor your body, His temple!

Through your relationship with Jesus Christ, you can set manageable goals and make them a priority. Through prayer and Bible study, the Holy Spirit will lead you to set the goals God designs for you. He will also help you stick to them. "I am able to do all things through Him who strengthens me" (Phil. 4:13).

Okay, are you ready to take some steps to begin a lifestyle that takes care of you? I'm including a work area at the end of this day's reading, because I know how important it is to write down your goals. It helps you take ownership and steers you toward a positive commitment. Spend some time thinking about where you need to improve. Perhaps you're good at taking a few rest breaks throughout the day, but you need to incorporate some exercise into your daily schedule. I know other women who take great pains to work in the exercise, but they quickly succumb to fast food because it's convenient to grab.

You will notice the greatest benefits from paying attention to each area. And success in one area can transfer to success in another! When I eat vegetables full of vitamins and minerals, for instance, I feel more like exercising than when I fill up on a meal of convenient fast food.

Please make it a point to get your Father's take on your goals. He loves you and wants you to succeed at managing your physical needs. In fact, He *wants* you to ask Him so that He can tell you how to do it!

My Goals for This Week

Exercise

1. _____

_____

2. _____

_____

3. _____

_____

Diet/Nutrition

1. _____

_____

2. _____

_____

3. _____

_____

Sleep/Rest

1. _____

_____

2. _____

_____

3. _____

_____

Date: _____

> Call to Me and I will answer you and tell you great
> and wondrous things you do not know.
> – *Jeremiah 33:3*

Today, Lord, I praise You for these things: _____

_____

_____

_____

_____

_____

Think About This

God understands your schedule and lack of time to take
care of yourself. He also knows it's critical that you honor
your body, His temple. Spend some time with Him right now,
seeking His direction in doing this. Write your thoughts below, asking Him to help you begin a new lifestyle of managing stress by paying attention to your physical needs.

_____

_____

_____

_____

_____

Today, I give You these details:

_____

_____

_____

_____

_____

_____

_____

_____

_____

_____

_____

_____

_____

_____

_____

_____

_____

_____

Today's Prayer

Lord, I know I should be taking better care of myself. I can't function my best without properly eating, exercising, and resting. Please show me the way. You hold the answer, so I'm seeking You right now. Speak to me. I love You.

Day 23: The Stress of Sin

Day and night Your hand was heavy on me;
my strength was drained as in the summer's heat.
Then I acknowledged my sin to You and did not conceal
my iniquity. I said, "I will confess my transgressions to
the Lord," and You took away the guilt of my sin.
Psalm 32:4–5

We have explored why we feel frazzled and how the effects of stress pile up when we don't take care of ourselves physically. But there's another kind of stress that can place great strain on us physically, mentally, and emotionally. Often it's even more painful and debilitating. It's the stress of unconfessed sin!

Donna often recalls the unrest she experienced several years ago. She remembers the day she went to her doctor because of shortness of breath, heart palpitations, and other physical discomforts. After an examination her doctor asked, "Are you under some kind of stress?"

Actually, Donna was suffering from the weight of unconfessed sin in her life. She didn't admit it at the time, but she now realizes that being out of harmony with God affected her emotionally, mentally, and physically.

Just as not attending to your physical needs can contribute to unwanted stress in your life, a complacent attitude toward sinful behavior can also lead to stress overload. Consider these damaging effects of unconfessed sins:

- sleeplessness
- loss of appetite
- loss of joy
- withdrawal from people
- lack of energy
- racing pulse
- physical aches
- inability to focus
- restlessness
- lack of interest
- moodiness

This is just a sampling of the physical upheaval in which we place ourselves when we allow unconfessed sin to linger within. David was right on target when he cried out, saying, "When I kept silence [before I confessed], my bones wasted away through my groaning all the day long. For day and night Your hand [of displeasure] was heavy upon me; my moisture was turned into the drought of summer" (Ps. 32:3–4 AMP).

David knew the agony of unconfessed sin. Before giving his sin to God, he experienced spiritual drought and heaviness. God did not want David (and He doesn't want you) to settle for anything less than a full and abundant life with Him. And that abundant life is contingent upon confessing our sins to our Heavenly Father and then turning in repentance to His thoughts and His ways. "A thief comes only to steal and to kill and to destroy. I have come that they may have life and have it in abundance" (John 10:10).

Sin is a thief that will rob you of God's blessings. When we are involved in personal sin, God may allow us to experience great physical, emotional, and mental discomfort. Discomfort is part of the refining process, drawing our wayward hearts back to Him. He is always working out His plan for our lives and is consistently leading us to the place of contentment and joy in His presence. But you and I will not enter that place of abundance in Him if there is willful and unconfessed sin in our lives!

Remember Donna and her doctor's visit? She did not come to terms with a particular sin area in her life until her doctor asked her, "Are you under some kind of stress?" Prior to her doctor's prodding, she had shrugged off her sin as no big deal. But unconfessed sin *is* a big deal and creates a barrier between you and God. Since the fall in the garden of Eden as described in Genesis 3, sin has been a reality for all of God's children. To rationalize sin and deny its existence in your life is to deny the truth of Scripture. "If we say, 'We have no sin,' we are deceiving ourselves, and the truth is not in us" (1 John 1:8). We need to acknowledge the reality of sin and our need to confess. We simply do not have to live with the burden of unconfessed sin! God has promised to forgive us and to restore our joy. "If we confess our sins, He is faithful and righteous to forgive us our sins and to cleanse us from all unrighteousness" (1 John 1:9).

Please don't misunderstand what I'm saying. Physical problems are not always indicative of unconfessed sin. Many things can cause sickness. It is important to realize, however, that physical pain and suffering are possible consequences to living a sinful lifestyle. Feelings of sadness, guilt, anger, embarrassment, shame, lethargy, sickness, and despair are often experienced as consequences of sin.

God does not desire you to stay in that place of hurt, but He will allow you to experience these ailments to bring you to repentance. You may need to repent of an attitude, a behavior, or even a lifestyle that is displeasing to Him. From my personal experience I can certainly attest that God will not allow me to enjoy His peace physically, mentally, and emotionally if I'm living out of His will.

I can also testify along with the psalmist that there is a sweet release when I bring my sin before the Lord, admitting it and asking for His forgiveness. As I read David's words, I can identify with the physical breaking of chains! A weight is lifted, and a burden is dropped when we come clean before our Lord. "Then I acknowledged my sin to You and did not conceal my iniquity. I said, 'I will confess my transgressions to the Lord,' and You took away the guilt of my sin" (Ps. 32:5).

Perhaps as you read these words again, you are being nudged to acknowledge and confess a sin area in your life that is displeasing to God. Often the most difficult step is taking ownership of the sin. We spend countless time and energy trying to rationalize and justify our sinful behavior while the choice that would bring us abundant life is right before us—the choice of acknowledging the sin, confessing it, and then turning in repentance to get on with living!

When I consider that the negative effects of sin might be the cause of my mental, emotional, and physical discomfort, I pray the prayer of the psalmist. Then if God reveals to me an area of displeasure to Him, I acknowledge it, confess it, and repent of it— accepting His grace and forgiveness so that I may move forward in the direction He chooses.

Date: _____

> Search me, God, and know my heart; test me and
> know my concerns. See if there is any offensive way
> in me; lead me in the everlasting way.
> – *Psalm 139:23–24*

Today, Lord, I praise You for these things: _____

_____

_____

_____

_____

_____

_____

Think About This

Dear friend, the stress of unconfessed sin will rob you of
God's blessings and joy. You simply cannot live in peace if
there's an area in your life that you have not turned over to
Him. I hope you'll search your heart right now and respond
to the Holy Spirit's nudging. Ask Him to reveal any areas in
your attitude and behavior that are not pleasing to Him.

_____

_____

_____

_____

Today, I give You these details:

_____

_____

_____

_____

_____

_____

_____

_____

_____

_____

_____

_____

_____

_____

_____

_____

_____

_____

Today's Prayer

Father, I thank You that You will never let be content with unconfessed sin in my life. Right now, I offer You my body, mind, and will. Reveal any area that causes You displeasure. Lead me into confession and repentance. Keep me deeply in love with You by examining my soul daily. I love You.

Day 24: My Identity

I sought the Lord, and He answered me and delivered
me from all my fears. Those who look to Him are radiant
with joy; their faces will never be ashamed.
Psalm 34:4–5

Bonnie was in the middle of the wellness seminar her supervisor had asked her to attend. She had looked forward to taking a break from phones, computers, and clients, and she did enjoy learning stress tips and strategies on how to begin an exercise program. Then the instructor asked the participants to do something that was a little difficult for Bonnie. "Write a brief paragraph describing who you are." The more Bonnie considered this assignment, the more confused she felt. She could describe what she *looked like* and tell *who she was at work*. She could describe her roles of being a woman, but none of these descriptions explained who she was. Perplexed and a bit disturbed, she began to ponder more deeply the question, "Who am I?"

Women often tell me they share this same confusion of figuring out their identities. When we get caught up in so many roles that take us all over the place (in mind and body) on any given day, it causes us to step back and wonder, "Well, who am I anyway?" And we often want to know, "When do I stop being this person and turn into another one?"

Whoa! Life's like that. It can throw you some real zingers along the way, causing you to flounder in confusion when God wants you to realize that your true identity is in Him! Colossians 3:3 says, "For you have died, and your life is hidden with the Messiah in God." This means that if Jesus Christ lives within you, then your earthly identity is not who you really are. That earthly person has died, so to speak, and the "real you" is nestled inside of Jesus and filled with His glory. It's hard to understand, and it's difficult to describe, but it's reality! By faith I choose to believe each day—and sometimes many times during the day—that my real life has nothing to do with what I do or who I am on this earth but everything to do with my position in Christ!

When life gets particularly stressful, I lose sight of that identity in Him. Notice I did not say I *lose* my identity, but I lose *sight* of it. Especially when I mess up in a certain area or feel inadequate to do something, it's so easy for me to define my self-worth within the context of that area. Know what I mean?

This identity battle originates in the mind, and we must fight to remember that our identity is in Jesus Christ, not in who we are or what we do. When people and circumstances get us down, it's important to fight hard to remember our true identity! Joyce Meyer, best-selling author and conference host, states:

I had a wandering mind and had to train it by discipline. It was not easy, and sometimes I still have a relapse. While trying to complete some project, I will suddenly realize that my mind has just wandered off onto something else that has nothing to do with the issue at hand. I have not yet arrived at a place of perfect concentration, but at least I understand how important it is not to allow my mind to go wherever it wishes, whenever it desires.[4]

When my mind wanders off, it's often in the realm of my identity, forgetting who I am in Christ and forgetting His power and authority to deal with each situation I face. I'm little by little training myself to remember *whose* I am and *who* I am. This discipline of remembrance helps keep me focused in Him as I go about my daily duties.

Another way that helps me remember my true identity is to picture myself in my holy attire! Read this description and visualize how you look dressed in God's righteousness:

I greatly rejoice in the LORD, I exult in my God; for He has clothed me with the garments of salvation and wrapped me in a robe of righteousness, as a bridegroom wears a turban and as a bride adorns herself with her jewels. (Isa. 61:10).

And according to King David, our glorious Father has placed a crown upon our heads! "For You meet him with rich blessings; You place a crown of pure gold on his head" (Ps. 21:3).

Dear sister in Christ, I plead with you to visualize yourself in your garments of salvation. This visual image will energize you and cause you to carry yourself boldly and regally in the midst of any trying circumstance! You may be a wife, a mom, a coworker, a volunteer, a referee, a nurse, an arbitrator, a counselor, the one in charge on the home front, but first and foremost you are a daughter of the King. And this reality, if you let it sink into your heart and soul, will greatly impact the moments of your days.

It's a fun challenge for me to visualize myself in my holy attire when I walk into the grocery store. Believe me, I walk in with a smile on my face and a spring in my step just thinking about my robe and crown! If you ask your Heavenly Father to help you remember your royalty, He will. Believe it or not, it even makes grocery shopping more pleasant.

Months ago I was on the road, leaving one Frazzled Female event and heading to another. I was tired, a little disturbed over a recent personal situation, and feeling pretty low on the "having it all together" scale. When I checked into the next hotel, the young man behind the desk said, "You are in the best room we have. In fact, you're in the bridal suite. Someone must really think a lot of you."

My heart jumped. I was overwhelmed with joy as the reality of who I am flooded throughout my body and soul. Yes! I'm His bride, and He thinks a lot of me. In fact, He loves me with an everlasting love and has reserved the best room (the bridal suite) in the house for me!

Come on, dear sister, use the creative mind God gave you and enter into the reality of who you are in Jesus. Then let this reality get all over you and splash out from your insides. Others will notice and wonder what's up with all that joy they see. Tell them!

Date: _____

For the Lord will comfort Zion; He will comfort all her waste places, and He will make her wilderness like Eden, and her desert like the garden of the Lord. Joy and gladness will be found in her, thanksgiving and melodious song. – *Isaiah 51:3*

Today, Lord, I praise You for these things: _____

_____

_____

_____

_____

_____

_____

Think About This

You will never find the answer to the question "Who am I?" by looking inside yourself. Only by looking to God will you discover your true identity and your purpose for living. God alone knows what His unique purpose for your earthly life is. Ask Him to give you His viewpoint about who you are. Record your thoughts below. _____

_____

_____

_____

Today, I give You these details:

_____

_____

_____

_____

_____

_____

_____

_____

_____

_____

_____

_____

_____

_____

_____

_____

_____

_____

_____

Today's Prayer

Lord, I so often get discouraged and do not view myself as You do. Thank You for loving me and for pursuing a deep love relationship with me. This fact alone makes my life significant. I choose today to love me, too! Help me grasp Your love for me. I love You!

Day 25: Yoked with Jesus

Christ has liberated us into freedom. Therefore stand firm
and don't submit again to a yoke of slavery.
Galatians 5:1

Liberated: set free, as from imprisonment or bondage. That's the
definition. But here's the reality: If Jesus lives in you, then you
have been set free—and will continue to be free. Even when you
don't *feel* free, you still are.

How is it then, that we become oppressed with the stresses of
life and submit again to that yoke of slavery . . . when we know
better?

Consider the yoke. In biblical times, the yoke joined animals
together so they could share the load of whatever they were pulling. What a wonderful device to be used by those tilling the field.
Each animal shared the heaviness of the load so that the labor
became easier for each to bear. The two operated as one unit,
bearing the load.

In using this metaphor, Paul helps us understand the negative consequences of getting tied down to the "yoke of slavery."

Instead of moving victoriously about in the freedom of Christ, we become attached and enslaved to all the stressors that are bombarding us.

On any given day, I'm faced with the reality of a life that's madly racing around the corners, bouncing off the walls, and skidding to abrupt halts to change directions when interrupted. Life's just like that and, from everything I'm experiencing, it's only going to get worse if I don't make some deliberate choices to calm the mayhem.

Recent journal entry: "5:30 a.m.—Dear Lord, right now as the moments of a new day unfold, my soul races ahead trying to sort out all the details of the morning and afternoon before me. So many things on my to-do list. Makes me tired just thinking about them. If I can just get to You, Jesus, I'll be okay!"

Stay with me here and focus on that line: "If I can just get to You, Jesus, I'll be okay!" Over and over, this thought, this concept, this *truth* surfaces to my conscious thinking. I choose to believe this message is straight from God's heart! He alone knows how a fresh encounter with Him can clear my thinking, slow my heart rate, and restore my sanity. The very day of that journal entry, I chose to enter into worship before attacking any of the items on my list. With sheer determination, I pushed the stressful thoughts aside and focused exclusively (well, as best I could) on worshiping my Lord.

That's not the first time I've made this choice. And just as before, by redirecting my thinking and energy to praise and worship,

I was filled with fresh life and energy. The day ahead began looking brighter and the discouragement eased away, being replaced by hope and gratitude that I was not going to have to face the day alone. He would be there, filling me with a positive mind-set, clear direction, and renewed strength to get done what had to be done. Being with Him in worship during those early-morning moments redirected my thoughts. And as the thinking goes, so goes the day!

There's no way around it. I've said it before and I'll remind you again. Personal contact with Jesus changes everything!

Deliberately choosing (and it does take strong determination) to be yoked with Jesus instead of being yoked to your to-do list will enable you to feel and move about in the freedom that is already yours. You see, the thief's goal is to keep you distracted from Jesus and focused on your stressful lifestyle. By yoking you with your stress, you and the stress become one, so to speak. And that makes you a partner and a slave to stress—yuk!

But when you follow Paul's admonition in Galatians 5:1 to stand firm, refusing to submit to a yoke of slavery, you are stepping forth in victory and moving throughout your day in the freedom that is yours as God's child. And when you share His yoke, He makes it easy for you.

Your choice: yoked to stress or yoked to Jesus.

I'm choosing Jesus!

Date: _____

> Come to Me, all of you who are weary and bur-
> dened, and I will give you rest. All of you, take up
> My yoke and learn from Me, because I am gentle
> and humble in heart, and you will find rest for your-
> selves. For My yoke is easy and My burden is light.
> – *Matthew 11:28–30*

Today, Lord, I praise You for these things: _____

_____

_____

_____

_____

_____

Think About This

You are choosing today whether to be yoked with stress or
yoked with Jesus. As I consider this choice, I wonder . . . why
would I ever choose to get linked up with stress instead of
Jesus? You can determine to hang onto your freedom today.
You can refuse to be yoked with stress. Ask Jesus to help
you bear your load. _____

_____

_____

_____

Today, I give You these details:

_____
_____
_____
_____
_____
_____
_____
_____
_____
_____
_____
_____
_____
_____
_____
_____
_____
_____

Today's Prayer

Dear Father, I'm choosing You today! You are my freedom, and I'm choosing to walk as a free daughter of the King! May others see the love of Christ in me as I exhibit Your peace in what the day holds. Thank You for freeing me from stress. Amen.

WEEK SIX

Near to the Heart of God

Humble yourselves therefore under the mighty hand of God,
so that He may exalt you in due time, casting all your care
upon Him, because He cares about you.
1 Peter 5:6–7

God is always close to me whether I feel like He is or not. I make a daily choice to recognize this fact and be persistent in staying close to Him.

I once heard someone say, "God is to you who you perceive Him to be." By this I don't mean that He's a figment of my imagination or that I can create Him in my own image, making Him anything I want Him to be, something other than the Bible says He is. But this comment got me to thinking about being more creative with my picture of God than I usually am. I have the type of personality that gets bored easily. So lots of times I change the way I do something just to keep from getting in a rut. Sometimes

I drive a different way to work or eat dessert first. I part my hair on the other side and change the furniture around.

I've discovered that keeping spontaneous in my approach to worshiping Jesus helps me draw closer to Him. There are lots of ways to be with Him, maybe ways you've never thought about. Sometimes I go for a walk with Him. I might sing to Him or write a letter to Him. Occasionally when my husband has to work late, I have dinner with Jesus, talking with Him as I eat and mulling over Scripture as I chomp on salad.

Now before you settle in on the notion that I'm totally weird, why don't you explore the idea of being creative in your relationship with Jesus? Take a look at what Gary Thomas says in his book *Sacred Pathways*, when he talks about people getting stuck in a rut in their relationships with God:

> Their love for God has not dimmed, they've just fallen into a soul-numbing rut. Their devotions seem like nothing more than shadows of what they've been doing for years. They've been involved in the same ministry for so long they could practically do it in their sleep. It seems as if nobody in their small groups has had an original thought for three years. They finally wake up one morning and ask, "Is this really all there is to knowing God?"[5]

Just as in my earthly relationships, growing my love for the Lord is enhanced when I try new things and change the ways I approach Him. After all, life's tough, and growing your love relationship with Jesus is the most powerful antidote available to the trials of life! It's worth taking the time to explore new ways to discover His freshness and His nearness.

In this last week of our time together, we're going to explore ways to keep going when your faith runs low and what to do if you experience deep depression. Then we'll finish up with the wonderful reality that Jesus is praying for you right this very minute!

I'm so excited for you and want to spur you on in your faith walk, knowing that if you desire Him with all your heart, soul, mind, and strength, you will find Him!

Day 26: The Faith Test

*May you be strengthened with all power, according to His
glorious might, for all endurance and patience, with joy.*
Colossians 1:11

I've had circumstances in my life when my feelings were so
intertwined around people and events, it just seemed I could not
muster up enough faith to see me through to the other side. Then
guilt sat on top of those other feelings, compounding the intensity and making me feel helpless and hopeless!

Have you ever felt you couldn't pass the faith test? You've
prayed, read your Bible, maybe even fasted, yet still you lack faith!
Then let me share some hopeful (and redeeming) news with you:
what you're experiencing may have nothing to do with faith at all
but everything to do with feelings! We're going to take a look at
the reality of faith and how our feelings can distract us and divert
our attention from Jesus. That's what happened to Peter:

Immediately He made the disciples get into the boat
and go ahead of Him to the other side, while He dis-

missed the crowds. After dismissing the crowds, He went up on the mountain by Himself to pray. When evening came, He was there alone. But the boat was already over a mile from land, battered by the waves, because the wind was against them. Around three in the morning, He came toward them walking on the sea. When the disciples saw Him walking on the sea, they were terrified. "It's a ghost!" they said, and cried out in fear.

Immediately Jesus spoke to them. "Have courage! It is I. Don't be afraid."

"Lord, if it's You," Peter answered Him, "command me to come to You on the water."

"Come!" He said.

And climbing out of the boat, Peter started walking on the water and came toward Jesus. But when he saw the strength of the wind, he was afraid. And beginning to sink he cried out, "Lord, save me!"

Immediately Jesus reached out His hand, caught hold of him, and said to him, "You of little faith, why did you doubt?" When they got into the boat, the wind ceased. Then those in the boat worshiped Him and said, "Truly You are the Son of God!" (Matt. 14:22–33)

Often there may be confusion during the storm! Peter had walked with Jesus long enough to experience His love, tenderness, and mighty power. He had listened intently to the parables about the farmer sowing on different types of ground, the mustard seed, and the net full of fish. He had seen Jesus miraculously feeding five thousand people who had followed Him. Peter experienced many miracles in the presence of Jesus, and the Master gave him authority to drive out evil spirits and heal diseases. How then, after walking on the water in those first few steps of faith, did Peter lose sight of Jesus and begin to sink?

It makes you wonder, doesn't it? How could he forget all the things he had seen Jesus do for others and for him personally!

But you know, I can identify with Peter. I have experienced many great events—and made it through them all—with the help of Jesus. He has helped me deliver babies and lead loved ones to salvation, given me unexplainable peace on many occasions, and allowed me to witness specific answers to prayers. Yet in spite of all those victorious moments, I've still been known to focus on the storm instead of keeping my focus squarely on Him. Did I lose my faith at these times? Did I forget about the power of Jesus? No, I don't think so.

Romans 12:3 tells us that "God has distributed a measure of faith to each one." If you are a child of God, it is in your spiritual nature to have faith. At times, however, you may confuse your *feelings* with your *faith*. Satan uses doubt and unbelief to make you think you have to work hard to have faith. And when you just can't seem to work hard enough, he tells you your faith is lacking. But the problem is not your lack of faith; it's Satan seeking to destroy your faith with lies.

For example, God provided Amy with a new job. He gave her the desire, the faith, and the ability to do her work well. She knew when she accepted the job that it was a gift from God. After a while, however, things started happening that made it difficult to enjoy her work the way she did at first. So Amy started to doubt and question herself, wondering if she really had heard from God in the first place. Was this really the job He wanted for her?

I sincerely believe that God places dreams and visions within our hearts. When He gives you a particular calling, He will also give you the desire, faith, and ability to carry it through. He may call you to start a new job, teach a Bible study, or begin a family. When you receive by faith God's call on your life, He wants you to know that He has your best interest at heart. He provides for your every need in that call. It may be trusting Him with the life of your child or trusting Him with your finances. He loves you and wants the best for you.

There may be times, however, when the journey gets rough, when you wonder if you really heard God in the first place. That's when you must rely on your faith instead of your feelings to seek the truth.

Think back to Abraham and his journey of faith. God made him a promise, and years later he still hadn't seen the results. Yet Abraham stood in faith. He must have been attacked by doubts and unbelief, but according to Scripture he stood steadfast and unmovable. "He did not waver in unbelief at God's promise, but was strengthened in his faith and gave glory to God" (Rom. 4:20).

During this time of waiting and watching and hoping that God's promise would come to pass, Abraham kept giving glory to God! And as he did, he grew stronger and became empowered. Perhaps, unlike Peter, who placed his mind on the storm at hand instead of focusing on the Master, Abraham just praised God and thanked Him for who He was.

It's a moment-by-moment choice to know that our God is in control. Storms, doubts, and confusion can intimidate you. In times of trial like these, feelings are unpredictable and unreliable. But choosing to have faith in God has little to do with how you feel. Remember that! Don't allow feelings of worry, doubt, and confusion to keep you from experiencing the peace God wants you to enjoy as you rest in His presence.

Persevere. Keep with Him. He will lead you in the way He wants you to go.

Date: _____

Let me experience Your faithful love in the morning,
for I trust in You. Reveal to me the way I should go,
because I long for You. – *Psalm 143:8*

Today, Lord, I praise You for these things: _____

_____

_____

_____

_____

_____

Think About This

If you've known the Lord for a while, it's likely you've experienced times when He's manifested His glory in your life.
You've sensed Him intervening in your circumstances and
have thanked Him for His nearness. However, there are certainly other times when you've not experienced His closeness. Describe one such event below. _____

_____

_____

_____

_____

_____

Today, I give You these details:

_____

_____

_____

_____

_____

_____

_____

_____

_____

_____

_____

_____

_____

_____

_____

_____

_____

Today's Prayer

Dear Lord, forgive me for relying on my feelings instead of my knowledge that You will never leave me or forsake me. Help me to recognize the difference between faith and feelings. Keep me believing when I'm not feeling Your nearness. I'm turning to You, trusting You, and loving You. Amen.

Day 27: More Than a Case of the Blues

My flesh and my heart may fail,
but God is the strength of my heart, my portion forever.
Psalm 73:26

Have you ever been unable to shake the blues? You keep trying and trying, but you can't quite seem to feel better? If I could beat on the drums and sound the trumpet right now, I would! Because I have good news for you, dear friend! Your body and mind may be fragile, but the Holy Spirit who lives within you is not!

I have such a heart for this topic of depression. Before experiencing it myself, I had no understanding of the debilitating effects of this illness. Being a committed Christian with a close relationship with the Lord, I felt I could pray my way out of anything. Whenever pressures stacked up in my life, I disciplined myself to increase my prayer time.

But as weeks turned into months, my physical, emotional, and mental condition spiraled downward. I felt guilty and helpless as I desperately tried to get a grip on my life. It never occurred to me that I was getting firsthand experience on how to deal with and later teach about clinical depression.

When I finally broke down (literally) and went to my doctor for help, he asked me about stress issues in my life. He wanted to know what kind of pressures I had been dealing with and for how long. As I described the nature of my stress and the symptoms I was experiencing, I realized I was pretty bad off. I had never admitted the severity of my problem, and certainly had never shared it with anyone else. I was Miz Superwoman Magnificat!

To this day, I am grateful for my doctor's words: "You should not feel guilty." Hearing him say these words helped me begin to release the feelings of guilt I had been heaping upon myself—the guilt of teaching everybody else how to keep it together when I was falling apart myself!

Now there's a smile that tickles my lips as I write about this time in my life. Yes, I was teaching stress management seminars and offering instruction on how to keep stress from becoming the unmanageable monster it can often become. Yes, I knew all about how to deal with stress!

Then adding to that guilt was the guilt I experienced because of my love for the dear Lord. I remember thinking that I must not really be as close to Him as I thought. I also reasoned that there was some fault in my spiritual character because I could not pray my way out of this situation. To say that I felt like I was at the bottom of a black hole with an elephant sitting on my chest is not exaggerating!

But to hear and then to accept the fact that I should not feel guilty was truly the beginning of my healing process. I later learned that many Christians who suffer from clinical depression experience this kind of guilt.

Paul speaks of how our earthly body makes us groan and long for our Heavenly one: "For we know that if our earthly house, a tent, is destroyed, we have a building from God, a house not made with hands, eternal in the heavens. And, in fact, we groan in this one, longing to put on our house from heaven" (2 Cor. 5:1–2).

Amen to that! There are many times I anticipate my new body with my Lord in Heaven, so thankful that this new body that awaits me will be my permanent dwelling place, not this one! Have you, dear sister, ever felt the burden of your body, mind, and emotions? Have you longed for your permanent dwelling place in Heaven where the demands of this life will no longer occupy your every thought and movement?

Rest assured. You are already provided for! "The One who prepared us for this very thing is God, who gave us the Spirit as a down payment" (2 Cor. 5:5). One day you'll make your residence with God in Heaven.

But meanwhile—yes—you are living in a physical body that is designed for life here on earth. Your body contains blood vessels, muscles, tissues, organs, ligaments, and various operating systems. Intricately and delicately designed, your body is your earthly tent, susceptible to earthly wear and tear. The body doesn't work one way for Christians and another way for non-Christians. Loving the Lord does not guarantee you will be immune to the attack of stress on your body, mind, and emotions.

If you have not experienced a time of depression in your life, chances are that you or someone close to you will. Developing a spiritual viewpoint on this sickness will help you respond in a biblical way.

The following Scripture offered much hope and strength to me during my dark days: "The LORD is near the brokenhearted; He saves those crushed in spirit" (Ps. 34:18). When I let go of my guilt and stopped trying to work my way out of my dark moods, I began to rest in the reality of His closeness. I began to sense His presence in the midst of my brokenness. I accepted that He was close to me and wanting to save my crushed spirit. What a comfort I began to experience! You can, too!

Date: _____

> How lovely is Your dwelling place, Lord of Hosts. I long and yearn for the courts of the Lord; my heart and flesh cry out for the living God. – *Psalm 84:1–2*

Today, Lord, I praise You for these things: _____

_____

_____

_____

_____

_____

Think About This

When you have ongoing stress, life can seem almost unbearable. If you've begun to notice prolonged periods of physical problems and lack of joy, it could be you are experiencing symptoms of clinical depression. How effective are you at dealing with stress issues in your life right now? Record your answers below. _____

_____

_____

_____

_____

_____

_____

Today, I give You these details:

_____
_____
_____
_____
_____
_____
_____
_____
_____
_____
_____
_____
_____
_____
_____
_____
_____
_____

Today's Prayer

Father, it takes You to heal broken hearts and mend fractured minds. I need You to direct me right now. Show me how to deal with the stress areas in my life. If I need to talk with my pastor or seek medical attention, please prompt me to do so. I trust You to lead me in the direction that's best for me. Amen.

Day 28: Help Is Available

But those who trust in the Lord will renew their strength;
they will soar on wings like eagles; they will run and
not grow weary; they will walk and not faint.

Isaiah 40:31

Diana was trying to believe what she was reading in her morning devotional. Phrases from Isaiah kept staring back at her from her Bible: *soar on wings like eagles, run and not grow weary, walk and not faint.* It had been some time since she had gotten excited about the promises of Scripture. In fact, she seemed never to have any excitement or joy about anything these days. Things that used to bring her happiness and fulfillment, like going places with her family, now only made her feel tired and bogged down. Everything was an effort, and nothing seemed to bring her pleasure the way it once did. As Diana read Isaiah's verses again, she couldn't help wondering, "If God gives strength to the weary, why do I feel so tired and rotten about life?"

Friend, if you have been in the throes of depression, then you understand exactly how Diana feels. Being in that place is intensified with lack of acceptance or understanding about the whole clinical depression ride. It's turbulent to say the least, causing upheaval to your psyche as well as your physical body.

Not understanding what's happening with your body, your mind, or your emotions can be exasperating and unsettling. Be confident that God knows and cares about your frustration! "The LORD is the everlasting God, the Creator of the ends of the earth. He will not grow tired or weary, and his understanding no one can fathom. He gives strength to the weary and increases the power of the weak" (Isa. 40:28–29 NIV).

One way He increases the power of the weak is by increasing their understanding. If I understand more about how my body functions, then I can begin to believe that the God who controls all the parts of my body is also in control of every frustration I have concerning my body.

The brain is housed in one of the most intricate systems in the body—the central nervous system. Just as the parts of a machine are subject to wear and tear, our body systems are also prone to breakdown. In my bout with clinical depression, my brain became the faulty part.

My doctor simply explained it to me this way. "When you go through a stressful situation for a long period of time, the chemicals in your brain may begin to alter. When that happens, the chemicals that were once balanced become unbalanced, and you could enter into a period of instability, causing you mental and emotional anguish."

Strength for the Journey is a wonderfully and strategically written Bible study for those wanting to get a biblical perspective on discouragement and depression. "Nearly all people face discouragement at some time. Discouragement lasts for several days, but most individuals gradually begin to feel more positive about themselves and their circumstances. Clinical depression, on the other hand, is a state of prolonged sadness and despair."[6]

According to the authors, Dr. James Porowski and Dr. Paul Carlisle, who adapted a list from the American Psychiatric Association, a person can be considered depressed if she experiences five or more of the following symptoms almost every day for a period of two weeks.

1. Depressed mood most of each day
2. Loss of pleasure in formally enjoyable activities.
3. Significant changes in weight or appetite.
4. Can't fall asleep at night or wakes up repeatedly throughout the night.
5. Fatigue or loss of energy.
6. Feelings of hopelessness.
7. Inability to concentrate or make decisions.
8. Recurrent thoughts of death or suicide.[7]

Dear sister, I'm not writing this to give you medical advice. I am not equipped to offer treatment plans or to tell you what should be done if you or a loved one is experiencing depression.

But I can offer you insight into this sickness by looking at its common symptoms like the ones listed above, which were the ones I experienced. If you are having these symptoms and have experienced them for a prolonged time, I lovingly encourage you to seek medical attention.

My treatment plan included medication and Christian counseling. I cannot tell you how grateful I am to have finally recognized what was going on in my brain so that I could get on the road to recovery. And full and complete recovery did occur. It was a gradual healing process, but it was one that my Lord brought me through moment by moment.

If you are experiencing depression, you simply must take care of yourself before healing can begin. Prayerfully consider these suggestions:

- Slow down. Don't try to do as much as you are accustomed to doing.

- Don't take on new activities.

- Delegate some of your responsibilities.

- Be kind to yourself when you can't accomplish what you normally accomplish.

- Plan additional time to relax during each day.

- Don't load your weekend with housework or other "catch-up" activities.

- Eat a well-balanced diet.

- Get enough sleep.

- Cut out some night activities.

- Refrain from making major decisions.

- Seek comfort from family and friends who love you.

- Spend quiet time with the Lord, resting in His presence, thinking about how much He loves you, being confident He will renew your strength.

Date: _____

> Do not fear, for I am with you; do not be afraid, for
> I am your God. I will strengthen you; I will help you;
> I will hold on to you with My righteous right hand.
> – *Isaiah 41:10*

Today, Lord, I praise You for these things: _____

_____

_____

_____

_____

_____

Think About This

Soaring on wings like eagles and running without growing
weary seems impossible at times. It's so important that you
take care of yourself physically with exercise, proper nutrition, and rest. If you can't seem to get it together and are
experiencing despair and hopelessness, then it's time to
get help. Today, you need to take care of yourself. What are
some ways you can begin? _____

_____

_____

_____

_____

Today, I give You these details:

_____

_____

_____

_____

_____

_____

_____

_____

_____

_____

_____

_____

_____

_____

_____

_____

_____

_____

_____

Today's Prayer

Dear Lord, I need You. I'm trusting You to speak to my heart right now. Show me what to do and I will do it. I'm trusting You. I will get help. I commit this to You. Amen.

Day 29: Jesus Is Praying for You

My God will supply all your needs according to
His riches in glory in Christ Jesus.
Philippians 4:19

Elijah was a great prophet of God, one who had been used mightily in the Lord's service, performing miracles and boldly proclaiming His righteous acts. Elijah's life is the picture of one who gave his all in service to the Lord. Then, in a radical turn, he became depleted and worn. Being tired and weary of life, he begged God to let him die. "He said, 'I have had enough! LORD, take my life, for I'm no better than my fathers.' Then he lay down and slept under the broom tree" (1 Kings 19:4–5).

The Father has often used this portrait of Elijah to assure me of His presence in my circumstances. Like Elijah, I have at times become weary of the circumstances of life. And there have been times when I, just like Elijah, being haggard and worn, have retreated to the resting place! And you know, it's often been in that resting place—that quiet place with the Lord—where I have heard His whisper! His whisper is unmistakable, loving, and strong!

He said, "Go out and stand on the mountain in the LORD's presence." At that moment, the LORD passed by. A great and mighty wind was tearing at the mountains and was shattering cliffs before the LORD, but the LORD was not in the wind. After the wind there was an earthquake, but the LORD was not in the earthquake. After the earthquake there was a fire, but the LORD was not in the fire. And after the fire there was a voice, a soft whisper. (1 Kings 19:11–12)

This passage speaks directly to my heart's need to hear from God. Many times when I pour out my longing to Him, He gives me His presence instead of my desire of the moment. And many times, my desire of the moment is likened to the rushing power and turbulence of the wind, the fire, and the earthquake. It's not that our Lord doesn't reveal Himself in these boisterous happenings of life. He does! But I'm finding that many times He calls me to quiet my soul and my racing heart so that He may speak to me in His whisper, full of power and grace and peace for the moment.

I remember as a teenager going through a particular event that caused me much anxiety and lots of tears. On one particular evening while I was tucked away in my bedroom crying, my older brother, Reg, came to me and offered these comforting words: "Did you know that Jesus is crying right now with you because you are so hurt and upset?" To think that Jesus really understood me and cared how I was feeling touched my heart in a way that has stayed with me through all these years into my adult life.

Think of the most wonderful gift you've ever received in your life. Remember the joy and gratefulness you felt upon receiving it. Then multiply that feeling infinitely, and you'll catch a glimpse—but only a glimpse—of how Jesus feels about you. He is joyful over you! In fact, we are told in Scripture that we are a "gift" to Jesus from the Father. Jesus said, "Father, I desire that they also whom You have entrusted to Me [Your gift to Me,] may be with Me where I am" (John 17:24 AMP).

Years after that experience in my bedroom, I learned not only that Jesus cares about me but also prays for me. Now *that* reality nearly blew me away, and to tell you the truth it still does!

I pray for them. I am not praying for the world but for those You have given Me, because they are Yours. All My things are Yours, and Yours are Mine, and I have been glorified in them. . . .

Now I am coming to You, and I speak these things in the world so that they may have My joy completed in them. . . .

I am not praying that You take them out of the world but that You protect them from the evil one. They are not of the world, as I am not of the world. Sanctify them by the truth; Your word is truth. As You sent Me into the world, I also have sent them into the world. I sanctify

Myself for them, so they also may be sanctified by the truth. . . .

Righteous Father! The world has not known You. However, I have known You, and these have known that You sent Me. I made Your name known to them and will make it known, so the love You have loved Me with may be in them and I may be in them. (John 17:9–10, 13, 15–19, 25–26)

My dear friend, I believe it is critical to your growing intimacy with your Lord and Savior to grasp the reality that Jesus loves you and is praying for you! Can you believe it? Yes, do! Let this divine truth get a hold on you and fill you to the depths of your being. The King of kings and Lord of lords is lifting you to our Father. He is praying for you!

Sometimes as I read that passage from John, I substitute the pronouns with my name. This helps me to further experience the tender, powerful, and unconditional love of my Lord. Knowing that Jesus is praying for me empowers me in ways I never thought possible.

Loving Jesus, pursuing a love relationship with Him, and desiring Him with all my heart, soul, mind, and strength continues to radically affect my life. Spending time daily with Jesus Christ changes everything about me!

Oh, it's my deep desire that you are being encouraged and filled with hope as you explore and commit to a lifelong, growing relationship with Jesus. He is pursuing your love and praying for you in your journey!

I encourage you to enjoy your relationship with Him, forever exploring His magnificent ways. Please know that as you're growing, His spirit is cheering you on and reflecting His love to those around you!

"We all, with unveiled faces, are reflecting the glory of the Lord and are being transformed into the same image from glory to glory; this is from the Lord who is the Spirit" (2 Cor. 3:18).

Date: _____

> He is always able to save those who come to God
> through Him, since He always lives to intercede for
> them. – *Hebrews 7:25*

Today, Lord, I praise You for these things: _____

_____

_____

_____

_____

_____

Think About This

Have you ever grasped the fact that Jesus is praying for
you? The Bible tells us He does, and it's true! Think of areas
in your life right now where you need the prayers of Jesus to
see you through. Talk to Him about it. _____

_____

_____

_____

_____

_____

Today, I give You these details:

_____
_____
_____
_____
_____
_____
_____
_____
_____
_____
_____
_____
_____
_____
_____
_____
_____
_____
_____

Today's Prayer

Lord, forgive me for taking Your great love for granted. I'm filled with new wonder as I think of You praying for me! Thank You for helping me understand that this is reality and that You love me more than I can possibly imagine. Today, I'm focusing on Your love.

Day 30: The Frazzled Female Complete

If I live, it will be for Christ, and if I die, I will gain even more.
Philippians 1:21 CEV

Upon finishing *The Frazzled Female* manuscript, it is time to take all my computer folders where I had worked on each part separately and now combine them into one document. Having done that, I will call this new file "The Frazzled Female Complete."

That's the very description of who I am in Jesus! Living in this world, I'm still a frazzled female, even at best. But with Jesus living inside of me, empowering me, loving me, and giving me His energy and zest for living, I'm complete in Him!

My yearning for you after you've journeyed through these thirty days is that you have allowed Jesus to birth in you—and then complete in you—an intense desire for a deep relationship with Him. I've truly prayed that you would recognize His yearning for that deep relationship with you in a way you've never experienced before. The longing of His heart is that you would pull aside with Him so that you may experience the depth of His love for you.

The benefits for you in reveling in the love of Jesus are unfathomable. As you go to that quiet place, perhaps frazzled on some days, you will emerge victoriously frazzled to face life on the good days . . . and on those that are not so good . . . and even on those days that seem worse than terrible.

Not too long ago, I heard a powerful illustration about growing in love with Jesus. As one of the speakers for a women's retreat in the glorious mountains of North Carolina, I was taking a dinner break and visiting with the women attending the conference. A beautiful woman in Jesus sat across the table from me and shared:

> I went to a wedding recently, and I realized a deep spiritual truth when I later reflected on the day's events. This was a day filled with lots of wonderful things with many people surrounding the bride and groom and joining in their celebration. In order to give birth to a new little life, however, it will be necessary for this young couple to pull aside from the crowd. That's true for me! It is necessary for me to pull aside from the crowd, my daily activities, and my earthy focus to experience the deep and intimate love of Jesus and to give birth to His ways in my life.

Oh, what a beautiful and accurate analogy. Yes, dear frazzled female friend, your Heavenly Father longs to help you give birth to His love, His glory, His power, and His peace, so that you may glorify Him as you go about your daily living. But in order for you to experience the depths of His love, you must be committed to a lifestyle of pulling aside with Him so that together you and Jesus will grow this gloriously intimate relationship!

Just know that as you continue to make this choice, I'm cheering you on. But more importantly, Jesus is daily pursuing you with a passionate love, praying for you to come close to His heart. "Father, I desire those You have given Me to be with Me where I am. Then they will see My glory" (John 17:24).

Bless you, my friend, on your journey!

Date: _____

> But from there, you will search for the Lord your God, and you will find Him when you seek Him with all your heart and all your soul – *Deuteronomy 4:29*

Today, Lord, I praise You for these things: _____

_____

_____

_____

_____

_____

Think About This

Jesus, in His Word, invites You to come away with Him to a quiet place and get some rest (Mark 6:31). My prayer is that you will realize His longing for you and that you will reciprocate in love, by spending time with Him each day. Are you growing deeper in love with Jesus? Write to Him about your love. _____

_____

_____

_____

_____

_____

_____

Today, I give You these details:

_____

_____

_____

_____

_____

_____

_____

_____

_____

_____

_____

_____

_____

_____

_____

_____

_____

_____

Today's Prayer

My Lord, it amazes me that You would desire a love relationship with me. I realize it's my choice to grow deeply in love with You. And I know You are praying for me to do so. I love You. Help me to love You more. Amen.

HOW TO BECOME
A CHRISTIAN

God wants us to love Him above anyone or anything else, because loving Him puts everything else in life in perspective. In God we find the hope, peace, and joy that are possible only through a personal relationship with Him. Through His presence in our lives, we can truly love one another because God is love. John 3:16 says, "For God loved the world in this way: He gave His One and Only Son, so that everyone who believes in Him will not perish but have eternal life."

In order to live an abundant life, we must accept God's gift of love. "I have come that they may have life and have it in abundance" (John 10:10).

A relationship with God begins by admitting we are not perfect. We continue to fall short of God's standards. Romans 3:23 says, "For all have sinned and fall short of the glory of God."

The price for these wrongdoings is separation from God. "For the wages of sin is death, but the gift of God is eternal life in Christ Jesus our Lord" (Rom. 6:23).

God's love comes to us right in the middle of our sin. "But God proves His own love for us in that while we were still sinners

Christ died for us!" (Rom. 5:8). He doesn't ask us to clean up our lives first. In fact, without His help we are incapable of living by His standards.

Forgiveness begins when we admit our sin to God. When we do, He is faithful to forgive and restore our relationship with Him. "If we confess our sins, He is faithful and righteous to forgive us our sins and to cleanse us from all unrighteousness" (1 John 1:9).

Scripture confirms that this love gift and relationship with God are not just for a special few but for everyone. "For everyone who calls on the name of the Lord will be saved" (Rom. 10:13).

If you would like to receive God's gift of salvation, pray this prayer:

> Dear God, I know that I am imperfect and separated from You. Please forgive me for my sin and adopt me as Your child. Thank You for this gift of life through the sacrifice of Your Son. I believe Jesus died for my sins. I will live my life for You. Amen.

If you prayed this prayer for the first time, share the news with someone! Talk to a pastor or to a Christian friend. And to begin growing in your Christian walk, begin cultivating your love for Jesus through Scripture study and fellowship with other believers. Welcome to God's family!

NOTES

[1] Gary Chapman, *The Five Love Languages* (Chicago: Northfield Publishing, 1992, 1995), 140.

[2] Charles Stanley, *Success God's Way* (Nashville: Thomas Nelson Publishers, 2000), 150, 155.

[3] Carole Lewis, *Back on Track* (Ventura, CA: Regal Books, 2003), 26.

[4] Joyce Meyer, *Battlefield of the Mind* (Tulsa, OK: Harrison House, 1995), 88.

[5] Gary L. Thomas, *Sacred Pathways* (Grand Rapids, MI: Zondervan, 2002), 15.

[6] James P. Porowski and Paul B. Carlisle, *Strength for the Journey* (Nashville: LifeWay Press, 1999), 23.

[7] Ibid., 24.

Manners and Customs
of
Bible Lands

Manners and Customs
of
Bible Lands

by
Fred H. Wight

MOODY PRESS

CHICAGO

ISBN: 0-8024-5175-6

38 39 40 Printing/EE/Year 92 91 90

Moody Press, a ministry of the Moody Bible Institute, is
designed for education, evangelization and edification. If we
may assist you in knowing more about Christ and the Christian life, please write us without obligation to:
    Moody Press, c/o MLM, Chicago, Illinois 60610.

Printed in the United States of America

Preface

IN THE SPRING of 1951, the author completed a thesis in partial fulfillment of the requirements for the degree, Master of Arts in Religion, at Pasadena College, California, under the title, "A Study of Manners and Customs of Domestic Life in Palestine as Related to the Scriptures." Desire was expressed by certain members of the faculty that additional material be added to the thesis, and that a general textbook be written on Oriental manners and customs bearing on the Scriptures. As a result of this, the manuscript for this book was completed. Chapters I through XI and XIII through XVII, plus a small portion of Chapter XXVI, are substantially the original thesis, the other chapters having been added.

The author is indebted to Dr. G. Frederick Owen, Professor of Archaeology and Biblical Literature at Pasadena College, for his assistance in the project. Dr. Owen has spent several seasons in Palestine doing research work, and his suggestions and criticisms have been a help to the author in writing. With Dr. Owen's permission, some material derived from class notes in a course taught by him in the summer of 1950 on the subject "Manners and Customs of Bible Lands," was included in the thesis and appears in the present work.

It is hoped that the bibliography in the back of this book

5

will be helpful to all those who desire to make a further study of the subject. Complete information about those books listed in the bibliography appears there, rather than in connection with any mention of them in the reference notes. But where books are referred to in the reference notes and are omitted from the bibliography, the full information about them appears in the reference notes.

Many months of research have been given to the preparation of this manuscript, and yet the result is not to be considered an exhaustive treatise on the subject. But the author will consider himself more than repaid for his efforts if, as a result of reading this book, Bible students will find in it real help in understanding and interpreting the Scriptures.

PERMISSIONS

The author wishes to express his appreciation to the following publishers for their permission to quote from their copyrighted publications. Acknowledgment of the author quoted, and the name of the book and its publisher, are given in the reference notes.

The Warner Press, Anderson, Indiana: *Palestine Speaks*, by Anis C. Haddad, 1936.

The Jewish Publication Society of America, Philadelphia, Pa.: *The Life of the People in Biblical Times*, by Max Radin, 1929.

Charles Scribner's Sons, New York, N.Y.: *Abraham; Recent Discoveries and Hebrew Origins*, by Sir Leonard Woolley, 1936.

Introduction

THE BIBLE WRITTEN BY ORIENTALS. It is easy for Occidentals to overlook the fact that the Scriptures had their origin in the East, and that each one of the writers was actually an Oriental. Since this is so, in a very real sense the Bible may be said to be an Oriental Book. But many are quite apt to read into the Scriptures Western manners and customs, instead of interpreting them from the Eastern point of view.

Knowing Oriental manners and customs necessary to understand the Bible. Many passages of Scripture that are hard for the Westerner to understand, are readily explained by a knowledge of the customs and manners of Bible lands. On the other hand, to ignore this subject is to deprive one's self of a thorough mastery of the Bible, both Old and New Testaments.

A study of the manners and customs of Arabs of Bible lands invaluable. For many years the Arabs were the custodians of Palestine. In the seventh century, an army of Arabs broke away from Arabia and invaded the Near East. They brought with them the habits of life inherited from countless generations before them. Since they have lived in these lands ever since, they have largely become the conservators of the manners and customs of Bible times.

During the centuries, Arab customs largely unchanged.
There are three classes of Arabs in these lands. First, there is
the Nomad or Bedouin Arab, who is a shepherd and lives in
tents. Second, there is the Peasant or Fellahin Arab, who is
a farmer and usually lives in a village one-room house. Third,
there is the City or Belladin Arab, who as a rule engages in
business in the larger cities. The Belladin Arab has come in
contact with western civilization more than the other classes,
and therefore his manner of life has undergone a certain
amount of change. On the other hand, the Peasant Arab has
changed his customs very little, and the Nomad Arab prac-
tically none at all. Through the centuries the Arabs have for
the most part considered it to be morally wrong to change
their ancient customs. For this reason the manners and customs of Bible-land Arabs are very much the same as the Jews
of Bible times. There are some exceptions to this rule, and
most of those have to do with religious observances.

*Sources of material about manners and customs of Bible-
land Arabs.* For information about the life-habits of the Arabs
of the Near East we are indebted to natives of Bible lands,
long time residents, missionaries, scholars, and travelers.

*What about the customs of the Jews who have returned to
the new nation of Israel?* The customs of the Jews who are
now returning from various parts of the world to the land of
their fathers, will not be of great value for this study, because
they are largely the customs of those lands from whence they
have come, and in many cases that means Western customs.
There may be a few of the returning Israelites and some of
those who have lived long in the land, who have the old-time
habits of life, especially religious observances, but those who
do are very much in the minority.

*Other sources of information about manners and customs
of Bible times.* Historians who have written about the time of
Christ or of the Apostles have often given information about
the manner of living of those days, and of even earlier days.

Also the findings of archaeologists have been a valuable source of knowledge on this subject. Things unearthed by the spade, such as pottery, various articles of household furniture, remains of old houses, inscriptions, and the like, often reveal secrets of how men in the long ago lived and acted. Ancient civilizations lost to the world for centuries have been revealed to men by the work of excavators in Bible lands.

Contents

Preface
Introduction
1. Tent Dwellings   13
2. Houses of One Room   20
3. Houses of More Than One Room   35
4. Foods and Their Preparation for Eating   43
5. Customs at Mealtime   55
6. Special Suppers and Banquets   61
7. The Sacred Duty of Hospitality   69
8. Daily Program of Activities   80
9. Dress and Ornamentation   91
10. Parental Position in the Home   103
11. Birth and Care of Children   107
12. Education of Youth   112
13. Religion in the Home   118
14. Marriage Customs   124
15. Some Special Events of Domestic Festivity   135
16. Sickness in Bible Lands   138

17. Death in Oriental Lands   142
18. Shepherd Life; The Care of Sheep and Goats   147
19. Growing and Harvesting Grain   169
20. Care of Vineyards   187
21. Olive and Fig Tree Culture   196
22. Trades and Professions   203
23. Vocal and Instrumental Music   229
24. The Oriental Town or City   238
25. Customs Regarding Property   246
26. Domestic Animals   251
27. Traveling on Land and Sea   270
28. Palestine Water Supply   280
29. Raids and Blood-Avenging   287
30. Slavery in Bible Times   290
31. Greek Athletics and Roman Gladiatorial Shows   294

Reference Notes   299
Bibliography   317
General Index   321
Scriptural Index   326

CHAPTER 1

Tent Dwellings

IN THE BIBLE, living in tents is of ancient origin. It goes back before the days of Abraham. The first reference in the Scriptures to tent life is concerning the man Jabal, of whom it is said, "he was the father of such as dwell in tents" (Gen. 4:20). Following the Flood the Sacred Record says, "God shall enlarge Japheth, and he shall dwell in the tents of Shem" (Gen. 9:27).

The patriarchs Abraham, Isaac, and Jacob lived most of their lives in tents, in and around the land of Canaan. It was said of Abraham that he "pitched his tent" in the vicinity of Bethel (Gen. 12:8), that Isaac "pitched his tent in the valley of Gerar" (Gen. 26:17), and Jacob "pitched his tent before the city of Shechem" (Gen. 33:18).

The Children of Israel lived in tents during their forty years in the wilderness. Moses said of them, "The children of Israel shall pitch their tents, every man by his own camp" (Num. 1:52). And Balaam "lifted up his eyes, and he saw Israel abiding in his tents according to their tribes" (Num. 24:2).

For many years after the entering of the Promised Land, Israel still lived in tents. In the days of David it was said to the king, "The ark and Israel and Judah, abide in tents" (II Sam. 11:11), indicating that many of the people at that time

13

were tent-dwellers. Even at the time of the revolt of the ten tribes under Jeroboam and their separation from Judah, the cry went forth, "To your tents, O Israel" (I Kings 12:16). When the tribes gathered together at such small places as Gilgal, and Shiloh, they undoubtedly brought their tents with them. And after the temple was built at Jerusalem the people would make their pilgrimages there to celebrate the feasts of the Lord, and many thousands of them would sleep in tents on the mountains surrounding the city.[1]

Like the Jews of old, the Nomad or Bedouin Arabs of Palestine, and especially those of Trans-Jordan, have been living in tents for centuries, and their manner of life is strikingly like unto that of the early Bible characters. A study, therefore, of these tent structures of Bible lands of today will throw much light on how the men of early Bible times actually lived. By such a study one can build the proper background for understanding the life and contributions of these men of the long ago.[2]

TENT MATERIAL

The Bedouin's home is his tent, which is made of black goat's hair. He calls it *beit sha'ar*, i.e., "house of hair." It is made of coarse, heavy fabric, and serves to protect the family in winter from the cold winds; in the summer the sides are usually lifted, and the tent serves as a sunshade.[3] This goat's hair cloth that is used in making these tents is porous when it is dry, but becomes waterproof after the first rains have shrunk it together.[4] The Song of Solomon refers to these black goat's hair tents thus: "I am black, but comely, O ye daughters of Jerusalem, as the tents of Kedar" (Cant. 1:5).

The material that makes up the Bedouin tent is the same as the sackcloth of Bible days. It must be remembered that this Oriental sackcloth is not at all like the Occidental burlap, but is rather a material made of prickly, coarse goat's hair.[5]

The Apostle John compares darkness to this sackcloth: "the sun became black like sackcloth of hair" (Rev. 6:12). In Bible times sackcloth was worn as a sign of sorrow (Gen. 37:34; II Sam. 3:31), as a sign of humility (I Kings 21:27; II Kings 19:1), or as a sign of repentance (Dan. 9:3; Jonah 3:5).

TENT ENCAMPMENTS AND MANNER OF SETTING UP OF TENTS

If the Bedouin Arabs live together as a tribe or a clan, as they often do, or if more than one family dwell with each other, then their tents are not pitched in a promiscuous cluster, but more likely in a large circle to make it possible for at least some of their flocks to be protected inside the circle. By the side of the sheik's tent stands a long spear as an emblem of his authority (cf. practice of King Saul in I Sam. 26:7). His tent is generally larger than the others.[6]

The Bible says that some of the sons of Ishmael lived in tent villages or encampments (Gen. 25:16, A. R. V.). The number of tents that made up the encampment of Abraham must have been large, for in his warfare against the confederacy of kings that took Lot captive, it is stated that he used a band of three hundred eighteen trained soldiers born in his household (Gen. 14:14). The arrangement of his tents was doubtless much like that of the wealthier Bedouin Arabs of today.

The main overhead portion of the Bedouin's tent is composed of one large awning which is held up by poles, and the ends of the tent cloth are drawn out by cords which are tied to pegs and driven into the ground.[7] It was one of these tent pins that Jael used in killing Sisera (Judges 4:21).

INSIDE ARRANGEMENT OF TENT

The Oriental tent is usually oblong in shape, and is divided into two, and sometimes three apartments by goat's hair cur-

Bedouin Goats'-Hair Tent

tains. The entrance leads into the apartment for the men, which also serves as the reception apartment. Beyond this is the apartment for the women and children. And sometimes there is a third apartment for servants or for cattle.[8]

The women in the inner apartment are screened from the view of those in the reception room, but they can hear what goes on in that room.[9] Thus Sarah in her apartment overheard what the angel guest said in the reception apartment of Abraham's tent (Gen. 18:10–15). In some cases there is a separate tent for the women. It took several tents to care for the large family of Jacob. Reference is made to Jacob's tent, to Leah's tent, to Rachel's tent, and to the tent of the two maidservants (Gen. 31:33).

INSIDE FURNISHINGS OF TENTS

The shepherd's tent is always subject to perpetual removals, as Hezekiah indicated in his song of thanksgiving, after his recovery from sickness (Isa. 38:12). Therefore, the furnishings of that tent must include only the necessities.

Rugs cover the ground, but at night the bedding is brought out, which is composed of mats, or carpets on which to sleep; and their outer garments worn by day become their coverings by night. Sacks of grain are apt to be piled around the middle tent posts. Sure to be about the tent some place are the hand-mill, and the mortar, in which the grain is pounded. And hanging from the poles will be the skin bags or bottles, for water and other liquids. Also there will be a leathern bucket with which to draw water from any well that may be available, and an earthen pitcher, used by the women to carry the water. Cooking utensils will not be many, but will include pots, kettles, and pans. Serving dishes will include mats, platters, or larger dishes, and there will be cups for drinking. A primitive lamp burning olive oil will illuminate the tent by night (see "lamp," pp. 27–30; 62–63). If the family is fortunate enough to have a camel, then the camel furniture will be used for sitting upon inside the tent, as Rachel was doing when her father searched the tents for the lost teraphim (Gen. 31:34; see also p. 119). Little else than these furnishings would be needed for the simple life of the tent-dwellers.[10]

The hearth is of course upon the ground. A hole is dug in the earth where there is a fire kindled, and several stones are put around it, and the cooking utensils are placed on these and over the fire. One of these hearths is inside the tent, and another one is outdoors, quite likely near to the women's quarters. In the hot weather the cooking is done outside rather than inside the tent.[11]

PATCHING A TENT AND ENLARGING THE QUARTERS

New tents are very seldom made among the Bedouins. About the only time this happens is when a young groom and bride set up housekeeping for themselves in a different location from that of the groom's parents, and this rarely happens. The usual procedure is to accumulate the goat clippings of a year or so, and with these make a new strip with which to repair the old tent. The women do this work. The section of the tent roof that is most worn is ripped out, and a new piece of the cloth replaces it. The old piece is then used for a side curtain. Each year new strips of cloth replace old ones and the "house of hair" is handed down from father to son without its being completely new or completely old at any one time.[12]

As the tent-dweller's family grows larger, or as he becomes richer and wishes to enlarge his tent, he does so by simply adding another section to his old tent, very much like the Occidental would build another room on to his house; but there is this difference: instead of building a new tent they just continue patching.[13] Isaiah had this process in mind when he compared the prophetic prosperity of Israel to a Bedouin tent. "Enlarge the place of thy tent, and let them stretch forth the curtains of thine habitations: spare not, lengthen thy cords, and strengthen thy stakes" (Isa. 54:2).

THE CHARACTER OF TENT-LIFE

The Westerner does not begin to appreciate the pilgrim character of the Oriental tent-dweller. One traveler among these nomads had this to say about them:

> The Arab's tent is his home: yet the word "home" does not mean to him what it means to us. Of our idea of home he has no conception . . . His home is the little spot where his tent is pitched and his flocks are gathered at night. His country—his fatherland—is the limited district over which he roams in summer.[14]

We must always remember that Abraham, Isaac, and Jacob were pilgrims in the Land of Promise. "By faith he became a sojourner in the land of promise, as in a land not his own, dwelling in tents, with Isaac and Jacob, the heirs with him of the same promise" (Heb. 11:9). And the writer to the Hebrews goes on to say of these patriarchs, "These all died in faith, not having received the promises, but having seen them and greeted them from afar, and having confessed that they were strangers and pilgrims on the earth" (Heb. 11:13, A. R. V.).

Tent-life with its simplicity, and so much of the time spent out-of-doors, has a real charm for those who are used to it. Most of them would not live otherwise if they had the choice to do so. And because the Jewish ancestors were tent-dwellers, their descendants considered such a life in the spirit of true dignity.[15] This explains the numerous references to tent-life in sacred poetry and prophecy (cf. Psa. 84:1–10; Cant. 1:5; Jer. 4:20, etc.).

CHAPTER 2

Houses of One Room

A<small>FTER</small> I<small>SRAEL</small> had been in the land of Canaan many years and had settled down from the nomadic life to the more stable agricultural pursuits, houses began to take the place of tents as places of abode. The average home of the common people was a one-room dwelling.[1] Dr. Thomson thinks that because the poor widow who entertained Elijah had an upper room in her house, it indicates she was not of the poorer class but was in straits only because of the terrible famine[2] (cf. I Kings 17:8–19).

P<small>URPOSES OF THE</small> H<small>OUSE</small>

In Bible times men did not build houses with the idea in mind that most of their daily living would be spent inside them. Their first interest was in spending as much time as possible in God's out-of-doors. The house served as a place of retirement. For this reason the outside walls of the humble house were not inviting. There was no effort to attract attention to this place of retirement.[3]

The purpose of these dwellings is borne out by the meaning of the Hebrew and Arabic words for "house." Rev. Abraham Rihbany, who was born in Syria and spent his early life there,

Peasant's One-Room House

has made a very illuminative statement about the meaning
and purpose of the Palestinian house:

> The Hebrew word *bavith* and the Arabic word *bait* mean
> primarily a "shelter." The English equivalent is the word
> "house." The richer term, "home," has never been invented
> by the son of Palestine because he has always considered
> himself "a sojourner in the earth." His tent and his little
> house, therefore, were sufficient for a shelter for him and
> his dear ones during the earthly pilgrimage.[4]

Because the Palestinians lived out-of-doors so much, the
sacred writers were fond of referring to God as a "shelter" or
as a "refuge," rather than as a "home." Such expressions in
connection with Deity are numerous in the Book of Psalms
and also in the prophetic writings[5] (cf. Psa. 61:3; Isa. 4:6).

FLOOR AND WALLS OF THE HOUSE

Concerning the nature of the floor of these Oriental houses, Dr. George A. Barton says:

> The houses generally had no floor except the earth, which was smoothed off and packed hard. Sometimes this was varied by mixing lime with the mud and letting it harden, and sometimes floors of cobblestones or stone chippings mixed with lime were found. In the Roman period mosaic floors, made by embedding small smoothly cut squares of stone in the earth, were introduced.[6]

The walls of the houses were often made of bricks, but these were not ordinarily burned, but were composed of mud dried in the sun.[7] Job speaks of these kinds of dwelling as "houses of clay" (Job 4:19). They are similar to the adobe houses so common in Mexico today, and often seen in the southwestern states of America, where the Spanish influence of the past is still felt.

But sometimes the walls were made of rough sandstones, so common in the land. These were of varying sizes and were set in mud. The joints between them were apt to be wide and irregular.[8] It was only the palaces or houses of the wealthy that were constructed of hewn stones, like the palaces of Solomon (I Kings 7:9), and the rich of Isaiah's day, who boasted they would replace fallen down brick walls with walls of hewn stones (Isa. 9:8–10).

CONSTRUCTION OF THE ROOF

The roof of these humble Palestinian houses is made by laying beams across from wall to wall, then putting on a mat of reeds, or perhaps thorn bushes, and over it a coating of clay or earth; sand and pebbles are scattered over this, and a stone roller is used to make it smooth and able to shed rain. This roller is usually left on the house top and the roof is rolled again several times, especially after the first rain, in order to keep it from leaking.[9]

A low parapet or wall, with spaces to allow the rain water to flow off, was expected to be built on these houses in Bible times, in order to prevent people from falling off. The failure to build such a wall in modern times has often caused accidents.[10] The law of Moses was very definite in commanding the erection of such. Its regulation says: "When thou buildest a new house, then thou shalt make a battlement for thy roof, that thou bring not blood upon thine house, if any man fall from thence" (Deut. 22:8). The common use of the house-roof for so many purposes, as shall be seen, made this law essential.

ITEMS OF INTEREST GROWING OUT OF THE
CHARACTER OF THE ROOF AND WALLS

Grass on the housetops. With the roofs of the houses made largely of dirt or clay, one can easily imagine how grass could grow on the tops of the houses as Bible references indicate. "Let them be as the grass upon the housetops, which withereth afore it growth up" (Psa. 129:6; see also II Kings 19:26, and Isa. 37:27). Examples of this in connection with similarly built roofs in modern times have often been seen. One book published in the latter part of the nineteenth century carries a picture of a Palestinian roof all covered with growing grass. The notation beneath the picture says: "This is a good example of the appearance of 'grass on the housetops.' After the winter rains, every flat and mud-roofed building is overgrown with grass and weeds, which soon perish."[11]

Leaky roofs. With a dirt roof it can be understood how natural it would be for a heavy rainfall to produce a leak, which would make it quite inconvenient for those inhabiting the house at the time. Travelers who stop for the night at one of these dwellings, have sometimes had to change their sleep-

Oriental Housetop

ing quarters, because of the dripping of the rain water.[12] The Book of Proverbs compares this dropping to a contentious woman (Prov. 19:13; 27:15).

Digging through of thieves. Since the walls of the houses are so often built of clay or dirt, or of stones with mud between them, it makes it an easy task for a robber to dig through and get into the house.[13] Job referred to this: "In the dark they dig through houses" (Job 24:16). Jesus also spoke of the same thing in His great Sermon on the Mount: "Lay not up for yourselves treasures upon the earth where moth and rust consume, and where thieves *dig through* and steal" (Matt. 6:19, A. R. V. margin; cf. Matt. 24:43, A. R. V. margin).

Snakes in house walls. Because the walls of the stone houses were built so that the joints between the stones were wide and irregular, therefore a snake might readily crawl into the crevices and unexpectedly come in contact with an inhabitant.[14] Concerning this kind of house the prophet Amos said that a man "leaned his hand on the wall and a serpent bit him" (Amos 5:19).

WINDOWS AND DOORS

Windows. The Oriental has few windows that open on the street side of the house, and those that do are usually high.

As a rule the window has wooden bars serving as a protection against robbers, while the lower half of the window is screened by a framework of latticework. The Book of Proverbs speaks of such a window: "For at the window of my house I looked forth through my lattice" (Prov. 7:6, A. R. V.). Wooden shutters close the windows at night. When the window is open, those inside may see out without themselves being seen.[15]

Latticed Window

Doors. The doors as well as windows were ordinarily built of sycamore wood. It was only for ornamental purposes of the wealthy that cedar wood was used[16] (cf. Isa. 9:10). These doors turned on hinges, as the familiar proverb about the sluggard makes mention of the turning of a door upon its hinges (Prov. 26:14). If the doors were fastened when shut, bars were usually used for this purpose (Prov. 18:19).

The door of the peasant's one-room house is opened before sunrise in the morning, and stays open all day long as an invitation to hospitality. The Apocalypse speaks thus: "Behold, I have set before thee an open door" (Rev. 3:8). For such a door to be shut would indicate the inhabitants had done that of which they were ashamed (cf. John 3:19). At sunset the door is shut and remains shut during the night (cf. Luke 11:7). The rule about the open door for the simple house does not hold for the city houses of more than one room. The reference to the Master knocking at the door has to do with such a door (Rev. 3:20; cf. pp. 39, 40). The distinction between the house of the villager and of the city dweller must always be made, in order to understand the scriptural references to houses.[17]

FURNISHINGS OF THE HOUSE

The furnishings of a one-room Palestinian house were and still are very simple. Mats and cushions are in use to sit on by day, and carpets or mats are slept on at night. There will be vessels of clay for household needs, with perhaps some cooking utensils of metal. There will be a chest for storing bedding, a lamp either placed on a lampstand or a bushel, a broom for house cleaning, and a handmill for grinding the grain, and the goatskin bottles in which liquids are kept. The fireplace would be on the floor often in the middle of the room. This gives a general picture of the furnishings of the average Palestinian home.[18] More details regarding some of these items will be given as the study proceeds.

SLEEPING ARRANGEMENTS

The Parable of the Importunate Friend which Jesus told, if understood in the light of an Oriental one-room house, will give information about sleeping arrangements.

And he said unto them, Which of you shall have a friend, and shall go unto him at midnight, and say unto him, Friend, lend me three loaves; for a friend of mine in his journey is come to me, and I have nothing to set before him? and he from within shall answer and say, Trouble me not: the door is now shut, and my children are with me in bed; I cannot rise and give thee (Luke 11:5–7).

Among the common folks of the Holy Land individual beds in separate bedrooms have been unknown. Instead the arrangements for sleeping in the parable, and today in Syria and Palestine among the peasants, have been thus described:

The cushion-mattresses are spread side by side in the living room, in a line as long as the members of the family, sleeping close together, require. The father sleeps at one end of the line, and the mother at the other end, "to keep the children from rolling from under the cover." So the man was absolutely truthful when he said by way of excuse, "My children are with me in bed."[19]

LIGHTING OF THE HOUSE

Biblical use of the word candle. The King James Version of the Bible frequently uses the word candle. This is because candles were so widely used at the time this version was made. A literal translation of the original words would use the word lamp or light. Bible characters knew nothing about candles, but were familiar with lamps.[20]

Character of the lamp. When the Children of Israel entered the Promised Land they adopted the lamp used by the Canaanites, which was an earthenware saucer to hold the olive oil, and a pinched lip to hold the wick. A thousand years later a Mesopotamian lamp was imported and used in some sections. This lamp had a closed tube for the wick, and thus could be carried about without spilling the oil so readily. In the fifth century B.C. Greek lamps of a beautiful black-glazed variety were imported and became popular. By the third century B.C. the old saucer-type lamp had all but disappeared, but in the second century, the Maccabeans revived the use of that type of lamp, as being more in line with the old Jewish traditions. But when the Roman Empire began to dominate the land of Palestine, the lamps in use were either imported, or made under foreign models. The Virgin's Lamp in use in the time of Christ was an improvement over the old saucer type, having sufficient covering to keep the oil from spilling.[21]

The lampstand. In early Bible times, lampstands were not in common use, and the lamps would be put on a place such as a stone projecting from the wall. In the days of Christ, lampstands were in quite general use. They were tall and were usually placed on the ground. Archaeologists have unearthed some bronze lampstands fourteen inches high that had been used in palaces. They were made for holding bowls or lamps. The poor no doubt had a less expensive type.[22]

If the family had no separate lampstand, the bushel placed on the ground upside down would serve for a lampstand, as well as a table from which the meal would be served. The lamp was to be put *on* the bushel and not *under* it[23] (Matt. 5:15).

The prophet's reference to smoking flax. Isaiah's prophecy concerning the Messiah was that "the smoking flax shall be not quench" (Isa. 42:3). Dr. Thomson tells of seeing ancient clay lamps in use illustrating this text. The wick was often made of a twisted strand of flax, and this was put into the olive oil in the shallow cup of the lamp. When the oil was almost used up it would give forth an offensive smoke. This was an indication it was time to replenish the supply of oil. The implication was that the quenching of the fire was sometimes done purposely. If the wick was well worn, the housewife would quench the fire, and then put a new wick in to take its place. God's servant would not thus treat the poor, weak, and despairing specimens of humanity. He would replenish the oil, trim the wick, and make the dimly burning flame to burn brightly. What a picture this is of our Saviour's desire to help the helpless and lift the fallen and save the lost.[24]

Using the lamp to find the lost coin. The Saviour's Parable of the Lost Coin (Luke 15) needs to be understood from the Oriental point of view. Abraham Rihbany as a boy often held an Oriental earthen lamp while his mother hunted for a lost coin or some other object of value. The house had one door and one or two small windows having wooden shutters. For this reason the house was always dimly lighted, and especially so in winter. The mats, cushions, and sheepskins covering the floor would be turned over, and the floor swept. When the lost coin was found, the women neighbors and friends would be called in to rejoice with her, because the loss of a coin would bring down upon the woman the wrath of her husband, and her women neighbors and friends would have a fellow-feeling for her, and would keep what had happened as a secret from the men folks.[25] Williams translates Luke 15:9: "And when she finds it, she calls in her *friends* and neighbors." (*See also* reference to the "lost coin," p. 99.)

The significance of light in a Palestinian house. A lamp is considered to be the Palestinian peasant's one luxury that is a necessity. When the sun sets in the West, the door of his house is shut, and then the lamp is lit. To sleep without a light is considered by most villagers to be a sign of extreme poverty. The Bible makes synonymous such terms as lamp, light, and life. A late traveler looks to see a light in a house, and then he knows there is life there. To wish that a man's light be put out would be to wish him a terrible curse.[26] Concerning the wicked man, Bildad in the Book of Job said: "The light shall be dark in his tabernacle, and his candle [lamp] shall be put out with him" (Job 18:6). But the psalmist considered himself blessed of the Lord when he said of himself in relation to God, "For thou wilt light my candle [lamp]" (Psa. 18:28). It was

to Orientals who appreciated the value of even a humble
earthenware lamp in the dark of night, or even in the ob-
scurity of a darksome house, that Jesus originally said, "Let
your light so shine before men, that they may see your good
works, and glorify your Father which is in heaven" (Matt.
5:16).

COOKING ARRANGEMENTS

The stove or fireplace. Like the Nomads who live in tents,
the peasants who live in one-room houses, carry on as much
of their meal-cooking outside as the weather will permit.
These operations are transferred inside only when the cold
winter weather makes it desirable. The Occidental would
hardly call what they use in cooking their meals either a
stove or a fireplace, but it serves the purpose. Often the place
for the fire is on the floor in the middle of the room. A small
open clay-baked box, or else a thick jar with holes at the sides,
is what usually serves as a stove.[27]

The fuel used. The peasant often uses dried dung as fuel
for his fire. Some of the poorer classes use this themselves, and
sell the sticks they find to those who can afford to buy them.[28]
A reference in the prophecy of Ezekiel indicates this use of
fuel was common in Bible times (see Ezek. 4:15).

In the Orient fuel is usually so scarce that dried grass and
withered flowers are apt to be carefully gathered into bundles
and used for making a fire.[29] There are Bible indications that
this was often done in those days of old. Jesus said: "The grass
of the field, which today is, and tomorrow is cast into the
oven" (Matt. 6:30; Luke 12:28).

Another popular fuel for fires in Palestine is thorns. There
are many kinds of thorny shrubs that grow there, and the
people gather them and make good use of them. Bible passages indicating such use of them are numerous (II Sam. 23:6,
7; Psa. 118:12; Eccles. 7:6; Isa. 9:18; Isa. 10:7; Isa. 33:12;
Nahum 1:10).

The widow of Zarephath was gathering sticks to build a fire (I Kings 17:10), but the fire built in the courtyard of the high priest's house, where Simon Peter warmed himself, was built of charcoal (John 18:18, Williams). Jesus cooked breakfast for His disciples on a charcoal fire (John 21:9, Williams).

The chimney. The Fellahin Arabs have various ways of taking care of smoke from the interior fires. Sometimes they have an opening in the ceiling that serves as a chimney, or an aperture in the side of the house will serve the purpose. Often, when the fireplace is in the corner of the room, there is a hood over it with an outlet for the smoke. Frequently, charcoal fires are started in a brazier outdoors, and when most of the smoking is over, and the coals are red hot, then it is taken indoors.[30]

The prophet Hosea refers to "smoke out of the chimney" (Hosea 13:3). Some translators render it, "smoke out of the window."[31] A high latticed opening in the wall of the house would serve both as window and chimney in certain of the peasant homes. But no doubt, most of the chimney arrangements used by the Arabs as mentioned above, were also in use in Bible times. The Psalmist's comparison of himself with "a bottle in the smoke" (Psa. 119:83), could be an indoor figure; other scriptural references to smoke, that are often spoken of as being indoors, could just as well be outdoors (Prov. 10:26; Isa. 65:5, etc.). It can safely be assumed that Bible houses were not always as full of smoke as many have assumed to be the case.

Kindling a flame. The method used in early Old Testament times to produce a fire was to make sparks by the striking of stone and flint, or by the friction of pieces of wood, afterwards igniting a blaze. There are indications that Israel in later times produced fire by striking steel against flint.[32] In Isaiah 50:11, where it speaks of kindling a fire, the Hebrew word translated "kindle" means "to strike," and evidently refers to the striking of flint on steel.[33]

USES MADE OF THE ROOF OF THE HOUSE

The roof of an Oriental house is used today for a great variety of purposes, much like it was used in the days of the prophets and of the apostles.

Used as a place to sleep. The roof is a popular place for the Oriental to sleep.

> For a great part of the year the roof, or "housetop," is the most agreeable place about the house, especially in the morning and evening. There many sleep during the summer, both in the city and the country, and in all places where malaria does not render it dangerous. The custom is very ancient.[34]

An example in the Bible of this practice, is the incident of Samuel calling Saul, who had slept on the house-top (I Sam. 9:26, A. R. V.).

Used as a place for storage. The flat Oriental roofs so exposed to the air and sunshine are well suited for storing grain or fruit to be ripened or dried. This custom is a common one in the East.[35] Rahab hid the spies with the stalks of flax which she had on her roof (Josh. 2:6).

Used as a gathering place in times of excitement. In Isaiah 22:1 the prophet says: "What aileth thee now, that thou art wholly gone up to the housetops?" Thus is described a typical Oriental city in the midst of a time of great commotion. Just as the Westerner at such a time gathers in the streets, so the Easterner goes to the housetops, where he can see down the streets, and discover what is happening.[36]

Used as a place for public proclamations. In the days of Jesus as well as in modern times the villages of the Holy Land have had town criers. The orders of local governors are thus proclaimed from the top of the highest house available. Such a proclamation is usually made in the evening, after the men have returned from their work in the field. The long drawn-out call becomes familiar to the residents, and they learn to listen for what follows.[37]

The call of the town crier is said to resemble a distant, prolonged railroad whistle.[38] Jesus must have often heard the call of the town crier. To his disciples he said: "What ye hear in the ear, proclaim upon the housetops" (Matt. 10:27, A. R. V.). As a warning against the impossibility of hiding our sins in the day of judgment, he said, "That which ye have spoken in the ear in closets shall be proclaimed upon the housetops" (Luke 12:3).

Used as a place of worship and prayer. The Scriptures indicate that roofs of houses were used for true worship of God, and also for idolatrous worship. The prophet Zephaniah speaks of "them that worship the host of heaven upon the housetops" (Zeph. 1:5). And Luke tells us that Peter at Joppa "went up upon the housetop to pray about the sixth hour" (Acts 10:9). It would be natural for those worshiping the heavenly bodies to do so on the roof, and no doubt Peter retired to the housetop where he could be alone with God.[39]

Used as a way of escape in time of evil. In a day when escape from evil was necessary, the inhabitants of villages in Christ's time could do so by going from roof to roof, because the houses were located so close to each other. Dr. Edersheim describes the situation thus:

> From roof to roof there might be regular communication, called by the Rabbis "the road of the roofs." Thus a person could make his escape, passing from roof to roof, till at the last house he would descend the stairs that led down its outside, without having entered any dwelling. To this "road of the roofs" our Lord no doubt referred in His warning to His followers (Matt. 24:17; Mark 13:15; Luke 17:31), intended to apply to the last siege of Jerusalem, "And let him that is on the housetop not go down into the house, neither enter therein."[40]

BETHLEHEM HOUSE AND MANGER

The humble scene of the birthplace of the Baby Jesus is so often interpreted with Occidental instead of Oriental flavor that it would be well for Westerners to have the description of the kind of a Bethlehem house in which the Saviour was doubtless born, as given by John D. Whiting.[41] Entering the door of this one-room Bethlehem dwelling one sees that two-thirds of the space is given over to a "raised masonry platform, some eight to ten feet above the ground and supported by low-domed arches."[42] This space that is raised is occupied by the members of the family, and the lower part of the house is for the cattle and flocks. Narrow stone steps lead up to where the family lives, and there are only two small windows in the room and these are high up from the ground. In winter weather the sheep and goats are kept inside the house, also a few work cattle, and perhaps a donkey. Primitive mangers for the cattle are to be seen around the walls, and these are "built of rough slabs of stone placed on edge and plastered up with mortar."[43] The owner of the animals often sleeps on a small raised place, where he can keep watch over newly born lambs.

> To know the heart of the land, to have learned the hospitality of its people, which is always offered, no matter how primitive or simple, makes it easy to picture Mary and Joseph returning from the inn, already filled with guests, and turning aside into a home such as we have described, the regular dwelling portion of which may have been none too large for the family which occupied it. It may have been crowded with other guests, but they find a welcome and a resting-place for the babe in a manger.[44]

CHAPTER 3

Houses of More Than One Room

Among the arabs of Palestine villages and towns, houses of more than one room are owned by those who are more or less prosperous. The Arabic word meaning "house" also means "a room." The same thing was true of the houses belonging to the ancient Hebrews. As a rule the houses of one room were in the villages, and those of more than one room were in the cities.[1]

Building a House of Two, Three, or More Rooms

If a house of two rooms is to be built, the Oriental does not place them side by side, as the Occidental builder would do. Rather the breadth of a room is left between the two rooms, and a wall is constructed between the ends, and as a result of this arrangement, the house has an open court. If the builder expects to have three rooms, then a room would be substituted for the wall at the end of the court, and there would be three rooms around a courtyard. If there are to be more than three rooms in the house, the additional rooms are added to those at the side, making the court of greater length.[2]

THE APPEARANCE AND ARRANGEMENT OF ROOMS

There is a great difference between an Oriental and Occidental house of more than one room. The exterior of the Occidental house is made to be as beautiful as possible, and especially the part that fronts on the street. But the exterior of the Oriental house presents an appearance that is mean and blank by comparison. The Oriental house fronts inwardly toward the court, rather than outwardly toward the street, as does the Occidental house. The general plan of the Oriental house is a series of rooms built around an open courtyard. The reason for this arrangement is that *seclusion* is the chief thought in mind.[3]

THE ORIENTAL COURTYARD

Open to the sky. It is important for the Westerner to realize that at the center of the Oriental house of several rooms is a courtyard that is open to the sky. The courtyard is an important part of the house. A person can be in the court and thus *in* the house, and yet he would be outdoors from the point of view of the Westerner. As an example, Matthew 26:69 says: "Now Peter sat without in the palace." Now this simply means that Peter was outside the rooms of the palace, and yet he was in the open courtyard, located in the central portion of the building.[4] Although the court is open to the air above, at times an awning is drawn over a portion of it.[5] And some houses have a gallery around the sides of the court.[6]

Often planted with trees, shrubs, or flowers. These Oriental courtyards are often made beautiful by the presence of trees, shrubs, or various flowers.[7] The Psalmist refers to such a practice with the familiar words: "I am like a green olive tree in the house of God" (Psa. 52:8). And again he said: "Those that be planted in the house of the Lord shall flourish in the courts of our God" (Psa. 92:13). He is illustrating divine truth by referring to trees so often planted in courtyards of houses. Actually trees were never planted in the Temple courts.[8]

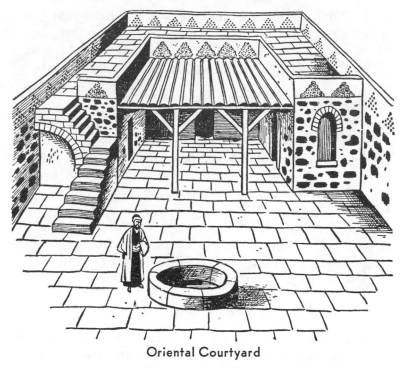

Oriental Courtyard

Cisterns often built in courts. The interesting story of two men in the days of David who hid from Absalom is told in II Sam. 17:18, 19. "But they went both of them away quickly, and came to a man's house in Bahurim, which had a well in his court; whither they went down. And the woman took and spread a covering over the well's mouth, and spread ground corn thereon: and the thing was not known." The "well" mentioned here was actually a "cistern" which is often dug in Oriental courtyards in order to catch the rain water. When these cisterns are dry, they make good places for fugitives to hide. Because the mouth of these cisterns is at the level of the ground, it makes it easy to cover it over with some article, and then spread grain over that, and thus the place of hiding can be kept secret.[9]

Fires often kindled in courts in cold weather. This practice is illustrated in Simon Peter's experience of denying Jesus. A fire was built in the courtyard of the high priest's house where Jesus was being tried. John 18:18 says: "And the servants and officers stood there, who had made a fire of coals; for it was cold: and they warmed themselves: and Peter stood with them, and warmed himself."

Courtyard as a bathing-place. When the Scripture says that David from his palace roof saw the beautiful Bathsheba bathing (II Sam. 11:2), it needs to be understood, that she was in the courtyard on the inside of her house, not visible to ordinary observation, yet the king from his palace roof saw her and was tempted to sin.[10]

Meals often eaten in the courtyard. Today, as in the days of Jesus, meals are often eaten in the interior court of the Oriental house. No doubt Jesus was entertained at meals which were served in the open court of his host's house.[11]

THE DOOR AND THE PORCH

Location and appearance of the door. The door or gate was located in the middle of the front side of the house. This entrance was usually so arranged that nobody could see into it from the street. Sometimes a wall was built in front of it to serve this purpose.[12]

Oriental gates, or large doors often have small doors like a panel within them. The small door is in use for ordinary occasions, and the large gate or door is opened only on extraordinary occasions.[13] Acts 12:13 speaks of Peter knocking "at the door of the gate," which doubtless means the smaller door within the larger gate.

The use of keys. The Oriental key of modern times is like the key of Isaiah's days, and most certainly not like the small occidental variety. Isaiah 22:22 says: "The key of the house of David will I lay upon his shoulder." Dr. Thomson tells of seeing different keys in Palestine that would be large enough to lay on the shoulder of a man. He saw one key about a foot and a half in length. The keys were usually made of wood. The lock is placed on the inside of the gate or door, and to make it possible for the owner of the house to unlock it, a hole is cut in the door, and he thrusts his arm through this hole, and then inserts the key. In Song of Solomon 5:4, the bride says: "My beloved put in his hand by the hole of the door." She saw him thrust his hand through the hole, that he might unlock the door and then go in.[14]

The porch and duties of the porter. The passageway inside the door and leading to the courtyard itself is called the porch. It is most often furnished with some kind of seats for the porter or for the servants.[15] It was in this porch that one of Peter's denials took place. "And when he was gone out into the porch, another maid saw him, and said unto them that were there, This fellow was also with Jesus of Nazareth" (Matt. 26:71; Mark 14:68).

It is the duty of the porter (or servant or member of the family serving in that capacity) to parley with any visitor who knocks on the door desiring admission.[16] The purpose of this is to give opportunity to recognize the *voice* of the visitor, and identify him as a friend. So it is not expected that the door will be opened as soon as the knock is heard. The one inside will call out, "Who?" And the outsider, instead of giving his name, will rather answer, "I." Acts 12:13, 14 says: "And as Peter knocked at the door of the gate, a damsel came to hearken, named Rhoda. And when she knew Peter's voice, she opened not the gate for gladness." When Rhoda had listened to Peter's voice then she recognized who it was outside the gate. The familiar words of Revelation 3:20 present the same idea: "Behold, I stand at the door and knock: if any man *hear my voice,* and open the door, I will come into him," (for additional light on Rev. 3:20, note Williams' translation of the word "guest" and then study the relation between host and guest as given in Chapter VII of this book). We must recognize the *voice* of the Saviour who is knocking. When Jesus came walking on the water to the fearful disciples in the storm, He did not say: "It is Jesus, be not afraid," but rather, "It is I; be not afraid" (Matt. 14:27; Mark 6:50; John 6:20). They heard His voice and recognized that it was the voice of Jesus. The Oriental is trained to listen to a voice and be able to recognize a friend.[17]

THE UPPER ROOM

The upper room or chamber is a well-known part of many Oriental houses today, and is frequently referred to in the Bible (cf. II Kings 1:2; 23:12; Acts 9:37; 20:8, etc.). Those who cannot afford such a room are content with booths or arbors on the roof of their houses. But when it is possible to do so they construct a room. It provides a place of coolness in the hot weather, a place of retreat, and a distinguished guest is given accommodations there. If more than one room is built on the roof, it is called a summer house, in contrast with the winter house which is downstairs.[18]

The most famous upper room of Old Testament times was the prophet's chamber built for Elisha, that he might have a place of retirement suited to a man of prayer. There was doubtless an outside stairway leading to it, so that the prophet might come and go without disturbing the people in the house. The furnishings of the room included a bed, a table, a stool and a lampstand (II Kings 4:10).

In the New Testament there are several notable uses of the upper room. Jesus sent two disciples to secure the use of a guest chamber for the Passover meal. A large upper room was put at their disposal. With thousands of Jews from all over Palestine in Jerusalem to celebrate the feast, it was expected that anybody having such a room would gladly let it be used for that purpose.[19] (See Mark 14:12–16; Luke 22:7–13.) And then the prayer meeting that preceded Pentecost was held in an upper room (Acts 1:13). The Revisers translate it "the upper room" rather than "an upper room." Perhaps it was the same room where Jesus had celebrated the Passover with them. At any rate, it had come to be their fixed place for meeting. Weymouth's translation reads: "They went up to the upper room which was now their fixed place for meeting." Upon the death of Dorcas, Luke says her body was washed and placed in an upper chamber, according to the custom of those times. The miracle of her being raised from the dead followed Peter's going up into that upper room (Acts 9:36–41).

LETTING THE SICK MAN THROUGH THE ROOF TO JESUS

A knowledge of the Oriental house is necessary in order to understand the story of the palsied man, who was let down through a hole in the roof, in order to get him to Jesus to be healed. Mark and Luke both give this aspect of the story. Mark says: "They uncovered the roof where he was: and when they had broken it up, they let down the bed" (Mark 2:4). Luke puts it this way: "And let him down through the tiling with his couch into the midst before Jesus" (Luke 5:19). These accounts present some difficulties, and several interpretations have been offered in solving them. The two most plausible ones will be given here.

The simplest explanation is that advocated by Dr. Thomson. He suggests that the sticks, thorn-bush, mortar, and earth of the roof were broken up, and thrown aside sufficiently, to let the sick man down into the house. He says that this could be done and the place could be repaired easily. Often this very thing is done in order to let grain, or straw or other things through. He testifies to having seen it done himself. The one difficulty about such a process, with the crowd below, would be the amount of dust caused.

It would seem that Luke's account mentioning the letting down of the man through the *tiling* presents a difficulty to this interpretation. But some have considered "the tiling" to be a reference to the ordinarily constructed roof in the Orient.

The Greek word for "tiling" means, "pottery ware," and such a word could describe a dirt roof when rolled and allowed to harden into clay.[21]

Other teachers of the Word have a different idea of what was done with the man. Advocating this view, Dr. Edersheim has this to say:

> It is scarcely possible to imagine that the bearers of the paralytic would have attempted to dig through this into a room below, not to speak of the interruption and inconvenience caused to those below such an operation. But no such objection attaches if we regard it not as the main roof of the house, but as that of the covered gallery under which we are supposing the Lord to have stood . . . In such case it would have been comparatively easy to "unroof" the covering of "tiles"; and then "having dug out" an opening through the lighter framework which supported the tiles, to let down their burden "into the midst before Jesus."[22]

In this connection Edersheim indicates that there were outside as well as inside stairways leading up to the roof.

MORE ELABORATE FURNISHINGS

The simple furnishings of a one-room house, where the common people lived, have already been described. Houses of more than one room were inhabited by those in a better situation. The wealthy usually had upper rooms as well as lower rooms, and of course, the furnishings were more elaborate. The divan or raised seat was located around the borders of the room. The rich adorned these and floored them. They were used for seats during the daytime, and beds were put on them at night. Amos speaks of the luxury of ivory beds in his day (Amos 6:4). The bed customarily in use was a mattress and pillow that could be placed where desired. In wealthy homes, carpets, curtains, and awnings were present in abundance. The Oriental custom was to sit on the divan with the lower limbs of the body crossed.[23]

CHAPTER 4

Foods and Their Preparation for Eating

WHAT KINDS OF FOOD did the ancient Jews eat? "The ordinary food of the average Hebrew of Bible times was bread, olives, oil, buttermilk and cheese from their flocks; fruits and vegetables from their orchards and gardens; and meat on rare occasions."[1] Only a few more varieties would have to be added to make this a complete list of foods eaten in those days.

THE USE OF RAW GRAIN AND PARCHED GRAIN

The eating of *raw grain* is a modern custom in Palestine that dates back to very ancient days. (*See also* "eating grain in the field" (p. 179). The Arabs today often pluck the ears of grain and rubbing them in their hands, eat them. The Mosaic Law said: "Ye shall eat neither bread, nor parched corn, nor *green ears*, until the selfsame day that ye have brought an offering unto your God" (Lev. 23:14; cf. Deut. 23:25; II Kings 4:42). The disciples of Jesus ate raw grain in the fields. "His disciples plucked the ears of corn and did eat, rubbing them in their hands" Luke 6:1; cf. Matt. 12:1, Mark 2.23).

So it can be readily seen that this custom of eating raw grain has prevailed for thousands of years.[2]

Another food common in the Orient today and in use in Bible times is *parched grain*. This is prepared from the grains of wheat that are not fully ripe. They are roasted in a pan or on an iron plate. Such grain is eaten either with or without bread. Jesse sent some of it to his sons in the army by the hand of David (I Sam. 17:17). Abigail included some of it in her present to David (I Sam. 25:18). And David received some of it from friends at the time he had fled from Absalom (II Sam. 17:28). These Scriptures show that parched grain has been in use for centuries.[3]

BREAD

Bread the principal food. In the Orient it has been estimated that three-fourths of the people live entirely upon either bread or upon that which is made from wheat or barley flour. It is unquestionably the principal food of the East.[4]

In the Bible such an expression as "eating bread" is often used when Occidentals would say: "eating a meal." When the Bible says, "The Egyptians might not eat bread with the Hebrews" (Gen. 43:31, 32), it means that they could not eat a meal with them (See also Gen. 37:25; Exod. 2:20; I Sam. 28:22–25).

Sacredness of bread. The Palestinians are brought up to think of bread as having a mystic sacred meaning. In some places they have such a reverence for bread that they will not arise to salute a guest, if they are in the midst of breaking bread together, but will wait till they are finished. Such is their attitude toward bread.[5]

It may be said that this attitude of the people toward bread is essentially religious. Everything about bread from the sowing of the seed to the baking of the loaves is done in the name of God. These Orientals sense the importance of the petition in the disciple's prayer: "Give us this day our daily bread" (Matt. 6:11). It was to men who really appreciate the value of bread, that Jesus first said, "I am the bread of life" (John 6:35).[6]

Since there is this attitude of sacredness in relation to "the staff of life," there grows out of it the universal Eastern custom of *breaking* bread and not cutting it. One who has lived in Palestine says about the natives of the country: "They never put a knife to bread, holding it to be absolutely wicked to cut it, but always break it into pieces with their fingers."[7] To cut bread would be thought of as cutting life itself. This custom of breaking bread rather than cutting it, is found throughout the Scriptures. In Lamentations 4:4 we read: "The young children ask bread, and no man breaketh it unto them." Thus the expression "breaking of bread" came to mean the taking of a meal whatever was included in the meal. Because Christ broke bread when he instituted the ordinance of the Lord's Supper, the expression came to refer to that ordinance. Matthew 26:26: "Jesus took bread, and blessed it, and brake it, and gave to his disciples." Thus we read in Acts 20:7: "And upon the first day of the week, when the disciples came together to break bread, Paul preached unto them."

Kinds of bread used. Two kinds of bread were in use in the days when Bible events were being enacted: wheat bread, and barley bread. Both of these are in use in Palestine today. There is this distinction between them: barley bread is used by the poorer classes, whereas if a family is able to have wheat bread, it is considered to have arrived at a place well up in the comfort scale.[8]

This same distinction was true in the Old Testament days and also New Testament times. When the "cake of barley bread tumbled into the host of Midian" in the dream of the Midianite soldier (Judges 7:13), it was an indication that the enemy despised Israel, as a more favored people eating wheat bread would despise eaters of barley bread, and yet God was to use the despised Israelites of Gideon's army to overpower those proud Midianites.[9] The lad who had his five barley loaves and gave them to Jesus, and saw him multiply them to feed five thousand (John 6:9), must have come from the poorer class, but his humble contribution made possible a great miracle, and the crowd was satisfied with that kind of bread.

Form of loaves. In the Holy Land where the old customs prevail, bread takes three forms. First, there are the small loaves which somewhat resemble the light bread biscuits of this country. It was this kind the lad had and gave to Jesus. Second, there are the larger loaves, nearly as heavy as the modern loaves of the West, but round instead of rectangular. The ten loaves which Jesse sent by David to the camp of Israel, were probably of this form (I Sam. 17:17). Third, there are the flat loaves which are thin like paper. These are something like American hot cakes only bigger around and much thinner. When served some of these, one man from the West thought they were napkins and started to use them as such. This kind of bread is used to take the place of the knife, fork, or spoon of the Occidental; Easterners "cup it up" and use it to dip into the food sauces (see pp. 59–60; 66–68). It is quite pliable, and the men fold it up and put it in their scrip, and take it with them, so they can eat it as needed.[10]

Baking of bread. The most primitive method of baking bread was the laying of cakes of dough on heated stones.[11] A Scriptural example of this is from the experience of Elijah. (I Kings 19:6, A. R. V. margin): "There was at his head a cake baken on hot stones."

Another simple method of baking is the digging in the ground of a hole four or five feet deep, and three feet in diameter, and after this oven is heated, the dough is rolled out until it is no thicker than a person's finger, and then it is struck against the oven's sides where it instantly bakes.[12]

Sometimes a great stone pitcher is used as an oven. In the

Bread-Baking

bottom of it a fire is made among small flints that retain the heat. The dough is placed on these and is quickly baked. Sometimes the dough is rolled out quite thin and is stuck on the outside of the hot pitcher where it bakes. Some have thought that it was this pitcher-oven that was meant in Lev. 2:4, where two types of unleavened bread were to be baked. The cakes of fine flour would be baked inside the pitcher-oven, and the wafers would be baked on the outside of it.[13]

Another type of simple oven is a large earthenware jar, into which the fuel is placed, and when the jar is hot enough the thin cakes are laid on the outside to cook.[14]

When bread was baked individually by each family in Bible days, some such method as has been described was probably used by the ordinary homes.

But often today, as in the days of Sacred Writ, bread was

and is baked in either a semipublic oven, or in the oven of a public baker. Sometimes each town might have several of these ovens. One type of such an oven consists of a big earthen tube, some three feet in diameter, and about five feet long. It is sunk in the ground inside a hut. The women take their turn in baking their bread. The fuel is thrown into the tube, and when the fire gets hot, and billows of smoke and tongues of flame come from the deep hole, the hut, without any chimney in it, begins to resemble an active crater. Malachi must have seen such an oven when he wrote the words, "For behold, the day cometh, that shall burn as an oven: and all the proud, yea, and all that do wickedly, shall be stubble" (Mal. 4:1).[15]

Another type of Oriental oven "is a long, low, stonebuilt vault, like half a railway-engine's boiler, with a stone pavement down the middle, and a long narrow strip at each side for the firewood."[16] Each night the ashes are taken out, and often the children of poor families will bring a piece of tin, or of a broken water jar, and carry home on this some of the embers of the fire with which to start the fire at home for the evening meal.[17] Hosea makes mention of "an oven heated by the baker" (Hosea 7:4). This would indicate that some of the people brought their bread to a baker to do the baking. The city of Jerusalem had its Baker's Street in the time of Jeremiah (Jer. 37:21).

VEGETABLES

The two most widely used vegetables in Bible times were *beans* and *lentils*. The prophecy of Ezekiel mentions both of these in one verse (Ezek. 4:9). Beans are included in the articles of food which David's friends brought to him when he was in flight from Jerusalem, because of Absalom's rebellion (II Sam. 17:28). The most famous Biblical use of lentils, was of course, the selling of Esau's birthright for a meal including lentils with bread (Gen. 25:33, 34, A. R. V.).

Thomson tells of being invited to a meal of lentils which he found to be very savory with its "appetizing fragrance and substantial taste, that to a hungry man must have been very tempting. In eating this dish, he did as his hosts did, doubled "some of their bread spoon-fashion," and then dipped it into the saucepan. He suggests that Esau no doubt used the same kind of spoon of bread in eating the pottage of lentils.[18]

The Israelites' Egyptian diet included the vegetables: leeks, onions, and garlic (Num. 11:5). Most of these were probably used sometimes in Palestine. The prophet Isaiah mentions a "garden of cucumbers" (Isa. 1:8). Gourds were also used, as suggested by two Scripture passages (Jonah 4:6–10; II Kings 4:39). The "pulse" which Daniel and his companions wanted as their diet, when they were captives, was probably vegetables (Dan. 1:12). The word means primarily, "something sown," and therefore would include edible seeds that are cooked, such as lentils, beans, peas, etc. It was a simple vegetable diet that was wanted instead of the rich, unwholesome food of the king's table.[19]

Dairy Products

Milk. Milk in Bible times was considered, not simply as something that was added to their food in cooking, but was regarded as a substantial food for all ages. Babies were fed mother's milk (Isa. 28:9). The Hebrews not only used cow's milk, but also sheep's milk (Deut. 32:14), goat's milk (Prov. 27:27), and, no doubt, camel's milk (Gen. 32:15). The Promised Land was often called "a land flowing with milk and honey" (Exod. 3:8; 13:5; Josh. 5:6; Jer. 11:5). This would indicate that Palestine's broad pasture lands would produce an abundance of milk.[20]

A form of milk that is in common use among the Arabs today is called by them "leben," which means, "white." It is like our sour milk curds. In order to make it, they pour milk in a dish and then put yeast in it, which starts it to working. They cover it over with a warm cloth, and after it sets for about a day it is ready to serve. The Arabs are very fond of it. They say of it, "It makes a sick man well." If they have money for only one dish, they would usually ask for leben.[21] It was probably this "leben" that Abraham gave to his guests (Gen. 18:8), and also that Jael gave to Sisera (Judges 4:19; 5:25).

Butter. It is generally agreed among Bible scholars, that in most of the cases where the word "butter" appears in our generally used translation, it does not mean the kind of butter known by the Westerner, but rather curdled milk or "leben." There are two passages that do refer to *butter*, but even that is in a different form from that used by those people who live outside the Orient.[22] The first passage mentions "butter of kine" (Deut. 32:14), and the second refers to the process of making butter, "the churning of milk bringeth forth butter" (Prov. 30:33). The Bible-time method of making butter was doubtless the same as used by the Arab Bedouins of today. Thomson describes the process and the resulting butter thus:

> What are those women kneading and shaking so zealously in that large black bag suspended from that tripod? That is a bottle not a bag, made by stripping off the skin of a young buffalo. It is full of milk and that is their method of churning. When the butter has come they take it out, and boil it, and then put it in bottles made of goatskins. In winter it resembles candied honey, in summer it is like oil. That is the only kind of butter they have in this country.[23]

Concerning the passage in Proverbs (30:33), "Surely the churning of milk bringeth forth butter, and the wringing of the nose bringeth forth blood," Thomson calls attention to the fact, that the word *churning*, and the word for *wringing* are the same word in the Hebrew. He says:

> It is the wringing of milk that bringeth forth butter, just as these women are squeezing and wringing the milk in that skin bottle. There is no analogy between our mode of

churning, and pulling a man's nose until the blood comes, but in this native operation the comparison is quite natural and emphatic.[24]

Buttermilk is not itself mentioned in the Bible, but it was without doubt used, because the process of churning, as has already been referred to, is mentioned.

Cheese. In Palestine the Arabs are fond of cheese. It is convenient for them to take cheese along with them. Their cheese is somewhat like Western slices, only larger and thicker. They are about as thick as a man's hand. They are found stacked up in the markets.[25] David's father gave him ten cheeses to take to the army captain (I Sam. 17:18). Also Barzillai brought cheese to King David (II Sam. 17:29).

MEAT

When meat was eaten and what kinds. As a rule, Bible characters, like Orientals in modern times, have not eaten meat, except on special occasions. When a stranger or guest was entertained, or when a feast was made, then meat would be served.[26] Kings and other wealthy men had meat often. The daily provision of meat for King Solomon's court is given in Scripture. Four kinds of meat for the king's daily menu are mentioned: beef, mutton, game, and fowl (I Kings 4:23). Abraham served veal to his guests (Gen. 18:7). Gideon's guest was provided with a kid (Judges 6:19). On the shores of the Sea of Galilee, fish was a common article of food in the days of Jesus. Christ referred to this when he spoke of a son begging his father for a fish (Luke 11:11). This Scripture might imply that these dwellers near the lake lived mostly on fish.[27]

How meat was cooked and served. The method of preparing meat has thus been described:

> Roasting on a spit was perhaps the oldest way of cooking flesh, but less common among the Israelites than boiling, roast flesh being used as a rule only by the rich and better classes, as is still the case in the East.[28]

The servants of Eli's sons said to those bringing offerings, "Give flesh to roast for the priest; for he will not have boiled flesh of thee" (I Sam. 2:15, A. R. V.). After the meat was cooked it was divided up into small pieces, and a broth was prepared to serve with it, and this would often have vegetables in it.[29] Such a broth was used in the days of Gideon and of Isaiah (Judges 6:19, 20; Isa. 54:4).

EGGS

Sometime between the days of Elijah and the time of Christ, the domestic fowl and the everyday use of eggs was introduced into Palestine.[30] There would seem to be one early Old Testament reference to what might be the egg of a hen. It is Job 6:6: "Is there any taste in the white of an egg?" But the marginal rendering of the American Revised text translates it: "Is there any taste in the juice of purslain?" It is doubtful if an egg is meant here. But we do know that the use of eggs, among the Galileans around the lake, was common in Christ's time, for Jesus speaks of a son asking for an egg from his father (Luke 11:12).

HONEY

God had promised Israel, "a land flowing with milk and honey" (Exod. 3:8; 13:5; Josh. 5:6; Jer. 11:5). The numerous references to honey or honeycomb in God's Word, are proof that Palestine abounded with the product of the bees. Without doubt, the Jews took care of bees in order to produce honey.[31] However, many of the Scriptural citations indicate that wild honey was very common. The favorite haunts of the bees were in the cavities of trees, where Jonathan discovered and ate some of the honey (I Sam. 14:25–27); in the holes of the rock, where it was often extracted (Psa. 81:16); and sometimes the dried carcasses of animals, as when Samson ate honey from the carcass of the lion he had slain (Judges 14:8, 9).

The poetical books of the Hebrew Bible abound with com-
parisons to honey. The judgments of God's Word are compared to it (Psa. 19:10). Pleasant words are likened unto it
(Prov. 16:24), as also knowledge and wisdom to the soul
(Prov. 24:13,14). And the bride and bridegroom of Solomon's Song speak of honey (Cant. 4:11; 5:1).

In New Testament times John the Baptist lived on locusts
and wild honey from the wilderness (Matt. 3:4). And when
Jesus wanted to prove to the disciples that His resurrection
body was a real body, He asked for food and was given a
piece of broiled fish with some honeycomb (Luke 24:41–43).

Dr. Thomson relates how "in the clefts of a precipice over-
hanging Wady el Kurn swarms of bees made their home."
A man was let down over the rock by ropes, and being protected from assault from the bees, he was able to extract a
large quantity of honey.[32] Such an incident is reminiscent of
the expression of Moses in his farewell song: "He made him
to suck honey out of the rock" (Deut. 32:13).

FRUIT

Olives and olive oil. Some use is made of the pickled berry
of the olive, but the bulk of the fruit is used to make oil. In
the Orient, olive oil usually takes the place of butter, and is
largely used in cooking meals. A survey of several Scriptures
will indicate how important a food olive oil was considered to
be. The widow who fed Elijah said to him: "I have not a cake,
but an handful of meal in a barrel, and a little oil in a cruse"
(I Kings 17:12). She had been depending largely on bread
and oil for her food, but the supply of both was about gone.
The miracle of Elijah was the multiplication of that supply,
"And the barrel of meal wasted not, neither did the cruse of
oil fail, according to the word of the Lord, which he spake
by Elijah" (I Kings 17:16). The Meal Offering of the Mosaic
law called for unleavened fine flour mingled with oil baked

in a pan (Lev. 2:5). And the prophet Ezekiel in reciting to Jerusalem all its past blessings from Jehovah said of her, "Thou didst eat fine flour, and honey, and oil" (Ezek. 16:13. *See also* section on "olive tree," pp. 196–200).

Figs. This fruit was often used in Old Testament times, especially dried figs. Abigail took two hundred cakes of figs to David (I Sam. 25:18). A cake of figs was given the Egyptian to revive him (I Sam. 30:12), and cakes of figs were brought to David at Hebron, at a time of great rejoicing (I Chron. 12: 40). (*See also* section on "the fig tree," pp. 200–202.)

Grapes and raisins. During the months of September and October, the fresh ripe grapes are eaten along with bread as one of the principal foods.[33] Canaan must have been a land of very fine grapes, for two of the spies brought back a great cluster of grapes on a branch carried on a staff between them, and secured from the Valley of Eshcol (Num. 13:23). Raisins were widely used in the days when the Jews lived in Palestine. Abigail gave David one hundred clusters of raisins (I Sam. 25:18). Raisins were brought to David at Hebron (I Chron. 12:40) and again, when he was fleeing from Absalom, he received a quantity of them (II Sam. 16:1). (*See also* section on "use of grapes," pp. 193–194).

Pomegranates. There are several varieties of sweet and sour pomegranates in the land. The juice of the sour variety is used in the absence of lemons for the purposes of that fruit. The pomegranate was greatly esteemed as a fruit in early Bible times, for it was mentioned by Moses as one of the excellencies of the Promised Land (Deut. 8:8). The Song of Solomon makes mention of the pomegranate fruit, trees, and spiced wine from its juice (Cant. 4:13; 6:11; 7:12; 8:2).[34]

CHAPTER 5

Customs at Mealtime

E ASTERN HABITS, connected with the eating of a meal, are such a decided contrast to Western habits, that much care should be given to the study of them, if the many references in the Bible to eating, are to be interpreted accurately.

WASHING OF HANDS BEFORE EATING

Orientals are careful to wash their hands before a meal, but they would think that the Occidental way of washing in the water already made dirty by the hands, to be very untidy and disgraceful. The servant or whoever takes his place, pours water on the hands to be washed as they are held over a basin. Often the basin has a concave cover with holes, so as to allow the dirty water to run through and thus be out of sight. The method of eating without knives, forks, or spoons, makes this washing a necessity.[1] That this method of washing was in vogue in the days of the prophets is seen by the way Elisha was characterized by the king's servants: "Here is Elisha the son of Shaphat, which poured water on the hands of Elijah" (II Kings 3:11). Elisha had served as Elijah's servant, and pouring water, so that his master could wash his hands, was an important part of his duties.

When the Pharisees complained against the disciples of Jesus, because they ate bread without washing their hands (Matt. 15: 1, 2; Mark 7:1–5), it was concerning a lengthy ceremonial washing of hands that they spoke. The Jewish hierarchy of that day had given forth a positive injunction as to exactly how this ablution should be done. It was not a law of Moses but a tradition of the elders. Jesus refused to sanction it as a rule that was binding. It was not the custom of washing hands before eating that Jesus objected to, but the authority the rabbis claimed to have in telling the people the exact and detailed manner in which it must be done.[2]

POSITION WHILE EATING

According to general Arabic custom, the seemly posture while eating is "to sit erect on the floor at the low table, with the legs either folded under the body, or thrown back as in the act of kneeling."[3] Thus in the desert tent of the Bedouin, or in the simple house of the Fellahin, this would be the position of those eating a meal. And we can be sure that this was the posture of the common people of Bible days in most cases. The exception to this rule is the custom of the wealthy, or the habit of the people on special occasions such as suppers or feasts; and this will be dealt with in a later section. It is easy to imagine Elisha and the sons of the prophets eating in the usual Oriental position, when it says concerning them: "And the sons of the prophets were sitting before him and he said unto his servant, Set on the great pot" (II Kings 4:38).

USE OF TABLE, CHAIRS, AND DISHES

Table. In many cases the Arab custom would seem to indicate to the Westerner that they use no table at all when serv-

Eating a Meal

ing a meal. Actually, a mat spread upon the ground serves the purpose of a table. This is especially true of the tent Arab.[4] This was the early Semitic table of Old Testament times, for the Hebrew word "Shool-khawn," usually translated "table," has as its root meaning, "a skin or leather mat spread on the ground."[5] With this sort of a table in view, the Psalmist can be understood when he said concerning his enemies, "Let their table become a snare before them." David's meaning would be, "Let their feet become entangled in it, as it is spread on the ground."[6]

If the Arabs use more of a table than this mat, then it is likely to be a polygon stool, no higher than about fourteen inches, and those eating would sit on the floor around this stool.[7]

Chairs. With such an Oriental table in general use, it would follow that Occidental chairs would be largely missing. In regard to making use of chairs in ancient Bible days it has been said: "On ordinary occasions they probably sat or squatted on the floor around a low table, while at meals of more ceremony they sat on chairs or stools."[8] The scriptural instances of chairs or stools used at mealtime, include Joseph's brothers sitting on seats at a banquet in Egypt (Gen. 43:33); and David's having a seat at the table of King Saul (I Sam. 20:5, 18). Both of these cases are connected with royalty or high position. On ordinary occasions the "chair" used by the vast majority of Israelites was the ground or floor on which would be spread a carpet or a mat.[9]

Dishes. At an Oriental meal the only dishes are those in which the food is placed on the table; there are no dishes given to each one having a part in the meal. Often there is only one dish for the food, and it is usually a tray of basketwork, or a copper dish.[10] Jesus spoke of His betrayer as "he that dippeth his hand with me in the dish" (Matt. 26:23; Mark 14:20). In entertaining his guest, Gideon put the meat in a basket, and the broth in a pot (Judges 6:19).

SAYING GRACE AT MEALS

Before the Arabs begin their meal each person repeats after the Master of the house some such a grace as, "In the name of God," or, "Praise Allah," or, "God be praised."[11]

In the Old Testament era the Jews were in the habit of saying grace at meals, and if a prophet was to be present he was expected to do it for them. Concerning Samuel when Saul was to eat the sacrifice with him, it was said, "He doth bless the sacrifice: and afterwards they eat that be bidden" (I Sam. 9:13).

In relating the miracle of Jesus feeding the five thousand John says, "And Jesus took the loaves and when he had given thanks, he distributed to the disciples . . ." (John 6:11). And concerning the feeding of the four thousand, Matthew is careful to include the blessing in his description: "And he took the seven loaves and the fishes, and gave thanks" (Matt. 15:36). Dr. Edersheim suggests that Christ may have prayed an extemporaneous prayer for grace, or he may have used the formula widely used by the Jews of his day as a mealtime grace. Here is the formula: "Blessed art Thou, Jehovah our God, King of the world, who causes to come forth bread from the earth."[12]

Also it was customary for the Jews in those days to have a second prayer of thanks at the end of the meal. Their authority for this was Deut. 8:10: "When thou hast eaten and art full, then thou shalt bless the Lord thy God for the good land which he hath given thee." In the saying of these graces it was customary for one of the guests to give the thanks in a loud voice, and for the rest to say Amen, or to repeat some of the words of the grace.[13]

USE OF HAND INSTEAD OF KNIFE, FORK, OR SPOON

In general it may be said that the Arabs in eating do not use knives, forks, spoons, plates, or napkins which are considered so essential in the West. They say: "What does a man want of a spoon when God has given him so many fingers?" Sheets of bread, about as thick as heavy flannel, take the place of spoons or forks to some extent. A piece from this bread is broken off and shaped so as to put some of the food on it.[14]

They use this bread to scoop up any partially liquid dish, such as soups, sauces, or gravies. Each torn off piece of bread that thus serves as a spoon is eaten along with the food it contains.[15]

Meat is usually served in a single large dish and is eaten with the fingers. Broth is served in a separate dish and it is used to moisten the bread. This method of eating is actually not as untidy as might be supposed.[16]

The invitation Boaz gave to Ruth to eat with his workers, indicates that these same customs must have been in operation in those days: "And at meal-time Boaz said unto her, Come hither, and eat of the bread, and dip thy morsel in the vinegar" (Ruth 2:14). And at the last supper Jesus said to his disciples, "He that dippeth his hand with me in the dish, the same shall betray me" (Matt. 26:23). Furthermore, he spoke of dipping a choice portion of the meat called the sop into the dish (John 13:26). More will be said of this under the section dealing with suppers and banquets. Suffice it to say, that most of the Oriental customs of today in regard to eating date back, not only to the days of our Saviour, but also to the Old Testament era.

WASHING AFTER THE MEAL

After a typical Oriental meal, washing the hands again is of course essential. If there is a servant, he is the one to bring in the pitcher of water and basin, and the water is poured over the hands of those who have eaten the meal. A napkin is placed over the shoulder so that the hands may be dried. They do this for each other if there is no servant to do it for them.[17] That this method of pouring water to wash hands was used in ancient times has already been seen concerning the washing of hands before eating.

CHAPTER 6

Special Suppers and Banquets

SINCE THE DAILY MENU of the ordinary Oriental meal is and always has been very simple, something needs to be said about those special occasions when a more elaborate and expensive meal is served. The Scriptures abound in accounts of these formal occasions, such as weddings, birthdays, or other times when special guests are invited and a sumptuous meal is served.

BANQUET INVITATIONS

In some parts of the East a custom of double invitations to an entertainment has been observed. Some time before the feast is to be served, an invitation is sent forth; and then, when the appointed time draws near, a servant is sent again, this time to announce that everything is ready.[1] There are several examples of this custom in the Bible. Ahasuerus and Haman were invited by Esther to a feast, and then when it was ready the king's chamberlains went to get Haman (Esther 5:8; 6:14). Another example is in the Parable of the Wedding of the King's Son. "The kingdom of heaven is like unto a certain king, which made a marriage for his son, and sent forth his servants to call them that were bidden to the wedding"

(Matt. 22:2, 3). Again, the Parable of the Great Supper has this double invitation in it: "A certain man made a great supper, and bade many: and sent his servant at supper time to say to them that were bidden, Come; for all things are now ready" (Luke 14:16, 17).

"Compelling" Guests to Attend

The following words of Christ's parable need to be understood from an Oriental point of view: "And the lord said unto the servant, Go out into the highways and hedges, and *compel them* to come in, that my house may be filled" (Luke 14:23). The usual brief invitation in America, and the ready acceptance of it would be considered in the East entirely undignified. In the East the one invited must not at first accept, but is expected rather to reject the invitation. He must be *urged* to accept. Although all the time he expects to accept, he must allow the one inviting him the privilege of "compelling him" to accept.[2] It was thus that Lydia must have extended, and Paul and his companions must have finally accepted hospitality. "If ye have judged me to be faithful to the Lord, come into my house, and abide there. And she *constrained* us" (Acts 16:15). When one of the Pharisees invited Jesus to a meal, the Saviour did not at first accept the invitation, although he did go finally: "Now one of the Pharisees *insisted* that he take a meal with him" (Luke 7:36, translation of A. T. Robertson). All of this was in keeping with Oriental customs.

Why Exclusion from a Feast Was Considered To Be So Terrible

Ancient banquets were usually held at night in rooms which were brilliantly lighted, and anybody who was excluded from the feast was said to be cast out of the lighted room into "the outer darkness" of the night.[3] In the teachings of Jesus, such exclusion is likened unto the day of judgment. "The children of the kingdom shall be cast out into outer darkness" (Matt. 8:12). "Bind him hand and foot, and take him away, and cast him into outer darkness" (Matt. 22:13). "And cast ye the unprofitable servant into outer darkness: there shall be weeping and gnashing of teeth" (Matt. 25:30). This expression "outer darkness" takes on new meaning, when it is realized what a dread the Oriental has for the darkness of the night. In the East a lamp is usually kept burning all night. To sleep in the dark as the Westerner usually does would be a terrible experience to the Oriental. Because of this fear of the darkness, the Saviour could have chosen no more appropriate words than "outer darkness" to represent the future punishment of the unrighteous.[4]

Posture While Eating at Feasts

It has already been observed that on ordinary occasions the people of the Bible age mostly sat or squatted on the floor around a low table at mealtime. In the king's circle, or at other times of special ceremony, seats were sometimes provided. The prophet Amos is the first sacred writer to refer to

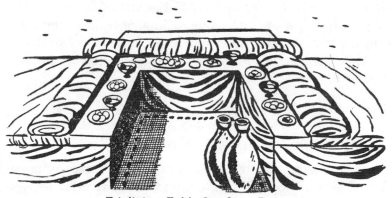

Triclinium Table Set for a Feast

the custom of "stretching themselves upon their couches" when eating (Amos 6:4). By the time of Jesus, the Roman custom of reclining on couches at supper had been adopted in some Jewish circles. The Roman table and couches combined was called a *triclinium*. There were three couches which were located on the three sides of a square, the fourth side being left open, so that a servant could get on the inside to assist in serving the meal. The guest's position was to recline with the body's upper part resting on the left arm, and the head raised, and a cushion at the back, and the lower part of the body stretched out. The head of the second guest was opposite the breast of the first guest, so that if he wanted to speak to him in secret he would lean upon his breast.[5]

This custom at a banquet table throws light on several passages from the four gospels. The Apostle John asked Jesus a question while in this position at supper (John 13:23–25). In the story of the Rich Man and Lazarus, when Jesus said that "the beggar died, and was carried by the angels into Abraham's bosom" (Luke 16:22), he doubtless meant to imply, that he was reclining at a heavenly table next to Abraham where he could lean upon his breast. This is clear in the light of Christ's description of that heavenly feast: "Many shall come from the east and the west; and shall *recline* with Abraham, and Isaac, and Jacob, in the kingdom of heaven" (Matt. 8:11, A. R. V. margin). Also this position of reclining at table explains how the woman could come during a dinner and take her position behind at the feet of Jesus and wash them (Luke 7:38).

PLACES OF HONOR AT THE TABLE

When the Pharisees were invited to a banquet, they were very covetous of having the highest places of distinction at the table. Jesus condemned them for this proud spirit. He said concerning them: "They . . . love the chief place at feasts" (Matt. 23:6, A. R. V.). When Jesus was guest at a meal in a Pharisee's house, he gave the guests a parable, when he noticed how they sought the chief places at the table. Here is the parable as given by A. T. Robertson's Translation of Luke's Gospel (Luke 14:8–10):

> When you are invited by anyone to a wedding-feast, do not recline in the post of honor, lest one more honored than you be invited by him, and lest the man who invited you both come and say to you, "Make room for this man"; and then you will begin with shame to take and keep the last place. But, when you are invited, go and recline in the last place, so that, when the man who has invited you comes, he will say to you, "Friend, come up much higher." Then you will have honor in the presence of all your fellow-guests.

In many native homes one room has a higher floor, and in this room the guests of honor are assigned places, and those of less honor on the lower floor or level.[6] A place of special honor would be on the right of the host, and the next highest place on his left. James and John asked for such positions in Christ's kingdom (Mark 10:35–37). But Jesus advised guests to take the last place. Where was this place located? It was on the lower level and nearest the door.[7] The guest who would take this humble place might be invited by the master of the house to take a place on a higher plane and farther from the door.

Food and Entertainment at Banquets

The prophet Amos, although he denounced extravagant luxuries and sinful excesses, nevertheless has given us a description of the eating, drinking, and other customs at an Oriental banquet. This is the way he describes it:

> And stretch themselves upon their couches, and eat the lambs out of the flock, and the calves out of the midst of the stall; that chant to the sound of the viol, and invent to them-

selves instruments of music, like David; that drink wine in bowls, and anoint themselves with the chief ointments (Amos 6:4–6).

The meat eaten at these suppers included the best lambs from the flock and calves that had been stall-fed. The drinking of wine at the feast was considered an important feature. Playing on stringed instruments was another activity, and the guests evidently vied with one another in anointing their bodies with very costly ointments.

Dancing was often a part of the entertainment at these feasts. When the Prodigal Son returned home, and his father celebrated with a feast, there was music and dancing (Luke 15:24, 25). Dancing was a social diversion of the Hebrew women and girls, especially when they made merry. Men did sometimes engage in it, as when David danced when the ark was brought to Jerusalem (II Sam. 6:14). But more often it was the activity of the fair sex (cf. Jer. 31:4). But there is no Scriptural record that the Jewish men danced with the women, as is the modern custom of the West. Neither is there indication that there were public female dancers, as is true in some Eastern places today. The dancing of the daughter of Herodias (Matt. 14:6) before men at a sensual banquet was the kind introduced among the Jews by corrupt Greek influence.[8]

DIPPING INTO THE DISH AND GIVING THE SOP

Oriental customs of eating must be kept in mind in order to understand the meaning of the words and action of Jesus, in relation to Judas Iscariot at the last supper. Mark's account reads:

> Jesus said, Verily I say unto you, One of you which eateth with me shall betray me. And they began to be sorrowful, and to say unto him one by one, Is it I? and another said, Is it I? And he answered and said unto them, It is one of the twelve, that dippeth with me in the dish (Mark 14:18–20).

Some have supposed that Judas was in the position where he would be dipping at the same time with Jesus into the dish, and that he was thus singled out as the betrayer. But this could hardly be, since the other disciples did not discover who the betrayer was from these words of Jesus. Since they all had been eating from the same large dish, these words of Jesus, "he that dippeth with me in the dish," did not identify any one of them. All of them, as well as Judas, had been dipping into the dish with Jesus. Jesus was simply informing them that one of them now eating with him would become his betrayer.[9]

Again, Christ's giving of the "sop" to Judas was in accordance with certain Eastern custom still observed in modern times. John reports what was done and said:

> He then lying on Jesus' breast said unto him, Lord, who is it? Jesus answered, He it is, to whom I shall give a sop, when I have dipped it. And when he had dipped the sop, he gave it to Judas Iscariot (John 13:25, 26).

What is meant by the "sop"? It is the most tasty morsel of food being served at the feast. It may be served in the "bread spoon," but is more often picked up by the host with his thumb and finger, and handed directly to one of the guests.[10]

But why is a sop given to one of the guests? A native and resident of Bible lands says that certain villagers there have this custom of giving the sop today, and he describes the purpose of the act thus:

> It is with them a mark of special respect for the master of the feast to hand to a guest portions of what is before him, or to insist on putting morsels or sops into his mouth with his own hand. I have had this done to me several times, when the intention was certainly to honor and manifest good will.[11]

The meaning of what Christ did then was most certainly to extend love and friendship to the very one who was going to betray him. The act has been described as if the Lord were saying to the traitor:

> Judas, my disciple, I have infinite pity for you. You have proved false, you have forsaken me in your heart; but I will not treat you as an enemy, for I have come not to destroy, but to fulfill. Here is my sop of friendship, and "that thou doest do quickly."[12]

CHAPTER 7

The Sacred Duty of Hospitality

ORIENTAL ATTITUDES ON ENTERTAINING A GUEST

EATING ALONE DISLIKED

IT IS A PART of Oriental etiquette to want to share hospitality with others. After a meal has been prepared, an Arab has been heard to call out three times from a high spot in the neighborhood, inviting men to come and partake of the meal. These men of the desert do not like to eat their meal alone.[1] The patriarch Job felt that way about it in his day: "Or have eaten my morsel myself alone, and the fatherless hath not eaten thereof" (Job. 31:17).

Guests believed to be sent by God. These men of the East believe that a person who becomes their guest is sent to them by God. Thus their hospitality becomes a sacred duty. When one such a host entertained Westerners, he was so happy that he wept tears of joy that "Heaven had sent him guests."[2] When Abraham entertained three strangers who proved to be angels, he showed much the same attitude. His enthusiasm in receiving the guests would indicate his belief, that those he was to entertain were sent to him by the Lord. It is said that he "ran to meet" the three men, that he "hastened into the tent unto Sarah" to get her to make ready food, that he "ran unto the herd," and that he "fetched a calf," and that he "hasted to dress it" (Gen. 18:2–7).

69

Kinds of Guests

Friends as guests. In the East a friend is always welcome to receive hospitality. The Romans of New Testament times had a token of hospitality between two friends, which consisted of a tile of wood or stone, which was divided in half. Each person wrote his name on one of the two pieces, and then exchanged that piece with the other person. These were often kept and handed down from father to son. To produce the counterpart of one of these pieces would guarantee the hospitality of a real friend.[3] The Book of Revelation no doubt refers to this custom in one of the promises to overcomers: "And will give him a white stone, and in the stone a new name written" (Rev. 2:17).

Strangers as guests. There is an Oriental proverb that says, "Every stranger is an invited guest." The Bedouin Arab of today, like Abraham of old, will sit in the entrance way of his tent, in order to be on the watch for stranger guests (Gen. 18:1).[4] The inspired apostle gave command concerning hospitality to this type of guest: "Be not forgetful to entertain strangers: for thereby some have entertained angels unawares" (Heb. 13:2). When Paul exhorted the Roman believers to be "given to hospitality" (Rom. 12:13), he was referring to the same thing, for the Greek word he used for hospitality, "fil-ox-en-ee-ah," means, "love to strangers."[5] (*See also* "entertaining fellow-believers in N.T. times," pp. 122, 123).

Enemies as guests. One remarkable feature of Oriental hospitality is that sometimes an enemy is received as a guest, and as long as he remains in that relationship, he is perfectly safe and is treated as a friend.[6] There are certain Oriental tribes of tent-dwellers who have the rule that an enemy who has "once dismounted and touched the rope of a single tent, is safe."[7]

PROVISION MADE FOR GUESTS

Among tent-dwellers. If a guest is entertained by one who lives in a tent, there is no separate place provided, nor would it be expected. Usually, the first section of the tent within the entrance is the regular guest apartment, which serves as dining room and sleeping quarters. The men eat with their guest and sleep with him.[8] It was in this guest-apartment of his tent, that Abraham entertained his angel guests, when Sarah in the adjoining woman's apartment, overheard what was said (Gen. 18:1–10).

In the villages and cities. If a village was not provided with a community guest room, then a guest would be entertained in one of the houses, and since most of these had but a single

Oriental Guest Room

room, that one room would serve as reception room, dining room, and sleeping quarters. This room would be much like the reception apartment of the tent.

But in many of the villages and cities, a public guest chamber is provided. The food for guests entertained here is supplied by the families providing the room. Often a servant is hired to care for the room. The guest-room may be an upper room, or in summer, the shade of a large tree might serve as the guest-room. This room is the social gathering place for the men of the village. Women are not allowed in these guest chambers. So if a man has his family with him when traveling, he does not go to this public reception room, but waits until someone invites them into his house.[9] The Book of Judges tells of a Levite traveling with his concubine and a servant, and how he was thus entertained by an old man (Judges 19:15-21). As many families sleep on the housetop in summer weather, a guest is often given that place for the night.[10] Saul was entertained overnight on the rooftop and Samuel called to him early in the morning (I Sam. 9:26, A. R. V.).

In the cities or where there are houses of more than one room, built around a courtyard, the guest-room is usually at the end of the court. As a rule this room is more open than other family rooms. This would correspond to the raised divan in some one-room houses, which serves as the place of honor for guests. In large houses a well-furnished room is provided near the door, so as not to disturb the family. If there is an upper room, a distinguished guest is often accommodated there.[11] The man of God was provided such a room as a place of retirement (II Kings 4:10).

CUSTOMS WHEN A GUEST ENTERS A HOME

Bowing. When a guest is received into an Oriental home, bowing between the guests and host is quite apt to take place. In Western lands such bowing would be of the head only, but in the East there is a more expressive custom of saluting with the head erect and the body a little inclined forward, by raising the hand to the heart, mouth, and forehead. The symbolic meaning of this action is to say something like this: "My heart, my voice, my brain are all at your service."[12]

But those who are used to this custom on many occasions enter into a more complete bow. They do not wait to do this only for royalty, but when they want to express thanks for a favor, or supplicate for a favor, and at many other times of meeting they often fall on their knees, and then incline the body touching the ground with their head, and kissing the lower part of the other person's clothing, or his feet, or even the dust at his feet. To those not acquainted with such manners, it would seem that one person was worshiping the other like he would worship God; but ordinarily, worship of this sort is not involved in the action.[13] Cornelius is said to have worshiped Peter: "And as Peter was coming in, Cornelius met him and fell down at his feet, and worshiped him" (Acts 10:25). Of course Peter rejected this lest it might involve divine worship. Concerning the enemies of the Philadelphian church, the Apocalypse records these words of our Lord: "I will make them of the synagogue of Satan . . . I will make them to come and worship before thy feet" (Rev. 3:9). The Revisers have a marginal note in explanation of the word "worship" in both of these Scriptures: "The Greek word denotes an act of reverence, whether paid to a creature or to the Creator." There are many examples in the Bible of this Eastern custom of bowing in varying degrees of intensity (cf. Gen. 18:2, 3; 23:7, 12; Matt. 18:26; Rev. 19:10).

Greeting. Upon entering an Arab house or a Bedouin tent, the greetings used are something like this: The host will say: "Salam alakum," which means, "Peace be on you." The guest will respond with the words: "Wa alakum es-salam," meaning, "And on you peace."[14] Knowing that these Arabic customs date back for centuries, how significant then are the in-

structions of Jesus to his disciples, who were to be entertained
in certain homes: "And into whatsoever house ye enter, first
say, Peace be to this house, and if the son of peace be there,
your peace shall rest upon it: if not, it shall turn to you again"
(Luke 10:5, 6).

Kissing. Guests in Holy Land homes expect to be kissed as
they enter. When entertained by a Pharisee, Jesus com-
mented on his reception by saying to him, "Thou gavest me
no kiss" (Luke 7:45). The difference between the Oriental
and the Occidental way of greeting each other is made clear
by one who lived in Palestine many years.

> Here men shake hands when they meet and greet, but in
> Palestine, instead of doing this, they place their right hand
> on their friend's left shoulder and kiss his right cheek, and
> then reversing the action, place their left hand on his right
> shoulder, and kiss his left cheek. In this country men never
> kiss each other's faces; there it may be constantly seen. But
> how the practice lights up the numerous allusions in Scrip-
> ture which are naturally lost to a Westerner! Once grasp the
> fact that their kiss answers to our hearty handshake between
> friends and social equals, and how much—how very much—
> becomes plain that was before obscure![15]

Scriptural examples of men kissing men might be multi-
plied. Jacob kissed his father (Gen. 27:27). Esau kissed Jacob
(Gen. 33:4). Joseph kissed his brothers (Gen. 45:15). Jacob
kissed the sons of Joseph (Gen. 48:10). Aaron kissed Moses
(Exod. 4:27). Moses kissed Jethro (Exod. 18:7). David and
Jonathan kissed each other (I Sam. 20:41). The Father kissed
the Prodigal (Luke 15:20). The elders of Miletus kissed Paul
(Acts 20:37). This custom is frequent in the Orient in modern
times.[16]

Removing the shoes. Upon entering a house to be entertained, a guest does as all Orientals would do, he takes off his
boots, shoes, or slippers before entering a room. This becomes
necessary since they sit on a mat, rug, or divan, with their

feet beneath them, and shoes would soil the couch and the clothes, and would also make a very uncomfortable seat. The idea of defilement from the shoes led to the custom of removing the shoes upon entering sacred places.[17] Thus at the burning bush the Lord told Moses, "Put off thy shoes from off thy feet, for the place whereon thou standest is holy ground" (Exod. 3:5).

Washing the feet. After bowing, greeting, and kissing, the Eastern guest is offered water for washing his feet. Wearing of sandals would naturally necessitate foot washing, but it is often done when shoes have been worn. A servant will assist the guest by pouring the water upon his feet over a copper basin, rubbing the feet with his hands, and wiping them with a napkin.[18]

When Jesus and his disciples were gathered together, the Saviour took the place of the servant, and washed the feet of His disciples, who themselves had disdained to do such a humble task. John tells us that He "laid aside his garments; and took a towel, and girded himself. After that he poureth water into a basin, and began to wash the disciples' feet, and to wipe them with the towel" (John 13:4, 5). Paul gave as a recommendation of a widow: "If she have washed the saints' feet" (I Tim. 5:10). This custom was also common in Old Testament days (Gen. 18:4; 19:2; 24:32; 43:24; I Sam. 25:41, etc.).

Anointing the head with oil. The custom of anointing guests with oil is an ancient one among nations of the East. Olive oil alone was often used, but sometimes it was mixed with spices. Simon the Pharisee was accused of lack of hospitality because he failed to anoint Jesus (Luke 7:46). This would indicate the custom was quite common in the days of the Gospel accounts. David immortalized the custom when he wrote his shepherd psalm and exclaimed: "Thou anointest my head with oil" (Psa. 23:5). Travelers in the Orient in recent times have discovered that this practice of anointing still exists in some quarters.[19]

CARING FOR A GUEST AFTER ENTRANCE

The guest given a drink of water. One of the first things done for a guest who has been received, is to offer him a drink of water. The doing of this is recognizing him as being worthy of peaceful reception. Thus to give a drink of water is the simplest way to pledge friendship with a person. When Eliezer, Abraham's servant, sought a welcome, he did so by requesting of the maiden who came to the well to draw water (Gen. 24:17, 18), "Give me to drink, I pray thee, a little water of thy pitcher." And when she made answer, "Drink, my lord," it was an indication that he was welcome to be a guest at the nearby home. With this significance attached to a drink of water, the promise of Jesus takes on new meaning (Mark 9:41), "Whosoever shall give you a cup of water to drink in my name, because ye belong to Christ, verily I say unto you, he shall not lose his reward."[20]

The guest served a meal. The sharing of food is in the East a very special act of hospitality. It means far more than it means in the West. It is a way of making a covenant of peace and fidelity.[21] When Abimelech wanted a permanent covenant with Isaac, the confirmation of that covenant came when Isaac "made them a feast, and they did eat and drink" (Gen. 26:30).

An Oriental considers as sacred the expression, "bread and salt." When it is said, "There is bread and salt between us" it is the same as saying, "We are bound together by a solemn covenant." A foe will not "taste the salt" of his adversary unless he is ready to be reconciled to him.[22]

In some rural districts of Syria today there is a custom that a person on a mission of importance will not eat bread and salt of his host until first the purpose of his errand is made known. They think that the covenant of "bread and salt" must not be entered into until the attitude of the host is known regarding the mission of the guest.[23] Thus Abraham's servant refused to eat at the table of Laban, until first he made known his mission of seeking a wife for Isaac (Gen. 24:33).

Dr. Thomson, Syrian missionary, was once guest in a Bedouin sheik's tent. The host dipped a bit of bread in some grape molasses and gave it to the missionary for him to eat. Then he said to him, "We are now brethren. There is bread and salt between us. We are brothers and allies."[24] When the Gibeonites sought a covenant of friendship with Israel in the days of Joshua, it was said that the Israelites "took of their victuals, and asked not counsel at the mouth of the Lord" (Josh. 9:14). Once having entered into this covenant, Israel was bound to keep it.

The guest made lord of the house. An Eastern proverb runs thus: "The guest while in the house is its lord." This is a true statement of the spirit of the hospitality of the East. One of the first greetings a Palestinian host will give his guest is to say, "Hadtha beitak," i.e., "This is your house." This saying is repeated many times. Thus actually the guest during his stay is master of the house. And whenever the guest asks a favor, in granting it the host will say, "You do me honor."[25]

There must have been the same attitude between host and guest in the days of Lot. The host was considered to be a servant, and the guest was lord. Thus Lot spoke of himself and his guests: "Behold now, my lords, turn in, I pray you, into your servant's house" (Gen. 19:2).

Privacy not expected by the guest. An Oriental guest would think he was ill-treated if he were left alone at any time. He does not need privacy at night, because he sleeps with his clothes on. He is happy to have others sleep with him. If a sleeping place is assigned to him in an upper room, then some of the family sons sleep alongside of him that he might have their companionship. He would feel he was being deserted if treated the way he would be if entertained in the West, just as a Westerner would feel oppressed by the constant attentions of an Oriental host.[26]

PROTECTING A GUEST

In the lands of the East, when a host accepts a man to be his guest he thereby agrees at whatever the cost to defend his guest from all possible enemies during the time of his entertainment. Dr. Cyrus Hamlin, an American missionary in the East, was entertained by a governor. The host took a piece of roast mutton and handed it to the missionary, saying as he did so, "Now do you know what I have done?" In answering his own question he went on to say: "By that act I have pledged you every drop of my blood, that while you are in my territory no evil shall come to you. For that space of time we are brothers."[27] The Psalmist felt utterly secure, though he had enemies close by him, when he knew that God was his host. "Thou preparest a table before me in the presence of mine enemies" (Psa. 23:5).

THE ABUSE OF HOSPITALITY

Among Eastern nations it is considered a terrible sin indeed for anybody who has accepted hospitality from a host to turn against him in the doing of an evil deed. This feeling goes back to very ancient times and is often alluded to by various writers.[28] The prophet Obadiah refers to this sin: "The men that were at peace with thee have deceived thee . . . They that eat thy bread have laid a wound under thee" (Obad. 7). The Psalmist David speaks of this terrible evil, "Yea, mine own familiar friend, in whom I trusted, which did eat my bread, hath lifted up his heel against me" (Psa. 41:9). And the Lord Jesus quotes this very passage from the Psalms as having its fulfillment in the treachery of Judas the betrayer, who ate at the same table with Him (John 13:18).

RENEWING A BROKEN COVENANT

Among oriental people, when a covenant of friendship has been once broken, it may be renewed by those involved once again eating together. After His resurrection, Jesus ate at least three times with various disciples of His, and this was no doubt done in order to renew the covenant, which had been broken by their disloyalty to Him during the days of His passion [29] (cf. Luke 24:30, 41–43; John 21:12, 13). In the Old Testament we have an example of this when Jacob and Laban were in strained relationship. They restored their friendship by eating together, as well as entering into an oath (Gen. 31:53, 54).

THE DEPARTURE OF A GUEST

When the time comes for a guest to depart, a Syrian host will do his best to delay the departure. He will beg him to stay for one more meal, or to wait until the morrow before he leaves. In Judges nineteen is the finest example in the Bible of this custom of delaying the guest. The host said to the guest: "Comfort thine heart with a morsel of bread, and afterward go your way." After the meal he urged him, "Tarry all night." The next day the guest was persuaded to tarry until afternoon. But when urged to stay over another night, the guest decided it was time to insist on departing, which he did. This is typical Oriental procedure (Judges 19:5–10).[30]

When a guest departs, the usual salutation is as follows. The guest will say: "With your permission." And the host will make answer, "Depart in peace."[31] Isaac must have used just such a salutation when Abimelech and his men departed, after having been entertained by Isaac at a meal. Scripture says: "And they departed from Isaac in peace" (Gen. 26:31).

When a host desires to do special honor to his departing guest, he will walk with him out of the town a distance. Sometimes this walk will last for an hour, and will come to an end only after the guest has urged his host that he need not go any farther.[32] Thus Abraham walked with his departing guests "to bring them on the way" (Gen. 18:16).

CHAPTER 8

Daily Program of Activities

EARLY RISING

Concerning the hour
of rising, one writer has summed up the matter thus:

> The habit of early rising is all but universal in Palestine.
> The climate makes this a necessity for the greater part of the
> year, the heat being so great that hard labor is oppressive a
> few hours after sunrise. At early dawn laborers go to their
> work and travelers start on their journeys.[1]

Many Bible passages indicate that the custom of early rising was practiced in those days. The Genesis account mentions an occasion when "Abraham rose early in the morning"
(Gen. 22:3). The Book of Exodus tells that "Moses rose up
early in the morning" (Exod. 34:4). And Scripture says that on
a certain day "Job rose up early in the morning" (Job 1:5).
Concerning the people who wished to hear Christ's teachings,
Luke says, "And all the people came early in the morning to
him in the temple, for to hear him" (Luke 21:38). And Mark
says of Jesus, "And in the morning, rising up a great while before day, he went out, and departed into a solitary place, and
there prayed" (Mark 1:35). Other such examples of early rising in Scripture times could be added.

GRINDING OF THE GRAIN BY THE WOMEN

The first sound to greet the ear in the early morning in many a Palestinian village will be the sound of the grinding of the grain. Today, as in the long ago, many of these people resort to the handmill for this purpose. A traveler passing by these humble homes will hear the hum of the handmill morning or evening and sometimes after dark. This sound of the grinding is not exactly musical, and yet many love to go to sleep under it. In the mind of those who live in the East this sound is associated with home, and comfort, and plenty. The women are the ones who engage in this task, and they begin it early in the morning, and it often requires half a day to complete.[2]

When Jeremiah foretold judgment upon Israel for her sins, he said concerning what God would take from her: "I will take from them the voice of mirth, and the voice of gladness, the voice of the bridegroom, and the voice of the bride, and *the sound of the millstones*" (Jer. 25:10). From this it can be seen that the sound of these handmills is an indication of life

Women Grinding Grain

and activity, and the absence of them would be a sign of utter desolation.

The Bible references to the grinding mills are true to Oriental customs. The task is for servants if the family has them, and if not the women do the job, but the men would consider it beneath them to engage in such a menial task. Part of the judgment upon Israel at the destruction of Jerusalem was that the enemy "took the young men to grind" (Lam. 5:13). And the Philistines punished Samson in this way, for it says of him, "and he did grind in the prison house" (Judges 16:21).

Although there are simple handmills made for the use of one person, more often two women operate one together. The mill is composed of two stones eighteen to twenty-four inches in diameter. The two women sit at these stones facing each other. The upper stone turns upon the lower one by means of an upright handle which the women alternately pull and push.[3] Here is how the process works:

> The upper stone rotates about a wooden pivot fixed in the center of the lower. The opening in the upper stone for the pivot is funnel-shaped to receive the corn, which each woman throws in as required with her disengaged hand. The flour issuing from between the stones is usually caught on a sheepskin placed under the mill.[4]

Job speaks of a heart being as "hard as a piece of the nether millstone" (Job 41:24). Thomson says that the lower millstone is not always harder than the upper, but he had seen the nether made of a very compact and thick sandstone, while the upper was of lava no doubt because being lighter it would be easier to drive it around with the hand.[5]

TIME OF MEALS

Meals are not always served at the same time in the Orient today, and the nature of the meals varies in different sections.[6] The same was also true in Biblical times. In the main it may be said that the Hebrews had only two meals a day, breakfast, and dinner. The time for breakfast varied all the way from early morning to noon.[7] Jesus served breakfast to a group of hungry fishermen early in the morning (John 21:12, A. R. V.). In commenting on the negligence of the guards of King Eglon (Judges 3:24), the Jewish historian Josephus says: "It was then summer time, and the middle of the day, when the guards were not strictly on their watch, both because of the heat, and because they were gone to dinner."[8] Attention is called to the fact that the word Josephus uses for "dinner" is the word meaning "breakfast" as used in the New Testament.[9] It would appear from this that the Jewish historian was indicating that sometimes breakfast was served as late as noon in his day. No doubt it was more often served in the middle of the morning. In the Parable of the Wedding of the King's Son, the message went forth to the invited guests, "I have prepared my breakfast" (Matt. 22:4, Twentieth Century N. T.). The marriage feast here would be similar then to the English "wedding breakfast."

Both meals of the Jews are mentioned by Jesus in an exhortation he gave his host, "When you give a breakfast or a dinner" (Luke 14:12, Twentieth Century N. T.). The evening meal would in most cases be the main meal, but not always, depending on the nature and place of the men's work. The custom in some modern cities of having breakfast anywhere from nine to twelve o'clock, and dinner in the evening, would correspond quite closely with the two meals of the Jews of Bible times.[10]

WEAVING CLOTH AND MAKING CLOTHES

The Jewish women were responsible for making the clothing for the family. The wool which was used came from their flocks. It had to be spun into yarn without the use of modern spinning wheels. Concerning this process, the Book of Proverbs in its tribute to the ideal mother, describes it thus: "She layeth her hands to the spindle, and her hands hold the distaff" (Prov. 31:19). The ancient Egyptians and Babylonians, being experts in weaving, had large looms, but for the most part the common people of Palestine used a very primitive loom and the weaving process was of necessity a slow and tedious one. Of course there were no sewing machines or steel needles. Their needles were coarse ones made of bronze or sometimes of splinters of bone that had been sharpened at one end, and with a hole through the other end.[11]

It is said that today most of the spinning in Syria is done by the older women. It gives occasion for these spinners to get together. And they spin while they talk, or even sometimes while they are eating in an informal way. When Scripture says, "She layeth her hands to the spindle, and her hands hold the distaff" (Prov. 31:19), it is the same way as saying, "She is never idle," or as the Syrians would say, "Her spindle is never out of her hands."[12]

WASHING CLOTHES

The Arab women in washing their clothes today usually go to nearby sources of water such as streams, pools, or watering troughs. They will dip their clothes in and out of the water, and then placing them upon flat stones which abound in Palestine, they will beat them with a club which is about a foot and a half long. They carry the water in goatskins and have a vessel for rinsing purposes.[13]

That this sort of process was used in the time of David is indicated by the prayer of his penitential psalm: "Wash me throughly from mine iniquity" (Psa. 51:2). His picture here comes from the process of washing clothes. Alexander Maclaren says concerning it:

> The word employed is significant, in that it probably means washing by kneading or beating, not by simple rinsing. The psalmist is ready to submit to any painful discipline,

if only he may be cleansed. "Wash me, beat me, tread me down, hammer me with mallets, dash me against the stones, do anything with me, if only these foul stains are melted from the texture of my soul."[14]

That soap was used in washing is clear from the Scriptures. The word occurs in the common translation of the books of Jeremiah and Malachi (Jer. 2:22 and Mal. 3:2). This form of soap was doubtless a vegetable alkali. Job said: "If I wash myself with snow water, and cleanse my hands with lye" (Job 9:30, A. R. V. margin). This was a vegetable alkali. There are two references in the Bible to mineral alkali which was called nitre (Prov. 25:20 and Jer. 2:22). This was probably the "natron" used so largely in Egypt.[15]

CARING FOR THE GOATS BY THE GIRLS

Among the Bedouin Arabs where camels engage the attention of the men folks, the task of caring for the goats is assigned to the young women of the home. These shepherdesses sometimes have a difficult time in watering their flocks, if perchance the camel herders come in from one of their five-day waterless periods of grazing. These girls are not apt to get much consideration from these men. The Sacred Record tells how Moses befriended Jethro's daughters when they had to fight for an opportunity to give water to their flocks. One of these girls afterwards became the wife of Moses (Exod. 2:15–21).[16]

THE MIDDAY SIESTA

In Palestine during the summer season the time of greatest heat is from noon to three o'clock in the afternoon. There is cessation of most activity during that time in many parts of the land. They rest at home or wherever they may be and can find a suitable place. A laundry or shop will often be discovered to be closed during those hours.[17]

This midday time of rest was common in Old Testament days. Genesis says that Abraham "sat in the tent-door in the heat of the day" (Gen. 18:1). Ishbosheth, Saul's son, was sleeping at midday. "Who lay on a bed at noon" (II Sam. 4:5). And when Saul entered the cave where David and his men were located, he no doubt did so in order to have his middle-of-the-day nap. "And Saul went in to cover his feet" (I Sam. 24:3).

DAILY CONVERSATION

Use of God's name in conversation. In Anglo-Saxon lands the name of God is seldom mentioned in daily conversation except by those who are profane. But among the Arabs of Bible lands, Gods' name is constantly on the lips of these people. An astonished person will exclaim, "Mashallah," i.e., "What has God wrought!" which is the very expression used by Balaam centuries ago (Num. 23:23). If a man is asked if he expects to do a certain thing, he will make answer, "If God wills." And this is the kind of answer recommended by James in his epistle (Jas. 4:15). If a baby is held up that you may admire it, the grandmother will say, "Behold the gift of God," words which are reminiscent of the Psalmist's declaration, "Lo, children are an heritage of the Lord" (Psa. 127:3). When a farmer greets his workers he says to them, "God be with you." And they will answer him, "God bless thee." These are the same greetings used centuries ago when Boaz came to his workers (Ruth 2:4). Such pious expressions, of course, could be used so constantly that they become meaningless, and on the lips of insincere people would soon lose their value. But such conversation is a great contrast to what is heard in the West.[18]

From the days of the patriarchs to the times of the Apostles, daily conversation among the Jews included many references to Deity. No doubt there were insincere lips that spoke the name of God carelessly, but when this custom was carried out by godly people, how beautiful it was! The Book of Ruth has a number of examples of such conversation, as for example, when Naomi's women friends exclaimed: "Blessed be the Lord!" (Ruth 4:14). It would be well if modern Christians had more of God in their daily conversation.

Use of figurative language and exaggerated expressions. Often the oriental manner of speech is to picture what is meant, or perhaps to demonstrate it. A good example of this is given us by Luke in his account of Paul's experiences:

> There came down from Judea a certain prophet, named Agabus. And when he was come unto us, he took Paul's girdle, and bound his own hands and feet, and said, Thus saith the Holy Ghost, So shall the Jews at Jerusalem bind the man that owneth this girdle (Acts 21:10–11).

If John the Baptist had spoken like some speakers in the West, he would have said, "Your pretensions to virtue and good birth far exceed your actual practice of virtue."[19] Being a real Oriental he actually said:

> O generation of vipers, who hath warned you to flee from the wrath to come? Bring forth therefore fruits meet for repentance. And think not to say within yourselves, We have Abraham to our father: for I say unto you, that God is able of these stones to raise up children unto Abraham (Matt. 3:7–9).

The large use of figures of speech in its teaching and conversation make the Book a typical Oriental book.[20]

The Oriental frequently makes statements that to the Westerner sound like uncalled-for exaggeration. One man will say to another, "What I say to you is truth, and if it is not, I will cut off my right arm." Or he will say, "I promise you this, and if I fail in fulfilling my promise, I will pluck out my right eye." In those lands nobody would ever dream that such a resolution would be carried out. The statement simply means that the speaker is in earnest.[21]

An Oriental can fully appreciate what Jesus meant when he said, "If thy right eye offend thee, pluck it out, and cast it from thee. If thy right hand offend thee, cut it off, and cast it from thee" (Matt. 5:29, 30). Many expressions of Jesus need to be understood in the light of daily conversation of his day. Here are examples of a few. "It is easier for a camel to go through the eye of a needle, than for a rich man to enter into the kingdom of God" (Matt. 19:24). "Ye blind guides, which strain at a gnat, and swallow a camel" (Matt. 23:24). "And why beholdest thou the mote that is in thy brother's eye, but considerest not the beam that is in thine own eye?" (Matt. 7:3). When reading such passages of Scripture, men from the Occident must remember the fondness of the Oriental for the hyperbole.

Dealing with delicate subjects in mixed company. Visitors to Palestine from other parts of the world are often embarrassed by the way the daily conversation of the natives may include matters never spoken of in polite circles in the West. The Oriental considers it to be perfectly proper to talk about anything that is natural in the presence of men, women, and children. And this is done in refined circles. A respectable woman from the Holy Land cannot understand why some critics of the Bible have condemned the Scriptural mention of certain matters deemed wrong for Westerners to talk about. The story told in Genesis of the details concerning the birth of twin boys, Esau and Jacob (Gen. 25:23–26), would be told in a public gathering in the East, with even more details, without a blush coming to any face. Several hundred years ago this same thing was true in England.[22]

Going of the Women for Water

It is the task of the women to go for the household water to the well or spring. And they do it today in many places in the East just like it was done when the Genesis account speaks of

Women Carrying Water Jars

it being "the time of the evening, even the time that women go out to draw water" (Gen. 24:11). The women are trained to do this from girlhood, for Saul and his servant "found young maidens going out to draw water" (I Sam. 9:11). The chief time for doing this is in the late afternoon or evening, although it is often done early in the morning. Earthenware pitchers (Lam. 4:2) are used for the purpose, and they have one and sometimes two handles.[23]

It has been customary for Syrian women to carry the pitcher of water on their shoulder, although sometimes it is carried on the hip. Most Arabs of Palestine carry it upon their head.[24] Scripture says that Rebekah carried her pitcher on her shoulder (Gen. 24:15).

Carrying a pitcher of water was all but universally done by women. It must have been a picturesque sight to see them going and coming with the pitcher poised gracefully upon the head or shoulder. When Jesus instructed two of his disciples, "Go ye into the city, and there shall meet you a *man* bearing a pitcher of water: follow him" (Mark 14:13), that would be an easy way of identifying the person, for it is exceedingly uncommon to see a *man* carrying a pitcher of water, which is a woman's task. When larger supplies of water are needed, men use large skins of sheep or goats for carrying the supply. The pitchers are reserved for the use of the women.[25]

There is nothing left at the well that may be used for drawing water from a depth. Each woman who comes for water brings with her, in addition to the pitcher in which to carry the water, a hard leather portable bucket with a rope, in order to let it down to the level of the water.[26] The Samaritan woman whom Jesus met at Jacob's well had brought all this with her, but Jesus did not have such equipment with him. Hence she said to him: "You have no bucket, sir, and the well is deep" (John 4:11, Twentieth Century N. T.). In response to his request for a drink, she drew from the well and gave to him.

CHAPTER 9

Dress and Ornamentation

THE STYLES OF DRESS in Anglo-Saxon lands are undergoing a constant change, whereas, in Eastern countries, the manner of dress today is largely the same as it was centuries ago. There is a prevalent view in Bible lands that it is morally wrong to change anything that is ancient. Thus the prevailing Palestinian dress of modern times (except of the Jews who have gone back to their land from various parts of the globe) is much as it was in the epoch that produced the Bible.[1]

THE INNER GARMENT—TUNIC OR SHIRT

The tunic (inappropriately translated "coat") was a shirt which was worn next to the skin. It was made of leather, hair-cloth, wool, linen, or in modern times, usually of cotton. The simplest form of it was without sleeves and reached to the knees or sometimes to the ankles. The well-to-do wore it with sleeves and extending to the ankles. Women as well as men wore it (see Cant. 5:3, A. R. V.), although there was no doubt a difference in style and pattern in what was worn by the two.[2]

Among the lower classes, the tunic was often the only dress worn in warm weather. Persons of higher rank might wear the tunic alone inside the house, but would not wear it without the outer garment outside, or when they were to receive a caller. In the Bible the term "naked" is used of men clad only with their tunic (cf. Isa. 20:2–4; Micah 1:8; John 21:7). To be dressed in such a scanty manner was thought of as "nakedness."[3]

As a rule the Jews of Christ's day had at least a change of apparel. A man would be considered poor to have only one garment.[4] Yet John the Baptist said to those who heard him, "The man who has two shirts must share with him who has none" (Luke 3:11, Williams). And when Jesus sent out the Twelve on a preaching and healing mission, He told them not to take an extra undergarment with them (Matt. 10:10, Williams).

The apparel which Jacob gave to Joseph (Gen. 37:3) is, after the Septuagint and Vulgate, rendered in our English translations, "coat of many colors." But the Hebrew expression here is the same as the one used for the garment worn by Tamar the daughter of King David, and translated in the Greek and Latin, "a sleeved tunic." (See II Sam. 13:18, A. R. V. margin.) For this reason many Bible scholars believe it was a long undergarment with sleeves: The working classes usually wore a short tunic, whereas the aristocracy wore a long tunic with long sleeves. Thus it would be a mark of distinction for Joseph to wear the latter. But some are inclined to think it was a robe worn over the tunic.[5]

The garment of Jesus for which the Roman soldiers cast lots, was a *tunic* without seam (Jno. 19:23, A. R. V. margin). It has often been referred to as a robe, but this is not correct, for it was not his outer garment, but rather his *undergarment*. Unfortunate translations have been responsible for this erroneous idea.

The Outer Tunic or Robe

In Bible times there was a looser and longer kind of tunic that was sometimes used but not by the ordinary people. Scripture indicates its use by kings (I Sam. 24:4), prophets (I Sam. 28:14), nobles (Job 1:20), and sometimes youths (I Sam. 2:19). Some Bible scholars believe it to have been a third garment, i.e., in addition to the ordinary tunic and outside mantle. But others have thought of it as a special robe that was worn over the undergarment, and thus might have taken the place of the mantle.[6]

The Girdle

If the tunic was ungirded it would interfere with a person's ability to walk freely, and so a girdle was always worn when leaving home for any kind of a journey (See II Kings 4:29; Acts 12:8). There were and are today two kinds of girdles. One, a common variety, is of leather, usually six inches broad and furnished with clasps. This was the kind of girdle worn by Elijah (II Kings 1:8), and by John the Baptist (Matt. 3:4). The other, a more valuable variety, is of linen (See Jer. 13:1), or sometimes of silk or embroidered material. It is generally a handbreadth wide. The girdle served as a pouch in which to keep money (II Sam. 18:11) and other things that might be needed (Mark 6:8). The girdle was used to fasten a man's sword to his body (I Sam. 25:13). Thus the girdle was a very useful part of a man's clothing.[7]

The Scriptures often make symbolic use of the girdle. When Jesus said to His disciples: "Let your loins be girded about" (Luke 12:35), it was as if He had said: "Be as men who have a long race to run; gather up the folds of your flowing robes, and fasten them with your girdle; that nothing may keep you back or impede your steps."[8] In Bible language, "to be girded" means: "to be ready for action" (cf. Psa. 18:39). The prophet

Isaiah spoke of righteousness as the girdle of Messiah's loins when He rules the world (Isa. 11:5). And Paul calls truth to be the Christian's girdle in his warfare with Satan (Eph. 6:14).

THE OUTER GARMENT, OR MANTLE

The outer garment which the Palestinian villager wears, is a large cloak which would serve the purpose of a Westerner's overcoat. It is made of wool or goat's hair and sometimes of cotton. It is dark brown and different shades with whitish perpendicular stripes. It serves as a shelter from the wind and rain, and as a blanket at night. It is a more or less common sight to behold a man walking on a hot day wearing his heavy cloak, and if he should be asked why he does so, his answer

Oriental Dress (Men)

would be, "What keeps out the cold, keeps out the heat also."[9]

It was this outer garment or mantle with which Elijah smote the waters of Jordan and crossed over with Elisha, and when he was taken up to Heaven this mantle became the property of Elisha (II Kings 2:8–13). The three young men who were cast into the fiery furnace were clad in their mantles as well as their tunics and other garb (Dan. 3:21, A. R. V.).

The Law of Moses contained an explicit commandment regarding this outer garment. This is the way the law reads:

> If thou at all take thy neighbor's raiment to pledge, thou shalt deliver it unto him by that the sun goeth down: for that is his covering only, it is his raiment for his skin: wherein shall he sleep? And it shall come to pass, when he crieth unto me, that I will hear; for I am gracious (Exod. 22:26, 27).

The need for this commandment is easily understood when it is known how the mantle is used at night. Going to bed at night is a very simple matter for the Bedouins or peasants. Mats, rugs, or mattresses are used to lie upon, but the host does not provide any covering. Each person provides his own which consists of his mantle. Being closely woven, it is warm, and if he sleeps out-of-doors, this covering is even waterproof.[10]

It was because this outer garment was a man's covering by night that the law did not allow anybody taking this as a pledge or security, for this would deprive him of his means of keeping warm while sleeping. Such a garment if taken at all had to be returned by sunset.[11]

A knowledge of this law and its purpose is an aid in understanding certain statements of Christ. On one occasion He said: "Do not keep back your undergarment from the one who robs you of your outer one" (Luke 6:29, translation of A. T. Robertson). This order is understood easily, because the outer garment would be the one most easily seized by a robber. But on another occasion He said. "If any one wishes to go to law with you and deprive you of your undergarment, let him take your outer one also" (Matt. 5:40, Weymouth). A Jewish court would not award an outer garment as judgment, because of the rule of the Law of Moses already referred to, but could award an undergarment. In such a case Jesus advocated going the "second mile" by giving the outer garment also.[12]

Because of the fullness of the mantle it served as a means of carrying various things therein. The lap was often filled with grain or fruit. Jesus said, "Give, and it shall be given unto you; good measure, pressed down, and shaken together, and running over, shall men give into your bosom" (Luke 6:38). Ruth could put six measures of barley into her mantle (Ruth 3:15, A. R. V.). Thus the upper garment served many useful purposes.[13]

HEADDRESS

The Jews of Bible times gave much attention to the care of their hair. The young people loved to wear it long and curled (Cant. 5:11, A. R. V. margin), and they were proud to have thick and abundant hair (II Sam. 14:25, 26). Middle-aged men and priests would occasionally cut their hair but very little. Baldness was scarce and suspicion of leprosy was often attached to it. Thus when the youth said of Elisha, "Go up, thou bald head" (II Kings 2:23), it was using an extreme curse, for the prophet being a young man, may not actually have been bald-headed. Men would not cut their beards, but allow them to grow long (II Sam. 10:4, 5). Beards would be anointed with oil often.[14]

In public the Jews always wore a turban, for at certain seasons of the year it is dangerous in Palestine to expose the head to the rays of the sun. This turban was of thick material and passed several times around the head. It was somewhat like our handkerchief and was made of linen, or recently of cotton.[15] The patriarch Job and the prophet Isaiah mention the use of the turban as a headdress (Job 29:14, A. R. V. margin; Isa. 3:23, A. R. V.). In place of the turban, the Palestinian Arabs today, for the most part, wear a head veil called "Kaffieh" which hangs down over part of their garment.

SANDALS

The shoes as worn by the majority in New Testament times were no doubt what we would call sandals. They consisted of a sole of either wood or leather, which was fastened to the foot by leather thongs. Some people wore that which was more like an Occidental shoe. With these, either the entire foot was covered, or the toes were left bare. Such shoes were probably considered to be a luxury, for the Bible references to footwear indicate the universal use of sandals.[16]

The Old Testament often makes mention of the sandals. The prophet Amos said, "Because of their selling for silver the righteous, and the needy for a pair of sandals" (Amos 2:6, Young). And Abraham spoke of the sandal thongs (Gen. 14:23). The New Testament references to sandals are also numerous. The angel told Peter, "Gird thyself and bind on thy sandals" (Acts 12:8). And John the Baptist refers to the latchet (thong, Robertson) of Messiah's sandals (Mark 1:7).

THE DIFFERENCE BETWEEN WOMEN'S DRESS AND MEN'S

The law of Moses forbade a man to wear a woman's clothing, and a woman to wear a man's clothing (Deut. 22:5). Among the Bedouin Arabs of Palestine there is a great care that either sex shall not imitate the other in matters of dress. A traveler one day discovered a Bedouin man who had put on a woman's garment while doing some rough work. He was hired to be a guide, but the man was very careful that none of his countrymen should see him in a woman's garb, and

Oriental Dress (Women)

hurried away as soon as possible to change into a man's apparel.[17]

The difference between the dress of women and men needs to be noted carefully.

> The dress of women was different in detail rather than in kind. They too wore tunic and cloak. We may suppose that in every case their dress was a little more elaborate. Doubtless they wore longer tunics, larger mantles than their menfolk. And if they did, they may be said to have had every right to them, for they generally made not only their own clothes but those of their lords.[18]

The *veil* was the distinctive female wearing apparel. All females, with the exception of maidservants and women in a low condition of life, wore a veil. They would usually never lay it aside, except when they were in the presence of servants, or on rare occasions. This custom has prevailed among the Eastern women down to the modern era. When traveling, women may throw the veil over the back part of their head, but if they see a man approaching, they place it back in its original position. Thus Rebekah, when she saw Isaac approaching her camel caravan, covered her face with her veil (Gen. 24:64, 65). When women are at home they do not speak to a guest without being veiled and in the presence of maids. They do not enter the guest's chamber, but rather, standing at the door, they make it known to the servant what is wanted (See II Kings 4:12, 13). It is well to remember that prostitutes went unveiled. Today, as in olden times, virgins and married women may be seen wearing veils in Bible lands.[19] The old customs are not being observed strictly by some Moslem women, for they are now going unveiled.

Although it was the custom for women to wear a veil entirely covering their head, when they were in public, this custom was not always strictly enforced among the Hebrew women. They were allowed more liberty than the Arab women are allowed today. The Egyptians saw Sarah's face (Gen. 12:14). While Hannah was praying, Eli "marked her mouth" (I Sam. 1:12). When a woman kept her veil down, it was forbidden for anyone to lift it, but she was free to do so if she chose. Jesus said, "Every one that looketh on a woman to lust after her hath committed adultery already with her in his heart" (Matt. 5:28). All these Scriptures indicate that women sometimes exposed their faces to view. Young girls were more apt to be veiled than married women.[20]

The headgear of Bethlehem women is of interest in throwing light on Biblical customs. It was of two parts. First, there was what might be called a high cap on the front of which have been sewn rows of gold and silver coins. It would have to be a dire circumstance that would ever cause her to part with any of these coins. If she lost one of these, an evil meaning would be attached to the loss, and so it would be considered a great shame. Thus the woman whom Jesus told us about (Luke 15:8–10), had not merely lost a coin that could be used for buying articles, she had lost a part of that which was an ornament to her and which was also her dowry. Reflection was cast upon her character. Second, there was the veil, which was quite a large affair perhaps six feet long and some four feet wide, and so placed over the cap as to cover the entire headgear, with the exception of the coins. Most of these veils are made of heavy white linen. Some have embroidery work on them, and some are nearly covered with needlework.[21]

ORNAMENTATION

As a rule, Jewish *men* did not indulge in extravagances of dress, and there was little ornamentation among them. They often carried a cane or staff, which would be ornamented at the top, but it served the useful purpose of protecting them from half-wild dogs that abounded in the country, and was not much of an ornament. Certain men wore a ring on their right hand, or suspended by a cord or chain around the neck.[22] Actually this was the *signet* ring or seal, and served as the personal signature of its owner, and so was not usually worn as an ornament. (For Scriptural examples of the ring, see Gen. 38:18; Cant. 8:6; Luke 15:22, etc.)

Among the *women* there was more apt to be ornamentation than among the men. Peter and Paul condemned an elaborate braiding of women's hair (I Peter 3:3, A. R. V.; I Tim. 2:9, A. R. V.), and the use of ornaments may possibly have been involved in the custom. Earrings were at one time worn by the women of Jacob's family (Gen. 35:4). And the golden earrings of the Israelitish women contributed to the making by Aaron of the golden calf (Exod. 32:2). These earrings as now worn in the East have as their main design the form of balls, long pendants, crescents, or disks. On behalf of his master, Abraham's servant had two bracelets ready to give Rebekah (Gen. 24:22). In recent years these are made of gold, silver, brass, or colored glass. In the third chapter of his prophecy, Isaiah lists many feminine ornaments. Necklaces or pendants are referred to also (Isa. 3:19, A. R. V.). Today they take the form of balls, squares, or hollow cylinders. Anklets, now having bells and disks attached, are also mentioned in this chapter (Isa. 3:18, A. R. V.). These are worn by Bedouin women today. Noserings also worn by these women were a part of Isaiah's list of feminine ornaments (Isa. 3:21). Amulets were worn in Isaiah's day (Isa. 3:20, A. R. V.), and still are worn in the East as a charm to protect a person from various kinds of evil.[23]

Special Dress of the Pharisees

The Pharisees in their religious garb, took two articles of dress which were worn by other Jews and emphasized them in a special way until they became their distinctive apparel. One of these was the *phylactery*. It was a little box of metal, or bands of parchment, which was fastened to the hand or forehead by straps. It contained passages of Scripture referring to the Passover and the redemption of the first-born from Egypt. The custom was based on certain Scriptural admonitions (Exod. 13:9, 16). And the Jews still bind them upon their arms and foreheads.[24]

The other special feature of the Pharisees' dress was the blue fringes placed at the corners of the mantle, as the law of Moses commanded (Num. 15:37, 38; Deut. 22:12). The Pharisees had unusually broad phylacteries, and very long fringes (Matt. 23:5). It was for this proud use of these things without an appreciation of their value, that Jesus condemned them so severely.[25]

THE DRESS OF CHRIST

How was Jesus Christ dressed? The famous artists, who have painted pictures of Him for us, have not always given an accurate view. One writer of the past century has attempted to describe His dress. It is worthy of careful study:

> Upon His head He must always have worn the turban, the national headgear, used alike by rich and poor . . . The turban He wore was probably white. It was fastened under the chin by a cord, and at the side fell down to the shoulders and over the tunic. Under His turban He wore His hair rather long, and His beard uncut. His tunic, the underneath vesture, was of one piece without seam, it was therefore of some value, and had probably been given Him by one of those women who "ministered to Him of their substance." Over this He wore the talith, loose and flowing. This mantle was not white, for we are told it became white during transfiguration. It was not red, for that was only the military color; it is possible it was blue, for blue was then very common; or it may have been simply white with brown stripes. In any case, Jesus had at the four corners of this mantle, the ciccith [fringe] . . . He wore sandals on His feet, as we learn from John the Baptist; and when He was traveling, going from place to place, He doubtless wore a girdle around the loins, and carried a stick in His hand.[26]

CHAPTER 10

Parental Position in the Home

Position of the Father

ORIENTAL MEANING attached to the word, *"father."* The Oriental idea of the family is a little kingdom within itself, over which the father is supreme ruler. Every company of travelers, every tribe, every community, every family, must have "a father," who is the head of the group. A man is said to be "the father" of what he invents. Jubal "was the father of all such as handle the harp and pipe." Jabal was "the father of such as dwell in tents and have cattle" (Gen. 4:20, 21). Because he was a preserver and protector, Joseph said that God made him "a father to Pharaoh" (Gen. 45:8). The Oriental mind cannot conceive of any band or group without somebody being "the father" of it.[1]

Supremacy of the father under the patriarchial system. Under the patriarchial administration, the father is supreme in command. This authority which the father has, extends to his wife, to his children, his children's children, his servants, and to all his household, and if he is the sheik, it extends to all the tribe. Many of the Bedouin Arabs of today are under no government except this patriarchial rule. When Abraham, Isaac, and Jacob lived in tents in the Land of Promise, they were ruled by this same system. And when the law of Moses was given to Israel, the authority of the parents, and es-

103

pecially the father, was still recognized. One of the Ten Commandments is "Honor thy father and thy mother" (Exod. 20:12). In many ways the father was the supreme court of appeal in domestic matters.[2]

Succession of authority. In a majority of cases, the great authority which the father had, was handed down to his eldest son, who took over the position of leadership upon the death of the father. Thus Isaac became the new "sheik" over his father's household upon the death of Abraham. He and Rebekah had been living in that household under his father's authority; but the succession of authority passed on to him as the son. Ishmael, being son of the handmaid, did not succceed to the place (Genesis 25). In some cases, the father bestowed the succession of authority on other than the eldest son, as when Isaac bestowed it upon Jacob instead of Esau (Genesis 27).

Reverence of the children for the father. Reverence of children for their parents, and especially the father, is well-nigh universal in the East down to modern times. Among the Arabs, it is very seldom that a son is heard of as being undutiful. It is quite customary for the child to greet the father in the morning by the kissing of his hand, and following this, to stand before him in an attitude of humility, ready to receive any order, or waiting for permission to depart. Following this, the child is often taken upon the lap of the father.[3]

Obedience to parents was demanded by the Mosaic Law, and a rebellious and disobedient son could be punished by death (Deut. 21:18–21). The Apostle Paul reiterated the injunction that children must obey their parents (Eph. 6:1; Col. 3:20).

Position of the Mother

Position of the wife in relation to the husband. The wife held a subordinate position to that of her husband, at least in office, if not in nature. The ancient Hebrew women did not have unrestrained freedom as the modern women of the Occident have. In the Orient, social intercourse between the sexes is marked by a degree of reserve that is unknown elsewhere. Dr. Thomson says, "Oriental women are never regarded or treated as equals by the men." They never eat with the men, but the husband and brothers are first served, and the wife, mother, and sisters wait and take what is left; in a walk the women never go arm in arm with the men, but follow at a respectful distance; the woman is, as a rule, kept closely confined, and watched with jealousy; when she goes out she is closely veiled from head to foot.[4]

This attitude toward women can be illustrated from the Bible. Notice how Jacob's wives when traveling were given places by themselves, and not with him (Genesis 32). And nothing is said about the prodigal's mother being present at the feast which the father served his son (Luke 15:11–32). All this is in keeping with Oriental custom.

But while these things are true, it must be understood that the Old Testament does not picture the wife as a mere slave of her husband. She is seen to exert tremendous influence for good or ill over her husband. And he showed great respect for her in most cases. Sarah was treated by Abraham as a queen, and in matters of the household, she ruled in many ways. Abraham said to her, concerning Hagar, who had given birth to Ishmael, "Behold thy maid is in thy hand; do to her as it pleaseth thee" (Gen. 16:6). The tribute to a Hebrew wife and mother in the Book of Proverbs indicates she was a person of great influence with her husband: "The heart of her husband doth safely trust in her" (Prov. 31:11). "She openeth her mouth with wisdom" (Prov. 31:26). "Her children arise up and call her blessed; her husband also; and he praiseth her" (Prov. 31:28).

Position of the mother in relation to the children. Children in the East show nearly the same respect toward the mother as they do toward the father. The mother is believed to be entitled to honor and to have authority from God. Actually, the father and mother are looked at, as being the representatives of God in the matter of authority. They are considered as having this position no matter how poorly they fulfill their obligations.[5] Hebrew children in general held their mothers in great respect, even when they became adults. This may be illustrated by the great influence exerted by queen mothers on the kings of Judah and Israel (I Kings 2:19; II Kings 11:1; 24:12, etc.).

Position of Jewish women superior to that of heathen women. The degradation of women in the Orient is a matter of common knowledge. In many cases she is more like a drudge, or a slave, or a plaything for the man, than she is the man's companion, as in the West. This situation has been in existence for centuries. But the position of Hebrew women was far superior to that of heathen women, long before Christianity had its origin among them. Concerning this superiority in relation to the Arabs, Dr. Thomson testifies:

> The position of women among them was far higher than with the Arabs, and the character of Hebrew women must have been, on the whole, such as to command and sustain this higher position. The Arabs can show no list of pious and illustrious ladies like those who adorn the history of the Hebrews. No Bedouin mother ever taught, or could teach, such a "prophecy" as King Lemuel learned from his; nor could the picture of "a virtuous woman," given in the last chapter of Proverbs, have been copied by an Arab. The conception by him of such a character was a moral impossibility.[6]

CHAPTER 11

Birth and Care of Children

DESIRE OF JEWISH WOMEN FOR CHILDREN

THERE WAS AMONG the Jewish wives a universal longing for, and joy in, the giving birth to children.[1] That longing was well expressed in the words of Rachel to Jacob, "Give me children, or else I die" (Gen. 30:1). The Lord had originally said to Adam and Eve, "Be fruitful and multiply" (Gen. 1:28). And the promise to Abraham was, "I will make thy seed as the dust of the earth" (Gen. 13:16). The law of God taught that children were a sign of God's blessing: "Blessed shall be the fruit of thy body" (Deut. 28:4). The Psalmist pictured a man blessed of the Lord, and says of him, "Thy wife shall be as a fruitful vine by the sides of thine house" (Psa. 128:3). Sterility in marriage was considered to be a divine visitation or curse. Hannah's barrenness was "because the Lord had shut up her womb" (I Sam. 1:6). To have a child after being a long time barren, as was the case of Elisabeth, meant that the Lord had taken away her reproach among men (Luke 1:25).

PREFERENCE FOR BOY BABIES

Among the Palestine Arabs there is always a desire on the part of the mothers and fathers that the baby shall be a

107

boy rather than a girl. A parting blessing often used by the Arabs is:

> May the blessings of Allah be upon thee,
> May your shadow never grow less,
> May all your children be boys and no girls.[2]

Boys are wanted because they tend to increase the size, wealth, and importance of the family group or clan. When they grow up and marry, they bring home with them their wives, and children of such unions perpetuate the father's house. If boys increase the house, girls are thought of as decreasing it. When they marry they usually go to live in the house of their husbands.[3]

This attitude among present-day Arabs, was also the attitude of the Hebrew people in Old and New Testament times. Except among the Christian Jews, there was an added reason why every Hebrew expectant woman wanted a boy. She always hoped that her son should be the Messiah. The Messianic promises of Holy Writ, no doubt, were often on the lips of Hebrew women. "The sceptre shall not depart from Judah, nor a lawgiver from between his feet, until Shiloh come" (Gen. 49:10). "There shall come a Star out of Jacob, and a Sceptre shall rise out of Israel" (Num. 24:17). These kept alive the hope of a coming Messiah, and caused the Hebrew mother to desire at each birth a boy baby, that perhaps she might be the mother of Shiloh.

CARE OF INFANT CHILD

For years the Orientals of Bible lands have cared for an infant child much as it was done when Jesus was born. Instead of allowing the young baby the free use of its limbs, it is bound hand and foot by swaddling bands, and thus made into a helpless bundle like a mummy. At birth the child is washed and rubbed with salt, and then with its legs together, and its arms at its side, it is wound around tightly with linen or cotton bandages, four to five inches wide, and five to six yards long. The band is also placed under the chin and over the forehead.[4]

The prophet Ezekiel indicated that these same customs at a child's birth were practiced in his day. "In the day thou wast born . . . thou wast not washed in water to cleanse thee; thou wast not salted at all, nor swaddled at all" (Ezek. 16:4, A. R. V.). And we are all familiar with the words of Luke, as to how they cared for the baby Jesus: "Ye shall find a babe wrapped in swaddling clothes and lying in a manger" (Luke 2:12, A. R. V.).

JEWISH RITES AND OFFERINGS AT BIRTH OF A CHILD

Jewish boys were circumcised eight days after birth. The one who circumcised the child spoke the following words: "Blessed be the Lord our God, who has sanctified us by His precepts, and given us circumcision." Then the father of the boy would go on with these words: "Who has sanctified us by His precepts, and has granted us to introduce our child into the covenant of Abraham our father." Because it was said that God changed the names of Abraham and Sarah, at the time He gave the covenant of circumcision, therefore they would name the boy on the day he was circumcised. After doing this they had a family meal.[5]

The rite of circumcision was the sign of the Abrahamic covenant. God had said to Abraham, "This is my covenant, which ye shall keep between me and you, and thy seed after thee" (Gen. 17:10). Jesus was circumcised the eighth day after birth and he was named "Jesus" at that time (Luke 2:21).

After childbirth, the Jewish mother passed through a period of purification of seven days for a boy and fourteen days for a girl, and then she still remained at home thirty-three days for a boy, and sixty-six days for a girl. Then she was to go up to the Temple to make her childbirth offerings. If she was rich she would bring a lamb to be offered, but if she was poor then she was allowed to present two young pigeons or a pair of turtledoves (Luke 2:21; cf. Leviticus 12).[6]

NAMING OF CHILDREN

The Arabs are fond of compounding the name of Allah into the name given their children. It was a very common custom for the Hebrews to include a name for God as a part of their children's names.[7]

A few samples of such Hebrew names are here given together with their meanings:

> Abijah—"Whose father God is"
> Ahaziah—"Held by Jehovah"
> Azariah—"Helped by Jehovah"
> Obadiah—"Servant of Jehovah"
> Daniel—"God is my Judge"
> Elijah—"My God is Jehovah"
> Elkanah—"Whom God created"
> Ezekiel—"God will strengthen"[8]

Another custom was practiced by Jews in naming their sons. After the birth of the first son, the father and mother were known as the father of so-and-so, and the mother of so-and-so. And the son added the father's first name after his own. Thus Jesus spoke of Peter as, "Simon Bar-jona" (Matt. 16:17), which means, "Simon, son of Jona." The Arabs giving such a name today would simply omit the word "son" and call the child "Simon Jona."[9]

Sometimes Jews had double names in Christ's time. This was true of Thomas. John's Gospel refers to him as, "Thomas, which is called Didymus" (John 11:16). Both of these names mean "a twin." The name "Thomas" was Aramaic, and the name "Didymus" was Greek. When traveling in foreign countries, Jews often assumed a Greek, or Latin, or other name, which had a meaning similar to their own.[10]

Jewish names given to girls, were often taken from beautiful objects in nature, or pleasant graces of character were used. "Bible examples are Jemima (dove), Tabitha or Dorcas (gazelle), Rhoda (rose), Rachel (lamb), Salome (peace), Deborah (bee), Esther (star)."[11] Naomi told the Bethlehem women, "Call me not Naomi, call me Marah." Our Bible margins give the meanings of these names thus: "Call me not, *Pleasant,* call me *Bitter*" (Ruth 1:20).

DUTY OF PARENTS IN TRAINING OF CHILDREN

It is quite clear from the Scriptures that the mother did most of the training of the children in their earlier years. The Book of Proverbs speaks of "The words of King Lemuel, the prophecy that his mother taught him" (Prov. 31:1). And concerning Timothy, Paul said, "From a child thou hast known the holy scriptures" (II Tim. 3:15). Earlier in the epistle, Paul refers to the faith of Timothy's mother and grandmother (II Tim. 1:5). Young children then were taught by their mothers. The daughters, doubtless remained under the guidance and oversight of their mothers until their marriage. As the boys grew up, they were more and more taught by their fathers, although they would never get away from the mother's training altogether. Proverbs often refers to a father's instruction of his son. "My son, hear the instruction of thy father" (Prov. 1:8). "My son, keep thy father's commandment" (Prov. 6:20). Only in well-to-do families was instruction turned over to tutors. King Ahab had tutors for his many sons (II Kings 10:1, 5). Schools for training boys were not in operation until comparatively a late date for Jewish youth in the land.[12]

CHAPTER 12

Education of Youth

A STUDY OF EDUCATION in Bible lands from early to late Biblical days will have bearing on the manners and customs of the people, and will throw light on certain Bible passages.

Schools at Ur when Abraham Was a Boy

The archaeological expedition conducted by Sir Charles Leonard Woolley at Ur of the Chaldees, from 1922 to 1934, has proven that there were schools in the city of Abraham's youth. Clay tablets were uncovered that indicate some of the subjects taught in these schools. The pupils had writing lessons on tablets, and dictation lessons in vocabulary. In arithmetic, they had the multiplication and division tables, and more advanced scholars had square and cube roots, with lessons in practical geometry. Grammar lessons included paradigms of the conjugation of verbs.[1] These revelations together with other discoveries at Ur, substantiate the view that Abraham came from a city of high civilization. No doubt he attended one of these schools.

It is certain that Abraham and Sarah were familiar with the laws of Hammurabi, having been taught this Babylonian law code from their youth. The explanation for Sarah's action in giving her maid Hagar to Abraham as a secondary wife (Gen. 16) is that the law of Hammurabi allowed such to be done. Similar action was repeated in Jacob's family relations (Gen. 30). But after the law of Moses came into being, this custom disappeared in Israel.[2]

SCHOOLS IN EGYPT WHEN MOSES WAS A YOUNG MAN

Stephen has given us the statement that Moses was "learned in all the wisdom of the Egyptians" (Acts 7:22). A wealth of information has come to us from the land of the Nile to let us know how valuable was the law-giver's education at the expense of Egypt.

Tradition has it that Moses went to school at the Temple of the Sun in Heliopolis. It was here then that he no doubt learned how to read and write. There is every indication that he had lessons in arithmetic, using duodecimal and decimal scales of notation. He must have studied geometry enough to make him familiar with the art of land-measuring. And his knowledge of mathematics would take in trigonometry. Astronomy was also studied by the Egyptians, as was architecture. The Egyptians had some proficiency in medical science and dentistry, and were acquainted with anatomy, chemistry, and had a knowledge of metals, for they had gold mines, and copper mines, and were familiar with the use of iron and the manufacture of bronze. Music was also an important subject in Egyptian schools. Moses must have been well educated according to the standards of ancient Egypt, which were of a high caliber.[3]

EDUCATION UNDER THE LAW OF MOSES

The duty of the educating of the youth was delegated by the Mosaic law especially to the Hebrew parents. The home was to be a school and the parents were to be teachers. The regulation read thus:

> And these words, which I command thee this day, shall be in thine heart: and thou shalt teach them diligently unto thy children, and shalt talk of them when thou sittest in thine house, and when thou walkest by the way, and when thou liest down, and when thou risest up. And thou shalt bind them for a sign upon thine hand, and they shall be as frontlets between thine eyes. And thou shalt write them upon the posts of thy house, and on thy gates
>
> (Deut. 6:6–9).

The feasts of the law such as the Passover were designed to cause the young to ask the question: "What mean ye by this service?" (Exod. 12:26), and thus give the parents an opportunity to explain its true meaning.

The Tabernacle, and later the Temple, were meant to be object lessons in divine truth. At each seventh year on the Feast of Tabernacles, the priests were to read the law before all the people. Thus the priests and Levites were also teachers in the land. And then an order of prophets arose, beginning with Moses, and continuing through a long and illustrious line, who were indeed valuable teachers of the youth of the land.[4] Special schools for the training of young prophets were developed by them, as will be seen.

THE SCHOOLS OF THE PROPHETS

Because of the moral decline of the priesthood under Eli and his wicked sons, Samuel was led to form a school of the prophets, wherein young men, mostly Levites, were trained to teach the Law of God to the people. There was such a school at Ramah, over which Samuel presided, and David fled there for a time when Saul sought to kill him (I Sam. 19: 18–21). There would seem to have been one at Gibeah where Samuel mentions "a company of prophets" (I Sam. 10:5, 10,

A. R. V., margin). In the days of Elijah and Elisha, reference is made to "the sons of the prophets" (I Kings 20:35), as living together at Gilgal, Bethel, and Jericho (II Kings 2:1, 3, 5; 4:38). About one hundred prophets ate with Elisha at Gilgal (II Kings 4:38–44). There may have been that many at Jericho, for mention is made of "fifty men of the sons of the prophets" (II Kings 2:7) that went to hunt for the body of Elijah. These schools were no doubt for the study of the law and history of Israel, and also the cultivation of sacred music and poetry. The writing of sacred history came to be an important part of the labor of the prophets. These young men were given mental and spiritual training in order that they might be able to exert a greater influence for good upon the people of their day.[5]

THE SYNAGOGUE SCHOOLS WHEN JESUS WAS A BOY

When Jesus grew up as a boy in the village of Nazareth, he no doubt attended the synagogue school. The Jewish child was sent to this school in the fifth or sixth year of his life. The pupils either "stood, teacher and pupils alike, or else sat on the ground in a semicircle, facing the teacher."[6] Until the children were ten years of age, the Bible was the one textbook. From ten to fifteen the traditional law was the main subject dealt with, and a study of theology as taught in the Talmud was taken up with those over fifteen years of age. The study of the Bible began with the Book of Leviticus, continued with other parts of the Pentateuch, and then went on with the Prophets, and lastly, the Writings. Because of the remarkable familiarity of Jesus with the Holy Scriptures, we may be fairly certain that His home in Nazareth had in it a copy of the Sacred Book as a whole. Doubtless He loved to ponder its pages at home after having studied its teachings in the school.[7]

THE RABBINICAL SCHOOL OF PAUL'S DAY

In the times of Paul, there were two rival schools of rabbinical theology, the school of Hillel which he attended at Jerusalem, and the school of Shammai. The former was the more liberal school as we would think of it today, and placed tremendous emphasis upon Jewish oral traditions. As a young man of thirteen years of age, Saul of Tarsus came to Jerusalem to begin his training under the great leader, Gamaliel. He graduated from this school to become a typical Pharisaical rabbi. Concerning his training he himself said: "I am verily a man which am a Jew, born in Tarsus, a city in Cilicia, yet brought up in this city at the feet of Gamaliel, and taught according to the perfect manner of the law of the fathers" (Acts 22:3).[8]

The training of Jesus as a boy had been under the other school, where there was less stress upon tradition, and more upon spiritual teachings of the law and the prophets. In his unconverted days, how Saul would have resented what Jesus said to the Pharisees, "Why do ye also transgress the commandment of God by your tradition?" and, "Thus have ye made the commandment of God of none effect by your tradition" (Matt. 15:3, 6)![9]

THE ROMAN SCHOOLS OF THE FIRST CENTURY

It is now known that there were twenty grammar schools in the great city of Rome when the Apostle Paul first visited the city. Girls as well as boys were allowed to go to school, but there is evidence that more boys than girls availed themselves of the privilege.[10]

Paul's reference to the "schoolmaster" (Gal. 3:24) of these Roman schools, was formerly misunderstood by many, until papyri writings threw light on his meaning. The individual called in our translation "schoolmaster" was actually not the headmaster or teacher, but rather a faithful slave whose duty it was to conduct his master's sons to and from school and prevent them from getting into mischief. Paul was comparing Christ with the real teacher, and the law was like the slave whose duty it was to conduct the pupil to the teacher.[11]

Discoveries of the archaeologists at Ephesus indicate that the School of Tyrannus that Paul engaged as a hall in which to preach (Acts 19:9) was probably an elementary school, where the teacher taught for a few hours early in the morning and for a while in the afternoon. Thus the room would be available for Paul's use when he wanted it. Such schoolrooms were usually adjacent to a street and thus would suit his purpose admirably.[12]

CHAPTER 13

Religion in the Home

The Father as Priest in Patriarchal Times

I_N THE DAYS_ of the early patriarchs, the father was the priest for the whole family, and this honor and responsibility of exercising the priesthood usually was bestowed upon the first-born son upon the death of the father. This practice continued until the law of Moses transferred this right to the tribe of Levi, which tribe then furnished the priests to Israel as a nation.[1]

The altar. The religion in the homes of those early days largely centered about an altar upon which animal sacrifices were offered unto God. Thus when Abraham came into the land and had pitched his tent in the vicinity of Bethel, the Scriptural record says of him, "And there he builded an altar unto the Lord, and called upon the name of the Lord" (Gen. 12:8). Later on it is recorded that he built an altar at Hebron (Gen. 13:18). It is said that Jacob built one at Shechem (Gen. 33:18–20). And then in obedience to the command of the Lord, he went to Bethel, and like his grandfather, built an altar to the Lord there. Anticipating doing this, he said to his family, "Let us arise, and go up to Bethel; and I will make there an altar unto God, who answered me in the day of my distress, and was with me in the way which I went" (Gen.

118

35:3). The altar in the home life of those early days helped to produce a sense of sin, a realization of God's holiness, and a knowledge that the way of approach to God was through a sacrifice. The altar was the forerunner of the family prayer life in a Christian home today, which is based upon forgiveness of sin through the blood of Christ, of which the animal sacrifice was a symbol.

The teraphim. In the land of Babylonia, from which Abraham had originally come, there was family worship of household gods, and the home had its altar along with clay figurines of these gods, which were called "teraphim." These family gods served as guardian angels of the home. At the death of a father, these household gods, or teraphim, would often be left to the oldest son, with the understanding that others of the family would have the right to worship them.[2]

When Jacob left the home of Laban in Haran, Genesis says, "Rachel stole the teraphim that were her father's" (Gen. 31: 19, A. R. V.). Laban was very much agitated over this theft. He pursued Jacob's party and said to him, "Wherefore hast thou stolen my gods?" (Gen. 31:30). But why was Laban so concerned about discovering those lost teraphim? Sir Charles Leonard Woolley, in charge of excavations at Ur of the Chaldees, tells of a tablet of that region which reveals a law that throws light on Rachel's theft. Dr. Woolley puts the law thus: "The possession of the household gods conferred the privilege of primogeniture."[3] Thus Rachel must have stolen her brother's birthright when she took her father's teraphim, and she was thereby seeking to make Jacob the legal heir to the wealth of Laban.[4] This ancient form of idolatry was vitally linked to family affairs. It would seem that Rachel brought forth those stolen teraphim when the family was about to move from Shechem to Bethel. Jacob said to his family at that time, "Put away the foreign gods that are among you and purify yourselves" (Gen. 35:2, A. R. V.). The presence of these relics of former days would indicate an effort

to combine the superstitions and heathen charms of an idolatrous worship along with the worship of the true and living
God. The teraphim appeared on several occasions in later
history of the Israelites.

RELIGIOUS EDUCATION UNDER THE LAW

The law of Moses was very definite in its requirement that
parents must train their children in the knowledge of God
and His laws. Concerning these divine precepts it said:
"Teach them thy sons, and thy sons' sons" (Deut. 4:9). Concerning the carrying out of this commandment, one writer
has said: "Religious education in the family became, as it has
continued, a special mark of Judaism."[5] It became the very
solemn duty of Hebrew parents to teach their children the
commandments of the law, and also to explain to them the
real meaning of the religious observances. No doubt it has
been this emphasis upon religious education in the family
which has contributed so largely to the permanence of the
Jew in history.[6] And it is also true that any failure of the Jews
to fulfill their God-given mission in the world may be traced
in part at least to their failure in family religious training.

FAMILY PILGRIMAGES TO THE SANCTUARY

A very important part of Hebrew family life was the pilgrimage made to the place of the sanctuary. "Thrice in the
year shall all your men children appear before the Lord God,
the God of Israel (Exod. 34:23). The whole family could go,
but the male members were required to go on this pilgrimage. The feasts of the Lord came at these three seasons of
the year. The element of thanksgiving was largely emphasized in most of them. The Lord made a special promise to
those going on such a pilgrimage to God's house. "Neither
shall any man desire thy land, when thou shalt go up to appear before the Lord" (Exod. 34:24). With so many of the men

folks gone from their homes, God promised to look after these homes against any possible attack from an enemy while the family was away on this pilgrimage.

The family of Elkanah was in the habit of making such pilgrimages. "And this man went up out of his city yearly to worship and to sacrifice unto the Lord God of hosts in Shiloh" (I Sam. 1:3). It was while on such a pilgrimage that Hannah prayed for a baby boy, and in due time Samuel was born.

The most famous example of a family pilgrimage to Jerusalem is of course that of Joseph, Mary, and Jesus. Luke reports it: "Now his parents went to Jerusalem every year at the feast of the passover. And when he was twelve years old, they went up to Jerusalem after the custom of the feast" (Luke 2:41–42). We can scarcely imagine how much that trip to the Holy City must have meant to the boy Jesus. The journey alone would be thrilling to any child, but to Jesus it was being in his Father's House that gave him the biggest thrill of all (Luke 2:49, A. R. V.).

Some Bible readers have been perplexed because Luke says that Joseph and Mary went a day's journey before discovering that Jesus was absent from them. But the present-day Syrian customs of family religious pilgrimages throw light on what actually took place. Luke says: "They sought him among their kinsfolk and acquaintance" (Luke 2:44). On such pilgrimages, kinsfolk and acquaintances travel together in large groups, and the young people of the party are considered to be perfectly safe as long as they are with this group. On these trips parents often go for hours at a time without seeing their sons. It is quite probable that Jesus was with the caravan when it started out, and then was detached from his kinsfolk and returned to the city and to the temple.[7]

THE BIBLE IN THE JEWISH HOME OF CHRIST'S TIME

In the days when Jesus grew up as a boy in his Nazareth home, whatever else of the Hebrew Scriptures the youth may have been acquainted with, they grew up to hear recited a prayer called "The Shema." This prayer was in reality the quotation of three passages from the Pentateuch. It was repeated morning and evening by the men. And Jewish boys when they became twelve years of age had to be able to repeat this prayer. The three Scriptures that made up the Shema were: Deuteronomy 6:4-9; Deuteronomy 11:13-21; and Numbers 15:37-41. It is quite likely that after Jesus returned from that pilgrimage to Jerusalem, He would borrow the manuscript from the synagogue of Nazareth (if He did not have a copy of the Scriptures in His own home) and study in it, especially the books of Moses and the prophets. In His teachings He often referred to these writers, and was especially fond of Isaiah and Jeremiah.[8]

The widespread use of the Shema in Christ's time became with many a mere form with little or no meaning. It was possible for this prayer to become as vain as a heathen prayer. Doubtless Christ was protesting such use of it when He said, "In praying use not vain repetitions, as the Gentiles do" (Matt. 6:7, A. R. V.).[9] The practice of the phylactery, which the Pharisees made such wide use of, was based on some of the Scripture in the Shema, and as used by them, was condemned by Jesus.[10]

Entertaining Fellow-Believers in New Testament Times

In the days of the apostles, great importance was attached to the religious duty of believers entertaining fellow believers who came to their town. In time of persecution, such hospitality would be of great value. Luke tells of one such time of persecution thus: "Therefore they that were scattered abroad went everywhere preaching the word" (Acts 8:4). How welcome a Christian home of refuge would be to one who had to flee from his home because of his testimony for Christ! The

Apostle Paul stayed in the home of Aquila and Priscilla, while he carried on his missionary work in Corinth (Acts 18: 1–3). One of the qualifications of a good bishop Paul gave in the words "given to hospitality" (I Tim. 3:2). And to laymen he stressed the importance of being "given to hospitality" (Rom. 12:13). Peter told the saints, "Use hospitality one to another without grudging" (I Pet. 4:9). The word translated *hospitality* here means "friendly to strangers." Peter was not thinking of believers entertaining their Christian friends, but rather of their entertaining traveling Christians who were in need of food and shelter.[11] The hospitality among the early Christians promoted Christian fellowship, and thus strengthened growth in the faith. It must have exerted a great influence upon the youth growing up in the homes where it was practiced. (*See also* Chapter VII, "The Sacred Duty of Hospitality.")

CHRISTIAN GATHERINGS IN THE HOME

The early gathering place for Christian worship was in the home. The earliest excavation of a church by archaeologists, where a date has been ascertained, is of a room within a house that was set apart for worship, and was thus furnished as a chapel. It dates back to the third century A. D.[12] It seems difficult for the twentieth century Christians to realize that most, if not all, of the earliest churches met in homes. Dr. A. T. Robertson lists some of those early gathering places:

> The church in Jerusalem met in the house of Mary (Acts 12:12), at Philippi in the house of Lydia (Acts 16:40), at Ephesus in the house of Aquila and Priscilla (I Cor. 16:19), and later in Rome (Rom. 16:5), and likewise there was the church that met in the house of Philemon in Colossae apparently (Philem. 2). The homes surely received a special blessing from that service. There was responsibility also.[13]

CHAPTER 14

Marriage Customs

POLYGAMY IN OLD TESTAMENT TIMES

THE MOSAIC LAW allowed polygamy among the Hebrew people. Wives were given certain protections against abuses, and there were various regulations regarding such marriages. There was, however, among the Israelites, a marked tendency toward monogamy. No doubt the main reason for this was that the custom of more than one wife was too expensive for most of the people.[1]

The law did forbid the multiplication of wives by the kings of Israel (Deut. 17:17). The cause of much of the trouble, in the lives of David and Solomon, as well as Ahab, was because of their following the example of the kings of their day in taking many, and especially heathen wives, rather than obeying God's law.

Old Testament influence in favor of monogamy is seen in two ways. First, pictures are painted of unhappy homes because of more than one wife in them. Trouble between rival wives, as in the case of Leah and Rachel (Genesis 30) and also Hannah and Peninnah (I Sam. 1:1–6) argues strongly in favor of monogamy. Second, monogamy among religious leaders and certain outstanding characters, sets the right example for the masses. Men like Adam, Noah, Isaac, Joseph,

Moses, and Job, had but one wife. Also the high priest (Lev. 21:14), and the prophets were, as far as we know, monogamous.[2]

DIVORCE IN OLD TESTAMENT TIMES

For centuries it has been possible for a husband in Arab lands, to divorce his wife by a spoken word. The wife thus divorced is entitled to all her wearing apparel, and the husband cannot take from her anything she has upon her own person. For this reason, coins on the headgear, and rings and necklaces, become important wealth in the hour of the divorced woman's great need. This is one reason why there is so much interest in the bride's personal adornment in Eastern countries. Such customs of divorce were no doubt prevalent in Gentile lands in Old Testament times. It was for this reason that the Law of Moses limited the power of the husband to divorce his wife, by requiring that he must give her a *written* bill of divorcement (Deut. 24:1). Thus the Jewish custom of divorce was superior to the Arabic.[3]

It is important to remember that the sin of adultery did not have anything to do with the matter of divorce under the Jewish law. That sin was punishable by death (Lev. 20:10; Deut. 22:22), and that by stoning. If a husband found any unseemly thing in his wife, he could give her a written bill of divorcement, which made it possible for her to marry another man (Deut. 24:2). A man guilty of unfaithfulness was considered to be a criminal only in that he had invaded the rights of another man. A woman was not allowed to divorce her husband. The prophet Malachi taught that God hated "putting away," and condemned severely any man who dealt treacherously with the wife of his covenant (Mal. 2:14–16). Such was the attitude of the Hebrew people on the subject of divorce.[4] The Lord Jesus swept away all grounds for divorce under the Law, and made unfaithfulness the lone grounds for divorce under the Christian dispensation (Matt. 5:31, 32).

CHOICE OF A WIFE THE PARENTS' PREROGATIVE

It is well known that in the East the parents of a young man select a bride for him. This custom goes back to early Old Testament times. When Esau married against the wishes of his parents, he caused ill-favor (Gen. 26:34, 35).

Reason for this parental privilege. Why did parents usually insist on their right to select a bride for their son? The new bride was to become a member of the bridegroom's clan, and therefore, the whole family was interested in knowing if she would be suitable. There is evidence that at least sometimes the son or daughter was consulted. Rebekah was asked if she was willing to go and become the wife of Isaac (Gen. 24:58). But the parents felt they had a right to make the choice.[5]

Love after marriage. Orientals look at the love between husband and wife very much as Occidentals would look at love between a brother and a sister. It is indicated that the former should love each other because God chose them for each other. Orientals would say that husband and wife love each other, because God through the parents, selected them for each other. In other words, the usual Oriental idea is that love comes *after* marriage.[6] When Isaac and Rebekah were married, they had never seen each other before. Yet the Sacred Record says, "Isaac brought her into his mother's tent, and took Rebekah, and she became his wife; and he loved her" (Gen. 24:67).

Love before marriage. Although it is true that most Oriental couples have no opportunity for love before marriage, yet the Bible gives some examples of that sort of love, that are worthy of note. The case of Jacob and Rachel is the most noted illustration of this. With him it was love at first sight (Gen. 29:10–18). Genesis describes his love for her with these memorable words: "And Jacob served seven years for Rachel; and they seemed unto him but a few days, for the love he had to her" (verse 20). Other examples of love before marriage would include Samson who loved "a woman in Timnath of the daughters of the Philistines" (Judges 14:2), and "Michal, Saul's daughter, who loved David," and afterwards became his wife (I Sam. 18:20).

CONDUCTING NEGOTIATIONS TO SECURE A WIFE

The customs of the Arabs in certain sections of Bible lands when they negotiate to secure a bride for their son, illustrate in many respects Biblical practices. If a young man has acquired sufficient means to make it possible for him to provide a marriage dowry, then his parents select the girl and the negotiations begin.[7] The father calls in a man who acts as a deputy for him and the son. This deputy is called, "the friend of the bridegroom" by John the Baptist (John 3:29). This man is fully informed as to the dowry the young man is willing to pay for his bride. Then, together with the young man's father, or some other male relative, or both, he goes to the home of the young woman. The father announces that the deputy will speak for the party, and then the bride's father will appoint a deputy to represent him. Before the negotiations begin, a drink of coffee is offered the visiting group, but they refuse to drink until the mission is completed. Thus Abraham's servant, when offered food by the parents of Rebekah, said, "I will not eat, until I have told mine errand" (Gen. 24:33). When the two deputies face each other, then the negotiations begin in earnest. There must be consent for the hand of the young woman and agreement on the amount of dowry to be paid for her. When these are agreed upon, the deputies rise and their congratulations are exchanged, and then coffee is brought in, and they all drink of it as a seal of the covenant thus entered into.[8]

THE MARRIAGE DOWRY

Reason for dowry for bride's family. In the Orient, when the bride's parents give their daughter in marriage, they are actually diminishing the efficiency of their family. Often unmarried daughters would tend the flock of their father (Exod. 2:16), or they would work in the field, or render help in other ways. Thus upon her marriage, a young woman would be thought of as increasing the efficiency of her husband's family and diminishing that of her parents. Therefore, a young man who expects to get possession of their daughter must be able to offer some sort of adequate compensation. This compensation was the marriage "dowry."[9]

It was not always required that the dowry be paid in cash, it could be paid in service. Because Jacob could not pay cash, he said, "I will serve thee seven years for Rachel" (Gen. 29:18). King Saul required the lives of one hundred of the enemy Philistines as dowry for David to secure Michal as his wife (I Sam. 18:25).

Reason for dowry for the bride herself. It was usually customary for at least some of the price of the dowry to be given to the bride. This would be in addition to any personal gift from the bride's parents. Leah and Rachel complained about the stinginess of their father Laban. Concerning him they said, "He hath sold us, and hath also quite devoured the price paid for us" (Gen. 31:15, A. R. V. margin). Laban had had the benefit of Jacob's fourteen years of service, without making the equivalent of at least part of it as a gift to Leah and Rachel.[10]

Since a divorced wife in the Orient is entitled to all her wearing apparel, for this reason much of her personal dowry consists of coins on her headgear, or jewelry on her person. This becomes wealth to her in case her marriage ends in failure. This is why the dowry is so important to the bride, and such emphasis is placed upon it in the negotiations that precede marriage.[11] The woman who had ten pieces of silver and lost one was greatly concerned over the loss, because it was doubtless a part of her marriage dowry (Luke 15:8, 9).

Special dowry from the bride's father. It was customary for fathers who could afford to do so to give their daughters a special marriage dowry. When Rebekah left her father's house to be the bride of Isaac, her father gave her a nurse and also damsels who were to be her attendants (Gen. 24:59, 61). And Caleb gave to his daughter a dowry of a field with springs of water (Judges 1:15). Such was sometimes the custom in olden times.[12]

THE BETROTHAL

Difference between a promise and a betrothal. A promise of marriage among the Jews of Bible times might mean an engagement without anything definite. There could be a number of engagements broken off. It was the betrothal that was binding, rather than a mere promise of marriage. The promise might be set aside, but a betrothal entered into was considered as final.[13]

The betrothal a covenant. Among the ancient Hebrews the betrothal was a spoken covenant. Ezekiel pictures God as marrying Jerusalem, and the following words are used of her: "I sware unto thee, and entered into a covenant with thee, saith the Lord God, and thou becamest mine" (Ezek. 16:8). After the exile, the betrothal included signing a written document of marriage.[14]

The ceremony of betrothal. The Jewish betrothal in Christ's time was conducted thus: The families of the bride and groom met, with some others present to serve as witnesses. The young man would give the young woman either a gold ring, or some article of value, or simply a document in which he promised to marry her. Then he would say to her: "See by this ring [or this token] thou art set apart for me, according to the law of Moses and of Israel."[15]

Difference between betrothal and marriage. The betrothal was not the same as the wedding. At least a whole year elapsed between the betrothal and the actual wedding. These

two events must not be confused.[16] The Law said, "What man
is there that hath betrothed a wife, and hath not taken her?"
(Deut. 20:7). Two events are differentiated here: betrothing
a wife, and taking a wife, i.e., in actual marriage. It was during
this period of about a year, between the betrothal and the
wedding, that Mary was found to be with child of the Holy
Spirit (Matt. 7:18, A. R. V.).

THE APPAREL OF GROOM AND BRIDE

When the night arrived for the wedding festivities to begin, and it was time to go for the bride, *the groom* was dressed
as much like a king as possible. If he were rich enough to
afford it, he wore a gold crown. Otherwise it would be a gar-
land of fresh flowers. His garments would be scented with
frankincense and myrrh, his girdle would be a silken one
brilliantly colored, his sandals would be figured and carefully laced, and all of this would give effect to the "flowing
drapery of the loose robes and to the graceful bearing peculiar
to the lands of the East. For the time, the peasant seemed a
prince among his fellows, and all paid him the deference due
to exalted rank."[17] This preparation of the groom for the wedding has been aptly described in the prophecy of Isaiah,
"He hath clothed me with the garments of salvation, he hath
covered me with the robe of righteousness, as a bridegroom
decketh himself with ornaments" (Isa. 61:10).

The adorning of *the bride*, was a very costly and elaborate
affair. Much time was given to the preparation of her person.
Every effort was put forth to make her complexion glossy and
shining with a luster like unto marble. The words of David
must have been their ideal for her: "that our daughters may
be as corner stones, polished after the similitude of a palace"
(Psa. 144:12). Her dark locks of hair were often braided with
gold and pearls. She was decked with all the precious stones
and jewels that the family had inherited from previous gen-

erations. Those who were too poor to afford much themselves would borrow what they could from their friends.[18]

The wedding festivities, and especially the bride's adornment, would always be remembered by her. The prophet Jeremiah made reference to this thought, "Can a maid forget her ornaments, or a bride her attire?" (Jer. 2:32). The Apostle John saw New Jerusalem "prepared as a bride adorned for her husband" (Rev. 21:2).

GOING OF THE GROOM TO GET THE BRIDE

Sometimes the bride's relations would conduct her from her father's house to the house of her fiancé, where her new home was to be. But more often, as was the case of the Ten Virgins in Christ's parable, the bridegroom himself went in person to bring her to his home for the wedding festivities to take place there. Before leaving the house that had been her home, she would receive the blessing of her relatives. Thus Rebekah's relatives sent her away with a typical Oriental marriage blessing, "Thou art our sister, be thou the mother of thousands of millions, and let thy seed possess the gate of those which hate them" (Gen. 24:60). The bride left her father's house adorned and perfumed, and with a crown on her head.[19] Ezekiel's description of the bride is very appropriate, "I decked thee also with ornaments, and I put bracelets upon thy hands, and a chain on thy neck. And I put a jewel on thy forehead, and earrings in thine ears, and a beautiful crown upon thine head" (Ezek. 16:11, 12).

THE WEDDING PROCESSION

The bridegroom set out with the bride from the house of her parents, and there followed a grand procession all the way to his house. The streets of Asiatic cities were dark, and it was necessary that anybody venturing forth at night should carry a lamp or torch (cf. Psa. 119:105). Those invited guests, who did not go to the bride's home were allowed to join the procession along the way, and go with the whole group to the marriage feast. Without a torch or lamp they couldn't join the procession, or enter the bridegroom's house.[20]

The Ten Virgins waited for the procession to arrive at the point where they were waiting; and five wise ones were able to proceed because they had a reserve supply of oil for their lamps; but the foolish virgins lacked that oil and so, not being ready, they were barred from the wedding feast (Matt. 25:1-13).

The lamps carried by these virgins have been described by Dr. Edersheim:

Oriental Bride

The lamps consisted of a round receptacle for pitch or oil for the wick. This was placed in a hollow cup or deep saucer, . . . which was fastened by a pointed end into a long wooden pole, on which it was borne aloft.[21]

In going from the bride's house to the groom's house, the bride allowed her hair to be loose and flowing, and she had her face veiled. Some of her own relations preceded her in the procession, and scattered ears of parched grain to the children along the way. There were demonstrations of joy all along the road to the destination. Part of the procession included men who played on drums or other musical instruments. And there was dancing along the way.[22] One of the punishments Jeremiah predicted for the Jews, because of their sins, was the taking away of wedding joys. "Then will I cause to cease from the cities of Judah, and from the streets of Jerusalem, the voice of mirth, and the voice of gladness, the voice of the bridegroom, and the voice of the bride" (Jer. 7:34).

ARRIVAL AT THE HOUSE OF THE BRIDEGROOM

The most important moment of the entire marriage festivity was that in which the bride entered her new home.[23] And as both groom and bride usually wore crowns, the Psalmist must have pictured this important moment in the marriage of the king:

> She shall be brought unto the king in raiment of needlework: the virgins her companions that follow her shall be brought unto thee. With gladness and rejoicing shall they be brought: they shall enter into the king's palace (Psa. 45:14–15).

After arriving at the bridegroom's house, some of the older women had the task of arranging the bride's hair. Her flowing locks were hidden beneath a thick veil. From this time on, the custom would dictate that her face was not to be unveiled in public. She was led to her place under a canopy, which was located either inside the house, or if the weather permitted, in the open air. Her place was beside her husband, where both would hear new words of benediction given by one of the fathers, or by some important person who might be present.[24] In the wedding at Cana of Galilee, Jesus was the most prominent guest present, and doubtless He was asked to pronounce His benediction upon the newlyweds (John 2:1-11).

THE WEDDING FEAST

Every guest that attended the feast was required to wear a wedding garment (Matt. 22:12). The wedding banquet was presided over by the ruler of the feast (John 2:8, 9). It was his duty to take care of the preparations, and during the feast he would get around among the guests, and see to it that they lacked nothing. He instructed servants in carrying out all the necessary details.[25] The expression, "children of the bride-chamber" (Matt. 9:15), used by Jesus, simply means the guests at the wedding. The governor or ruler of the feast returned thanks at the dinner and pronounced benedictions at appointed times. He also blessed the wine. It was customary to tell riddles at these feasts like Samson did at his wedding (Judges 14:12-18). During the meal mirthfulness prevailed, and the guests were expected to exalt the bride.[26]

There was no religious ceremony at the feast. In place of this were the benedictions of relatives and friends. The benediction of those who witnessed wedding arrangements for Ruth and Boaz is a good example of what would be included in such a benediction (Ruth 4:11). It corresponds to the well wishing of Western wedding guests. After the wedding feast was over the husband was escorted by his friends into the apartment where his wife had previously been conducted. These wedding festivities with relatives and friends lasted for a whole week (cf. Judges 14:17), but the entire number of what was called "the days of the marriage" was thirty.[27]

CHAPTER 15

Some Special Events of Domestic Festivity

DEDICATION OF A NEWLY BUILT HOUSE

THAT THERE WAS a generally accepted custom among the Jews of dedicating a newly constructed dwelling is indicated from the words of the Mosaic Law: "What man is there that hath built a new house and hath not dedicated it" (Deut. 20:5). No doubt the social and also the devotional elements entered into the occasion. A similar custom was in use in other ancient and in some modern lands of the East.[1]

The title of the Thirtieth Psalm reads, "A Psalm; Song at the dedication of the house of David." This would seem to reveal that David celebrated the entering into his house with a special service or festivity of dedication. Spurgeon quotes Samuel Chandler as saying concerning this custom:

It was common when any person had finished a house and entered into it, to celebrate it with great rejoicing, and keep a festival, to which his friends are invited, and to perform some religious ceremonies, to secure the protection of Heaven.[2]

WEANING OF A CHILD

The weaning of a child is an important event in the domestic life of the East. In many places it is celebrated by a festive gathering of friends, by feasting, by religious ceremonies, and sometimes the formal presentation of rice to the child.[3]

Among the peasant Arabs of Palestine, babies are often nursed for two years, and sometimes for four or even five years. When it is being weaned, various dainties are given the child to sweeten the gums and make it to forget the mother's milk[4] (cf. Psa. 131:2).

The old time Hebrew mothers also weaned their infants late. One such mother said to her son: "My son, have pity upon me that carried thee nine months in my womb, and gave thee suck three years, and nourished and brought thee up unto this age" (II Maccabees 7:27). It was probably at this age of three, or possibly even later, that Hannah weaned Samuel and brought him to God's sanctuary, where offerings were made to God, and he was presented to the Lord (I Sam. 1:23). The Scriptural example of a weaning feast was the one celebrated for Isaac. Scripture says of it: "And the child grew, and was weaned: and Abraham made a great feast the same day that Isaac was weaned" (Gen. 21:8). It must have been a time of great rejoicing and dedication of the child to the Lord.

HARVEST HOME

In the Orient, the harvest time is always a time of great festivity. To the Jews of Bible days, it was also a time of great joy. The prophet said, "They joy before thee according to the joy in harvest" (Isa. 9:3). The law provided two feasts that were harvest festivals (Exod. 23:16). The first of these was called at one time The Feast of the Harvest, and later named The Feast of Pentecost. This feast was celebrated after the grain harvest. It was designated to express thanksgiving to God for the harvest that had been gathered. It was a time of rest from labor (Exod. 34:21). Also it was a time of feasting (Exod. 23:16). The second of these feasts was sometimes called The Feast of Ingathering, being held after all the grain, fruit, wine, and oil had been gathered in. It, too, was a time of thanksgiving and joy over the harvest. It was also called the Feast of Tabernacles (Lev. 23:39–43), because they dwelt in booths to remind them of the wilderness days of the past.[5]

Sheep-Shearing

It would seem from two Bible references that sheep-shearing was another time of special festivity in the ancient Hebrew home. It was at a sheep-shearing time that the affair between David and wealthy Nabal took place (I Sam. 25:4). Concerning Nabal's celebration Scripture says: "And Abigail came to Nabal; and, behold, he held a feast in his home, like the feast of a king" (I Sam. 25:36). The other example is the sheep-shearing feast of Absalom, at which time the murder of Ammon was perpetrated (II Sam. 13:23 f.). These two examples of this sort of a feast would not by themselves indicate that it was anything but a time of festivity alone. But without doubt, in many pious homes it was a time of thanksgiving to God for the wool provided from the flocks.

CHAPTER 16

Sickness in Bible Lands

Promises of health through obedience to the law. Through their wilderness experiences and after they were in the Land of Promise, the Hebrew families could look to the promise God originally gave to them about health for their bodies:

> If thou wilt diligently hearken to the voice of the Lord thy God, and wilt do that which is right in his sight, and wilt give ear to his commandments, and keep all his statutes, I will put none of these diseases upon thee which I have brought upon the Egyptians, for I am the Lord that healeth thee (Exod. 15:26).

Health was promised upon condition of obedience to the law of God.

Sickness as punishment for disobedience. The law also taught Israel that sickness could be expected when God's law was disobeyed. The twenty-eighth chapter of the Book of Deuteronomy lists many curses that would come upon the people of Israel because of disobedience. Among them are these:

> He will bring upon thee all the diseases of Egypt, which thou wast afraid of; and they shall cleave unto thee. Also every sickness, and every plague, which is not written in the

book of this law, them will the Lord bring upon thee, until thou be destroyed (Deut. 28:60, 61).

The families of Israel who were acquainted with the Hebrew Bible would be brought up on the idea that health was the reward for obedience, and sickness the punishment for disobedience.

What Old Testament Jews Did in Time of Sickness

Ordinarily, the ancient Hebrews did not go to physicians when they were sick. There are surprisingly few references to physicians in Old Testament days. Job mentions the existence of such when he says, "Ye are all physicians of no value" (Job 13:4). King Asa was criticized by the sacred writer who says of him, "He sought not to the Lord, but to the physicians" (II Chron. 16:12). The prophet Jeremiah asked the question, "Is there no balm in Gilead; is there no physician there?" (Jer. 8:22). It is quite probable, that any physicians referred to in these days were foreigners, and not Jews of the land.[1]

There are many examples of prayer to God for healing of sickness under the dispensation of law. Moses prayed for the healing of the Israelites bitten by the snakes (Num. 21:7). The Sixth Psalm is David's prayer in time of sickness, and one which God heard. One of the great thanksgiving Psalms has a section in it dealing with gratitude to God for healing of the sick (Psa. 107:17-21). King Solomon in his dedicatory prayer for the temple, encouraged the people to expect God to answer their prayer for healing of sickness (II Chron. 6:28-30). And King Hezekiah was healed in answer to prayer (II Kings 20).

Jewish Attitude Toward Sickness in Christ's Time

The Jews of that day were largely lacking in a scientific knowledge of medicine. This fact may be accounted for in their belief that sickness was caused by either the sin of the sick person, or of his relations, and that it was sent as punishment for that sin. Concerning the blind man, the disciples asked Jesus, "Master, who did sin, this man, or his parents, that he was born blind?" (John 9:2). Also, sickness was usually attributed to demons. Therefore, they considered that the cure was the casting out these evil spirits. Among them, it was the most pious rather than the most educated man who would have this power. Jesus referred to this practice when the Pharisees wrongly accused him: "If I by Beelzebub cast out demons, by whom do your sons cast them out?" (Matt. 12:27, A. R. V.) These facts explain the Jewish lack of medical knowledge in those days.[2]

Mark adds an interesting fact in his report of Christ healing the woman with the issue of blood. He says that she "had suffered many things of many physicians" (Mark 5:26). One writer quotes the Talmud of Babylon as authority for the fact that some of the rabbis themselves posed as physicians, and very queer remedies indeed were prescribed by them for a woman with this ailment. If one course of procedure did not succeed in healing, another one was suggested. One of these was this:

> Dig seven pits, and burn in them some vine branches not yet four years old. Then let the woman, carrying a cup of wine in her hand, come up to each pit in succession, and sit down by the side of it, and each time let the words be repeated: "Be free from thy sickness."[3]

PREVALENCE OF SICKNESS IN PALESTINE
IN CHRIST'S DAY AND IN MODERN TIMES

The Gospel records tell of the presence of a multitude of sick people in the land, and how these were brought in great numbers to Jesus to be healed. "And at even . . . they brought unto him all that were diseased . . . and all the city was gathered at the door. And he healed many that were sick of divers diseases" (Mark 1:32–34). In the days before the British occupation of the land, and before the modern Jews brought scientific medical skill in the healing of disease, the Land of Israel was overrun with all kinds of afflicted people. One traveling through the land would scarcely ever be out of sight of blind beggars, or crippled people, or lepers, etc. Such a situation has served to illustrate the conditions under which the ministry of Christ was carried on so effectively, in meeting the need in the homes where sickness was present.[4]

Expectation of Supernatural Power to Heal by a Representative of God

Dr. Trumbull has called attention to a very interesting situation which he discovered in the Orient. He says:

> Another fact that sheds light upon the work of Jesus and His disciples in their ministry of healing, is the universal expectation, in the East, of the cure of disease through the supernatural power of some reputed representative of God. So it is, and so it has been.[5]

A multitude of people lay about the pool of Bethesda expecting an angel to trouble the waters and cure their sicknesses (John 5:1–4). A blind beggar was given an orange and a crust of bread, but he pointed to his sightless eyes, and asked Dr. Trumbull to cure his blindness. He thought that this traveler was a representative of God who could heal him. Such is the faith that exists in the East, in modern times. This universal faith in divine power to heal, in Messianic times, presented Jesus and His apostles with a marvelous opportunity to demonstrate the healing power of a compassionate God.[6]

CHAPTER 17

Death in Oriental Lands

THE ATTITUDE OF THE PEO-
PLE of the East toward death, and their behavior at such
times, is so strikingly different from the attitude and behavior
in the West that the Bible student will do well to sudy such
customs.

THE DEATH WAIL

As soon as a death has taken place in the Orient, a wail is
raised that announces to all the neighborhood what has happened. This is a sign for the relatives to begin demonstrat-
ing their sorrow.[1] This death wail is referred to in connection
with the first-born of Egypt, "And Pharaoh rose up in the
night, he, and all his servants, and all the Egyptians; and
there was a great cry in Egypt; for there was not a house
where there was not one dead" (Exod. 12:30).

Such a death-wail heard in an Eastern desert has been thus
described as, "a sharp, shrill, ear-piercing shriek." This shriek
is followed by prolonged wails. When this is heard, everybody knows a death has occurred.[2]

LAMENTATION

From the time the death wail is heard, until the burial takes
place, relatives and friends continue their lamentation. The

prophet Micah compares it to the cry of wild beasts or birds: "I will make a wailing like the jackals, and a lamentation like the ostriches" (Micah 1:8, A. R. V.). Such lamentation was in the house of Jairus when Jesus entered it: "And he cometh to the house of the ruler of the synagogue, and seeth the tumult, and them that wept and wailed greatly" (Mark 5:38).

In connection with the lamentations, there are apt to be certain exclamations of sorrow used. David mourned over the death of Absalom: "O my son Absalom, my son, my son Absalom! would God I had died for thee, O Absalom, my son, my son!" (II Sam. 18:33). Certain words are repeated over and over again. The exclamations concerning the disobedient prophet who died, were: "Alas, my brother!" And in mourning the death of a king, the words were used, "Ah lord!" and "Ah his glory!" (Jer. 22:18).

The Hebrew prophets mention professional mourners, who were called in at the time of sorrow to express mourning for the dead. "Call for the mourning women, that they may come; . . . and let them make haste, and take up a wailing for us" (Jer. 9:17, 18). Another reference is to "such as are skillful of lamentation" (Amos 5:16). The presence of such a group of mourners hired for the occasion seems out of place to the Occidental mind; but certainly such professional wailers are no more lacking in helpfulness to the Easterner than are non-religious professional singers at a Western funeral service.[3]

EXPRESSIONS OF SORROW AND COMFORT

Since Orientals are so very demonstrative and emotional, it is difficult for those not acquainted with their customs to appreciate their method of expressing their sorrow, and their attempts to be comforted.[4] In times of grief and sorrow, sackcloth is worn, and they often rend their garments in order to let people know how deep is their grief (II Sam. 3:31). The beating of the breast is another method of expressing sorrow

(Luke 23:48). Tears flow freely at such times and are considered to be a definite means of bringing comfort to sorrowing hearts (John 11:33).

PREPARATION OF THE BODY FOR BURIAL

In Syria the custom has prevailed of wrapping the dead. Usually the face is covered with a napkin, and then the hands and feet are bound round with linen cloth. The body is then put upon a bier, with a pole at each corner, and thus carried on the shoulders of men to the tomb for burial.[5] The description of Lazarus, when Jesus called him forth from the tomb, indicates that the same custom was practiced in those days: "Out came the dead man, his feet and hands tied with wrappings, and his face tied up with a handkerchief" (John 11:44, Williams). Also we know that the body of Jesus was thus wrapped by Joseph of Arimathea and Nicodemus: "Then took they the body of Jesus, and wound it in linen clothes with the spices, as the manner of the Jews is to bury" (John 19:40). Embalming spices were used when they could be afforded.

EASTERN FUNERALS

Burial follows death quickly. The burial of the dead in the East takes place soon after death, usually the same day. The people of these regions have a primitive idea that the spirit of the one who dies, hovers near the body for three days after death. Mourners think of this spirit as being able to hear the wailing calls of grief. Martha, no doubt, thought it would be hopeless to think of reviving her brother's body, because he had been dead four days (John 11:39).[6]

Burial in caves, tombs, or graves. Today there are thousands of rock-cut tombs scattered over the land of Palestine, to bring to mind past decades. Such tombs were made by the wealthy. Not being able to afford these, the poorer folks buried their dead in graves. Some of these tombs had many chambers in them. They were closed by a rolling-stone which ran down an inclined plane in front of the mouth of the sepulcher. In the vicinity of ancient Gadara (Luke 8:27), there are many rock-hewn tombs today, bringing to mind the experience of Jesus when he met the demoniac who lived in the tombs.[7]

Often the dead were buried in graves dug in the earth, as in the case of Deborah, Rebekah's nurse, who was buried under an oak at Bethel (Gen. 35:8). Natural caves were sometimes utilized, as in the case of the cave of Machpelah, where Abraham, Sarah, Isaac, Rebekah, Leah, and Jacob were placed (Gen. 49:31; 50:13). When they could afford to do so, families had a sepulcher. Gideon was buried in the sepulcher of Joash his father (Judges 8:32). Only prophets and kings were buried within the limits of a city, as Samuel, who was buried in his house at Ramah (I Sam. 25:1), and David, who was buried in the city of David (I Kings 2:10). A graveyard for poorer people was located outside Jerusalem (II Kings 23:6). Many of the villages had graveyards outside their limits, as for example Nain, where Jesus raised the widow's son (Luke 7:11-17). There is a graveyard located there today.[8]

Custom following burial. In Bible times it was quite customary for the sorrowing ones to fast up to the time of burial. Then, following the funeral, they would be offered bread and wine as a comforting refreshment. Such was called a mourning feast, which had as its real purpose the comforting of the mourners. The prophet Jeremiah refers to this custom: "Neither shall men break bread for them in mourning, to comfort them for the dead; neither shall men give them the cup of consolation to drink for their father or for their mother" (Jer. 16:7, A. R. V.). This mourning feast brought to an end the period of deepest sorrow and strict fasting.[9]

BIBLICAL EXPRESSIONS OF ORIENTAL MOURNING

The Psalmists, Prophets, and Apostles often make use of expressions referring to Oriental mourning. Some of these cannot be appreciated by the Occidental, unless the highly emotional character of the Easterner is understood, and also his fondness for figurative language. The Psalmist says: "Rivers of waters run down mine eyes, because they keep not thy law" (Psa. 119:136). The prophet exclaims, "Oh that my head were waters, and mine eyes a fountain of tears, that I might weep day and night for the slain of the daughter of my people!" (Jer. 9:1). And it was to Orientals that Paul said, "Weep with them that weep" (Rom. 12:15). It will pay the Bible student dividends if he will read the Word from the Oriental point of view.

CHAPTER 18

Shepherd Life;
The Care of Sheep and Goats

SHEEP IN THE LAND OF ISRAEL

Large number of sheep in palestine. From the days of Abraham down to modern times, sheep have abounded in the Holy Land. The Arabs of Bible lands have largely been dependent through the centuries upon sheep for their living. The Jews of Bible times were first shepherds and then farmers, but they never abandoned entirely their shepherd life. The large number of sheep in the land can be understood when it is realized that Job had fourteen thousand sheep (Job. 42:12), and that King Solomon at the Temple's dedication, sacriced one hundred and twenty thousand sheep (I Kings 8:63).

Fat-tailed sheep the variety mostly in use. The fat tail provides reserve strength for the sheep, much like the hump does on a camel. There is energy in the tail. When the sheep is butchered, this fatty tail is quite valuable. People will buy the tail, or part of it, and use it for frying. That this variety of sheep was in use in ancient times is seen by references in the Pentateuch to the fat tail of the sheep. "Also thou shalt take of the ram the fat, and the fat tail, and the fat that covereth the inwards" (Exod. 29:22, A. R. V.). "The fat tail entire, he shall take away hard by the backbone" (Lev. 3:9, A. R. V.).[1]

Fat-tailed Sheep

THE SHEPHERD

Youngest boy often the shepherd. The youngest boy in the family becomes shepherd of the sheep, especially when the Arab peasant is a shepherd as well as being a farmer of grain. As the older son grows up he transfers his energies from sheep raising to helping the father with sowing, plowing, and harvesting the crops, and passes on the shepherd's task to the next younger boy. And so the job is passed from older to younger until the youngest of all becomes the family shepherd.[2] Such must have been the custom when Jesse raised his family of eight sons. "And Samuel said unto Jesse, Are here all thy children? And he said, There remaineth yet the youngest, and behold, he keepeth the sheep" (I Sam. 16:11). David, being the youngest of eight sons, became the family shepherd. His experiences as a shepherd lad were often used to illustrate his beautiful psalms. His Shepherd Psalm has become the classic of the ages.

The shepherd's garb. The dress of an Arab shepherd lad is a simple tunic of cotton that is girded around his body by a leathern girdle, and his outer garment, called *aba*, is often of camel's hair, like that of John the Baptist (Matt. 3:4). The *aba* keeps the boy warm, is able to shed the rain, and at night is used as a blanket in which to wrap himself.[3]

The shepherd's scrip. This is a bag made of dried skin. When he leaves home to go and tend the sheep, his mother will put into it some bread, cheese, dried fruit, and probably some olives.[4] It was into this bag that David placed the five smooth stones when he went to battle with the giant Goliath (I Sam. 17:40).

The shepherd's rod. It is like a policeman's club. It is often made of oak wood and has a knob on the end of it. Into this knob nails are sometimes driven so as to make a better weapon. It is very useful for protection, and no shepherd would be without it.[5] It was no doubt the rod that David used in protecting his sheep from wild animals (I Sam. 17:34–36). He mentions both the rod and the staff in his Shepherd Psalm (Psa. 23:4).

The prophet Ezekiel refers to the custom of the sheep passing under the shepherd's rod for the purpose of counting or inspecting them. "I will cause you to pass under the rod" (Ezek. 20:37). The law of Moses speaks of tithing the flock for a specific purpose at such a time. "And concerning the tithe of the herd, or of the flock, even of whatsoever passeth under the rod, the tenth shall be holy unto the Lord" (Lev. 27:32). To do this Jewish writers tell us that the shepherd allowed the animals to come by him as they would under the rod at a narrow entrance. The head of the rod was dipped into some coloring fluid and was allowed to come down upon every tenth one that passed by, thus marking him as the one to be given to the Lord for sacrificial purposes.[6]

The *scepter*, which the ancient kings of the East usually had with them, had its origin in the *shepherd's rod.* Kings were considered to be shepherds of their people. Thus the scepter, or rod, of the king became a symbol of protection, power, and authority. Young translates Micah 7:14: "Rule thou thy people with thy rod, the flock of thine inheritance."[7]

The shepherd's staff. David mentions the staff along with the rod in his Shepherd Psalm (Psa. 23:4). It is a stick five or six feet long and sometimes but not always has a crook at the end of it. It is used like Western men would use a cane or walking stick. It is useful in handling the sheep, and also for protection.[8]

The shepherd's sling. It was a simple affair, being composed of two strings of sinew, rope, or leather, and a receptacle of leather to receive the stone. It was swung a time or two around the head and then was discharged by letting go one of the strings.[9] The shepherd, in addition to using his sling against wild animals or robbers, found it very handy in directing the sheep. A stone could be dropped close to a sheep that was lagging behind and startle it into coming along with the rest of the flock. Or if one would get away in another direction, then a stone would be slung so as to drop just beyond the straying sheep, and thus bring him back. It was the shepherd's sling that young David used in slaying the giant Goli-

Shepherd and His Flute

ath (I Sam. 17:40–49). In her plea to David, Abigail was no doubt contrasting two items of his shepherd's equipment when she said, "The soul of my lord shall be bound in the bundle of life with the Lord thy God; and the souls of thine enemies, them shall he sling out, as out of the middle of a sling" (I Sam. 25:29). The "bundle of life" could be translated either "the pouch of life," or "the bag of life," and most probably refers to the shepherd's scrip. David's enemies were to be like the stones in his sling, being that which was to be thrown away; whereas David's soul would be like the provisions in his scrip, which were to be kept and guarded by the Lord himself.[10]

The shepherd's flute. A dual-piped flute of reed is generally carried by the Arab shepherd. It is true that minor strains of music come from this flute, but the heart of the shepherd is stirred, and the sheep of the flock are refreshed by the invigorating music that comes from this simple instrument. There can be little question but that David used such an instrument when he was with his flock, in the same way the shepherd lads have done for centuries around Bethlehem. It is of interest to know that the word in the Arabic language which is the equivalent of the Hebrew word for "psalm" is *mazmoor*, which means "played on a pipe or flute."[11]

FOOD AND WATER FOR THE FLOCK

Food planned for the flock. One of the principal duties at all seasons of the year is for the shepherd to plan food for his flock. In the springtime there is an abundance of green pasture, and usually the sheep are allowed to graze near to the village where the shepherd's home is located. After the grain is reaped, and the poor have had an opportunity to glean what is left for them, then the shepherd brings in his flock, and the sheep feed on certain fresh growths, or dried blades, or an occasional ear of grain that the reapers may have left, or was overlooked by the gleaners. When this source of food is exhausted then the pasture is sought in other places. The

wilderness of Judea which is located along the western side
of the Jordan Valley is carpeted in the spring with a certain
amount of grass and this turns into standing hay as the hot
weather comes, and this becomes food for the sheep during
part of the summer.[12]

Scripture often refers to shepherds looking for pasture for
their flocks. "And they went to the entrance of Gedor, even
unto the east side of the valley, to seek pasture for their flocks"
(I Chron. 4:39). The Psalmist thanks God for the pasturage
which the Lord as Shepherd provides for His people: "So we
thy people and sheep of thy pasture will give thee thanks for
ever" (Psa. 79:13).

In the late autumn or winter months, there are times when
the shepherd can find no pasturage that is available for his
flock, and then he must become responsible for feeding the
animals himself. If the flock is small there may be times when
it is stabled within the peasant house, and the family lives on
a sort of mezzanine floor above it. At such seasons of the year
the shepherd must provide the food. This is what Isaiah
meant when he said: "He shall feed his flock like a shepherd"
(Isa. 40:11). In some sections of Syria, flocks are taken at this
season to places in the mountain country, where the shepherd
busies himself with the bushy trees, cutting down branches
that have green leaves or tender twigs, that the sheep and
goats can eat.[13] Micah was probably speaking of this custom
of providing food for the sheep, when he said: "Feed thy
people with thy rod, the flock of thine heritage" (Micah 7:14).

Water provided for the flock. In selecting pasturage for the
flock, it is an absolute necessity that water be provided, and
that it be easy of access. Often flocks are stationed near to a
stream of running water. But the sheep are apt to be afraid
of drinking water that moves quickly, or that is agitated.
Therefore the shepherd looks for pools of water, or provides
some quiet place where they may quench their thirst. How
appropriate then are the words concerning the divine Shep-

Shepherd Leading the Flock

herd: "He leadeth me beside the still waters" (Psa. 23:2). But when all such watering places are dried up in the heat of summer, as is often the case in Palestine, then wells are used. Usually a large rock is placed over the mouth of the well and this must be removed, as Jacob did, before the sheep can be watered (Gen. 29:8–10). Noontide is usually the time for watering the sheep. When Jacob was at the well, he said, "Lo, it is yet high day . . . water ye the sheep" (Gen. 29:7). The matter of water supply plays an important part in locating the flock for pasturage.[14]

THE SHEEPFOLD

A simple improvised sheepfold. Such is sometimes made by the shepherd when he is a distance from his home, or especially when he may be in the territory of mountains. It is a temporary affair that can be taken down easily when it comes time to move on to another location. A fence is built of tangled thorn bushes or rude bowers. This is all the protection that is needed, as the shepherds often sleep with their flocks when the weather permits. Ezekiel mentions such a sheepfold when he predicts the future of Israel: "I will feed them in a good pasture, and upon the high mountains of Israel shall their fold be" (Ezek. 34:14).[15]

Sheepcotes in connection with caves. There are many caves in the Holy Land, and when one of these is available it is utilized as a sheepcote. During stormy weather, and at night, the sheep retreat into the cave, but at other times they are kept in the enclosure immediately in front of the cave's mouth. This enclosure is generally constructed of loose stones piled up in a circular wall, with thorns on the top.[16] The cave into which King Saul went to rest, and David and his men were already within it, was a cavern with a fold built in connection with it. "And he came to the sheep cotes by the way, where was a cave; and Saul went in to cover his feet" (I Sam. 24:3).

More permanent sheepfolds. Such shelters are usually built by the shepherd in a valley, or else on the sunny side of a hill where there is protection from cold winds. This fold is a low building with arches in front of it, and a wall forming an outdoor enclosure, joining the building. When the weather is mild, the sheep and goats are allowed to be in the enclosure during the night, but if the weather is stormy, or the evenings are cold, then the flock is shut up in the interior part of the fold, with its protection of roof and walls. The walls of the enclosure are about three feet wide at the bottom, and become narrower at the top. They are from four to six feet high. Large stones are used in constructing the outsides of the wall, and they are also placed on the top, and then the center is filled with smaller pieces of stone, of which there is much in the land. Sharp, thorn bushes are put on the top of this wall to protect the sheep from wild animals or robbers. There is a gate guarded by a watchman.[17]

Jesus made reference to the familiar sheepfold of Palestine when He spoke those memorable words of His: "He that entereth not by the door into the sheepfold, but climbeth up some other way, the same is a thief and a robber. But he that entereth in by the door is the shepherd of the sheep. To him the porter [watchman] openeth" (John 10:1-3).

HANDLING AND GATHERING THE SHEEP

Several flocks sometimes allowed to mix. More than one flock may be kept in the same fold, and often flocks are mixed while being watered at a well. For the time being, no attempt is made to separate them. Jacob saw such a mixture of flocks: "Then Jacob went on his journey, and came into the land of the people of the East. And he looked, and behold, a well in the field, and lo, there were three flocks of sheep lying by it" (Gen. 29:1-3).[18]

Ability to separate the sheep. When it becomes necessary to separate several flocks of sheep, one shepherd after another will stand up and call out: "Tahhoo! Tahhoo!" or a similar call of his own choosing. The sheep lift up their heads, and after a general scramble, begin following each one his own shepherd. They are thoroughly familiar with their own shepherd's *tone of voice.* Strangers have often used the same call, but their attempts to get the sheep to follow them always fail.[19] The words of Jesus are indeed true to Eastern shepherd life when he said: "The sheep follow him, for they know his voice. And a stranger will they not follow, but will flee from him: for they know not the voice of strangers" (John 10:4, 5).

Gathering scattered sheep. The shepherd knows how to gather sheep that have been scattered. Especially is this necessary when the sheep must be led back to the fold, or when they are to be guided to another pasture. It is accomplished

by his standing in the center of his scattered sheep, and giving them the call which serves as the notes of a bugle do to an
army of men. Pebbles are sent by means of his slingshot in the
direction of and beyond members of the flock that fail to heed
the call, in order to get their attention and then bring them
back. He does not commence to lead them away until he
knows they are all there.[20] Ezekiel predicts that the Lord as
Shepherd of Israel will one day gather His people that have
been scattered, and will bring them back to their own land of
Palestine.

> As a shepherd seeketh out his flock in the day that he is
> among his sheep that are scattered; so will I seek out my
> sheep, and will deliver them out of all places where they
> have been scattered in the cloudy and dark day. And I will
> bring them out from the people, and gather them from the
> countries, and will bring them to their own land, and feed
> them upon the mountains of Israel (Ezek. 34:12, 13).

The use of dogs. Some shepherds make use of dogs. When
dogs are possessed, they are of value in handling the flock.
When traveling, the shepherd usually walks ahead, and the
dogs are allowed to bring up the rear. They bark furiously
at any intruder among them, and therefore warn of possible
danger to the flock. When the sheep are in the fold, then the
dogs become the guardians against any possible attack by
an enemy. Many a foe of the sheep has been frightened away
by the defiant barking of these animals.[21] The patriarch Job
spoke of shepherd dogs: "They that are younger than I have
me in derision, whose fathers I would have disdained to have
set with the dogs of my flock" (Job 30:1).

INTIMATE RELATIONSHIP BETWEEN SHEPHERD AND SHEEP

When we learn of the intimate relationship that exists between the shepherd and his sheep, the figure of the Lord as a
Shepherd of His people takes on new meaning.

Giving names to the sheep. Jesus said concerning the shepherd of his day: "He calleth his own sheep by name" (John 10:3). Today, the eastern shepherd delights to give names to certain of his sheep, and if his flock is not too large, all of his sheep may be given names. He knows them by means of certain individual characteristics. He names one: "Pure White"; another, "Striped"; another, "Black"; another, "Brown"; and still another, "Gray-eared." All this indicates the tender affection which he has for every one of his flock.[22]

Guidance for the sheep. The Eastern shepherd never drives his sheep as does the Western shepherd. He always leads them, often going before them. "And when he putteth forth his own sheep, he goeth before them" (John 10:4). This does *not* mean that the shepherd is *always* in front of his sheep. Although he may be usually in that position when traveling, he often walks by their side, and sometimes follows behind, especially if the flock is headed for the fold in the evening. From the rear he can gather any stragglers, and protect such from a sly attack from a wild animal. If the flock is a large one, the shepherd will be in front, and a helper will follow behind.[23] Isaiah speaks of the omnipresent Lord in a double relationship to His people: "For ye shall not go out with haste, nor go by flight: for the Lord will go before you; and the God of Israel will be your rereward [rear guard]" (Isa. 52:12).

The skill of the shepherd, and personal relationship to them is clearly seen when he guides his sheep along narrow paths. The Shepherd Psalm says: "He leadeth me in the paths of righteousness" (Psa. 23:3). The grain fields are seldom fenced or hedged in Bible lands, and sometimes only a narrow path runs between the pasture and these fields. The sheep are forbidden to eat in the fields where crops are growing. Thus in guiding the sheep along such a path, the shepherd must not allow any of the animals to get into the forbidden area, because if he does, he must pay damages to the owner of the grain. One Syrian shepherd has been known to guide a flock of one hundred fifty sheep without any help, along such a narrow path for quite a distance, without letting a single sheep go where he was not allowed to go.[24]

Straying sheep restored. It is very important that sheep should not be allowed to stray away from the flock, because when by themselves they are utterly helpless. In such a condition, they become bewildered, for they have no sense at all of locality. And if they do stray away, they must be brought back.[25] The Psalmist prayed the prayer: "I have gone astray like a lost sheep; seek thy servant" (Psa. 119:176). The prophet Isaiah compared man's waywardness to that of sheep: "All we like sheep have gone astray" (Isa. 53:6). David sang of his divine Shepherd: "He restoreth my soul" (Psa. 23:3).

Playing with the sheep. The shepherd is so constantly with his sheep that sometimes his life with them becomes monotonous. Therefore he will occasionally play with them. He does this by pretending to run away from his sheep, and they will soon overtake him, and completely surround him, gamboling with great delight.[26] Sometimes God's people think He forsakes them when trouble comes their way. They say: "The Lord hath forsaken me" (Isa. 49:14). But actually their divine Shepherd says to them: "I will never leave thee, nor forsake thee" (Heb. 13:5).

Intimate knowledge of the sheep. The shepherd is deeply interested in every single one of his flock. Some of them may be given pet names because of incidents connected with them. They are usually counted each evening as they enter the fold, but sometimes the shepherd dispenses with the counting, for he is able to *feel* the absence of any one of his sheep. With one sheep gone, something is felt to be missing from the appearance of the entire flock. One shepherd in the Lebanon district was asked if he always counted his sheep each evening. He replied in the negative, and then was asked how then he knew if all his sheep were present. This was his reply: "Master, if you were to put a cloth over my eyes, and bring me any sheep and only let me put hands on its face, I could tell in a moment if it was mine or not."[27]

When H. R. P. Dickson visited the desert Arabs, he witnessed an event that revealed the amazing knowledge which some of them have of their sheep. One evening, shortly after dark, an Arab shepherd began to call out one by one the names of his fifty-one mother sheep, and was able to pick out each one's lamb, and restore it to its mother to suckle. To do this in the light would be a feat for many shepherds, but this was done in complete darkness, and in the midst of the noise coming from the ewes crying for their lambs, and the lambs crying for their mothers.[28] But no Oriental shepherd ever had a more intimate knowledge of his sheep than Jesus our great Shepherd has of those who belong to His flock. He once said of Himself: "I am the good shepherd, and know my sheep" (John 10:14).

The difference between the shepherd and the hireling. Concerning the hireling, Jesus said: "The hireling fleeth, because he is an hireling, and careth not for the sheep" (John 10:13). When the flock is small, the shepherd handles his sheep without any help but if the flock becomes too large, then it becomes necessary for him to hire someone to help him with the sheep. One man can usually handle from fifty to one hundred sheep, but when he has more than one hundred, he usually seeks a helper. The hireling does not usually have the personal interest in the sheep that the shepherd has, and so cannot always be trusted to defend the flock in the way the shepherd himself would do.[29] "He that is an hireling, and not the shepherd, whose own the sheep are not, seeth the wolf coming, and leaveth the sheep, and fleeth: and the wolf catcheth them, and scattereth the sheep" (John 10:12).

CARING FOR THE SHEEP IN SPECIAL TIMES OF NEED

The love of the shepherd for his sheep is best seen when times of special need call forth unusual acts of care for members f the flock.

Crossing a stream of water. This process is most interesting. The shepherd leads the way into the water and across the stream. Those favored sheep who always keep hard by the shepherd, plunge boldly into the water, and are soon across. Others of the flock enter the stream with hesitation and alarm. Not being close to their guide, they may miss the fording place and be carried down the river a distance, but will probably be able to clamber ashore. The little lambs may be driven into the water by the dogs, and they are heard to bleat pitifully as they leap and plunge. Some manage to get across, but if one is swept away, then the shepherd leaps quickly into the stream and rescues it, carrying it in his bosom to the shore. When they all arrive over the stream, the lambs will gambol about with joy, and the sheep will gather around their shepherd as if to express their thankfulness to him.[30] Our divine Shepherd has a word of encouragement for all His sheep who must pass through streams of affliction: "When thou passest through the waters, I will be with thee; and through the rivers, they shall not overflow thee" (Isa. 43:2).

Special care of baby lambs, and sheep with young ones. When lambing time comes, the shepherd must take great care of his flock. The task is made more difficult because it so often becomes necessary to move to a new location to find pasturage. The sheep that are soon to become mothers, as well as those with their young ones, must be kept close to the shepherd while in transit. Little helpless lambs that cannot keep up with the rest of the flock, are carried in the bosom of his undergarment, the girdle turning it into a pocket.[31] Isaiah pictures this activity in his famous passage: "He shall feed his flock like a shepherd: he shall gather the lambs with his arm and carry them in his bosom, and shall gently lead those that are with young" (Isa. 40:11).

Care of sick or wounded sheep. The shepherd is always on the lookout for members of his flock that need personal attention. Sometimes a lamb suffers from the rays of the sun, or its body may have been badly scratched by some thornbush. The most common remedy he uses with these sheep is olive oil, a supply of which he carries in a ram's horn.[32] Perhaps David was thinking of such an experience when he wrote of the Lord, "Thou anointest my head with oil" (Psa. 23:5).

Watching sheep at night. In weather that permits, the shepherds often keep their flocks in the open country. One group of shepherds provided simple sleeping places for themselves by placing "a number of oblong circles of stones, inside of which rushes were collected for bedding, according to the Bedouin fashion in the desert. These simple beds were arranged in a circle, and sticks and roots were collected at the center for a fire."[33] With this arrangement they were able to keep watch over their sheep by night. It was in such a way as this that the Bethlehem shepherds took turns watching and sleeping on the hills outside Bethlehem, when the angels visited them announcing the Saviour's birth. "And there were in the same country shepherds abiding in the field, keeping watch over their flock by night" (Luke 2:8). When Jacob cared for Laban's sheep, he spent many a night in the out-of-doors, looking after the flock. "Thus I was; in the day the drought consumed me, and the frost by night; and my sleep departed from mine eyes" (Gen. 31:40).

Protection of sheep from robbers and wild animals. The sheep need to be guarded against *robbers* not only when they are in the open country, but also when they are in the fold. The bandits of Palestine are not apt to pick locks, but some of them may manage to climb up over the wall, and get into the fold, where they cut the throats of as many of the animals as possible and then sling them over the wall to others of their band, and all of them attempt to escape without being caught.[34] Jesus described just such operations: "The thief cometh not, but for to steal, and to kill, and to destroy" (John 10:10). The shepherd must be on guard constantly for such an emergency, and must be ready for quick action to protect his rights in the flock.

The *wild animals* of Palestine today include wolves, panthers, hyenas, and jackals. The lion has not lived in the land since the days of the Crusaders. The last bear was killed over half a century ago. David as a shepherd lad experienced the coming of a lion and of a bear against his flock, and by the Lord's help, he was able to slay both of them (I Sam. 17:34–37). Amos tells of a shepherd attempting to rescue one of the flock from the lion's mouth: "As the shepherd taketh out of the mouth of the lion two legs, or a piece of an ear" (Amos 3:12). One experienced Syrian shepherd is reported to have followed a hyena to his lair and compelled the animal to give up his prey. He won his victory over the wild beast by himself howling in characteristic fashion, striking on rocks with his heavy staff, and flinging deadly stones with his slingshot. The sheep was then carried in his arms back to the fold.[35] The faithful shepherd must be willing to risk his life for the sake of the flock, and perhaps give his life for them. As our Good Shepherd Jesus not only risked his life for us, He actually gave Himself on our behalf. He said: "I am the good shepherd: the good shepherd giveth his life for the sheep" (John 10:11).

Seeking and finding lost sheep. Being responsible for anything that happens to one of his flock, the Eastern shepherd will spend hours if necessary in traversing the wilderness or mountain side, in search of a sheep that has strayed away and is lost. After weary hours of hunting for it, it will usually be found in some waterless hollow in the wilderness, or in some desolate mountain ravine. The exhausted creature will be borne home on the shoulders of the sturdy shepherd.[36] And what happens then is best described by the Parable of Jesus: "And when he cometh home, he calleth together his friends and neighbors, saying unto them, Rejoice with me; for I have found my sheep which was lost" (Luke 15:6).

SHEEP PRODUCTS

Sheep in Palestine and vicinity have always been valuable because of the important products that are derived from them.

Wool. Wool has been a valuable product in Bible lands. In ancient times most of the clothing which the Israelites wore was made of wool. The large outer garment or mantle was usually woolen. The shearing months in Palestine are May and June.[37] The sheep are washed before they are sheared. Solomon's Song speaks of "a flock of ewes that are newly shorn, which are come up from the washing" (Cant. 4:2, A. R. V.). The color of the wool varies somewhat according to the color of the animal shorn, but white wool is considered to be most valuable. The prophet compares sins forgiven with the whiteness of wool (Isa. 1:18).

Sheepskins. From ancient times to modern days it has often been customary for pastoral people to make for themselves coats out of the skins of the sheep with wool still adhering to the skins. The Epistle to the Hebrews tells of the persecuted heroes of faith, saying of some of them that they "wandered about in sheepskins" (Heb. 11:37). The skin of sheep was at times tanned and then used as leather, but the skin of the goats was superior to that of sheep for this purpose.[38]

Sheep for meat or sacrificial purposes. Sheep were often eaten when meat was desired. For the ordinary person, meat was not on the daily menu, but was only used on special occasions of rejoicing, as when a feast was prepared, a wedding supper, or when a guest of honor was being entertained. The animal was usually cooked as soon as it was killed, and then was often boiled, although sometimes it was roasted.[39]

The sheep was used in Bible times more than any other animal for sacrificial purposes. A young male lamb was used in most cases as a thanksgiving offering, as atonement for transgression, or as redemption of a more valuable animal. The offering of the Passover Lamb was the most important religious act of the year. This lamb had to be a male, which was selected after minute examination, in order that it be free from any blemish, and it was to be a first year lamb. It was killed on the fourteenth of the month Abib (after the Babylonian captivity Nisan, about the equivalent of our April), and the blood was sprinkled with hyssop. In Egypt the blood was sprinkled on the lintels and doorposts of the houses, but in Canaan it was sprinkled on the altar. The meat was roasted with fire, rather than boiled, and not a bone was broken, as was customary when it was boiled. It was eaten by the entire household in the spirit of haste, as if a journey was being started. Anything left of it was burned with fire, and not left over for the next day.[40] The Feast of the Passover was the most important of all the Jewish annual feasts, and formed the background for the Christian ordinance of the Lord's Supper (cf. Exod. 12; Lev. 23:5 f.; Matt. 26:17–29).

Milk. Milk from the sheep is especially rich, and in the Orient is considered to be of more value than that of the cattle. Milk is seldom drunk in its fresh condition, but rather is made into "leben," or into cheese. Buttermilk is also much used.

Rams' horns. The horns of the rams are considered to be of great value. In many Western lands, growers of sheep have endeavored to develop a hornless breed, but in the East the horns are thought of as an important part of the animal. The ram's horn has been used chiefly as a vessel in which liquids have been carried. For carrying purposes a wooden plug is driven into the large end of the horn so as to close it, and sometimes it is covered with raw hide to hold it in place. The small part of the pointed end of the horn is cut off, and the opening closed with a stopper. The ram's horn was used in

Bible times to carry oil.[41] Samuel was told to take his horn
of oil and anoint David to be the future king (I Sam. 16:1).
Solomon was anointed king by the oil in the horn of Zadok
the priest (I Kings 1:39). Reference has already been made
to the shepherd's use of oil with his sheep, and this was carried in a ram's horn.

The ram's horn was also made into a trumpet and has been
called by the Jews, *Shofar*. The Mosaic Law called for the
sounding of rams' horns at certain times. Each year of Jubilee
was ushered in by the blowing of these horns. "Then shalt
thou cause the trumpet of the jubilee to sound on the tenth
day of the seventh month, in the day of atonement shall ye
make the trumpet sound throughout all your land" (Lev.
25:9). In connection with the Feast of Trumpets there was to
be "a day of blowing the trumpets" (Num. 29:1). The most
famous use of the rams' horns was in connection with the en-
circling and destruction of the city of Jericho by Joshua's
army. "And seven priests shall bear before the ark seven
trumpets of rams' horns; and the seventh day ye shall compass the city seven times, and the priests shall blow with the
trumpets" (Josh. 6:4). The trumpets were also used as signals
to gather the people (Jer. 4:5).

The ram's horn trumpet measures about eighteen inches
long and is in one piece. It is made from the left horn of the
fat-tailed sheep, which is "not spiral but flattish, curved back-
wards, and forming nearly a circle, the point passing under
the ear. This structure, added to the large size of the horn,
adapts it well for its purpose. In order to bring it to the proper
shape, the horn is softened by heat (i.e. hot water) and then
modeled into the very form which was used by the Jewish
priests."[42]

GOATS

Care of goats—leadership ability. There are many goats
being cared for by Bible land shepherds. A shepherd looks
after them much as he would care for a flock of sheep. Some-

times the goats belong to one flock along with the sheep, and in this case:

> It is usually a he-goat that is the special leader of the whole (Jer. 50:8; Prov. 30:31), walking before it as gravely as a sexton before the white flock of a church choir. It is from this custom that Isaiah speaks of kings as "the he-goats of the earth" (Isa. 14:9, A. R. V., M.), a name applied to them by Zechariah also (Zech. 10:3), and to Alexander the Great by Daniel, who describes him as a he-goat from the west, with a notable horn between his eyes (Dan. 8:5): a fitting symbol of his irresistible power at the head of the Macedonian army.[43]

How goats differ from sheep. Most of the Palestinian and Syrian sheep are white, whereas most of the goats are black. The goats like the slopes of the rocky mountains, whereas the sheep prefer the plains or mountain valleys. The goats are especially fond of young leaves of trees, but the sheep would rather have grass. Goats will feed during all the day without the heat of summer affecting them; but when the sunshine is hot, the sheep will lie down under a tree, or in the shade of a rock, or in a rude shelter prepared by the shepherd for that purpose. Song of Solomon makes mention of this rest time for the sheep: "Tell me, O thou whom my soul loveth, where thou feedest, where thou makest thy flock to rest at noon" (Cant. 1:7). The goats are bolder, more venturesome, more playful, more apt to clamber to dangerous places, more apt to break into the grainfields, more headstrong, more vigorous, and more difficult to control than are the sheep.[44]

Separating goats from sheep. At certain times it becomes necessary to separate the goats from the sheep, although they may be cared for by the same shepherd that cares for the sheep. They do not graze well together, and so it frequently becomes necessary to keep them apart from the sheep while they are grazing. Dr. John A. Broadus, when visiting Palestine, reported seeing a shepherd leading his flock of white sheep and black goats all mingled together. When he turned into a valley, having led them across the Plain of Sharon, he turned around and faced his flock: "When a sheep came up, he tapped it with his long staff on the right side of the head, and it quickly moved off to his right; a goat he tapped on the other side, and it went to his left."[45] This is the picture the Saviour had in mind when he spoke the solemn words: "And before him shall be gathered all nations: and he shall separate them one from another, as a shepherd divideth his sheep from the goats; and he shall set the sheep on his right hand, but the goats on the left" (Matt. 25:32–33).

Use of goat's milk. The milk derived from goats is especially excellent and rich. Most of the "leben" used today and in Bible times is made from goat's milk. Buttermilk and cheese are also utilized as milk products. The book of Proverbs speaks of the importance of goat's milk to the Hebrew people: "Thou shalt have goat's milk enough for thy food, for the food of thy household, and for the maintenance of thy maidens" (Prov. 27:27).

Use of the meat of kids. The meat of an adult male goat is of course rather tough, and so not ordinarily used. The female goats are seldom killed because they are needed to increase the flock. Thus it is the meat of the young male kid that is largely used in Bible lands. In Old Testament times, when visitors were entertained, often a kid was made ready for the meal (cf. Judges 6:19). The prevalence of the flesh of kids in Christ's day is brought out by the reference of the Prodigal's brother. "And he answering said to his father, Lo, these many years do I serve thee, neither transgressed I at any time thy commandment: and yet thou never gavest me a kid, that I might make merry with my friends" (Luke 15:29). There is sarcasm in this reproval, for the kid was of less value at a banquet than would have been a lamb, and considerably inferior to the *fatted calf*, which was killed and served on only special occasions to do honor to a very special guest. The brother was objecting to the father serving the fatted calf at the banquet honoring the return of the Prodigal, whereas he as the elder brother had not been given even *a kid* to make merry with his friends.[46]

Use of goats' hair and goats' skin. The *hair* of the goat was considered to be of great value to the Hebrew people. When the materials were brought for the construction of the Tabernacle in the Wilderness, only the finest and the costliest that could be obtained were accepted; and goats' hair was included in the list of materials the children of Israel offered unto the Lord (See Exod. 35:23). Tabernacle curtains were made of goats' hair (Exod. 26:7). The tents of the Bedouin Arabs are made of goats' hair, just as were similar dwellings in Old and New Testament times. Goats' *skins* have been used widely in Bible lands for leather, and are considered to be better for this purpose than the skin of sheep. This leather is used in making the Oriental "bottle" for carrying or storing water or other liquids.

Use of goats for sacrifices. The Levitical Code often allowed the Hebrews a choice of a sheep or of a goat for the offering. "If his offering be of the flocks, namely, of the sheep, or of the goats, for a burnt sacrifice" (Lev. 1:10). On the Day of Atonement, it was required that a goat be sacrificed by the high priest, and that another goat should be "the scapegoat." "And the goat shall bear upon him all their iniquities unto a land not inhabited: and he shall let go the goat in the wilderness" (Lev. 16:22). Moses had ordered that the scapegoat should be taken out into the wilderness and turned loose. But in order to prevent its return to Jerusalem, it became customary to lead the creature to the height of a mountain, where it was pushed over and would be certainly killed.[47] This was the symbol of the forgiveness of sin through the sacrifice of Christ. Although John the Baptist spoke of Jesus as the Lamb of God, he may have had in mind also the picture of the scapegoat when he said: "Behold, that is God's Lamb, who takes and bears away the sin of the world" (John 1:29, Centenary, Montgomery).

CHAPTER 19

Growing and Harvesting Grain

T

HE NUMEROUS REFER-
ENCES to the growth of grain, which are found in the law of
Moses, indicate that it was expected that the Israelites would
become an agricultural people after entering the land of
Canaan, and that the cultivation of grain would become one
of their chief industries. It is a remarkable fact that the
methods used by them in growing and harvesting this crop
are' virtually the same as those that have been used by the
Palestinian Arab peasants for centuries down to the present
day.

PRELIMINARY PREPARATION FOR PLANTING THE GRAIN

Waiting for rain before beginning to plough. In Palestine,
ploughing is done after the early rains have softened the
earth (cf. Psa. 65:10). These rains usually come the latter part
of October or the first part of November. If they do not come
then, the farmer must wait for them before he can plough his
ground. Job said, "They waited for me as for the rain" (Job
29:23). Jeremiah described lack of rain thus: "There was no
rain in the earth, the ploughmen were ashamed, they covered
their heads" (Jer. 14:4). Once the rain has come, the industrious farmer will start his ploughing. "The sluggard will not
plough by reason of the cold" (Prov. 20:4). Such a man will
retreat into his home and enjoy the warmth of his fire, but he

will miss the harvest. Dr. Thomson tells of one year when the farmers waited until the month of February for sufficient rain to enable them to plough the ground for the grain crop. The harvest came late, but was abundant.[1]

Getting ready for ploughing. The farmer gets ready for ploughing after the first rain starts falling, if he has not already done so before. He will spend the time making sure that his plough is in good repair and ready for action. He may need to cut and point a new goad to use in prodding his team of oxen. He must also see to it that his yoke is smooth and fits the necks of the animals. An ill-shaped or heavy yoke would gall them. The Lord Jesus spoke of "the easy yoke" promised to His obedient followers (Matt. 11:30). When the ground has been softened sufficiently by the rain, then the ploughing can begin.[2]

EQUIPMENT USED IN PLOUGHING

The Plough. One type of Syrian or Palestinian plough is made up of two wooden beams which are joined together, and at the front end it is hooked to a yoke, and at the rear end it is fastened to a crosspiece, the upper part of which serves as the handle, and the lower part holds the iron ploughshare or colter.[3] Even today many may be seen in Bible lands plowing with what we might term a "forked stick." Bible writers often mention iron ploughshares (I Sam. 13:20, etc.). These ploughs could without much work be changed into swords for warfare. Thus the prophet Joel said: "Beat your ploughshares into swords" (Joel 3:10). Exactly the reverse of this prophecy was suggested by both the prophets Isaiah and Micah in predicting the Golden Age (Isa. 2:4; Micah 4:3).

The yoke. The yoke is a rude stick that fits the necks of the cattle. Two straight sticks project down each side, and a cord at the end of these sticks and underneath the cattle's necks holds the yoke on the necks.[4] These yokes of wood are often spoken of in the Scriptures (Jer. 28:13, etc.).

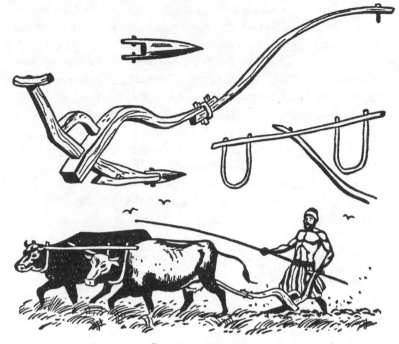

Primitive Plowing

The goad. A goad is carried by the native ploughman to-day, and was also used in Bible times. It is a wooden rod varying in length from five to seven feet, with a sharp point at one end. With this the farmer can hurry up his slow-moving animals.[5] It was such an ox-goad that was used by Shamgar in slaying six hundred Philistines (Judges 3:31). The conviction of sin that came to Saul of Tarsus and led to his conversion was compared to the pricks of an oxgoad: "It is hard for thee to kick against the goad" (Acts 26:14, A. R. V.).

ANIMALS USED IN PLOUGHING

Use of oxen. In Bible times oxen were used almost exclusively for ploughing. For this reason the expression "a yoke" was used by the Hebrews to mean the measure of land which a yoke of oxen could plough in a day (cf. I Sam. 14:14, and Isa. 5:10). "Oxen" as the Hebrews used the term, meant both sexes of the animal, cows being used as well as bulls for purposes of draught, but the latter were castrated.[6] This explains the reason for the law specifying concerning a heifer to be used for sacrificial purposes, that it be one "upon which never came yoke" (Num. 19:2). The law of Moses forbade ploughing with an ox and an ass yoked together (Deut. 22:10). The Apostle Paul spoke of "the unequal yoke" in connection with partnership between believers and unbelievers (II Cor. 6:14) Today, the Arabs usually make use of oxen in ploughing, but sometimes utilize camels, and occasionally yoke together an ox and a donkey, or a camel and a donkey.[7]

PREPARING THE SOIL FOR THE CROP

Ploughing. The ploughing of the ground in Oriental fashion is quite primitive. The plough, which at best is a slight implement, can be carried if necessary two miles to the farmer's place of work. Of course by comparison with modern ploughs, it could be said merely to scratch the surface of the soil. The ploughman holds the one handle of the plough with one of his hands, while he carries the goad in the other hand, with which to prod the animals. Jesus said, "No man, having put his *hand* to the plough, and looking back, is fit for the kingdom of God" (Luke 9:62). He described the operation accurately in saying *hand,* i.e. *one hand,* rather than two hands, as is the case with a Western farmer. It would be fatal for the Palestinian farmer to look back, because his implement is so light that the worker often has to press down with all his weight upon it to keep it from leaving the furrow.[8]

The Eastern farmers will sometimes plough together, each man having his own plough and team of oxen, and one following close behind the preceding one. This sort of farmer's club is adopted as a protection from roving Bedouin robbers, and also because co-operation is desired when the wheat farms are large.[9] Thus Elisha was found ploughing with eleven other ploughmen and a total of twenty-four oxen (I Kings 19:19).

Use of pickax or mattock. Where the ground is hard, or on the rocky hillside, it is not possible to use the plough. In such places, if the peasant farmer is industrious, he will prepare the soil by using the pickax or mattock. Isaiah speaks of "hills that shall be digged with the mattock" (Isa. 7:25). By using such an implement, all the available ground is utilized for the crop.[10]

Fertilizer seldom used. The Eastern farmer seldom adds fertilizer to his soil in raising grain. Many a hillside used by the farmer for his crop has a quantity of small, soft lime-stones scattered over it. Part of the lime in the stones is dissolved with each rainstorm, and mixing with the soil, makes it better qualified for a good stand of grain. These stones take care of liming the soil.[11] Modern Jews, returning from the West to farm their land, are adding various chemicals from the Dead Sea as fertilizer for their soil. But there is no mention in the Bible of fertilizing the ground for a grain crop. Jesus did mention in one of his parables about the fertilizing of a fig tree (Luke 13:1-9).

SOWING THE SEED

Kinds of grain sown. There are various kinds of grain used in the Orient. The word "corn," as used in English translations of the Bible, is actually the family name for *cereal grains,* because the "maize" or "Indian corn" of modern days was doubtless unknown to Bible writers. The two principal grains cultivated in ancient Palestine were wheat and barley. There is one mention in the Old Testament of the use of millet (Ezek. 4:9). The Revisers in the A. R. V. have changed the word "rye" in Exodus 9:32 and Isaiah 28:25 to mean "spelt." In modern times, both rice and maize or Indian corn are used in Palestine, although the former is largely imported.[12]

How and when the seed is sown. The farmer usually carries his seed to his field in a large sack on the back of his donkey, and then the leather bag which he carries under his arm is replenished with seed from the sack.[13] As a rule, the seed is scattered broadcast on the ground, and then it is covered over by the ploughing. Often the sower walks along, scattering his seed, and then one of his family, or a servant if he has one, follows directly with the plough.[14] The Biblical word "to sow," as used in the Pentateuch (Gen. 26:12; Lev. 25:3, etc.), means, "to scatter seed."[15]

Sowing as illustrated by the parable of Jesus. The process of sowing, and what happens to the seed, is well illustrated by the Parable of the Sower. No better picture could be given of the Oriental process of sowing the grain than that given by Jesus in this parable (Matt. 13:3–8; Mark 4:3–8; Luke 8:5–8).

"Behold, a sower went forth to sow; and when he sowed, some seeds fell by the way side, and the fowls came and devoured them up" (Matt. 13:3, 4). Palestine had few roads in the modern sense of the word until the Romans built their roads, and these only connected the most important places. Because traveling was either on foot, or by means of donkeys, or camels, a simple footpath was usually all that was necessary. These paths were given over to public use by ancient custom. If a farmer had such a path running across his land, he would plough the earth to the edge of the narrow path, but would leave it for the use of travelers.[16] The Synoptic Gospels tell of Jesus and His disciples traveling in this manner through a grainfield (Matt. 12:1; Mark 2:23; Luke 6:1). Hedges or fences were seldom erected along such a footpath. When the farmer scattered his seed, some was quite apt to fall on this "way," and not being covered by the plough soon enough, the birds would discover it and eat it.

"Others fell upon the rocky places, where they had not much earth: and straightway they sprang up, because they had no deepness of earth: and when the sun was risen, they were scorched; and because they had no root, they withered away" (Matt. 13:5, 6, A. R. V.). The thought here is not of a soil that is mingled with stones, but rather a thin layer of mould covering a rock. Under such conditions, the grain would spring up quickly, but lacking depth of root, would be scorched by the sun, and fail to mature.[17]

"And some fell among thorns; and the thorns sprung up, and choked them." In Palestine and Syria, there are many thornbushes present that are apt to grow adjoining the grain-fields, and some of them will spring up in the midst of the grain. The native farmer uses these thornbushes in the summer for the outdoor fires for cooking the meals. Hence he is not so careful to get rid of them in the near vicinity, and so some of these will choke the wheat or barley shoots.[18]

"But other fell into good ground, and brought forth fruit, some an hundredfold, some sixtyfold, some thirtyfold." The native farmers of Bible lands often have poor returns on the seed they sow, because their methods are primitive. But there are instances of good crops in modern times. Rev. George Mackie, who was a missionary to Syria, has said: "The soil is in many places exceedingly fertile, and the return corresponds to the standard cited in the parable."[19] When Isaac farmed in the rich Negeb section of Southern Canaan, Scripture says: "Then Isaac sowed in that land, and received in the same year an hundredfold" (Gen. 26:12).

ENEMIES OF THE GRAIN

Birds. The birds of the air are foes of the grain. In the East, large flocks of birds often follow the farmer as he sows his seed in order to snatch up, if they can, what he has scattered. Some of the grain is therefore lost before the plough can succeed in covering it up. That which chances to fall on the path would readily be devoured by them (Mark 4:4).[20]

Tares. The tares are also enemies of the grain. In his Parable of the Tares, Jesus said: "While men slept, his enemy came and sowed tares among the wheat" (Matt. 13:25). In the Holy Land, tares are something called "wild wheat," because they resemble wheat, only the grains are black. Thomson has this to say about the tares:

> The Arabic name for tares is *zawan*, and they abound all over the East, and are a great nuisance to the farmer. The grain is small, and is arranged along the upper part of the stalk, which stands perfectly erect. Its taste is bitter, and when eaten separately, or when diffused in ordinary bread, it causes dizziness, and often acts as an emetic. In short, it is a strong soporific poison, and must be carefully winnowed, and picked out of the wheat, grain by grain, before grinding, or the flour is not healthy. Of course the farmers are very anxious to exterminate it, but that is nearly impossible.[21]

Fire. Fire is another enemy of the grain farmer. In Palestine, the Arabs let the wheat become dead ripe, and therefore as dry as tinder, before they cut it. Thorns usually grow all around the wheat fields and intermingle with the grain, and thus it would be easy for a fire starting with the thorns to spread to the wheat, and it would be difficult to keep a whole field from being burned.[22] The law of Moses had a wise regulation regarding fire in relation to the grain fields: "If fire break out, and catch in thorns, so that the stacks of corn, or the standing corn, or the field, be consumed therewith; he that kindled the fire shall surely make restitution" (Exod. 22:6).

Locusts. The locusts are a dreaded enemy of the grain farmer. Perhaps these creatures are the most hated enemy of the Palestinian farmer. These locusts are very much like the large grasshopper with which the Westerner is acquainted. When they reach the proportion of a plague, they are indeed a vast multitude (cf. Judges 6:5; 7:12). They will occupy a space as large as ten or twelve miles long, and four or five miles wide. They are said to march like an army. The Book of Proverbs indicates this interesting fact about them: "Locusts have no king, but they march all in ranks [i.e., in orderly array]" (Prov. 30:27, tr. of C. H. Toy).[23] When the weather is cold and the air is moist, or if they become wet with the dew, then they will stay where they are until the sun has warmed and dried them. The prophet Nahum describes them thus: "Which camp in the hedges in the cold day, but when the sun ariseth they flee away" (Nahum 3:17). The prophet Joel describes the judgment of the Day of the Lord in terms of an invasion of locusts. The plague of locusts shuts out the light of the sun because of their great numbers (Joel 2:2). Before their coming, the land might be like the Garden of Eden, but after they leave, it has become a desolate wilderness (Joel 2:3). Their appearance is compared to horses because the form of their head resembles that of a horse (Joel 2:4). They make a loud noise when they are eating (Joel 2:5). The consternation which they cause to the people of the land may well be understood: "Before their face the people shall be much pained" (Joel 2:6). They are able to pass over walls, and to enter windows or doors of houses (Joel 2:9). The terrible fact is that sometimes one swarm of locusts after another may invade the same section of land.[24] Dr. Keil believes that this is what Joel 1:4 describes, rather than different stages in the development of the locust. He gives a literal translation of the verse thus: "The leavings of the gnawer the multiplier ate, and the leavings of the multiplier the licker ate, and the leavings of the licker, the devourer ate."[25]

Thieves. Thieves are also great foes of the grain farmer. This has been especially true in modern times when the government has not been stable and efficient, as sometimes under the Turkish rule. Under those conditions, when the crop of grain has been planted a distance from the villages where the Fellahin farmers have lived, or if it was planted near to the territory of some of the wild tribes of Bedouin Arabs, there has been risk of losing the crop or at least a portion of it.[26] In Bible times, Israel many times lost grain to her enemies. This was especially true in the days of the Judges. "And so it was, when Israel had sown, that the Midianites came up, and the Amalekites, and the children of the east" (Judges 6:3). With enemies nearby, crops may be lost to them, and even the seed is often taken. If therefore the peasant farmer is very poor, and his supply of seed to plant is not large, he would go forth to sow his seed with a certain amount of fear and trembling, wondering if he would get a harvest from his scattering, or if the enemy would take it from him. As the feelings of the Oriental are easily moved, one can imagine him going forth with tears to sow, and if a harvest was actually reaped, what great rejoicing would be his![27] This is the picture the Psalmist had in mind when he wrote: "They that sow in tears shall reap in joy. He that goeth forth and weepeth, bearing precious seed, shall doubtless come again with rejoicing, bringing his sheaves with him" (Psa. 126:5, 6).

RAIN AND THE MATURING OF THE CROPS

The Palestine grainfields are largely dependent upon the rain that falls, for their fruitfulness. No rain falls in the land from May to September. *The former rain,* spoken of in Scripture, falls in the latter part of October or the first part of November usually. It is this rain that is the signal for the farmer to begin his ploughing and plant his seed. The Bible also speaks of *the latter rain,* which ordinarily falls in March and April, and it is this rain that is of so much value in maturing the barley and the wheat crops. *The heavy winter rains* come the latter part of December and during January and February. The prophecy of Joel mentions all three of these kinds of rain: "And he will cause to come down for you the rain, the former rain, and the latter rain in the first month" (Joel 2:23). The word *rain* here means heavy, gushing rain that falls in winter months, and the rainy season starts with the *former rain* in the fall, and ends with the *latter rain* in the spring.[28] Barley harvest is usually in April and May, and wheat harvest in May and June. Thus we see that Jeremiah was quite correct in his order of seasons in relation to the harvest time, when he said: "The harvest is past, the summer is ended, and we are not saved" (Jer. 8:20).

THE FARMER'S LAW OF HOSPITALITY

Eating grain in the field. When the grain in the wheatfield has passed the "milk stage," and has begun to harden, it is then called "fereek" and is considered to be delicious to eat raw. Natives of the land will pluck the heads, and then rub them in their hand and eat them. For centuries the unwritten law of hospitality has been that wayfarers may eat of the wheat as they pass by or through a field, but they must not carry any away with them.[29] The law of God allowed this same privilege. "When thou comest unto the standing corn (i.e. grain) of thy neighbor, then thou mayest pluck the ears with thine hand; but thou shalt not move a sickle unto thy neighbor's standing corn" (Deut. 23:25). When the Pharisees criticized the disciples, it was not for eating wheat as they passed through a wheat field, but rather for doing it on the sabbath day (Luke 6:1, 2).

Grain left for the poor. The Mosaic Law also had a provision in it to help take care of the poor, in connection with the grain harvest. "And when ye reap the harvest of your land, thou shalt not make clean riddance of the corners of thy field when thou reapest, neither shalt thou gather any gleaning of thy harvest: thou shalt leave them unto the poor, and to the stranger" (Lev. 23:22). Ruth the Moabitess made use of this provision as a stranger in the land, and so gleaned in the field of Boaz (Ruth, Chapter 2). The Arab farmers of today still carry out this ancient custom, although they may not be acquainted with the Biblical precept concerning it. They would not think of touching the corner of their field when harvesting. It is left for the poor and stranger. It may be

Carrying Sheaves to the Threshing Floor

collected later into a great heap, but it is then given to the poor, or used to maintain a guest chamber.[30]

Cutting and Transporting the Ripened Grain

Cutting the ripened grain. The ripe grain is cut with a sickle. In early times sickles were made of flint, which material was abundant and therefore cheap. In later periods there were some made of bronze or of iron, but the former were more prevalent in all periods. The flint was at first set in the jaw-bone of an animal, or in a curved piece of wood.[31] The prophet Jeremiah speaks of "him that handleth the sickle in the time of harvest" (Jer. 50:16). And the prophet Joel commands: "Put ye in the sickle, for the harvest is ripe" (Joel 3:13).

Binding the grain into sheaves. The cut grain is gathered on the arms and bound into sheaves. The Psalmist makes reference to the mower filling his hand, and the binder of sheaves filling his bosom (Psa. 129:7). And Song of Solomon speaks of an heap of wheat (Cant. 7:2), and Joseph in his dream saw "binding sheaves in the field" (Gen. 37:7). Thus the cut grain was gathered in the arms and bound into sheaves.

Transportation of grain to the threshing floor. The usual method of transporting the grain to the threshing floor is as follows: two large bundles of the grain are made secure by a network of rope and then placed a few feet apart. Then a camel is made to kneel in the space between them, and then the bundles are fastened to the animal's packsaddle. The driver gives his signal, and the camel rises and begins to march off to the threshing floor, which is usually located not far from the village. Here he kneels again and is relieved of his burden of grain, and goes back for another load.[32] When a camel was to be had, this was the method of transportation that was doubtless used in Bible times. Otherwise the much-used donkey was utilized for the purpose. When sheaves of grain are loaded on the donkey, a sort of cradle is suspended to the flat saddle, and the cut grain is thrown over this and tied by a rope.[33] The brothers of Joseph used asses to carry sacks of grain and also straw for them to eat (Gen. 42:26, 27).

THRESHING THE GRAIN

Threshing floor. A typical Oriental threshing floor has been described by Thomson thus:

> The construction of the floors is very simple. A circular space, from thirty to fifty feet in diameter, is made level, if not naturally so, and the ground is smoothed off and beaten solid, that the earth may not mingle with the grain in threshing. In time, the floors, especially on the mountains, are covered with a tough, hard sward, the prettiest, and often the only, green plots about the village, and there the

Threshing Grain

traveller delights to pitch his tent. Daniel calls them summer threshing floors; and this is the most appropriate name for them, since they are only used in that season of the year.[84]

Methods of threshing. Three methods of threshing were in use in ancient times, and in some places in the East today. (1) *A flail* was used for threshing small quantities of grain. Ruth must have used such a wooden instrument. "And beat out that she had gleaned: and it was about an ephah of barley" (Ruth 2:17). And without doubt Gideon was also using such an instrument when he was threshing a small amount of wheat secretly, for fear of the enemy. "Gideon was beating out wheat in the winepress, to hide it from the Midianites" (Judges 6:11, A. R. V.).[35]

(2) *A threshing instrument* was often used. One type that has been used in Bible lands in modern days, is composed of

two wooden planks joined together, about three feet wide and six feet long, and underneath has rows of cut square holes, and sharp stones or pieces of metal are driven into these. Isaiah well describes such a threshing instrument: "Behold, I will make thee a new sharp threshing instrument having teeth" (Isa. 41:15, A. R. V.). This threshing board is pulled by the oxen over the grain, and the thresher sits or stands upon the instrument, with his goad in his hand to hurry up the animals.[36] Another type of threshing instrument takes the form of a small wagon with low cylindrical wheels that serve as saws.[37] The prophet must have been thinking of this sort of instrument when he mentioned "the cart wheel" in connection with the threshing activity of the farmer (Isa. 28:27, 28).

(3) *The oxen alone* were driven over the grain in order to thresh it. This method was the most common method used by the Jews in Old Testament times. The animals were turned over the layer of grain as it lay upon the threshing floor, and their hoofs did the work of threshing. Many of the Fellahin today will say that this is the best way of threshing. "This must have been the same in Bible days, for the Hebrew verb 'to thresh' is *doosh*, which has as its root-meaning 'to trample down,' 'to tread under foot' "[38] (cf. Job 39:15; Dan. 7:23).

The oxen not muzzled while threshing. Even today the Arab peasant farmer does not muzzle his oxen while they are treading the grain on the threshing floor. He says it would be a great sin to do so.[39] This agrees with the teaching of the Mosaic Law. "Thou shalt not muzzle the ox when he treadeth out the corn [grain]" (Deut. 25:4). The Apostle Paul quotes this Scripture to enforce his argument that "the laborer is worthy of his hire" (I Cor. 9:9; I Tim. 5:18).

What the threshing process accomplishes. What happens has been described as follows:

> As these heavy sledges are drawn over the layer of straw and ears, they rub out the grain. This by its form and weight, sinks immediately through the straw, and thus escapes being

hurt. The straw, which by its lightness remains on the surface, is slowly broken and crushed into tiny pieces. Thus a
double process goes on by means of this simple but effective
treatment. Not only is the corn threshed out, but the straw is
at the same time prepared for cattle and camel fodder. In
this crushed state it is called "teben" and is used to mix with
the barley with which all their animals are fed, just as we
mix chopped hay with oats; but this crushing is far superior
to our chopping as a means of preparing cattle food.[40]

WINNOWING THE GRAIN

Winnowing was accomplished by the use of either a broad
shovel or of a wooden fork which had bent prongs. With this
instrument, the mass of chaff, straw, and grain was thrown
against the wind. Because there was generally a breeze blowing in the evening, this was the time when it was normally
done.[41] So Naomi said to Ruth concerning Boaz: "Behold, he
winnoweth barley tonight in the threshing floor" (Ruth 3:2).

When the Bible speaks of the farmer's *fan*, it does not mean
that some instrument was used to increase the wind. Rather,
the fan was the shovel or wooden fork used when unseparated
grain and straw was thrown against the wind.[42] The prophet
Jeremiah tells of God using a fan to winnow His people Israel:
"I have winnowed them with a fan in the gates of the land"
(Jer. 15:7, A. R. V.).

When the grain and straw, not as yet separated, are thrown
into the air, the wind causes the mass of material to fall as
follows: Since the grain is the heaviest, it naturally falls beneath the fan. The straw is blown to the side into a heap, and
the lighter chaff and the dust are carried beyond into a
flattened windrow.[43] This gave to the Psalmist his figure:
"The ungodly are not so, but are like the chaff which the wind
driveth away" (Psa. 1:4). The chaff is burned as Scripture
often indicates. "And the flame consumeth the chaff" (Isa.
5:24). John the Baptist was familiar with the winnowing
process and the burning of the chaff. He said: "Whose fan is

Measuring Grain

in his hand, and he will throughly purge his floor, and gather his wheat into the garner; but he will burn up the chaff with unquenchable fire" (Matt. 3:12; Luke 3:17).

Dr. Lambie reports seeing an additional process used by Bible land Arabs. After being thrown against the wind, the grain is placed on a rock and the farmer uses a mat about eighteen inches square with which to fan the grain, while a helper keeps turning it over, in order to get rid of any remaining chaff.[43a] There is no definite reference to such a practice in the Bible, but it is possible this method may have been used in olden times as an additional means of cleaning the grain, or perhaps it was employed when the winds were quiet.

SIFTING THE GRAIN

When the winnowing process is over, then comes the sifting of the grain. The wheat or barley will still be more or less mixed with certain amounts of chaff, little stones, and perhaps some tares. Sifting is therefore necessary before the grain can be ground into meal. This is the task of the women. The sifter seats herself on the floor, and shakes the sieve which contains the grain, until the chaff begins to appear on the top, and this is blown away by lung power. The stones are removed as are also the tares.[44] The Lord Jesus made reference to the "sifting" of Simon Peter. He said: "Simon, Simon, behold, Satan hath desired to have you, that he may sift you as wheat: But I have prayed for thee, that thy faith fail not; and when thou art converted, strengthen thy brethren" (Luke 22:31).

STORING THE GRAIN

Smaller quantities of grain are often stored away for future use by the family, in "barrels" made of a combination of clay and wickerwork. If there is a larger quantity of grain it is sometimes placed in a dry cistern under the ground, and the location of the place is kept a secret by covering over the opening.[45] Actually there were no flour *barrels* in the homes of Old Testament characters. The Revisers have correctly changed the word "barrel" to "jar." Earthenware jars were used to store grain or flour (see I Kings 17:12, 14, 16; 18:33, A. R. V.).

Both underground storage places for grain and buildings above ground have been in use in modern times. In the Bible, three words are used in our English translations for grain storage places: the storehouse, the garner, and the barn (Deut. 28:8; Matt. 3:12; Prov. 3:10). These places were often located below the surface of the ground, but were sometimes above ground. The barns of the rich fool Christ told about, must have been of the latter type, because he said: "I will pull down my barns and build greater" (Luke 12:18). When excavators uncovered the city of Gezer, they discovered that granaries had been important buildings in ancient times. Some of them were connected with private homes, while others were evidently public storehouses. Most of them were circular in shape, like some that have been in use on the maritime plain of Palestine in recent years. Their size varied greatly.[46]

CHAPTER 20

Care of Vineyards

THE DESCRIPTION OF A VINEYARD
BY ISAIAH AND BY JESUS

IN ISAIAH'S PARABLE of the Vineyard, and in Christ's Parable of the Wicked Husbandman, taken together, we get an accurate picture of an Oriental vineyard. Isaiah wrote: "My well beloved had a vineyard in a very fruitful hill: and he digged it, and gathered out the stones thereof, and planted it with the choicest vine, and built a tower in the midst of it, and also hewed out a winepress therein" (Isa. 5:1–2, A. R. V.). Jesus spoke thus: "There was a certain householder, which planted a vineyard, and hedged it round about, and digged a winepress in it, and built a tower, and let it out to husbandmen" (Matt. 21:33). These two accounts list eight interesting facts that are true of many vineyards in Bible lands. They are often located on a hillside, they usually have a hedge or fence around them, the soil is cultivated by hoeing or spading, large stones are gathered out of the ground, choice vines are planted, a watch-tower is built, a winepress is constructed, and sometimes vineyards are rented. These points suggest the main features that need to be noticed in a study of the Oriental vineyard.

Terraced Vineyard

LOCATION OF VINEYARDS

Hillsides often used. Although vineyards are to be found in various locations in Palestine, it has been customary during past years for the hillsides to be utilized for the purpose, or the ground at the foot of a hill that slopes gently. Grapevines like a sandy or loose soil. They need plenty of sunshine and air by day, and dew by night, and their roots will penetrate deep crevices of rock to get nourishment.[1] It was "in a very fruitful hill" that Isaiah's vineyard grew (Isa. 5:1).

Sections where most of the grapes grow. The favorite places for vineyards in Bible lands are Southern Palestine, especially in the vicinity of Hebron where there are many hillsides; and in Syria and the foothills of the Lebanon Mountains in the north. It has been reported that one variety of grape grown in the vicinity of Hebron sometimes develops fruit so that one bunch may weigh as much as twenty-four pounds. Two natives will carry such a bunch on a pole, which reminds us of the spies sent by Moses into Canaan.[2] "And they came unto the brook Eshcol, and cut down from thence a branch with one cluster of grapes, and they bare it between two upon a staff" (Num. 13:23).

PREPARATION FOR A VINEYARD

Terraces necessary for many vineyards. This has to do with those located on the hillsides. A series of low stone walls above each other, are constructed along the side of the hill, to keep the soil in place, and at the right level for growing grapes. Remains of old terraces in various places indicate that this custom has been practiced for many centuries.[3]

A hedge or wall usually built around a vineyard. An Eastern vineyard is usually surrounded with a ditch, and the earth from the digging of it is thrown along the inner side of the ditch, and upon this a fence of posts, branches, and twigs is built with thorn-branches on top. Oftentimes a wall of either stones or sun-dried mud takes the place of the fence. This serves as protection from foxes, jackals, or other animals, as well as from any thieves.[4] In the parable of Jesus, the owner of the vineyard "hedged it round about" (Matt. 21:33). The Psalmist recounted what would happen to a vineyard whose hedges were broken down: "Why hast thou then broken down the hedges, so that all they which pass by the way do pluck her? The boar out of the wood doth waste it, and the wild beast of the field doth devour it" (Psa. 80:12, 13). The lover in the Song of Solomon speaks of "the foxes, the little foxes, that spoil the vines" (Cant. 2:15).

Large stones gathered out of the land. After putting a hedge or wall around the vineyard, the next task is to gather out stones. Isaiah's parable says: "And he fenced it, and gathered out the stones thereof" (Isa. 5:2). It is not the small stones that are taken out, because their presence is important to aid in the retaining of moisture in the vineyard's soil. Rather the large boulders must be removed that would be a hindrance to the growing vines. Much of Palestine's land has had these rocks present, and they must be laboriously moved in preparation for a crop of grapes.[5]

The soil prepared for planting. The ground for hillside vineyards is not usually ploughed on account of its rocky character. Rather is the more arduous method of hoeing or spading by hand used. Isaiah pictures the process of cultivation of the soil in the words, "and he digged it" (Isa. 5:2, A. R. V.). If the farmer in charge of the vineyard does not have a small vineyard, he will probably need to have some workmen to help him, as was the case of the householder in Christ's Parable of the Laborers in the Vineyard (Matt. 20:1–3), and in such a case it is to the marketplace that he will go to secure his workers.

The construction of a booth or tower. For centuries Palestinian vineyards have had watchmen, whose duty it has been to be on the lookout for marauders of any kind. Sometimes a simple booth is constructed for him, on a high spot where he can view the entire vineyard. This is made of branches and boughs of trees, and provides a shelter from the rays of the sun. This place becomes the home for the watchman for the summer months of the year. In the winter months this booth is deserted. Isaiah said: "The daughter of Zion is left as a booth in a vineyard" (Isa. 1:8, A. R. V.). Often a more durable abode is made for the watchman, especially if his family is to live with him for the summer. Isaiah's Song of the Vineyard mentions the building of a tower "in the midst" of the vineyard (Isa. 5:2). Jesus' Parable of the Wicked Husbandmen speaks of the building of a tower in the vineyard (Matt. 21:33). Also when Christ told of the man who did not count the cost of building a tower, it was doubtless a vineyard-tower to which he was referring (Luke 14:28–30). These towers were of varying height, all the way from ten feet to an occasional

Vineyard Watch-Tower

forty feet. These towers were not the same as the ones connected with the city walls. Nor are they the same as the more modern towers now in use by the Jews returning to the land of their fathers, who use them as a protection for their agricultural colonies.[6]

PLANTING OF THE GRAPEVINES

The vineyard of Isaiah's song was planted, "with the choicest vine" (Isa. 5:2). Although the slips are usually planted closer together, they are sometimes set about twelve feet apart in order to give plenty of space for the branches to run. As a rule the young vine is trimmed back and does not bear grapes until following the third year. The grape blossom comes out in April and May and gives out a delicate sweetness.[7] Solomon's Song says: "The vines with the tender grape give a good smell" (Cant. 2:13).

CARE OF A VINEYARD

Parable of the sluggard. A good indication of the care required in growing a vineyard may be derived by looking at this parable as given in the book of Proverbs. "I went by the field of the slothful, and by the vineyard of the man void of understanding; and, lo, it was all grown over with thorns, and nettles had covered the face thereof, and the stone wall thereof was broken down" (Prov. 24:30, 31). The sluggard failed to keep his vineyard-wall in repair, and he failed to keep his growing vines free of thorns and weeds. These two activities are absolutely necessary. As in the case of raising a crop of grain, the native farmer does not usually fertilize the ground of his vineyard. Liming of the ground is dependent upon the many small and soft limestones so often present in Palestine. Some of the lime in the stones is dissolved with each rainstorm, and mixing with the soil helps it in the growth of the grapes.

Pruning of the grapevines. Before the arrival of springtime, the keeper of the vineyard prunes off every superficial branch, every branch that is sickly or feeble, so that the sap may flow into the healthy ones that will bear fruit. The branch that is located nearest the trunk or root usually bears the most grapes.[8] Jesus indicates his familiarity with the pruning of the grapevines, in his famous allegory of the vine and the branches: "I am the real vine, and my Father is the cultivator. He cuts away any branch on me that stops bearing fruit, and He repeatedly prunes every branch that continues to bear fruit, to make it bear more. You are already pruned because of the teaching that I have given you" (John 15:1–3, Williams).

HARVESTING OF GRAPES

The vintage begins in the month of September in the Holy Land, and at this period, from ancient times, the inhabitants of many a village move out to the vineyards, where they live in tents or in lodges. Concerning the men of Shechem, the Book of Judges says: "They went out into the fields, and gathered their vineyards" (Judges 9:27). Jeremiah tells us about the gathering of the grapes by means of baskets: "Turn back thine hand as a grape-gatherer into the baskets" (Jer. 6:9). Isaiah predicts judgment as being a time when "there shall be no singing" in the vineyards (Isa. 16:10). Thus the gathering of the grapes into the baskets was done with great joy and much singing. Whole families entered into the happiness of this harvest time. This is true among Oriental grape farmers today.

USE OF GRAPES AND MAKING OF GRAPE PRODUCTS

Fresh grapes and raisins. During the months of September and October, the fresh ripe grapes are eaten along with bread as one of the principal foods, in Bible lands. Then the grapes are dried in a level corner of the vineyard. While being dried they are turned over and sprinkled with olive oil to keep the skin moist. Then they are stored for winter use.[9]

The Mosaic Law allowed the eating of grapes from a neighbor's vineyard, but none could be taken away in a vessel (Deut. 23:24). Today, in the Arab villages of Palestine, there is an unwritten law of hospitality that everyone passing by a vineyard may help himself, but nobody would think of imposing on this kindness by carrying off any grapes.[10]

Raisins were widely used in the days when the ancient Hebrews lived in Palestine. Abigail gave David one hundred clusters of raisins (I Sam. 25:18). Raisins were brought to David at Hebron (I Chron. 12:40), and again, when he was fleeing from Absalom, he received a quantity of them (II Sam. 16:1).

Grapesyrup or "dibs." The Arabs take the juice of grapes, and boil it until it is as thick as molasses. They call this "dibs," and they are very fond of eating it with bread, or they thin it with water and drink it. This grapehoney was in use in Bible times. It was probably this that Jacob sent to Joseph in Egypt (Gen. 43:11), and which was purchased by the Tyrians from the land of Palestine (Ezek. 27:17). Three hundred pounds of grapes will make one hundred pounds of dibs.[11]

The Oriental winepress. The winepress of Isaiah's parable was constructed by hewing it out of rock (Isa. 5:2, A. R. V.). Those seen today are composed of two depressions hewn out of solid rock. The one is higher than the other one, and is also larger. The grapes are put into this one, and then trodden by the feet of men, women, and also children, usually whole families working together. The juice flows into the lower depression. Usually each vineyard of any size has its own winepress.[12] This work of treading the grapes was customarily accompanied by shouts and songs of happiness. Jeremiah speaks of judgment in terms of the absence of this happiness. "And joy and gladness is taken from the plentiful field, and from the land of Moab; and I have caused wine to fail from the winepresses: none shall tread with shouting; their shouting shall be no shouting" (Jer. 48:33).

The winepress as a figure of divine judgment. Isaiah describes the nations as being put in God's winepress where He treads upon them until His garments are sprinkled with their lifeblood (Isa. 63:3–6). There is a graphic picture of the destruction of the army of Antichrist in the Apocalypse. The coming Redeemer is described as being "clothed with a vesture dipped in blood," and He is said to tread "the winepress of the fierceness and wrath of Almighty God" (Rev. 19:13, 15).

The Renting of a Vineyard

Vineyards that are large are often rented out to one or more families. When this is done, the peasant who rents the

The Winepress

vineyard agrees to give half or more of the products of the grapes. When harvest-time comes, the owner will send his servant to secure his share of the grapes, raisins, wine, or dibs.[13] This illustrates Christ's Parable of the Wicked Husbandmen, for Jesus in telling his parables was making use of familiar practices among the people. "There was a certain householder, which planted a vineyard . . . and let it out to husbandmen, and went into a far country: and when the time of the fruit drew near, he sent his servants to the husbandmen, that they might receive the fruits of it" (Matt. 21:33, 34).

CHAPTER 21

Olive and Fig Tree Culture

THE OLIVE TREE

Abundance of olive trees in bible lands. For centuries the olive tree has been growing in lands bordering on the Mediterranean Sea, but its growth in Palestine has been quite abundant. Moses told Israel that Canaan was "a land of oil olive" (Deut. 8:8). He also told them that they would acquire olive trees which they had not planted (Deut. 6:11). From that day down to the present day, the growth of the olive tree, and the use of its products, have played an important part in the history of the land.

Characteristics of the olive tree. The young olive tree only bears olives after seven years of growth, and it is about fourteen years before the crop reaches its maturity. Because of the injurious method of harvesting the olives by using sticks to knock off the fruit, the trees only bear a full crop every other year. Some twenty gallons of oil are often derived from the olives of one tree. The berries are harvested in the month of October.[1]

After the olive tree reaches its maturity, its fruitfulness lasts for many years. Its longevity is one of the remarkable charac-

196

teristics of the tree. It lives and bears fruit for centuries. The old olive tree is often seen to have several thrifty young shoots springing up all around it from its roots. It was this picture that the Psalmist had in mind when he wrote: "Thy children like olive plants round about thy table" (Psa. 128:3).

The olive tree thrives in Palestinian soil which has so many rocks in it. Thomson says of it: "It insinuates its roots into the crevices of this flinty marl, and draws from thence its stores of oil."[2] Doubtless it is to this that the song of Moses alludes: "He made him to suck honey out of the rock, and oil out of the flinty rock" (Deut. 32:13).

To the Occidental, the olive tree with its dull grayish color of foliage, does not seem to be a particularly beautiful tree, but the Oriental sees in it many charms.[3] Writers of Scripture often speak of the beauty and attractiveness of the olive. Concerning Israel, the prophet Jeremiah said: "The Lord called thy name, A green olive tree, fair, and of goodly fruit" (Jer. 11:16). The prophet Hosea said, "His beauty shall be as the olive tree" (Hosea 14:6). And David asserted concerning himself: "I am like a green olive tree in the house of God" (Psa. 52:8).

Olive trees have a remarkable number of blossoms, many of which fall without ever maturing into fruit. Sometimes the breeze blows upon the tree and the falling blossoms look like a shower of snowflakes.[4] The book of Job makes a comparison to this characteristic of the olive blossoms: "And shall cast off his flower as the olive" (Job 15:33).

Grafting of the olive tree. In the western part of Asia the olive tree often grows wild, and so when the trees are cultivated they must be grafted. A graft of a cultivated olive tree is inserted into the stem of the wild olive tree, and then the wild olive tree is cut down close to the ground, and the part below becomes root and feeder for the inserted shoot.[5] This is the customary process of grafting. But the Apostle Paul, for sake of argument, speaks of grafting contrary to the natural process. He tells of God grafting the wild olive of the Gentiles on the good stock of the Jewish nation, which is a reversal of custom (Rom. 11:24).

Harvesting the olive crop. The Arabs harvest their crop of olives in the Holy Land by beating the trees with sticks in order to knock off the fruit. Instead of hand picking them, they beat the limbs and thus cause the fruit to fall. The tender shoots that would ordinarily bear fruit the following year are thus apt to be damaged, so as to interfere greatly with the next year's crop. This is no doubt the reason for the trees yielding a good crop only every other year. The reason why this method is used is because their forefathers have always done it this way, and they don't believe in change of customs.[6] As a matter of fact, Moses indicates that the same method was used by Israel when he gave the law concerning leaving some of the olive berries for the poor: "When thou beatest thine olive tree thou shalt not go over the boughs again: it shall be for the stranger, or the fatherless, and for the widow" (Deut. 24:20). Isaiah also speaks of the obtaining of berries left by the olive harvesters: "Yet gleaning grapes shall be left in it, as the shaking of an olive tree, two or three berries in the top of the uppermost bough, four or five in the outmost fruitful branches thereof" (Isa. 17:6).

Use of olives for eating. The natives of Bible lands have made large use of a form of dried olives. The pickled olive berry so much used in the Occident, is gradually being introduced by the returning Jews. It has been said that bread and olives are used in Syria today, much like porridge and milk are used in Scotland.[7] The workingman of the East usually has some olives in his bag when he leaves home for his daily work.

The process of making olive oil. Olive mills are used for making oil. There have been many of these instruments for the manufacture of oil located in Palestine.

Oil-presses comprised, in addition to the vat, an upright stone with a large hole in it. In this hole a beam was inserted. This beam rested on the olives which were to be pressed, extending far beyond the receptacle containing the olives, and weights were hung on the end farthest from the stone.[8]

The Garden of Gethsemane was in reality an olive orchard, and the word, "Gethsemane," means "Oil-Press." Another Bible-time way of making oil was to tread the olive berries with the feet. This primitive method was mentioned by the prophet Micah: "Thou shalt tread the olives, but thou shalt not anoint thee with oil" (Micah 6:15).

The wide use of olive oil in Bible lands. Olive oil was considered to be one of the great sources of wealth in the days of King Solomon (cf. I Kings 5:11; II Chron. 2:10). Solomon gave to Hiram each year in return for services rendered by his men, among other things, twenty thousand baths of oil, one bath being about seven and one-half gallons.[9] The prophets Ezekiel and Hosea make mention of the exporting of oil to other lands (Ezek. 27:17; Hosea 12:1). Oil has been used for a great variety of purposes in the Orient. It largely took the place of butter in eating, and for cooking purposes it was used in place of animal fat. Ezekiel mentions three important items of diet of which oil is one, and flour and honey are the other two (Ezek. 16:13). And olive oil was used almost exclusively for light in lamps. The most famous example of this is "the ten virgins, which took their lamps, and went forth to meet the bridegroom" (Matt. 25:1). Also oil is used today in Bible lands in the manufacture of soap, and it is quite likely that it was so used in Bible days. And oil was often used for anointing the body. Naomi told Ruth, "Wash thyself therefore, and anoint thee, and put thy raiment upon thee, and get thee down to the floor" (Ruth 3:3). Then oil was many times used in various religious ceremonies. It formed a part of the meal offering (Lev. 2:1, A. R. V.). The prophet was anointed with oil when he took over his duties (I Kings 19:16). The priest was also anointed with oil when he took over his duties (Lev. 8:12). And the king was anointed either by a prophet or by the priest (I Sam. 16:13; I Kings 1:34). In New Testament times the sick were anointed for the healing of their bodies (Mark 6:13; Jas. 5:14).

The use of olive wood. Wood from the olive tree is often used in the East. It is close-grained and has a yellow tint. The Oriental carpenter is fond of using it. It is especially utilized in the construction of cabinets. King Solomon had the cherubim of the temple, and the inner and outer doors and posts of the sanctuary, all made of olive wood[10] (I Kings 6:23, 31, 33).

The symbolic meaning of the olive. The olive tree has been thought of as a symbol of peace, ever since the dove sent out by Noah from the ark came back, and "Lo, in her mouth an olive leaf plucked off" (Gen. 8:11). Throughout the Bible, oil is often used symbolically of the Holy Spirit. And when the Apostle John speaks of the "anointing which ye have received" (I John 2:27), he means by it the enduement with power of the Holy Spirit. Also oil was considered a symbol of abundance (Deut. 8:8), and a lack of it was a symbol of want (Joel 1:10).

THE FIG TREE

Three crops of figs in Palestine. The early figs, not very many in number, but large in size, are ripe a month before the main crop; the summer or main crop is used in August and September; and the winter figs remain on the trees until late in the fall of the year. Mention is made in Scripture of the firstripe figs as being desirable (Hosea 9:10), and the ease with which they are secured when the tree is shaken (Nahum 3:12). The summer crop that is not eaten as fresh fruit is dried on the housetops, and then used in the winter months.[11]

The fig tree a sign of the season. The fig tree shows sign of foliage later than some of the other fruit trees of Palestine.

The unfolding of the fig leaves and the deepening of their color is thought of as a sign that summertime is at hand.[12] Jesus made reference to this idea: "Now learn a parable of the fig tree; when his branch is yet tender, and putteth forth leaves, ye know that summer is nigh" (Matt. 24:32; Mark 13:28). The lover in the Song of Solomon indicated that winter was past and summer was at hand because "the fig tree putteth forth her green figs" (Cant. 2:11–13).

Christ and the fig tree. In order to understand why Christ cursed the fig tree one day, it is necessary to know the custom of the fig tree's growth of leaves and fruit. The normal habit of the fig trees is that fruit begins to form on the tree as soon as leaves appear. Leaves and fruit also disappear together. But it was said of this fig tree which Jesus and his disciples saw on the Mount of Olives, "for the time of figs was not yet" (Mark 11:13). Actually this was no excuse for this fig tree, because if it was not the time for figs, it was also not the time for leaves to appear. By a show of leaves, it was like many people, pretending to have fruit which was not there. It was like the Pharisees who professed to be very religious, but whose lives were fruitless. Therefore Christ cursed this tree as an object lesson to all not to be hypocritical.[13]

Jesus also gave us the Parable of the Barren Fig Tree.

> A certain man had a fig tree planted in his vineyard; and he came and sought fruit thereon, and found none. Then said he unto the dresser of his vineyard, Behold, these three years I come seeking fruit on this fig tree, and find none: cut it down; why cumbereth it the ground? And he answering said unto him, Lord, let it alone this year also, till I shall dig about it, and dung it: and if it bear fruit, well: and if not, then after that thou shalt cut it down (Luke 13:6–9).

Here was a fig tree that failed for three years to bear fruit, when its owner had a right to expect a crop. The gardener suggested patience with the tree, and proposed additional cultivation and fertilization for it, giving it another chance to bear figs. It will be noted that this fig tree had been planted in the midst of a vineyard. This is often done in Palestine.

Use of figs in the Old Testament. Figs were often used in the history of Israel, especially dried figs. Abigail took two hundred cakes of figs to David (I Sam. 25:18). A cake of figs was given the Egyptian to revive him (I Sam. 30:12). And cakes of figs were brought to David at Hebron at a time of great rejoicing (I Chron. 12:40). When King Hezekiah was sick, Isaiah told him to put a lump of figs on his boil, and the Lord healed him (II Kings 20:7). Jeremiah refers to the characteristic of figs, that some of them can be very good, and then again, they can be very bad (Jer. 24:1, 2).

Sitting under one's own fig tree. Several times the Old Testament makes use of this expression with the addition of the vine. It is used in various ways. In the prosperous reign of King Solomon it was said, "And Judah and Israel dwelt safely, every man under his vine and under his fig tree, from Dan even to Beer-sheba, all the days of Solomon" (I Kings 4:25). This was another way of saying that there was prosperity and peace in the land, that every family enjoyed the possession of his father's inheritance, which was symbolized by the fruits of the vine and fig tree belonging to each home. The prophet Micah used the expression to picture the universal peace and prosperity which would characterize the coming Golden Age: "Nation shall not lift up sword against nation, neither shall they learn war any more. But they shall sit every man under his vine and under his fig tree; and none shall make them afraid" (Micah 4:3, 4). It is a picture of enjoying the blessings of peace.

CHAPTER 22

Trades and Professions

THE POTTER

THE GREAT DEMAND FOR POTTERS IN THE ORIENT. This is because copper vessels are so expensive, because leather bottles are not suitable for some domestic purposes, and because earthenware vessels are so easily broken and must therefore be replaced often. Porous earthenware jars are in much demand to keep drinking-water cool through the process of evaporation. In a warm climate, courtesy usually demands that "a cup of *cold* water" be given (Matt. 10:42).[1]

Ceramic quarters in Jerusalem. The prophet Jeremiah speaks of visiting one potter in Jerusalem, but the writer of Chronicles tells of a ceramic quarter in the city. "These were the potters . . . there they dwelt with the king for his work" (I Chron. 4:23). Thus it would seem that there were in ancient times families or guilds of potters, and also royal potters.[2]

Preparation of the clay for the potter. It was trodden by the feet in order that it might become of the right consistency.[3] The prophet Isaiah speaks of this action when he says: "He shall come upon princes as upon morter, and as the potter treadeth clay" (Isa. 41:25).

203

The Potter at His Wheel

The equipment and method of the potter. Today the potter plies his trade in many sections of the East, just like his predecessors have done for centuries. His workshop is very rude. He works behind a coarse wooden bench. His equipment consists of two wooden discs or wheels, with an axle standing up from the center of the lower disc. The upper wheel thus turns horizontally when the lower one is put into action by the foot. He keeps a heap of clay lying on his bench, and from this he places a lump of clay that has been previously softened, upon the upper wheel. He makes this wheel spin around, as he shapes the clay with his hands into a cone-shaped figure. Then he uses his thumb to make a hole in the top of the whirling clay, and keeps opening it until he can put his left hand inside of it. As it is necessary, he sprinkles the clay with water from a vessel which he keeps beside him.

He uses a small piece of wood with his right hand to smooth the outside of the vessel as it continues to rotate. He is thus able to make the vessel into whatever shape he desires in keeping with his individual skill.[4]

Jeremiah referred to the work of the potter in his message, the inspiration of which came while he was visiting the potter's house: "O house of Israel, cannot I do with you as the potter? saith the Lord. Behold, as the clay is in the potter's hand, so are ye in mine hand, O house of Israel" (Jer. 18:6).

The Apocrypha contains an interesting description of the potter and his work in that day:

> So is the potter sitting at his work, and turning the wheel about with his feet, who is always anxiously set at his work, and all his handiwork is by number; he will fashion the clay with his arm, and he will bend its strength in front of his feet; he will apply his heart to finish the glazing; and will be wakeful to make clean the furnace (Ecclesiasticus 38:29, 30).

Marring the vessel. Dr. Thomson visited a large pottery at Jaffa and watched a potter work much like the one whom Jeremiah saw in his visit to the potter's house. The prophet of old noted one thing: "And the vessel that he made of clay was marred in the hand of the potter: so he made it again another vessel, as seemed good to the potter to make it" (Jer. 18:4). The Palestinian missionary says he had to wait a long while before he saw the same thing happen, but at last it did. Perhaps because of some defect in the clay, or because he had used too little of it, the potter very suddenly crushed the jar that had been progressing, into a shapeless mass of mud; and then, starting all over again, he set out to make something different.[5] Paul refers to such action in his Epistle to the Romans, "Shall the thing formed say to him that formed it, Why hast thou made me thus? Hath not the potter power over the clay, of the same lump to make one vessel unto honor, and another unto dishonor?" (Rom. 9:20, 21).

Baking the pottery. After the potter is through working

with the vessel on the wheel, he places it on a shelf where there are rows of other vessels, and where they are kept from the direct rays of the sun, and yet where they are exposed to the wind from all directions. The brickkiln where they are baked is a shallow well of stone or brick around four feet deep and eight to ten feet in diameter, which has a small brick oven at its base. The vessels are piled up over this oven in cone-shape, sometimes to a height of twelve feet. It is then covered thickly with brushwood in order that the heat may be kept in and that there may come no sudden chilling. The fire is made to burn until the pottery is hardened sufficiently.[6] The prophet Nahum refers to the preparation for baking pottery when he says: "Make strong the brickkiln" (Nahum 3:14). Sometimes inferior products are made by insufficient burning of vessels.

The fragility of pottery. Eastern pottery is indeed very brittle, especially when modern methods of glazing are unknown. Many times the young woman going for the family water supply has had to come home without it, because she put down her water pitcher too suddenly. The writer of Ecclesiastes has this in mind when he says: "The pitcher be broken at the fountain" (Eccles. 12:6). When only a slight blow will break pottery into pieces, intentional dashing of a vessel of clay to the ground will result in complete ruin, and this is the picture often used by Biblical writers of divine judgment upon God's enemies, or upon His people who disobey Him.[7] "Thou shalt dash them in pieces like a potter's vessel" (Psa. 2:9). "He shall rule them with a rod of iron; as the vessels of a potter shall they be broken to shivers" (Rev. 2:27). "Thus saith the Lord of hosts; even so will I break this people and this city, as one breaketh a potter's vessel, that cannot be made whole again" (Jer. 19:11).

Use of broken fragments of pottery. Broken pieces of earthen vessels are to be seen about a potter's place, and also in many other places in the East. Some of these pieces which happen to be of suitable size and shape are of practicable use for the peasants. Isaiah gives two uses for them: "And he shall break it as the breaking of the potter's vessel that is broken in pieces; he shall not spare: so that there shall not be found in the bursting of it a sherd to take fire from the hearth, or to take water withal out of the pit" (Isa. 30:14). In the evening time it is a common sight to see children coming to the public ovens with sherds of pottery in their hands, and go away with a small amount of hot coals or hot embers, which the baker has placed on each child's sherd, in order that the homes represented might be able to warm up their evening meal. Then at the spring, well, or cistern, sherds that are of the right size and shape to hold water are often left there that they might be used as ladles for filling the container, or as drinking cups.[8] In ancient times when parchment was so expensive to possess, peasants would use fragments of pottery on which to scratch memoranda of business transactions. Many of these have been uncovered by archaeologists, and have proven to be of great value in revealing past history. They are called "ostraca."[9]

THE CARPENTER

Palestine carpenters. Oriental carpenters have plied their trade in the Holy Land in much the same way through the centuries. Visitors to towns like Nazareth or Tiberias have found these workmen to be quite primitive. About the only modern innovation they have adopted has been to have a workbench instead of sitting on the floor beside their working board, as some men, engaged in related crafts, actually do even in modern times. Instead of working, however, always at this bench, they are seen to do much of their work at the doorsill where the light is much better.[10] This occupation has undergone little change from the days when they said of the young Messiah, "Is not this the carpenter?" (Mark 6:3).

Carpenter's tools. With but few exceptions, the tools used

Carpenter Working with Primitive Bow-Drill

by the carpenter in Bible times are those used by these primitive Palestinian carpenters of today. The prophet Isaiah names four instruments used by the carpenter of his day. "The carpenter stretcheth out his rule; he marketh it out with a line; he fitteth it with planes, and he marketh it out with the compass" (Isa. 44:13). The "rule" was no doubt a *measuring line;* the "line" was a *marking tool* or *stylus,* taking the place of our *pencil;* the "plane" was a scraping tool; and the "compass" was an *instrument for making a circle,* as it is today. The "ax" was used in olden times to shape timber as well as to fell trees. It had an iron head usually fastened by means of thongs to a wooden handle, and so it was easy for the head to slip off (cf. Deut. 19:5 and II Kings 6:5).[11]

Excavations at the city of Gezer revealed that the people of Palestine in Bible times had developed ribbon-flint knives into saws by making their edges irregular. Finds there also indicate that they used saws that were made of thin, flexible strips of metal that had been set in frames of wood.[12] Isaiah mentions the use of the saw: "Shall the saw magnify itself against him that shaketh it?" (Isa. 10:15). Jeremiah refers to the use of hammers and nails: "They fasten it with nails and with hammers that it move not" (Jer. 10:4). The archaeologists have found an abundance of bronze and iron nails. The hammers they have brought to light were made mostly of stone. Thus Christ must have made use of both hammer and nails in his Nazareth carpenter shop.[13] The Bible mentions twice the use of the *awl* (Exod. 21:6; Deut. 15:17). These boring instruments as found at Gezer were usually set in bone handles. Chisels found there were made either of bronze or iron. Christ must have used this tool also.[14]

Products of the carpenter. There are several products of the Eastern carpenter's skill. Many have wondered what Jesus as a carpenter made. There is an old tradition that has come down to us, that he was a maker of *plows* and *yokes*.[15] The yoke, and most of the plow, with the exception of the iron ploughshare, are constructed of wood, and so would be the task of the carpenters. As there were many farmers among the ancient Hebrews, as there are among the Arab peasants today, there would be a great demand for yokes and plows. Other products of the carpenter would include wooden locks and wooden keys for houses, doors, roofs, windows, low tables, chairs or stools, and chests for storage use. The carpenter's most ornamental work would include panelling of the roof, latticework for windows, and decorative art on house doors.[16]

The skill of the Oriental carpenter. Because of the use of what seems to the Westerner to be very crude and primitive tools, some have thought that these workmen are lacking in skill, but this is not so. In many ways he is able to use his simple tools in a way that displays great skill. Much personal attention is given the product, and great pride is taken in the resulting handiwork.[17]

HUNTERS

Nimrod the first hunter recorded by Scripture. He was called "a mighty hunter before the Lord" (Gen. 10:9). Of Ishmael it is said that he "dwelt in the wilderness, and became an archer" (Gen. 21:20). Esau was "a cunning hunter" (Gen. 25:27). Isaac said to Esau, "Take, I pray thee, thy weapons, thy quiver and thy bow, and go out to the field, and take me some venison" (Gen. 27:3). Hunting was common in Egypt, and Israel must have been acquainted with it when she dwelt there. There was also, no doubt, some hunting of the Israelites during the wilderness wanderings on the Sinai Peninsula. Upon entering Canaan, it was necessary for Israel to engage in hunting since otherwise their occupation of the land would have been made more difficult. The Lord had said to them, "I will not drive them out from before thee in one year; lest the land become desolate, and the beast of the field multiply against thee" (Exod. 23:29). The Law of Moses made provision for hunting for food. "And whatsoever man there be of the children of Israel, or of the strangers that sojourn among you, which hunteth and catcheth any beast or fowl that may be eaten; he shall even pour out the blood thereof, and cover it with dust" (Lev. 17:13).

Hunting to protect the sheep. Hunting has been undertaken through the years in Palestine of necessity as a means of protecting the flocks of sheep and goats. In Bible times the chief enemies of the sheep included the lion, the bear, the leopard, the wolf, and the hyaena. The shepherd's activities along these lines have already been dealt with.

Animals killed for food. Among the wild animals, different species of the deer were sought after especially by the Jewish hunters for food. It was venison that Isaac asked Esau to bring him (Gen. 27:3). The Law refers to the roebuck (gazelle) and the hart as being desired by Israel for meat (Deut. 12:15). The dinner table of King Solomon was served with the meat of harts, roebucks, and fallowdeer (I Kings 4:23).

Fowl killed for meat. God's wholesale supply of quail for Israel in the wilderness is indication of the popularity of that kind of meat among ancient hunters. The Arabs today have often captured quantities of this bird, and after much of the meat is consumed, the rest of it is preserved for future use by being split and then laid out for the sun to dry it.[18] This is just what Israel did with its excess supply of quail meat: "And they spread them all abroad for themselves round about the camp" (Num. 11:32). Doves and pigeons were also popular as food among the Israelites. Many of them were tamed, but wild ones were often sought after for food as well as for sacrificial purposes. The Bible speaks of their nesting in the clefts and holes of the rocks. "O my dove, that art in the clefts of the rock" (Cant. 2:14).

The methods used by hunters. In modern times, the use of the gun is gradually doing away with ancient customs of hunting with more primitive weapons in Bible lands. But the Bible has given us a clear picture of those methods which have been practiced for years. *Pitfalls* for larger animals were often employed. These pits were covered over with a thin covering of rushes and brush so as to hide their presence, and sometimes approaches were constructed to the place of the pit, which made it possible to force the animal into the hole.[19] The prophet Ezekiel tells of this method of catching a lion. "And she brought up one of her whelps: it became a young lion, and it learned to catch the prey; it devoured men. The nations also heard of him; he was taken in their pit" (Ezek. 19:3, 4).

Some animals such as the wild bull or antelope were sometimes caught by using a *net*. Isaiah mentions this method. "As

a wild bull [antelope] in a net" (Isa 51:20). The net used by
the Hebrews was probably of two varieties. The one was
long and had several ropes and was supported on poles that
were forked and were of different lengths according to the
inequalities of the ground which the net covered. The other
type of net was smaller and was utilized in order to stop
gaps.[20]

When the pitfall or net was not used, then the hunter made
use of one of the following methods: the arrows, slingstones,
the spear, or the dart. All of these are referred to in the Lord's
message to the patriarch Job: "The arrow cannot make him
flee: the slingstones are turned with him into stubble. Darts
are counted as stubble: he laugheth at the shaking of a spear"
(Job 41:28–29).

In catching birds, the *snare* was often used. David was evidently acquainted with bird traps, for he compared his escape
from his enemies to the escape of a bird from a trap. "Our soul
is escaped as a bird out of the snare of the fowlers: the snare
is broken, and we are escaped" (Psa. 124:7). This bird trap was
made in two parts and when set, and spread upon the ground,
was fastened slightly by means of a trap stick. When the bird
touched this stick, the parts flew up and enclosed the bird in
the net.[21]

Hide-outs for wild animals. Palestine and Syria have their
hide-outs for wild animals and fowl. Wild beasts have lived in
the wild parts of the Lebanon Mountains to the north of the
Holy Land through the years, but this was more the source
of these animals for Syria rather than for the main part of
Palestine itself. The marshes immediately north of Lake
Merom have through the centuries been the haunt of many
waterfowl, and the reeds thereby have provided lairs for various animals, especially the wild buffalo. When Herod the
Great was a young man he used to come here to hunt game.[22]
Today, the Jews are busy draining much of this swampland
that it may be used for agricultural purposes. The principal

hide-out for wild animals that bother the citizens of Palestine, and especially Judea and Samaria, is the *Zor* of the Jordan Valley. The Jordan Valley between the Sea of Galilee and the Dead Sea is called by the Arabs, *The Ghor*, i.e., "the Rift." Within the *Ghor* is a narrow and deep valley called *The Zor*, in the center of which the river flows. For much of this distance *the Zor* is a jungle of tropical plants, shrubs, and trees. It is thus a hideout for all kinds of wild animals. During the part of the year when the river overflows, the wild beasts are driven from their haunts, but return there when the river recedes.[23] Most of the wild animals that have raided the habitable parts of Palestine through its history have come from these haunts in Jordan Valley. Thus Jeremiah says: "Behold, he shall come up like a lion from the swelling of Jordan against the habitation of the strong" (Jer. 49:19). The scene of the temptation of Jesus was doubtless the Wilderness of Judea. Mark says of Jesus: "And he . . . was with the wild beasts" (Mark 1:13). Quite probably most of these animals had come up from the *Zor* which was near at hand.

FISHERMEN

Places for fishing. In Palestine the main fishing places have been along the Mediterranean coast, and in the Sea of Galilee, with some little done in the streams of water. The Israelites in the wilderness said: "We remember the fish, which we did eat in Egypt" (Num. 11:5). Most interest centers in the Galilee fishing, because of the Gospel incidents connected with the Lord Jesus and his early fishermen disciples. The Jews engaged in a large fishing business in the days of Jesus in the waters of Galilee. A few years ago A. C. Haddad, a native of Syria and a twentieth century resident of Palestine, counted sixty men, all of them Arabs, as earning their living as Peter did, by fishing in the Sea of Galilee.[24] Their methods of work have been very similar to those used

Galilee Fishermen

by the disciples of Jesus. Such methods will fast disappear from this region now, since the new state of Israel controls this body of water, and up-to-date Western fishing equipment is taking the place of former more primitive methods. The new government has subsidized the fishing industry on Galilee.

Angling. It is not thought probable that the disciples in Galilee used this method of fishing very extensively. That it was used on occasions is seen from the account of Peter's catching a fish with a hook, and discovering the coin in its mouth with which he paid the temple tax (Matt. 17:27). Isaiah speaks of it in connection with fishing in the streams: "The fishers also shall mourn, and all they that cast angle into the brooks shall lament" (Isa. 19:8). Amos makes reference to this type of fishing when he says, "He will take you away with hooks, and your posterity with fishhooks" (Amos 4:2). The excavation at the mound of Gezer brought to light an actual fishhook, indicating the ancient use of the angling method of fishing.[25]

Spearing of fish. The book of Job refers to this method of fishing. "Canst thou fill his skin with barbed irons? or his head with fish spears?" (Job 41:7). That such method was practiced in Egypt is proven by inscriptions picturing Egyptians using fishing-spears.[26]

The cast net, or hand net. Two of the disciples were busy with such a net when Jesus called them to be fishers of men. "Now as he walked by the Sea of Galilee, he saw Simon and Andrew his brother casting a net into the sea: for they were fishers. And Jesus said unto them, Come ye after me, and I will make you to become fishers of men" (Mark 1:16, 17). This sort of net is in circular form about fifteen feet in diameter, with fine meshes. Around the edge it has lead sinkers. A long piece of line is attached to the center of the net. This line is held by the left hand, and the net is gathered up in the right hand, and is cast with a broad sweep of that arm over shallow water near the shore wherever a shoal of fish is observed to be. The middle of the net is then drawn by the cord, and the fisherman is able to wade into the water to get what he has caught.[27]

The dragnet, or drawnet. Jesus used this sort of fishing as the basis for one of his parables. "Again the kingdom of heaven is like unto a net, that was cast into the sea, and gathered of every kind: which, when it was full, they drew to shore, and sat down, and gathered the good into vessels, but cast the bad away" (Matt. 13:47, 48). This net is a long one, sometimes hundreds of feet in length and about eight feet broad. Ropes are furnished the ends of the net. Corks are attached along one of the long sides of the net to keep it buoyed up, whereas the other long side has lead sinkers attached to it to make it sink. Sometimes the net is set between two boats in the sea, being stretched between them. The boats are rowed so as to enclose a circular space and when the boats meet, then the net is hauled into the boats, the circle becoming smaller. The bottom rope is pulled in faster than the top one and thus the fish are enclosed in a bag and are pulled into the boats. Sometimes the net is set and then drawn from the land. The one end is then taken as far as possible by a boat seaward. Then this boat brings that end of the net around with a sweep to the place of starting, where men use the same method of pulling in the nets and landing the fish. Again, two boats sometimes stretch the net between them at a distance from shore, and then they will sweep in to the shore, forcing the fish to come with them. There must be no rocky obstructions for this method to be successful.[28]

This way of fishing illustrates the value of co-operative effort. A number of men will work together. Some of them will row the boats, some will have to pull the rope with great strength, and some will throw stones or in other ways seek to keep the fish from getting away by frightening them. As they get close to the shore, the edges of the net are held, and it is dragged to land and the fish must be seized. Afterward the fish caught are sorted, as indicated in the parable of Jesus. What an illustrative lesson this is in co-operative soul-winning![29]

Fishing at night. Galilee fishermen often have fished at night. They light their way with a blazing torch, and sighting fish they let fly their fishing spear, or fling their net into the sea.[30] But sometimes they fish all night with no results, as was the case with Simon Peter and his comrades. "Master, we have toiled all the night, and have taken nothing" (Luke 5:5).

The location of shoals. A Galilee fisherman was seen one day to use his hand net as he waded into the waters of the sea. He cast his net several times and it came up empty. But presently the man's companion on the shore shouted to him to cast to the left, and when this was done, the net was drawn up with fish in it. Shoals of fish are sometimes seen by those on the shore when they are hidden from the view of the fishermen in the water.[31] Such was what happened with Jesus and his disciples as reported by John: "But when the morning was now come, Jesus stood on the shore: but the disciples knew not that it was Jesus. Then Jesus saith unto them, Children, have ye any meat? They answered him, No. And he said unto them, Cast the net on the right side of the ship, and ye shall find. They cast therefore, and now they were not able to draw it for the multitude of fishes" (John 21:4–6). This ability to see from the shore what the fishermen in a boat fail to see, does not do away with a miracle taking place with the disciples. It was the power of Jesus that brought the great number of fish to the particular spot where the disciples could catch them in their nets.[32]

MASONS

Expert masons have always been in demand in Bible lands through the years. The building of house walls and terrace walls usually called for stone or brick. This trade is of interest to the student of Scripture because of the numerous illustrative references to it in the Bible.

Foundations and cornerstones. In building foundations it is important to get down to rock or otherwise the shrinkage and expansion due to the summer heat and the winter rains will do damage to the construction. Jesus tells of a good mason who "digged deep, and laid the foundation on a rock" (Luke 6:48). Deep trenches are dug, and filled with stone and lime, and this is allowed to settle all it will. All this being below the surface of the ground is invisible afterwards, and therefore it is considered a lack of courtesy for one man to build upon another man's foundation, as Paul mentions (Rom. 15:20). The cornerstone is another important part of the mason's work of which Scripture speaks. When the first layer of oblong stones is laid on the foundation, a broad square stone is selected for each corner where two walls meet. A thinner square block is usually put at each corner of the top rows of stones where the roof-beams are to rest. When trimming the oblong stones forming the bulk of the walls, it is easy for the mason to pass by the stone suitable for the cornerstone because of its uninviting shape. Thus the Psalmist said: "The stone which the builders refused is become the head stone of the corner" (Psa. 118:22).[33]

The mason's equipment. The plumbline is composed of a small inverted lead cone which is fastened by a cord to a cylindrical piece of wood made of the same diameter. The mason puts the wood to the newly set stone, and the suspended lead should barely touch the wall. To be a permanent one, every wall must stand the test of the plumbline. The prophet Amos compared the Lord's test of Israel to the mason's use of a plumbline. "Behold, I will set a plumbline in the midst of my people Israel" (Amos 7:8). The prophet Ezekiel describes a man making use of a measuring reed (Ezek. 40:3). This was used by a mason in laying the foundation and in the construction of the walls. It is a straight cane around twenty feet long, and is used to measure wall spaces, especially between windows and doors. Sometimes a shorter reed is also used. The prophets said of the Lord, "I will stretch over Jerusalem the line of Samaria" (II Kings 21:13). Evidently this was a leveling line which was strung from stones at each end of the wall being built. It was used in conjunction with the plumbline.[34]

METAL WORKERS

A study of working with metal would need to begin with "Tubal-cain, the forger of every cutting instrument of brass [copper] and iron" (Gen. 4:22, A. R. V.). The Orientals who lived three to four thousand years ago were very advanced in the mechanical arts. Some of the work of those skilled ancient workmen, as brought to light by archaeologists, is superior to anything the world has produced since.[35]

Blacksmiths. In the days of King Saul the Philistines put a ban on Hebrew blacksmiths. "Now there was no smith found throughout all the land of Israel: for the Philistines said, Lest the Hebrews make them swords or spears" (I Sam. 13:19). The Philistines required the Hebrews to bring their coulters and mattocks to the vicinity of Ramle to be sharpened, and this district in the Valley of Ajalon for many years afterward came to be known as the Valley of Smiths.[36] But Jewish blacksmiths were active in the days of Isaiah, for he said: "The smith with the tongs both worketh in the coals, and fashioneth it with hammers" (Isa. 44:12). Isaiah refers to the blacksmith's anvil (Isa. 41:7), and Jeremiah makes mention of his bellows (Jer. 6:29). The primitive type of anvil that has been in use for centuries is simply a cube of iron that has been inserted in a block of oak log. The old type of bellows, which is worked by hand, is made of the skin either of a goat or of a cow with the hair left on it.[37]

Coppersmiths. Moses described the land of Canaan as being "a land whose stones are iron, and out of whose hills thou mayest dig brass [copper]" (Deut. 8:9). Deposits of copper and iron have been discovered along the length of Wadi Araba which leads to the Gulf of Akaba. An excavation at Tel el Kheleifeh, which is the site of ancient Ezion-geber, King Solomon's port city, has revealed that some of Solomon's copper and iron refineries were located there. The builders of the smelters at Ezion-geber faced their furnaces toward the prevailing wind which was northwest. Winds that continued steadily blew through flue holes and kept the fire in the furnace rooms burning. Thus in those days the same principle essentially was employed as that of the Bessemer blast furnace of modern times.[38] Solomon must have carried on a thriving business in copper. Scripture says: "And the pots, and the shovels, and the basons: and all these vessels, which Hiram made to King Solomon for the house of the Lord, were of bright brass [i.e., burnished copper]" (I Kings 7:45).

Silversmiths and goldsmiths. Nehemiah mentions the presence of goldsmiths (Neh. 3:8), and the most famous example of a silversmith is Demetrius, whose business was interfered with by the evangelistic work of the Apostle Paul (Acts 19:24). The Apostle Peter used the goldsmith's task as an illustration of the trial of the Christian's faith. "That the trial of your faith, being much more precious than of gold that perisheth . . . might be found unto praise and honor" (I Pet. 1:7). The apostle is describing an old-time goldsmith who places his crude ore in a crucible and then applies the heat to melt it. When the impurities come to the surface they are skimmed off. When the workman is able to see his face reflected clearly in the surface of the molten liquid, he takes it away from the fire, and knows that he has pure gold left.[39]

Tanners and Dyers

The tanning business. This has always been an important business in Bible lands. Peter stayed at the house of Simon the tanner when he was at Joppa (Acts 9:43). In recent years the important tanneries have been located at Hebron and at Jaffa. Sheepskins are sometimes used for making shoe leather, although goatskin leather is generally considered to be superior to that made from sheepskins. Goatskins are used largely for the making of bottles for carrying water or other liquids. Except for the neck, legs, and tail, the goatskins are stripped off whole. The holes where the legs and tail were located are sewn up, and the end where the neck was, becomes the mouth of the bottle. These goatskins when laid out in rows for the sun to cure them, look much like pigs with head and legs missing. Sheepskins are treated in a similar way and made soft, and then they are dyed a yellow or red color when used in the making of shoes.[40]

Oriental dyeing. The Orientals have some very fine dyes. Their favorite color is a brilliant crimson, and the dye they use to make this color comes from a worm or grub that feeds on oak and other plants. Indigo is made from the rind of pomegranate. Purple is made from the murex shellfish which can still be found on the beach at the city of Acre.[41] Luke tells of Lydia, "a seller of purple, of the city of Thyatira" (Acts 16:14). She was a merchant who sold the purple dye to tanners, weavers, and others. This business of dyeing with which she was connected, had long been centered in the city of Thyatira. Inscriptions have been discovered that refer to "a guild of dyers" that was located in that vicinity.[42]

TENTMAKERS

Because of the large use of tents by the Hebrew people, there has been a great demand for tentmakers. Besides the ordinary tent used as a dwelling, many portable tents were made for the use of travelers. In New Testament times it was the custom to teach every Jewish boy some trade. As Jesus was a carpenter, so Paul was a tentmaker. Paul practiced this trade in company with Aquila at Corinth (Acts 18:1–3). Rough goat's hair was used in making these tents, and Paul had learned to cut the cloth straight, even as he did the "straight interpretation of God's word"[43] (cf. II Tim. 2:15). Dr. Edersheim says: "In Alexandria the different trades sat in the synagogue arranged into guilds, and St. Paul could have no difficulty in meeting in the bazaar of his trade with the like-minded Aquila and Priscilla with whom to find a lodging."[44]

MERCHANTS

The merchant's place of business. In the Oriental city or village, the market place is an important place for the doing of business. It is not always located in the same place. It may be near the city gates, or it may be in the open streets of the

Oriental Market Place

town. The market is not always in operation in some districts, but is open for business whenever there is something to be sold. The arrival in town of a camel caravan would be one great occasion for setting up the market place and the selling of produce, especially the "blessed grain."[45] Also, many goods are sold in the oriental bazaar. This is usually a covered arcade containing a row of narrow shops on each side, and those of like trade often having their shops together, such as those selling dry goods, grocery items, tin utensils, leather goods, sweetmeats, etc. Jeremiah speaks of the bakers' street (Jer. 37:21).

Oriental buying and selling. This is quite different from purchasing in the West. No fixed price is put upon whatever is to be sold. Ordinarily the buyer must expect to spend from a few minutes to an hour or so to complete a purchase. The merchant begins by asking a high price and the buyer by offering a low price. Then the bargaining continues in earnest. To a stranger this process of "striking a bargain" is a tedious one indeed, but the true Orientals enjoy it greatly. Among them, haggling over prices, and controversy, argument, and excitement usually become heated.[46] When the sale is made, the buyer will go away to boast of his splendid bargain, and will be greatly admired by the seller. The Book of Proverbs pictures such a purchaser: "It is bad, it is bad, saith the buyer; but when he is gone his way, then he boasteth" (Prov. 20:14, A. R. V.).

Payment for goods. Payment is not always in cash or coins for goods purchased. Barter and trade originally took the place of money. There was exchange of goods in kind. In early Old Testament times the giving of money took the form of weighing precious metals to be given the seller. Thus "Abraham weighed to Ephron the silver, which he had named in the audience of the sons of Heth" (Gen. 23:16). This was the purchase price for the Cave of Machpelah. Concerning the money in the sacks of Joseph's brethren, Scripture says: "Every man's money was in the mouth of his sack, our money in full weight" (Gen. 43:21). The first coins did not appear until about 700 B. C. The New Testament refers to the coinage of the Roman Empire which was in general use in those days for business transactions. But the Oriental seller does not always receive cash. Debt is common among many. Sometimes a poor peasant will sow seed he has borrowed, on borrowed land, using borrowed tools, and will even live in a borrowed house.[47] The parable Jesus told of the unjust steward refers to men who owed their lord various amounts such as "an hundred measures of oil," and "an hundred measures of wheat" (Luke 16:5–7).

Oriental method of measuring grain. In selling grain in Bible lands it is the custom that each measure must run over.

Likewise such liquids as oil or milk should run over a small amount into the buyer's vessel. A bushel measure is used for measuring the grain. As this measure begins to be full to the brim, the grain is pressed down, and then two or three shakes are given from side to side to settle the grain. The man who is doing the measuring then puts more grain on top, and repeats the shaking process until the measure is actually full clear to the brim. He then presses gently on the grain and makes a small hollow place on top and taking additional handfuls of grain he makes a cone on the surface. He builds up the cone until it can hold no more, some of it beginning to run over. Following this the grain is emptied into the buyer's container. Such is Oriental measure.[48] Jesus said, "Give, and it shall be given you; good measure, pressed down, and shaken together, running over, shall they give into your bosom [lap]. For with what measure ye mete it shall be measured to you again" (Luke 6:38, cf. A. R. V.). The word translated "bosom" should be "lap," because it is not in his bosom but in the skirt of his garment that there is ample room, and there the Oriental carries his grain, like a woman among us might carry things in her folded apron.[49]

MONEY-CHANGERS AND BANKERS

Money-changers. Although the modern section of Jerusalem has had its Western type of banks with capital running into the millions of dollars, the old section of the city has always had its money-changers. These men change people's money from one type of currency to another, and also provide change within the same currency. The money-changer sits beside the narrow street and behind a little glass-top table, under which his coins are on display. A charge of about ten per cent is made for the transaction. This profession has been necessary because of the great variety of coinage in Palestine and Syria, and also because of so many tourists from all over the world.[50]

In the days of Jesus, the money-changers sat in the spacious Court of the Gentiles, or in one of the adjoining porches of the Jerusalem temple, and carried on their business there. When the Jewish nation was numbered, it was required by the law of Moses that every male Israelite who was twenty years or older, pay into the temple treasury a half-shekel as an offering to the Lord (Exod. 30:13-15). This had to be paid by using the exact Hebrew half-shekel, and the money-changer provided the right coins for the multitudes that came to Jerusalem for the feasts. The Jewish Talmud says that the rate of twelve per cent was charged by the changers for each transaction. In addition to the need for the half-shekel tribute money, the money-changers would provide the exact coins necessary to purchase the animals or doves required for the sacrifices for the temple. It has been estimated that these changers would reap a profit of from forty to forty-five thousand dollars.[51] The business of money-changing was considered to be a legitimate business, although there were unscrupulous practices connected with it, but Jesus condemned these men largely because of bringing their business into the temple courts where men should have come in the spirit of true prayer and worship.

Bankers. Borrowing money at a rate of interest has been practiced in Palestine in modern times among the natives. Two references from Jesus indicate it was done in his day: "Thou oughtest therefore to have put my money to the exchangers, and then at my coming I should have received mine own with usury [interest]" (Matt. 25:27). "Wherefore then gavest not thou my money into the bank, that at my coming I might have required mine own with usury [interest]" (Luke 19:23).

The Greek word for *bank* means "table" or "bench" across which the money was paid out or received. The Phoenicians invented the money-lending system, and it was in full operation in the various provinces of the Roman Empire in Christ's time. The law of Moses did not allow the Israelites to lend to one another upon interest (Deut. 23:19, etc.). But it did allow them to charge interest upon loans made to Gentiles (Deut. 23:20). Jesus did not here condemn the charging of interest by a bank, for the word translated "usury" should be translated "interest."[52]

TAXGATHERERS

Taxcollection under the Turkish government. In the days when the Turkish government controlled Palestine, a system of farming out import and export duties, excise taxes, and government produce tithes, was in force. A company would guarantee the government a certain sum for a tax, and then, having the monopoly of this, would charge the public enough to make sure a good profit for the deal. Much oppression and injustice was fostered by such a system, but it was continued so long that the public finally accepted it as a necessary evil.[53]

Taxcollection under the Roman Empire. A somewhat similar system to the Turkish system was in operation in the Roman Empire in New Testament times. The office of *publican,* or *taxcollector,* was in itself legitimate enough, as it was necessary to have government taxes, and important to collect them. But there was resentment on the part of the Jews against paying taxes to a Gentile government. This resentment was increased all the more because among these taxcollectors there was much graft and oppression, as charged by John the Baptist: "Then came also publicans to be baptized, and said unto him, Master, what shall we do? And he said unto them, Exact no more than that which is appointed you" (Luke 3:12, 13). Because of this situation, the publicans came to be associated by the Jews with notorious sinners. Such expressions as "the publicans and the harlots," and "publicans and sinners" were in common use among them (Matt. 9:11; 21:31). Because Jesus sought to be friendly with, and bring help to, the lowest of men, certain men of His day gave Him the title, "friend of publicans and sinners" (Matt. 11:19).

Matthew was a publican who had his customs office not far from Capernaum on the road from Damascus to Acre, where he could examine the goods of travelers along this highway, and could collect the required taxes. Holding this office he had of necessity to violate the Pharisaical Sabbath observances, and would therefore cause wrath to be upon him. But Jesus called Matthew to follow Him. "And saw a publican, named Levi, sitting at the receipt of custom: and he said unto him, Follow me" (Luke 5:27). Zaccheus was not an ordinary taxcollector, but rather a taxcommissioner, who farmed out a whole district, and had other taxcollectors under his jurisdiction. His conversion was so thorough that he agreed, "If I have taken anything from any man by false accusation, I restore him fourfold" (Luke 19:8).[54]

PHYSICIANS

Physicians among Orientals today. Orientals have two names for their men who practice the art of healing. They call him "the wise man," and also term him, "the holy man." The first title indicates the skill they think necessary in him, and the second shows their belief that a holy man has power from God to heal. Often one after another doctors are summoned, which reminds one of the poor woman who "had suffered many things of many physicians" (Mark 5:26), before she was healed by Jesus. The most common ailments from which the people of the East suffer include: eye infections, skin diseases, consumption, and malarial and typhoidal fevers. The Orientals have a proverb which emphasizes the importance they attach to faith: "Have faith, though it be only in a stone, and you will recover." They have a strong conviction that, although they believe it a duty to use what means are available, the real power to heal is Divine.[55]

Physicians in Old Testament times. Physicians were present from early Bible times. The Code of Hammurabi, under which Abraham grew up as a young man in Babylonia, specified that if a surgeon should operate on a man's eye, using a copper lancet, and the man should lose his eye because of the operation, then the doctor's eye should be put out with a copper lancet.[56] Job talks of "physicians of no value" (Job 13:4) when referring to his friends who were trying to comfort him. The law of Moses contained an ordinance providing that a man wounded in a brawl should have his loss of time paid for by the one responsible for his wounds, and adds, "and shall cause him to be thoroughly healed" (Exod. 21:19). Circumcision was an operation in surgery. The Sacred Writer indicates that King Asa put his confidence in physicians instead of the Lord when he reports: "And Asa in the thirty and ninth year of his reign was diseased in his feet, until his disease was exceeding great: yet in his disease he sought not to the Lord, but to the physicians. And Asa slept with his fathers" (II Chron. 16:12, 13).

Physicians in New Testament times. In New Testament times there were many physicians. Among them were, no doubt, many who were not worthy of the name. Concerning the poor woman who had been to many doctors, Mark adds, "and was nothing bettered, but rather grew worse" (Mark 5:26), indicating that these physicians had harmed her rather than helped her. But there were sincere practicing physicians, and Luke was a notable example. In his Epistle to the Colossians, Paul called him: "Luke, the beloved physician" (Col. 4:14). In the ruins of the city of Pompeii, there "was found a number of instruments exactly such as our best surgeons now use."[57] The Bible recognizes the presence of physicians, but does not give a prominent place to them. God's power to heal sickness is emphasized in both the Old and New Testaments. (*See also* Sickness in Bible Lands, Chapter 16.)

CHAPTER 23

Vocal and Instrumental Music

ORIGIN OF MUSICAL INSTRUMENTS

JUBAL, THE PIONEER MUSI-
CIAN. Concerning him Scripture says: "He was the father of all such as handle the harp and pipe" (Gen. 4:21, A. R. V.). Doubtless this means he was the inventor of these musical instruments, and as he was not many generations removed from Adam, we may infer that music has always played an important role in the history of mankind.

Babylonian musical instruments preceding Abraham. Since Abraham spent his early life in Ur of the Chaldees, it is more than likely that some of the musical instruments used by the patriarchs had their origin in that land. Woolley's excavations at Ur brought to light from one of the death pits in connection with a royal tomb, four harps or lyres, one of which was a magnificent specimen. The artistic beauty of these gold and mosaic musical instruments emphasizes the fact that the musical art was at a high level in those ancient days.[1] A cylinder-seal of a queen of the land of Abraham's birth, who reigned about a thousand years before his time, reveals the fact that *timbrels* were being used at banquets and at religious gatherings.[2] Jacob's father-in-law Laban, lived in Babylonian territory, and when Jacob left him in haste, he said to

229

him: "Wherefore didst thou flee away secretly . . . that I might have sent thee away with mirth, and with songs, with tabret, and with harp?" (Gen. 31:27). This suggests the possibility that some of these musical instruments as used in Babylonia found their way into the life of the early Hebrews.

Egyptian musical instruments influencing Moses and Israel. Moses received a thorough education at the hands of the Egyptians, and music was an important part of his training. Music was greatly emphasized in Egyptian religious services. The following instruments were used by them: the harp, the lyre, the flute, the tambourine, and cymbals. Dancing was commonly connected with the use of musical instruments.[3] Some phases of Egyptian musical customs most probably followed the Israelites from Egypt into the land of Canaan.

MUSICAL CELEBRATION OF RED SEA VICTORY

After the miraculous crossing of Israel through the Red Sea, the victory over the Egyptians was fittingly celebrated with music. "And Miriam the prophetess, the sister of Aaron, took a timbrel in her hand; and all the women went out after her with timbrels and with dances" (Exod. 15:20). There was the singing of a song, the words of which Moses gives us. This was accompanied by the use of the timbrel, and along with it was dancing. This timbrel was a circular hoop, made of either wood or brass, and covered with skin tightly drawn, and with small bells hung around it.[4]

ISRAEL'S USE OF TRUMPETS

The trumpets as used by the Hebrews were in three forms. The earliest form was made from the horn of an ox or a ram. A second form was a curved metallic trumpet. And a later form was the straight trumpet, a representation of which is seen on the Arch of Titus.[5] Moses was commanded of the Lord to make two silver trumpets which were to be sounded forth "for the calling of the assembly, and for the journeying of the camps" (Num. 10:2). Also God told them: "If ye go to war in your land against the enemy that oppresseth you, then ye shall blow an alarm with the trumpets" (Num 10:9). The fiftieth year, or the Year of Jubilee, was ushered in on the Day of Atonement by the blowing of the trumpets (Lev. 25:8, 9). Throughout the history of Israel, trumpets were used to gather the people together in times of war that they might go to battle, and usually in times of peace that they might come to the sanctuary for the purpose of divine worship.

SPECIAL OCCASIONS FOR THE USE OF MUSIC

Among the Hebrews, vocal and instrumental music together with dancing were employed on most occasions of great joy. Victories in battle were thus celebrated. In this way the women of Israel celebrated the victory of young David and the army of Saul over the Philistines. "And it came to pass as they came, when David returned from the slaughter of the Philistines, that the women came out of all the cities of Israel, singing and dancing, to meet King Saul, with timbrels, with joy, and with instruments of music" (I Sam. 18:6, A. R. V.). At the coronation of the boy King Joash, music was prominent. "And all the people of the land rejoiced, and blew trumpets, the singers also played on instruments of music, and led the singing of praise" (II Chron. 23:13, A. R. V.). Music was also part of the entertainment at banquets. "And the harp, and the viol, the tabret, and pipe, and wine, are in their feasts." Thus wrote Isaiah about the feasts of his day (Isa. 5:12).

THE PROPHETS' USE OF MUSICAL INSTRUMENTS

Beginning with Samuel, the prophets of Israel made much use of music and musical instruments in connection with their prophesying. Samuel told Saul, "Thou shalt meet a company of prophets coming down from the high place with a psaltery, and a tabret, and a pipe, and a harp, before them; and they shall prophesy" (I Sam. 10:5). Music helped to create the right atmosphere for spiritual exercises of devotion. Concerning Elisha the prophet it was said: "But now bring me a minstrel. And it came to pass, when the minstrel played, that the hand of the Lord came upon him" (II Kings 3:15).

THE CONTRIBUTION OF DAVID TO THE MUSIC OF ISRAEL

David the boy musician. Through the centuries Palestine shepherd boys have played their simple dual-piped flutes made of reed, in the presence of their flocks. The strains of the music are minor, but it appeals to both the shepherd and the sheep. No doubt David's musical experience began with this instrument, when he cared for the family flock. But in addition to playing on this shepherd's instrument, young David became famed for his ability to use what our Bible versions have called "a harp." Now the instrument was not large enough to be like what Westerners today would call a harp. It would be more appropriate to call it "a lyre." Such an instrument is actually a modified form of harp, being portable. The sound-chest forms the base of it. "From the end of this arise two rods curved or straight connected above by a cross-piece, and the strings are stretched upward from the base to the crosspiece."[6] When Saul's servants were asked to look for someone who could play on this instrument with ability, one of their number said: "I have seen a son of Jesse the Bethlehemite, that is cunning in playing" (I Sam. 16:18). And thus David came to play for King Saul when he had one of his fits of sadness, in order to refresh him.

David the writer and collector of psalms. David not only played on instruments, he also under all kinds of situations, penned beautiful psalms that helped to make up the Hebrew hymn book, we call the Book of Psalms. He drew upon his boyhood experiences to write his immortal Shepherd Psalm (Psa. 23). He wrote of his experiences when he fled from the hand of King Saul and hid in a cave (Psa. 57). And he celebrated the deliverance which the Lord gave him over all his enemies by writing Psalm 18. When he repented of his great sin, he gave to the world his Penitential Psalm (Psa. 51). Thus in writing down under the Spirit's inspiration his personal experiences, men and women through the centuries have been spiritually blessed. But it must be remembered that these Psalms of David (and of other Hebrews) were originally *songs of Israel*. No doubt many of the Psalms not written by David were collected by him and inserted in the king's musical selection of poems for use in divine worship.

David the originator of certain musical instruments. The chronicler of the Hebrew kings says of David, "Four thousand praised the Lord with the instruments which I made, said David, to praise therewith" (I Chron. 23:5). And again, "And the Levites stood with the instruments of David" (II Chron. 29:26). Either King David was himself the inventor of these instruments for worship, or at least he was responsible for their invention, for they were called his instruments.

David the organizer of Hebrew musical worship. It would appear that the Hebrew liturgy for many years following David's life was what was originally prescribed by him. The musical service rendered by the Levites in the worship of the sanctuary was organized by David. He was responsible for appointing certain ones to this task. "And with them Heman and Jeduthun with trumpets and cymbals for those that should make a sound, and with musical instruments of God" (I Chron. 16:42). We are told that Heman had fourteen sons and three daughters. And "all these were under the hands of their father for song in the house of the Lord, with cymbals, psalteries, and harps, for the service of the house of God, according to the king's order to Asaph, Jeduthun, and Heman. So the number of them, with their brethren that were instructed in the songs of the Lord, even all that were cunning, was two hundred fourscore and eight" (I Chron. 25:6, 7). No doubt these singers and players sang psalms accompanied by instruments. When King David became organizer and director of Hebrew sacred music, it may be said that he made his nation famous for its music for years to come.[7]

CHARACTER OF SOME OLD TESTAMENT
MUSICAL INSTRUMENTS

It has already been indicated that the Old Testament word "harp" is better rendered "lyre." The word "organ" is translated by the Revisers "pipe," and is more like our *flute* than any other instrument. The "psaltery" and "viol" are stringed instruments, there being much uncertainty concerning their exact nature. "The cymbal consisted of two large and broad plates of brass, of a convex form; which being struck against each other, made a hollow ringing sound. They form in our days, a part of every military band."[8] The "dulcimer" (Dan. 3:5) is rendered in the margin (A. R. V.), "bagpipe."

SOME SONGS OF THE HEBREW BIBLE

In addition to the Book of Psalms, there are numerous Hebrew poems that were originally sung as songs and are now a part of the Hebrew Bible. Some editions of the Scriptures print these in poetic form. The Song sung by Moses and Miriam at the Red Sea is one such a song (Exod. 15). When God gave Israel water in the wilderness, they sang the Song of the Well (Num. 21:17, 18). And Moses put his final warnings and instructions to Israel into a song which he taught them (Deut. 32). The Song of Deborah (Judges 5) was sung in order to celebrate a victory over the Canaanites. The Song of Hannah (I Sam. 2) was sung as a mother's thanksgiving for the birth of her son Samuel. And the Song of Solomon was a song celebrating the love between the Lord and Israel His bride. Other songs might be added to this list.

ABSENCE OF MUSIC IN THE CAPTIVITY

In predicting the judgment of the captivity days for Israel because of her sins, the prophet said: "The mirth of tabrets ceaseth, the noise of them that rejoice endeth, the joy of the harp ceaseth" (Isa. 24:8). Music largely ceased among the captive Hebrews in Babylonia. The exiles composed a psalm in which they said:

> By the rivers of Babylon, there we sat down, yea, we wept, when we remembered Zion. We hanged our harps (lyres) upon the willows in the midst thereof. For there they that carried us away captive required of us a song; and they that wasted us required of us mirth, saying, Sing us one of the songs of Zion. How shall we sing the Lord's song in a strange land? If I forget thee, O Jerusalem, let my right hand forget her cunning (Psa. 137:1-5).

The Babylonian captors had heard of the songs of Zion for which Jerusalem was noted, and asked their captives to sing one of them for them. But the Jewish religious singing was so vitally connected with the temple of Jerusalem that they refused to sing such a song in a foreign land.

REFERENCES TO MUSIC IN THE LIFE OF JESUS

There are four references to music in the ministry of Jesus.[9] The first of these has to do with music used in mourning the death of a loved one. When Jesus came into the home where the ruler's daughter had died, Matthew says: "He saw the flute-players" (Matt. 9:23, A. R. V.). In the Orient even today, professional mourners are called in to express sorrow for the loss of the deceased one. And if the family can afford to do so, as would be true of the ruler, flute-players are also brought in to express mourning through these instruments.[10]

A second reference is when Jesus spoke of the children playing in the market place. "We played the wedding march for you, but you did not dance. We sang the funeral dirge, but you did not mourn" (Luke 7:32, Williams). There are two groups of children represented here. One of them has a pipe, perhaps a shepherd's flute, and plays upon it as is done at a wedding procession all the way to the feast, saying: "Let's play wedding." But the other group refuses to join in the play. Then the one group begins to sing and wail as is done in a funeral procession, suggesting, "Let's play funeral," but the other group continues obstinately to refuse to co-operate.

A third reference to music is in Christ's famous story of the Prodigal Son. When the wayward boy returned home, his father celebrated with a banquet. And when the elder brother came in from the field it is said "he heard music and dancing" (Luke 15:25). It was customary at banquets to have singers and players on instruments, especially flute-players, along with dancers.

The fourth reference is what happened at the end of the Last Supper. The record reads: "And when they had sung an hymn, they went out into the Mount of Olives" (Mark 14:26). Unquestionably what Jesus and his disciples sang was from the Psalms. It was the custom of the Jews to sing at the close of the Passover meal Psalms 115 to 118. The manner of singing was what we would call chanting, and the music itself was in the minor key. Orthodox Jews today observe similar customs.[11]

New Testament Songs and Music

The New Testament contains a number of songs, not all of which are ordinarily considered to be songs. There is the Magnificat, or Song of Mary, sung in anticipation of the birth of Jesus (Luke 1:46–55); and the Benedictus, or Song of Zacharias, sung after the birth of John the Baptist (Luke 1:67–79); and the Song of the Angels, sung to the Bethlehem shepherds upon the birth of Jesus (Luke 2:14); the Apostle Paul's Hymn of Redemption (Eph. 1:3–14)[12]; and a Hymn of the Early Church (I Tim. 3:16). John's book of Revelation contains several references to songs and music. "A new song" is sung in Heaven in chapter 5:9, 10. "The Song of Moses" and "The Song of the Lamb" are sung in chapter 15:3, 4. Babylon's fall is described graphically, and concerning it John said: "And the voice of harpers, and musicians, and of pipers, and trumpeters, shall be heard no more at all in thee" (Rev. 18:22).

In his vision of Heaven John "heard the voice of harpers harping with their harps," and a song was sung before God's throne (Rev. 14:2, 3). The word for "harp" used here is not the equivalent of the Old Testament word, more correctly rendered "lyre," which was a portable harp. Rather it is indeed a harp, the music of which is sweeter than that of earth's most beautiful instruments.

CHAPTER 24

The Oriental Town or City

WALLS

DIFFERENCE BETWEEN CITY AND VILLAGE, AS TO WALLS. In early Old Testament times the *villages* were smaller places of abode without walls around them, whereas the *cities* or *towns* were larger places that had walls around them. The Mosaic Law made such a distinction: "If a man sell a dwelling house in a walled city" (Lev. 25:29). "But the houses of the villages which have no wall round about them" (Lev. 25:31). The villages were often located near a fortified city upon which they were more or less dependent. Thus the city was the metropolis of the villages. We often read in the Bible of "cities and their villages," and sometimes a literal translation would give us the expression: "cities and their daughters," indicating a mother-city, and her dependent villages surrounding her (cf. Joshua 15:45 and 17:11, A. R. V. margin).[1]

Walls a part of city fortifications. In Bible times most cities were walled and fortified for protection against an enemy. Those living in a city without walls would be interested in having walls built for them. Often when the Bible says that a certain character built a city, what is meant is not that a new site was located and a new city was built, but rather that a city already inhabited was supplied with walls entirely around its confines.[2] It was thus that Solomon built "Beth-horon the upper, and Beth-horon the nether, fenced cities, with walls, gates, and bars" (II Chron. 8:5).

GATES

Character of gates. The gates of an Oriental city were of course connected with the walls; nevertheless, they were in a sense a structure by themselves. They were usually made of wood or stone, or wood that had been armored with metal. The Psalmist speaks of gates of brass (copper), and gates of iron (Psa. 107:16). Often they were two-leaved (Isa. 45:1), and were provided with heavy locks and bars (I Sam. 23:7). Sometimes a city or town had two walls and therefore two gates with a space between them. A sentinel was stationed in

City Gates

the tower of the first gate. When David was at Mahanaim awaiting the result of the battle with Absalom, Scripture says: "And David sat between the two gates: and the watchman went up to the roof over the gate unto the wall, and lifted up his eyes, and looked, and behold a man running alone" (II Sam. 18:24). This space between the gates was used for many purposes.[3]

Gateway as a meeting-place. The gateways of ancient walled cities and the open spaces near them, were popular meeting places for the people. They seemed like large halls that could care for great assemblies of people. Being vaulted, they provided a cool place to meet on a hot day.[4]

Variety of uses for gates. These city gates had many uses. "The openings of the gates" are described by Proverbs as "the chief place of concourse" (Prov. 1:21). The city gate was used as a public gathering place for the giving of an address or proclamation. Concerning King Hezekiah it was said: "And he set captains of war over the people, and gathered them together to him in the street of the gate of the city, and spake comfortably to them" (II Chron. 32:6). David speaks of his persecutors gossiping about him at the city gates (Psa. 69:12). Mordecai sat in the king's gate in order to attract attention from the sovereign (Esther 2:21). The prophets often preached their sermons in the gates of the city. Thus the Lord told Jeremiah, "Go and stand in the gate of the children of the people, whereby the kings of Judah come in, and by the which they go out, and in all the gates of Jerusalem" (Jer. 17:19).

City gates a place for holding court. One of the most important uses of the gates of an ancient city was for holding court. Stone seats were provided for the judges. Thus Lot sat in the gate as a judge (Gen. 19:1). The city gates of those days would be like our modern courthouse. It was there that Boaz went to redeem the estate of Elimelech and thus receive Ruth to be his wife (Ruth 4:1). The prophet Amos preached to Israel to "establish judgment in the gate" (Amos 5:15). The Mosaic law recognized the city gates as the place of justice: "Judges and officers shalt thou make thee in all thy gates, which the Lord thy God giveth thee, throughout thy tribes, and they shall judge the people with just judgment" (Deut. 16:18). Thus it can be seen that one of the most important places in an ancient city was the gates of that city.[5]

Symbolic references to the city gates. The Bible often refers to the gates of the city in a symbolic way. Sometimes the gates are used to represent the city as a whole, as when the Lord said to Abraham, "Thy seed shall possess the gate of his enemies" (Gen. 22:17). The Psalmist was no doubt thinking of the temple gates when he said: "Open to me the gates of righteousness" (Psa. 118:19). It is customary for the city gates to be closed at sunset, and John alludes to this by way of contrast in his description of the New Jerusalem (Rev. 21:25).

TOWERS

The Oriental city has had two types of towers located in it. *First* was the tower constructed as a part of the city wall. At this point the wall was built higher and served as a fortification. The approach of an enemy could be sighted from here, and weapons hurled down upon men who attempted to take the city. Almost every gate of any consequence would have a tower over it. Then towers were often built where the wall turned a corner. These were called "corner towers." King Uzziah made use of such towers: "And he made in Jerusalem engines, invented by skilful men, to be on the towers and upon the battlements [A. R. V. margin: "corner towers"] to shoot arrows and great stones withal" (II Chron. 26:15). *Second* was a citadel tower or fortress which was built apart from the wall and on higher ground than the rest of the city, and thus served to defend the city. The tower of Shechem referred to in the story of Abimelech was doubtless this sort of tower (Judges 9:46).

STREETS

The words used in the Hebrew Bible for streets would indicate that there were three varieties of them. The usual street was long, narrow, and winding (Josh. 2:19 etc.). Those near the city gates or those in front of a public building, or where one crossed another were broad squares (Neh. 8:1). A third kind was the short street more like our alley (Prov. 7:8). As a rule, Eastern streets today are narrow, and everything would indicate that they were narrow in ancient times. In the cities some of them are paved (usually with stone), but in the villages they are seldom paved. David said, "I did cast them out as the dirt in the streets" (Psa. 18:42). Isaiah refers to the "mire of the streets" (Isa. 10:6). The city streets usually paved in Bible days would include those connected with the temple or some public building. The Oriental appreciates greatly the description of Heaven, "wherein the streets are paved with pure gold as it were transparent glass" (Rev. 21:21).[6]

THE MARKET PLACE

The market place is not only a place for the purchase of goods, it is also a place for the people to gather for many other purposes. It is one of the most popular places in an Oriental city. (See section on "Merchants" p. 221 f. especially: *The merchant's place of business*.)

The market place as a social gathering place. Business transactions are usually preceded by a social visit with the customer. The important people as well as the ordinary people love to come there and meet their friends and greet them in true Oriental fashion, which always takes much time. Jesus said to his disciples: "Beware of the scribes, which love to go in long clothing, and love salutations in the market places" (Mark 12:38). Discussions of various kinds are entered into at the market. The Apostle Paul took advantage of such an opportunity when he was at Athens. "Therefore disputed he

Heavily laden Porter

... in the market [place] daily with them that met with him" (Acts 17:17). The market place was an ideal location for heralding the gospel.[7]

The heavy-laden porter in the market place. In many Eastern cities, carriages or carts are not allowed to enter the city gates and carry loads to the market place. These loads of produce are carried by porters. These men are, as a rule, taken from the poorest of men. What a sight it is to see them laden down with tremendous burdens on their backs! Sometimes two of these porters will stand back to back with their loads locked together and thus rest their tired bodies for a time before proceeding on their way.[8]

Jesus condemned the lawyers of his day with words that doubtless refer to their treatment of these porters. "Woe unto you also, ye lawyers! for ye lade men with burdens grievous to be borne, and ye yourselves touch not the burdens with one of your fingers" (Luke 11:46). Perhaps Paul was thinking of porters when he said to the Galatians, "Bear ye one another's burdens, and so fulfill the law of Christ" (Gal. 6:2). And Jesus must have had in mind especially the poor porters of his day so laden down with burdens, when he gave that most gracious invitation, "Come unto me all ye that labor and are heavy laden, and I will give you rest" (Matt. 11:28).

Children in the market place. In the Orient children always love to go to the market place, where so many interesting things are happening. They watch with keen interest everything that happens there. They may play pranks, and of course they have their games. Jesus used a crowd of such youngsters as an illustration in one of his sermons. When the suggestion was made by some of them that they "play wedding," and later that they "play funeral," the rest of them balked at both suggestions. Jesus said: "But whereunto shall I liken this generation? It is like unto children sitting in the markets, and calling unto their fellows, and saying, We have piped unto you, and ye have not danced; we have mourned unto you, and ye have not lamented" (Matt. 11:16, 17).[9]

Laborers in the market place. In the Eastern city men who want employment stand in groups in the market place, waiting for someone to hire them. It was here that the man in the parable of Jesus went to secure workmen for his vineyard. "And he went out about the third hour, and saw others standing idle in the market place, and said unto them; Go ye also into the vineyard" (Matt. 20:3, 4). These men do not apply for work as is done in the Occident, rather they wait in the market place for some man to come and hire them.[10]

Rulers in the market place. At certain times members of the city council will be found there, and they will listen to the case of those who are in trouble. What is done there is of course unofficial because the real court is at the city gates, or

as we would say, the courthouse.[11] Paul and Silas were taken
before the magistrates in Philippi: "They caught Paul and
Silas, and drew them into the market place unto the rulers"
(Acts 16:19).

PRESENCE OF BEGGARS

In Eastern cities there are usually many beggars. *In Old
Testament times* the idea of a beggar going from door to door
to ask for alms was little known among the Jews. The law of
Moses provided for the needy by requiring that the Jews purposely leave some of the harvest for the poor. Also mortgaged
property was returned to the original owner at the year of
jubilee. However, beggars were not entirely unknown, for
Hannah speaks of them in her song of thanksgiving (I Sam.
2:8). The Psalmist promised that beggary would be the lot
of the wicked (Psa. 109:10), and also that the righteous would
be kept from the necessity for it (Psa. 37:25).[12]

In New Testament times beggars were usually the blind,
maimed, or diseased. Thus blind Bartimeus "sat by the highway side begging" (Mark 10:46). The impotent man "was carried, whom they laid daily at the gate of the temple which is
called Beautiful, to ask alms of them that entered into the
temple" (Acts 3:2). The beggar Lazarus, who was diseased,
was laid at the gate of "a certain rich man" (Luke 16:19, 20).
Thus did these needy ones ask alms of those who passed their
way. Today in the East a poor sick man is sometimes placed in
a booth alongside the door of a rich man's house, and lives by
means of the gifts of those who pass by him.[13]

CHAPTER 25

CustomsRegarding Property

MEASURING AND ALLOTTING THE LAND

MEASURING THE LAND. It has been the custom even in modern times in parts of northern Palestine and in the Plain of the Philistines to assign land periodically for farming purposes. The land thus assigned is measured by a cord.[1] The Psalmist indicates that this same method was used for measurement of the land of Canaan when it was assigned to the tribes of Israel. "He cast out the heathen also before them, and divided them an inheritance by line" (Psa. 78:55). The prophet Amos predicted that the land would be similarly measured and assigned by the foreign foe after its capture. "Thy land shall be divided by line" (Amos 7:17).

Allotting land. When land has been measured, "the lot" determines what section each man will secure. Those wishing to farm this land gather together usually at a threshing floor, where the man in charge of operations has a bag and pebbles. A certain distinguishing mark is put on each pebble to indicate the portion of land it represents. Then these small stones are put in the bag, and the bag is given to a small boy, who takes out the pebbles one by one, and hands one to each man desiring the use of the land. Each man upon receiving his "lot," says: "May God maintain my lot." This reminds the Bible reader of the words of the Psalm writer: "Thou maintainest my lot" (Psa. 16:5). Each man soon discovers whether his portion is desirable or not. David used this as an illustration of God's goodness to him, when he said, "The lines are fallen unto me in pleasant places; yea, I have a goodly heritage" (Psa. 16:6). It would seem, then, that the method used for allotting land by certain Arabs in modern days is similar to that used by the Jews in the days of the Old Testament.[2]

THE IMPORTANCE OF LANDMARKS

In Bible lands, when those who have the old-time customs, want to prove the extent of their property, whether it is held temporarily or permanently, landmarks hold an important place. The boundary line is marked by a double furrow, but at each end of the furrow a heap of stones, called "the stones of the boundary," is placed. If the rain does away with the furrow line, the landmark is still there to indicate the boundary. To remove one of these landmarks is considered to be a great sin.[3] Sometimes small community wars have been precipitated by the removing of a landmark. The law of Moses had this statute: "Thou shalt not remove thy neighbor's landmark, which they of old time have set in thine inheritance" (Deut. 19:14).

PURCHASING OF LAND

Transfer of property and recording of deeds in ancient times. Jeremiah's account of his purchase of a field gives us the procedure in Old Testament times. Here is the way he describes it:

And I bought the field of Hanameel my uncle's son, that was in Anathoth, and weighed him the money, even seventeen shekels of silver. And I subscribed the evidence, and sealed it, and took witnesses, and weighed him the money in the balances. So I took the evidence of the purchase, both that which was sealed according to the law and custom, and that which was open: and I gave the evidence of the purchase unto Baruch the son of Neriah, the son of Maaseiah, in the sight of Hanameel mine uncle's son, and in the presence of the witnesses that subscribed the book of the purchase, before all the Jews that sat in the court of the prison (Jer. 32:9–12).

Several ancient customs are indicated here. The money was not in the form of coins. Coinage did not come into use until later than the prophet's day. Rather the money was silver that was *weighed.* The purchase was witnessed by certain Jews who "sat in the court." There were duplicate copies of the deed made out. It was doubtless customary to seal one of these and deposit it in a safe place, which usually meant it was buried on part of the land purchased. The other copy that was open, i.e., unsealed, was placed in the public place designated for recording deeds, where it could be referred to when necessary. However, in the case of Jeremiah's purchase, both copies of the deed were preserved in an earthen vessel because the city of Jerusalem was to be destroyed.[4]

Specific inclusions noted in transfer of property. When purchasing property in the East, especially from the Arabs, it is important to indicate in detail just what is included in the purchase. If this is not done the new owner will discover he is not the owner of all he thought he purchased. In the Orient it sometimes happens that a man owns a well in the middle of a field belonging to another man. The reason for this is that the man in buying the field did not specify that he was buying the well located in the field.[5] When Abraham purchased the cave of Machpelah as a burying place for Sarah, he was careful to make clear what was included. Scripture says: "The field, and the cave which was therein, and all the trees that were in the field, that were in the borders round about, were made sure unto Abraham" (Gen. 23:17).

BURYING AND DISCOVERING VALUABLES

Through its entire history, Palestine has been a land where its inhabitants have often buried treasure in its ground. Foreign foes have many times swept through the land to plunder. In more recent years robber bands from the desert have many times rushed in to rob the inhabitants. A feeling of insecurity has caused the people of the country to seek a place to hide away valuable possessions. Therefore, many times have valuable possessions been buried in secret places. This was often done by men before leaving for battle, or before going on a long journey. If they returned safely they would be able to reclaim their buried treasure. But if they died in battle, or for any other reason failed to return, the place where the valuables were hidden would remain a lost secret. Because of this situation, there always has been a looking for hidden treasure by certain people all over the Holy Land.[6]

The Bible contains numerous references to this pursuit. Thus it was that in the days of Job it was said: "The bitter in soul . . . long for death, but it cometh not; and dig for it more than for hid treasures" (Job 3:20, 21). One of Solomon's proverbs uses the comparison of seeking for hidden treasure: "Yea, if thou criest after knowledge, and liftest up thy voice for understanding; if thou seekest her as silver, and searchest for her as for hid treasures, then shalt thou understand the fear of the Lord, and find the knowledge of God" (Prov. 2:3–5). The most famous reference to this custom is the parable Jesus told: "The kingdom of heaven is like unto treasure hid in a field; the which when a man hath found, he hideth, and for joy thereof goeth and selleth all that he hath, and buyeth that field" (Matt. 13:44). The important consideration in this story is that hidden treasure that is discovered belongs to the man who owns the property where it is found. Hence the man in the parable sold all he possessed that he might be able to buy the field where the treasure was found, and thereby become owner of the treasure he had discovered.

REDEEMING LOST INHERITANCES

The Old Testament law provided a way through which an inheritance that had been lost could be redeemed through a "go-el" or *kinsman-redeemer*. If a man through poverty was forced to mortgage his property, and then was unable to meet the payment on the date of maturity of the mortgage, then the man holding the mortgage could hold the land until the year of jubilee (which came every fifty years), at which time it reverted automatically to its former owner. But before this date a kinsman-redeemer (nearest male blood relation) could go into the civil court and by payment, recover the land for his relative. If the relation had died without an heir, then it became the duty of the kinsman-redeemer to marry his widow, and raise up the name of his brother.[7]

The story of Ruth and Boaz is the Bible example of this ancient custom. Boaz redeemed the estate of the deceased Elimelech, Naomi's husband, by marrying Ruth, the widow of one of Elimelech's sons. There was a kinsman nearer in relation than Boaz, but he chose not to be redeemer, and this left the way open for Boaz, who was next in line to become the kinsman-redeemer. In completing the transaction whereby the inheritance was redeemed and Ruth became his wife, an interesting old custom was observed. The account says: "Now this was the manner in former time in Israel concerning redeeming and concerning changing, for to confirm all things; a man plucked off his shoe, and gave it to his neighbor: and this was a testimony in Israel. Therefore the kinsman said unto Boaz, Buy it for thee. So he drew off his shoe" (Ruth 4:7, 8). Boaz took off his sandal and gave it to the owner of the mortgage as evidence of completing his act of redemption. This custom was usual in the transfer of inheritances.

CHAPTER 26

Domestic Animals

THE CAMEL

VARIETY OF CAMELS IN BIBLE LANDS. The Arabian or dromedary camel, which has one hump on its back, is the one in use in Syria and Palestine today, and is the kind found among the desert Arabs of the East. The Bactrian camel, that has two humps, comes from another region altogether, and is rarely seen in Bible lands. It was the Arabian camel that was used in Bible times.

By whom the camel was used. The camel was used largely by the early Hebrew patriarchs.[1] These men measured their wealth by the number of domestic animals they possessed, and camels were included among them. "Abram had sheep, oxen, she-asses, and camels" (Gen. 12:16). Rebekah rode on a camel on her trip to become the bride of Isaac (Gen. 24:64). "Jacob had much cattle, asses, and camels" (Gen. 30:43). It was a company of Ishmeelites with their caravan of camels that carried Joseph down into Egypt (Gen. 37:25, 28). The patriarch Job had three thousand camels before his testing experience, and this number was doubled afterwards (Job 1:3; 42:12).

The Hebrew people as a whole during most of the Old Testament times did not make large use of the camel. Living in hilly country, and being a pastoral and agricultural people,

Camel Caravan

they did not have so much need for the camel. Their kings usually possessed camels which were used for travel and transport purposes. Thus Scripture says King David had many camels, some of which had been captured in war (I Sam. 27:9).

The camel's use of water. Surely, this animal was divinely designated for desert country. Its remarkable characteristic is of course its ability to go for a long time without drinking water. This does not mean that it can get along with less water than other animals, but simply that it has the ability to store up water in a series of cells or sacks with which its interior region is furnished. The camel is able to consume as much as nine gallons at a single drink, and this water taken in in a few minutes will last it for several days. A camel that is thirsty for water has been known to scent water at a great distance, and will go at great speed to the spot where the water is located. When camel caravans unexpectedly run out of water, the men will sometimes kill one of the camels and extract from its stomach water enough to save the life of the people in the caravan.[2]

The process of watering the camels. Genesis tells how Rebekah watered the camels of Abraham's servant: "And she hasted, and emptied her pitcher into the trough, and ran

again unto the well to draw water, and drew for all his camels"
(Gen. 24:20). The Bedouin Arabs of the desert do not water
their camels at all in winter if their grazing is good. When the
weather begins to warm up, they water them every week or
nine days. As the summer becomes hotter, the camels are
watered oftener, until the very hot weather when they are
watered under ordinary conditions every other day. Leather
buckets are usually utilized to draw the water out of the well,
and a leather receptacle serves as trough, out of which the
camels drink the water poured therein. This trough is supported by wooden stands, and is kept in the tent of the desert
Arab ready for use when it comes time to water the camels.[3]

The camel's food. Under ordinary conditions, the camels
are fed *teben,* which is the short straw that comes from the
Oriental threshing floors. Each camel caravan will carry some
of this packed closely in bags. But when on a journey and it
becomes necessary, the camel often lives on what can be
found by it along the way, even in desert country. It is able
to make good use of the scanty herbage to be found in those
regions. Under these circumstances its favorite food is a
shrub that is called *ghada,* that has slender little green twigs.
It also makes use of a thornbush which it is able to devour because it has a hard and horny palate. Camels have been
known to travel for twenty days without receiving anything
as food except what they discovered for themselves along the
way.[4]

The camel's feet. These are indeed made for desert traveling. They consist of two toes that are long and that rest upon
hard elastic cushions that have a horny and tough sole. The
soft cushions of their feet cause their tread to be as noiseless
as that of a cat. Thus the camels do not sink in the desert
sands, and the toughness of their feet enables them to stand
the burning soil, and the stones that are often mixed with the
sand.[5]

The camel's hump. This serves important purposes. It makes it possible for the back of the animal to receive burdens that are to be transported. And the fatty matter that accumulates in the hump provides a supply of reserve energy which can be utilized by the animal as occasion demands. The condition of the hump is always examined when an Oriental buys a camel.[6]

Mounting a camel. This is not an easy art for a Westerner to learn. It would be impossible to do this while the animal is standing, and so it is trained to kneel and stay in this position until the rider has mounted it. It is natural for the camel to kneel because it is born with warts on the legs and breast which serve as cushions to rest its weight when kneeling. When it kneels it begins by dropping on its knees, and then on the joints of the hind legs, then it drops on its breast, and finally on its hind legs that are bent. In rising, the process is reversed: the hind quarters rise first, tending to throw the rider forward, after which the front quarters rise rapidly, tending to throw the rider backward, then the forward movement of the animal would tend to throw the rider forward again. An experienced camel rider sways to and fro, yielding his body to the movements of the animal. This movement of the camel causes some inexperienced riders to have "seasickness." Most Westerners who attempt to ride the camel find the journey to be a very uncomfortable one.[7] Abraham's servant "made his camels to kneel down without the city by a well at the time of the evening, even the time that women go out to draw water" (Gen. 24:11).

The equipment used by desert Arabs for travel by camel. This includes a camel saddle which has two tall pommels in front and behind; large saddlebags that hang down on each side of the saddle, a leather apron that hangs down in front of the saddle, stretching down on the sides of the camel's neck almost to its knees; the camel stick; a leather bag containing dates; and other bags with supplies.[8]

Camel furniture for women. Sometimes the women ride the camels in the same way that the men do, but more often a special arrangement of saddle takes care of them. "Camel furniture" was a part of Jacob's traveling equipment for his womenfolk, and when such was placed in Rachel's tent, she hid the stolen teraphim therein (Gen. 31:34, A. R. V.). They often sit in large basket-like appendages which have been slung on each side of the animal.[9] Another common arrangement for the wives of sheiks was:

> One made of two slabs, or planks of wood, about ten feet in length, which were fastened upon the frame of the saddle and at right angles to it. From the end of those, ropes were stretched over upright posts fixed above the middle of the saddle, to support an awning under which the women sat upon quilts and cushions.[10]

Such an arrangement served the same purpose as a western umbrella.

Camel ornaments. These have been widely used in the East. Owners of camels often put various ornaments on their favorite animals. Sometimes they cover the collars with cowrie shells which are sewn on them according to a pattern. Ornaments that are crescent-shaped are sewn on red cloth and make a jingling sound with each step of the animal. Often, ornaments of silver are displayed on the camel's neck. Concerning Gideon, Scripture says: "And Gideon arose, and slew Zebah and Zalmunna, and took the crescents that were on their camels' necks (Judges 8:21, A. R. V.). Thus the camel's ornaments of that day were the same as used by the Arabs of today.[11]

The camel as a beast of burden. Through the centuries the camel has been used for carrying burdens. In the Bible, "forty camels' burden," is referred to in one passage (II Kings 8:9); and in another, bread was carried on "asses, and on camels, and on mules, and on oxen" (I Chron. 12:40). In still another, treasures were to be carried on the humps of camels (Isa. 30:6). A special packsaddle is used when the animals carry loads.

A narrow bag about eight feet long is made, and rather loosely stuffed with straw or similar material. It is then doubled, and the ends firmly sewn together, so as to form a great ring, which is placed over the hump, and forms a tolerably flat surface. A wooden framework is tied on the pack-saddle, and is kept in its place by a girth and a crupper. The packages which the camel is to carry are fastened together by cords, and slung over the saddle. They are only connected by those semiknots called "hitches," so that when the camel is to be unloaded, all that is needed is to pull the lower end of the rope, and the packages fall on either side of the animal. So quickly is the operation of loading performed, that a couple of experienced men can load a camel in very little more than a minute.[12]

Camel caravans. It is camel caravans that have been largely used to transport goods from one country to another in Bible lands, or to go a great distance especially in desert territory. Isaiah prophesied to the Dedanites, who were caravan merchants between the shores of the Persian Gulf and Palestine: "In the forest in Arabia shall ye lodge, O ye caravans of Dedanites" (Isa. 21:13, A. R. V.). The number of camels in a caravan in modern times has differed widely, but one writer tells of joining a caravan which was divided into four companies, and the first three of these numbered sixteen hundred camels.[13] The usual arrangement of a caravan is a string of camels with each one tied to the one before it, and the leader of the caravan either riding on the back of, or walking by the side of a donkey. A cord from the first camel in the line, is tied to a ring that is fastened to leather strips on the hips of the donkey. Thus the camels learn to follow implicitly the donkey that heads the procession.[14]

The social influence of the caravans. In ancient times as well as today, in large sections of the Orient, the caravans take the place of newspaper, telephone, and radio. Ordinarily, the knowledge of what was going on was limited on the part of the women to what they heard at the village oven, or the village well; and on the part of the men, to what they heard at the village guest room, or at the gates of the city. But when a caravan arrived in the village, it was an event of great importance, because there was always news brought from a distance.[15] The familiar proverb must have referred to such an event: "As cold waters to a thirsty soul, so is good news from a far country" (Prov. 25:25).

The swift Arabian camel. This animal is often called the *deloul*, has long and wiry limbs, and is without superfluous fat. Its shoulders are broad and its hump small, although hard and firm. It is an ungainly looking creature, but the Arab is very fond of this animal. The ordinary camel travels along at the rate of about three miles an hour, whereas the *deloul* if not heavily loaded will traverse nine or ten miles an hour. Some of the natives even claim that this animal can outrun a race horse. Jeremiah the prophet speaks of "a swift dromedary traversing her ways" (Jer. 2:23). The movements of this swift animal are hard on the rider, who usually prepares for the trip by "belting himself tightly with two leathern bands, one just under the arms, and the other round the pit of the stomach."[16]

Various camel products. The Arab of today makes use of camel meat and camel milk. The Mosaic law forbade the Jews to use camel meat "because he cheweth the cud, but divideth not the hoof; he is unclean unto you" (Lev. 11:4). It is possible that they did use the milk, at least in patriarchal times (cf. Gen. 32:15). Camel's hair serves many purposes in the Orient. At the right season of the year it is removed in tufts and the women spin it into strong thread. Various coarse fabrics are made from this thread. The Bedouin tents are sometimes made of camel's hair, as are also carpets, rugs, "abayas" or the outer garments, and other items. Matthew says of John the Baptist that he "had his raiment of camel's hair" (Matt. 3:4). The camel's skin is made into leather and from this material are made sandals, leggings, and water bottles. Even the dung of camels is commonly used for fuel.[17]

Two references to the camel in Christ's sermons. The first reference is given by all three synoptic Gospel writers: "It is easier for a camel to go through the eye of a needle, than for a rich man to enter into the kingdom of God" (Matt. 19:24; Mark 10:25; Luke 18:25). It must be remembered that Orientals are very fond of exaggeration as a figure of speech, and so would appreciate this hyperbole that Jesus used. In Luke's account, the word ordinarily referring to a surgeon's needle was the one used by the writer of the third Gospel, who was himself a physician.[18] The words that Jesus added, need to be taken with his statement: "With men this is impossible; but with God all things are possible" (Matt. 19:26). The other reference to the camel was given when Jesus was denouncing the Scribes and Pharisees, and said to them: "Ye blind guides, that strain out the gnat, and swallow the camel!" (Matt. 23:24, A. R. V.). The reference here is to the ancient custom of filtering wine. The gnat and the camel are in striking contrast to each other in size. The use of the camel here was obviously a hyperbole, but was appropriate, not only because of its great size, but because to the Jews it was an unclean animal (because it does not divide the hoof, although it does chew the cud). The Pharisees were careful to strain out the smallest creature, but swallowed the larger one. They were scrupulous about small things, but very careless about the more important matters.[19]

THE DONKEY

The donkey as the Oriental pack animal. He has been the beast of burden from time immemorial. The packsaddle used with this animal differed somewhat according to the load being carried. When firewood was carried, a crosstree was used as a saddle. No doubt Abraham loaded his donkey in this way with wood for the sacrifice he was to make (Gen. 22:3). When sheaves of grain were carried by the donkey, a kind of cradle was either suspended to the crosstree or to the flat saddle. This saddle had as its under layer thick felt, and as its

Traveling by Donkey

upper layer haircloth, with a padding of straw or sedges between. When sacks of grain or cut straw are carried, they are thrown over this saddle and tied with a rope going under the beast's breast. The sons of Jacob probably packed their donkeys in this way (Gen. 42:26, 27). Large baskets are used for carrying bread and other provisions. If fruit is being taken, two boxes are slung in a similar way. Jesse and Abigail doubtless packed their donkeys in such a way when they sent their presents (I Sam. 16:20; I Sam 25:18). Children are often carried in larger boxes on the donkeys. Sacks of grain are sometimes slung across the bare back of the donkey.[20]

The donkey sometimes utilized for ploughing. The ox has been more generally used for this purpose, but occasionally the donkey becomes the animal to pull the Oriental plough. The prophet Isaiah speaks of both the ox and the donkey being used thus: "Blessed are ye that sow beside all waters, that send forth thither the feet of the ox and the ass" (Isa. 32:

20). The law of Moses forbade the mixed yoke, i.e., ploughing with an ox and a donkey together, or any other combination (cf. Deut. 22:10).

The donkey sometimes used for grinding grain. Here again, the usual method of grinding the grain is for the women to use smaller stones for their mills. The larger mill is elevated so that a singletree becomes suitable for the work. A camel may be used in place of a donkey. It was this type of a mill that the Philistines required Samson to pull (Judges 16:21). Jesus referred to this larger type of millstone when he said: "But whoso shall cause one of these little ones that believe on me to stumble, it is profitable for him that a *millstone turned by an ass* should be hanged about his neck, and that he should be sunk in the depth of the sea" (Matt. 18:6, A. R. V. margin). The size and weight of this stone made its illustrative use by Jesus very forceful.[21]

The donkey used for riding. Before the tenth century B. C. it was used more than any other animal for this purpose. At that time, the mule came into use, especially among the rich, but the donkey has continued to be in use by many through the years.[22]

Riding the donkey not considered a mark of humility. Rich people and important people rode on this animal. Of Abraham Scripture records that he "rose up early in the morning, and saddled his ass" (Gen. 22:3). Concerning one of the judges it was said, "And after him arose Jair, a Gileadite, and judged Israel twenty and two years. And he had thirty sons that rode on thirty ass colts, and they had thirty cities" (Judges 10:3, 4). Also Achsah, the daughter of Caleb (Judges 1:14), and Abigail, the wife of wealthy Nabal (I Sam. 25:23), each rode on an ass.

White donkeys used by persons of high rank. "Speak, ye that ride on white asses, ye that sit in judgment, and walk by the way" (Judges 5:10). These white donkeys are used today in many places in the East by people of high social standing

They are usually larger animals and are supposed to be swifter.[23]

The donkey used as a symbol of peace-times. The horse has usually symbolized times of war, but the donkey, times of peace. In Old Testament times this was especially true from the days of King Solomon. This fact helps to explain the words of the prophet about the Messiah that were fulfilled in the triumphant entrance of Jesus into Jerusalem: "Rejoice greatly, O daughter of Zion; shout, O daughter of Jerusalem: behold, thy king cometh unto thee; he is just, and having salvation; lowly, and riding upon an ass, even upon a colt the foal of an ass" (Zech. 9:9; cf. John 12:15). Here the use by Jesus of the donkey was to signify that He was Prince of Peace, rather than Captain of an army, when He entered the Holy City.[24]

Drivers sometimes used for donkeys. When women rode on donkeys, it was customary at times to have a driver for the animal. Thus it says concerning the trip made by the woman of Shunem: "Then she saddled an ass, and said to her servant, Drive, and go forward; slack not thy riding for me, except I bid thee" (II Kings 4:24). On the journey made by Moses and his family (Exod. 4:20), his wife and sons were mounted on their donkey while Moses no doubt walked along beside the animal. Because of this arrangement of travel for the journey of Moses and his family, it is believed by many that Mary and the child Jesus rode on the donkey (Matt. 2:13–15), and Joseph walked alongside in their flight into Egypt.[25] However, in the Orient, many times husband and wife are seen to ride both of them on the backs of a donkey.

Special donkey riding-saddles. Those used in the Orient today are rather large. A cloth of wool folded several times is spread over the animal's back. On this is placed a thick pad of straw which is covered with carpet. It is flat on top instead of being rounded. The pommel is quite high, and a cloth or carpet of bright color is often thrown over the saddle. This usually has fringed edges and tassels. It is quite likely that the saddle of Bible times was much simpler than this arrangement. It was probably a simple covering of cloth or skin which was used for the convenience of the rider, and especially to protect the animal from chafing.[26]

MULES

Mules used by the Arabs of Bible lands. They scarcely ever breed the mule themselves, but instead import them from either the Lebanon district of Syria, or from Cyprus. The Arabs very seldom use the mule for the purposes of agriculture, but rather use it for riding or for carrying of burdens particularly in rocky country.[27]

Mules used in later Old Testament times. The mule is not mentioned in the Bible until the reign of King David.[28] The law of Moses prohibited the rearing of any animals which were the result of the union of different species (Lev. 19:19). So the Jews never bred mules, but evidently they thought the law did not prohibit them from using them. From the days of King David, they came to be used as beasts of burden, and for the saddle, and were imported from other countries, especially Egypt. Included in the tribute which King Solomon received from other nations was a quantity of "mules, a rate year by year" (I Kings 10:24, 25; II Chron. 9:24). The first Scriptural reference to the mule is in connection with the sheep-shearing feast planned by Absalom for the plot against Amnon. It says: "All the king's sons arose, and every man got him up upon his mule, and fled" (II Sam. 13:29). Each prince had a mule for his personal travel use, and thus this animal had taken the place of the donkey for such use. The mule was used by King David when he traveled in state, and to ride upon the mule belonging to the king was considered to be much the same thing as sitting upon the throne of the king. Thus David said concerning Solomon whom he wanted to make king to succeed him: "Take with you the servants of your lord, and cause Solomon my son to ride upon mine own mule, and bring him down to Gihon" (I Kings 1:33). When

Adonijah, who attempted to usurp the throne against the wishes of his father, heard that Solomon had ridden on the mule of David, he knew thereby that he had been made the new king (I Kings 1:44f). By the time of Isaiah, the mule was in common use. The prophet says: "And they shall bring all your brethren for an offering unto the Lord out of all nations upon horses, and in chariots, and in litters, and upon mules, and upon swift beasts, to my holy mountain Jerusalem" (Isa. 66:20). Kings had especially made use of them, as Ahab who was much concerned about keeping his mules alive in time of famine (I Kings 18:5). The Bible does not anywhere mention the obstinate disposition of the mule. A reference by the Psalmist says: "Be ye not as the horse, or as the mule, which have no understanding: whose mouth must be held in with bit and bridle, lest they come near unto thee" (Psa. 32:9). But this is not a reference to that trait of character for which the mule is noted today in the West.[29] The New Testament does not mention the mule.

Horses

Bible time horse same as Arab horse today. Assyrian and Egyptian sculpture would indicate that the horse of Bible times was the same as the Arabs use today. In those days the horse was used mainly for war purposes, although Isaiah, in connection with threshing, speaks of the use of horses (Isa. 28:28), thus indicating that to a limited degree at least, horses were used in agriculture. But today the Arabs make much use of horses for riding. The horse is looked upon as part of the Arab's family. Although it is heavily bitted, the reins are rarely used. It is controlled by the rider's voice. When the camp or oasis is reached, the horses are unsaddled or unharnessed and allowed to roam free. They will graze around the place and always come when called. Hoofs of the Arab horses are never shod, this practice being made useless by the hot climate.[30] In ancient days the same thing was true. In Scripture the quality of a horse was judged partially by the hardness of its hoofs. Isaiah said: "Their horses' hoofs shall be counted like flint" (Isa. 5:28). Micah wrote: "I will make thy hoofs brass" (Micah 4:13).

Care of horses. In Old Testament days the horse was cared for much as it is by the Arab today. In addition to the use of grass in grazing, the horses were fed barley and cut straw. Thus both "barley also and straw for the horses" (I Kings 4: 28), were in use in King Solomon's time. The Psalmist indicates the use of bit and bridle: "Be ye not as the horse . . . whose mouth must be held in with bit and bridle" (Psa. 32:9). And the Book of Proverbs speaks of "a whip for the horse" (Prov. 26:3).

Horses and chariots used in Egypt from early times. Joseph rode in "the second chariot" which King Pharaoh had (Gen. 41:43). When the Israelites made their escape from the bondage of Egypt, they were pursued by "all the horses and chariots of Pharaoh, and his horsemen, and his army" (Exod. 14:9). In later years, Egypt was the main source for the supply of horses used by the kings of Israel (I Kings 10:28, 29).

Regulation in the law of Moses concerning horses. The Book of Deuteronomy was explicit about the use of horses by future kings of Israel. Concerning a ruler it was said: "But he shall not multiply horses to himself, nor cause the people to return to Egypt, to the end that he should multiply horses: forasmuch as the Lord hath said unto you, Ye shall henceforth return no more that way" (Deut. 17:16).

Use of horse and chariot impractical in much of Canaan. This was due to the mountainous character of much of the country. This was especially true of most of Judea and Samaria, except on the main roads through this territory. This is the reason for their absence in the battles that took place there.

Horses and chariots not used in conquest of Canaan. Joshua did not make use of them in his conquest of Canaan. There is no record that he made use of either cavalry or of chariots in his warfare. But Moses had predicted that Israel would have to face enemies that did have their horses and chariots. "When thou goest out to battle against thine enemies, and seest horses, and chariots, and a people more than thou, be not afraid of them: for the Lord thy God is with thee, which brought thee up out of the land of Egypt" (Deut. 20:1). When Joshua went against such foes and conquered them, he was commanded by God to cut the hamstrings of captured horses, and to burn the chariots thus secured. The Bible records his obedience to this command (Josh. 11:6, 9).

War chariots used by Israel's enemies in the days of the Judges. When the Canaanites oppressed Israel in those days "the children of Israel cried unto the Lord: for he [i.e., the Canaanitish king] had nine hundred chariots of iron" (Judges 4:3). But the Lord gave Israel victory over these chariots without the Hebrews themselves using such implements of warfare.

King David's use of horses. David made some use of horses in battle. On the occasion of his victory over Hadadezer, King of Zobah, "David houghed all the chariot horses, but reserved of them for an hundred chariots" (II Sam. 8:3, 4). Doubtless he wanted these chariots and their horses for battle use on the flat ground of his country.

King Solomon's excessive use of horses. He disregarded the Law of Moses, and began to import great numbers of horses and chariots from the land of Egypt. "And Solomon had horses brought out of Egypt . . . and a chariot came up and went out of Egypt for six hundred shekels of silver, and an horse for an hundred and fifty" (I Kings 10:28, 29). He had many stalls made for his large number of chariot horses and cavalry. These animals were stationed in chariot cities where the stalls were constructed (I Kings 4:26; II Chron. 1:14; 9:25). Archaeologists have uncovered the ancient city of Megiddo, which was one of Solomon's chariot cities, and there in the southeast corner of the tell (ancient mound) was discovered that which gives every evidence of being the stables of Solomon. Between four and five hundred of these stables were laid bare with nearby quarters for the grooms who cared for the horses. A manger was located in front of each horse. Massive stone hitching posts remain with holes in them for inserting the hal-ter-shanks.[31]

Use of horses and chariots by kings of Judah and Israel. Fol-lowing the example of Solomon, the kings that followed dur-ing the history of the divided kingdom, made use of horses and chariots. King Ahab died in his battle chariot in war with the Syrians (I Kings 22:35). And the prophet Isaiah warned the kings of his day against going down to Egypt for help in securing horses for the day of battle. "Woe to them that go down to Egypt for help; and stay on horses, and trust in chari-ots, because they are many; and in horsemen, because they are very strong, but they look not unto the Holy One of Is-rael" (Isa. 31:1).

Use of horses and chariots in time of peace. It was mainly kings or men of wealth or position who used chariots drawn by horses in times of peace. As prince, Absalom rode in a char-iot, and King Rehoboam and King Ahab had their chariots in which they rode in state (II Sam. 15:1, Absalom; I Kings 12:18, Rehoboam; I Kings 18:44, Ahab). And Jeremiah made this prophecy concerning the city of Jerusalem: "Then shall there enter into the gates of this city kings and princes sitting upon the throne of David, riding in chariots and on horses, they, and their princes" (Jer. 17:25). In New Testament times the use of chariots was also limited to men of prominence. The Ethiopian eunuch of Queen Candace rode in a chariot when Philip joined him and won him to Christ (Acts 8:28 f). In the Apocalypse, the noise of the judgment locusts is compared to "the sound of chariots of many horses" (Rev. 9:9).

Description of ancient chariots. There have been numbers of pictorial representations of ancient chariots discovered by archaeologists. These give a fair idea of what they were like. These implements so often used in warfare were very simple in style and yet very uncomfortable for the occupants. They were "semicircular boxes on wheels and of very small size. They were hung very low, so that the occupants could step in and out without trouble."[32] There were no springs, but the floor was made of a network of rope stretched so as to be elastic and thus overcome some of the effects of the jolting. Often two horses pulled one chariot. In battle it was customary to have two men in each chariot, one to drive the horses, and the other to do the fighting.[33]

Figurative use of chariots and white horses. Chariots and white horses were often used as figures of speech in the Bible. Chariots are referred to as symbols of power. Thus God "maketh the clouds his chariots" (Psa. 104:3). The Lord is said to have his army of angels and many chariots: "The chariots of God are twenty thousand, even thousands of angels" (Psa. 68:17). And concerning the coming of the Lord, Isaiah prophesied: "The Lord will come with fire, and with his chariots like a whirlwind" (Isa. 66:15). The coming of Christ to fight the battle of Armageddon is predicted to be on a white horse, and the armies that follow him from Heaven will be upon white horses (Rev. 19:11, 14). Generals of armies have usually been known to ride upon white horses, and so as General of a great army, Christ will ride such an animal; and since His saints share with Him in the victory, it is appropriate that they too shall ride upon white horses.

CATTLE

The domestic cattle of Palestine have been much like those raised in the West, only there have not been as many kinds of breed. In the time of Israel's prosperity, cattle were much more numerous than they have been among the Arabs today, and were probably better developed animals. The ancient Jews used the cattle for sacrifices, and for this purpose they had to be without flaws. The Arabs do not use cattle for meat very much, but rather use sheep and goat meat. Various words are used in our English Bible to indicate cattle. The word "ox" is often used, and it is sometimes indicated that this animal was especially fatted for table use. "Better is a dinner of herbs where love is, than a stalled ox and hatred therewith" (Prov. 15:17). The words "bull" or "bullock" are used in Scrip-

ture to designate the male cattle. The bullock was one of
the animals that could be offered under the law of Moses as
a burnt offering (Lev. 1:5). Milk-giving cows, sometimes
called "milch kine," were in common use (I Sam. 6:7; Deut.
32:14). Bull calves were often used in Bible times for meat.
But the chief use of oxen was by the farmer in his various activities. The Jews used the oxen where the modern farmer
has used the horse. Oxen were put under the yoke and made
to pull the plow. Cows as well as bulls were utilized, the latter having been castrated. "Elisha was plowing with twelve
yoke of oxen" (I Kings 19:19). Oxen were used in threshing
grain. "Thou shalt not muzzle the ox when he treadeth out
the corn [grain]" (Deut. 25:4).

During part of the year, the cattle in Palestine are allowed
to graze. In the thickly populated sections, a boy will act as
herdsman to see that they do no harm. But in the thinly populated districts, the farmers will sometimes turn their herds
loose and let the cattle forage, hunting their own pasturage.
While doing this they take on some of the characteristics of a
wild animal. The Bible refers to some of these habits. The
Psalmist cried: "Many bulls have compassed me, strong bulls
of Bashan have beset me round. They gaped upon me with
their mouths, as a ravening and a roaring lion" (Psa. 22:12).
The prophet Joel referred to the custom of turning herds loose
to search for their own pastures: "How do the beasts groan!
the herds of cattle are perplexed, because they have no pasture" (Joel 1:18). Under the dire conditions described by the
prophet, the cattle could find no pasturage.[34]

Special use of the fatted calf. The "fatted calf" as used by
the Jews served a special purpose. This calf was stall-fed as
is indicated by the prophet Malachi: "And grow up as calves
of the stall" (Mal. 4:2). This animal is not only allowed to eat
all that he wants to eat, but he is forced to eat more. The
whole family, and especially the children, are interested in
feeding it. It is fattened up in order that it may be killed for
some special occasion.[35] Two occasions called for the slaying

of this animal. First, if a special guest was to be received and thus honored, the calf was then killed. When the witch of Endor entertained King Saul with a meal, the account says that she "had a fat calf in the house; and she hasted, and killed it" (I Sam. 28:24). The well-known New Testament example was when the prodigal's father said to his servants, "Bring hither the fatted calf, and kill it; and let us eat, and be merry" (Luke 15:23). It was the custom to kill the animal, cook it, and then eat it, in quick succession. Abraham, Gideon, Manoah, the witch of Endor, as well as the prodigal's father, are examples of this. The Bedouin Arabs do this today when unexpected guests arrive. These Orientals would appear to be expert in the art.[36] Second, the "fatted calf" was sometimes slain as a special sacrifice or offering unto the Lord. The prophet Amos mentions "the thank offerings of your fatted calves" (Amos 5:22, Keil).[37]

Dogs

There are two kinds of dogs that are referred to in the Bible. *First,* there is the wolf-like, short-haired creature, that stands guard over the tent or the house, and which barks fiercely at strangers that come that way. He will eat whatever garbage is tossed to him, and in the evening he is usually heard barking about the city (cf. Psa. 59:6). Sometimes he is allowed to be under the table ready to receive scraps given to him (cf. Matt. 15:27). *Second,* there is the shepherd dog that goes out with the shepherd to help him in rounding up the sheep. Job speaks of these animals as "the dogs of my flock" (Job 30:1). Because dogs were so often regarded as mere scavengers, the Bible does not use the word "dog" as Westerners are accustomed to think of this animal. The price of a dog was never brought to the house of the Lord (Deut. 23:18). To call anybody "a dog" was to consider him as very low down indeed (Rev. 22:15). The attitude of the Orientals toward dogs needs to be kept in mind in interpreting the Scriptures that refer to them.[38]

CHAPTER 27

Traveling on Land and Sea

Character and Conditions of Oriental Traveling

THE EXPENSE, DISCOMFORT, AND DANGER OF TRAVEL. In the Orient, where modern Western customs have not displaced old-time methods, to travel is a great expense, it means much discomfort, and it involves great danger. Therefore it is done only when absolutely necessary. When a traveler sets out on his journey he must "pay all debts, provide for dependents, give parting gifts, return all articles under trust, take money and good temper for the journey, then bid farewell to all, and be merciful to the animal he rides upon."[1] The traveling of the Apostle Paul emphasized the hardships of journeying in the East. "In journeyings often, in perils of waters, in perils of robbers, . . . in perils in the wilderness, . . . in weariness and painfulness, . . . in hunger and thirst, . . . in cold and nakedness" (II Cor. 11:26, 27).

Wherever it is possible to do so men travel in large groups so that they can help each other in case they meet with robbers or wild animals along the way. A guide or someone who knows the way, and especially one who is acquainted with the locations of wells or springs of water or other watering places, is invaluable to the travelers. Sometimes they depend upon a spring of water and then discover upon arrival that

270

it has dried up. Isaiah spoke of "a spring of water, whose waters fail not" (Isa. 58:11).[2] The Psalmist (Psa. 107:4–7) told of a caravan of travelers that lost their way in the desert, running out of food and water. After prayer, the Lord guided them to "a city of habitation."

Methods of travel. Traveling is sometimes done on foot, but more often on the backs of horses, mules, or donkeys, and when traveling in the desert, camels are mostly used. In order to avoid the intense heat, and to escape detection by robber tribes, traveling is often done by night. The guide will get his direction from the stars. Summer is the usual time for traveling in order to avoid the many inconveniences connected with the winter months.[3]

Food taken by travelers. Travelers going a distance will carry food with them, which will include bread, parched grain, dried olives, dried figs, and dates. Most travelers in the East now, as in the days of Jesus, will not go any distance from home without taking barley bread or meal or parched grain sufficient to last for one or two days. When Jesus performed the miracle of feeding the four thousand, he said, "I have compassion on the multitude, because they continue with me now three days, and have nothing to eat: and I will not send them away fasting, lest they faint in the way" (Matt. 15:32). According to custom, the multitude would have a day or two's supply of food with them when they flocked to hear Jesus. But on the third day, seven loaves and a few small fish was all that was left.[4]

How distances are often measured in the Orient. In traveling in Bible lands, it is often customary to measure distances in units of time rather than in terms of space. One village is said to be three hours distant from another village, because it takes that long to travel from one to the other. In Old Testament days distance in traveling was similarly noted. It was "three days' journey," "seven days' journey," etc. (Gen. 30: 36; 31:23). In New Testament times, "a day's journey" is mentioned, and also "a sabbath day's journey" (Luke 2:44; Acts 1:12). Among the Jews a day's journey was twenty to thirty miles, but when there was a large company it would be only ten miles. A sabbath day's journey would be a little less than two miles.[5]

NATURE OF EASTERN INNS

Old Testament Inns. The inns of Old Testament days were merely stopping places for travelers overnight. In the first two books of the Bible, the word "inn" in the King James Version is translated "lodging-place" by the Revisers (Gen. 42:27; 43:21; Exod. 4:24, cf. with A. R. V.). The word refers only to a resting-place for the night, and a tent or perhaps a cave would most likely serve the purpose.[6]

New Testament Inns. The inns of New Testament times were not like Western hotels. It was because hospitality was considered to be a religious duty that therefore the modern type of hotel was unknown in olden days, and also does not exist today in many sections of Bible lands. If parties of travelers are not too many in number, they will be entertained at a Bedouin tent encampment, or in a village guest room. When Mary and Joseph came to Bethlehem, Luke says: "There was no room for them in the inn" (Luke 2:7). Some Bible scholars have thought that this inn was actually a guestchamber, because the same word is used for such a place on another occasion (Mark 14:14; Luke 22:11). But surely, with so many out-of-town visitors in the village, the guest room would long ago have been utilized. This inn was most probably a place where travelers might camp overnight, and so would have to provide their own food, cooking utensils, and other provisions. There might or might not have been an innkeeper. But there was simply no space left for Mary and Joseph at this inn. (*See also* "Bethlehem house and manger," p. 34).

Sometimes the inn had an *innkeeper*. Luke tells us how the Good Samaritan brought the poor man he was helping "to an

Oriental Caravansary or Inn

inn, and took care of him." In this case a "host" or "innkeeper"
is mentioned (Luke 10:34, 35). It would be the duty of this
man to supply a few of the necessary provisions for the travelers who spent the night there.

The Oriental "caravansary" or "khan" is probably the equivalent of at least some of the "inns" of New Testament times.
The "caravansary" is a large building and is usually located
in a city, although sometimes it serves as a shelter in the desert. The courtyard of these buildings serves as a place to un-
mount and unload the animals, and the ground floor becomes
a place for the beasts to be cared for, while the travelers themselves are put upstairs. The "khan" is a smaller building which
serves the same purpose, but is located in a village. Most of

these are but one-story buildings, where travelers sleep close to their animals. Many of these Eastern "inns" are without any furniture, innkeeper, or food for either man or animal. The traveler under these conditions is provided shelter only, and he himself must provide everything else. When the inn does have an "innkeeper," he will sell to the travelers coffee or other provisions, and furnish fire and the means by which they may cook their own meals. He may also provide food for the animals. Where the inn is located at a strategic center, such as where caravan routes intersect each other, it may become a public gathering-place on account of bazaars and markets being held there. Animals are sometimes killed and the meat sold at these places, and often travelers can purchase many other things at the inn.[7]

ORIENTAL SALUTATIONS AMONG TRAVELERS

When travelers in the Orient meet each other on the way, they love to engage in salutations that to the Westerner seem complicated, tedious, and time-consuming. Wordy questions will be asked each other seeking such information as this: From where have you come? Where are you going? What is your name? How many children have you? How many men belong to your clan? What enemies does your clan have? etc., etc. While such salutations are entered into, business and everything else can wait. For this reason, when Jesus sent the seventy disciples on a healing and preaching mission, he said to them: "Salute no man by the way" (Luke 10:4). To engage in such extensive salutations as were customary would have interfered with the urgent business of the Lord.[8]

TRAVELING BY SEA IN ANCIENT TIMES

The attitude of the ancients toward the sea. Ancient people had a great fear of the ocean, and truly there was reason for this dread, since the mariners had no chart of the seas or

Oriental Salutations

compass to guide them. Travel by ship was usually inconvenient, and windstorms often necessitated great delay in arrival at the desired port. Ordinarily the Mediterranean Sea was closed to sea travel during the winter months.[9] The ship in which Paul was to sail for Rome got into difficulties because those in charge risked getting the ship to another harbor before winter set in. "And because the haven was not commodious to winter in, the more part advised to depart thence also, if by any means they might attain to Phenice, and there to winter" (Acts 27:12). The Psalmist has given us a graphic description of a storm at sea and God's deliverance from it (Psa. 107:25–30). The Apostle John's inspired description of Heaven was originally given to men who greatly feared the grave dangers and horrors of sea-experiences, and to them he wrote concerning the new earth: "And there was no more sea" (Rev. 21:1). Travel by sea in early days was undertaken only when absolutely necessary.

Ship routes. It is important to remember that in Bible times, vessels that traveled in the Mediterranean Sea kept as close as possible to land. Thus the trade routes were along the coast or from one headland to another one.[10] When the Apostle Paul was returning from one of his missionary journeys, he traveled by ship from Ephesus to Caesarea. His ship would keep near the coast going from city to city, and Paul sometimes stopped off and visited friends (Acts 21:1–8). In those days the small size of the ships often made it necessary for passengers to go ashore for the night, and finding a place there to sleep, join the ship the next day.[11]

Shipping nations. Egyptian ships early plied the Mediterranean Sea, and light-weight "vessels of papyrus" (Isa. 18:1, 2, A. R. V.), were piloted by both Egyptians and Ethiopians on the Nile River. The Phoenicians were the most famous sea-merchants and travelers of ancient times. The ship in which Jonah took his voyage was no doubt navigated by these seamen (Jonah 1). The Islands of Crete and Cyprus became famous shipping centers, and the Philistines of old had their ships upon the waters of the Mediterranean. In New Testament times it was the Greeks and Romans who were especially noted for their shipping activities.[12] But what about the Hebrews? Were they seamen? The patriarch Jacob made this prediction concerning the tribe of Zebulun: "He shall be for an haven of ships" (Gen. 49:13). But the Palestine seacoast was not occupied at all times by the Hebrew people. Other nations became navigators, and for the most part the Jews probably contented themselves with occasionally hiring out to these foreign sea captains as sailors. The Psalmist says: "They that go down to the sea in ships, that do business in great waters" (Psa. 107:23).

Israel did have one great experience with ships during the reign of King Solomon. David had conquered the Edomites and so came into possession of the two ports of Eloth and Ezion-geber on the Red Sea. Thus Solomon inherited good harbors for ships. Arrangements were made for Hiram, King of Tyre, to send carpenters to build ships for Solomon, "and Hiram sent in the navy his servants, shipmen that had knowledge of the sea, with the servants of Solomon. And they came to Ophir, and fetched from thence gold . . . and brought it to king Solomon" (I Kings 9:27, 28). A few years later King Jehoshaphat of Judah joined with King Ahaziah of Israel on a similar shipping expedition, but the Lord did not approve of this alliance, and so "the ships were broken at Ezion-geber" (I Kings 22:48). While King Jehoram, Jehoshaphat's successor, was reigning, the Edomites freed themselves from the Hebrew yoke, and came into possession of their Red Sea ports.[13] This ended Israel's shipping experience in ocean waters for many generations to come, although Eloth has become an important port for the modern nation of Israel. In New Testament times boats were used to cross the waters of the Sea of Galilee.

How ships were propelled. Two methods were used. Ships of war, although furnished with sails, were propelled mainly by means of oars. Merchant vessels depended for the most part on sails, but many of the navigators resorted to oars when it became necessary.[14] Thus the men who piloted Jonah's ship, which was a merchant ship, "rowed hard to bring it to the land; but they could not" (Jonah 1:13). The storm was too great for them. The ship that Paul was in when the storm broke on the Mediterranean Sea was a sailing ship without oars for men to row (Acts 27).

The Phoenician ship in which Jonah sailed. The first chapter of the book of Jonah gives interesting information about ancient ships. This ship was traveling from Joppa to Tarshish as a merchant ship, for when the storm came, the men "cast forth the wares that were in the ship" (verse 5). Exclusively passenger ships were little known in those days, most traveling, if not all, being done on merchant ships. Passengers, of course, paid fare for their trips, as did Jonah (verse 3). When the storm arose, the sailors discovered that "Jonah was gone down into the sides of the ship" (verse 5). This means he had gone "below deck," into the lower room of the ship. The word "shipmaster" used in verse 6 means the chief of the sailors, or as we would say, the captain of the ship. Verse 13 mentions the use of oars when the ship was in the storm, in a futile effort to bring it to shore.

Luke's account of Paul's voyage to Rome. Luke's report of Paul's sea journey in Acts 27 and 28 is the most accurate account of a sea voyage that has come to us from olden times. We gain more knowledge of these ships from this story than from any other source.[15] In the second half of the nineteenth century, Mr. James Smith made a detailed study of Paul's voyage, traveling by ship himself where Paul's trip took him. By means of admiralty charts and a study of the tides, etc., he was able to prove how remarkably accurate Luke was in what he wrote.[16] Lieutenant Edwin Smith of Canada was in the Mediterranean waters in 1918–1919 in command of a ship on special service. He also had opportunity to test out Luke's accuracy and make a study of shipping in Paul's day.[17] What were these ancient ships like? Lieutenant Smith makes this answer:

> In general outline they did not differ so much from sailing ships of fifty years ago, especially in their under-water parts, with the exception that the bow and stern were very much alike . . . Perhaps the greatest difference between these ancient ships and all classes of modern ships, is in the steering arrangements. The ancient ships were not steered as those in modern times, by a single rudder hinged to the stern post, but by two great oars or paddles, one on each side of the stern; hence the mention of them in the plural num-

ber by St. Luke (Acts 27:40). They were operated through two hawse holes, one on either side, which were used also for the cables when the ships were anchored by the stern.[18]

James speaks of only one rudder on a ship (Jas. 3:4, A. R. V.), but this is because the pilot would only make use of one of the two rudders at a time.[19]

In Acts 27:17, A. R. V., Luke tells us that the sailors lowered the sail in the storm, and in verse 40, he informs us that they hoisted up the foresail. This latter was a small sail which the seamen were in the habit of substituting for the mainsail in storms.[20] Verse 17 also says: "They used helps, undergirding the ship." When it became necessary, chains or cables were placed around the hull at right angles to the length of the ship, and then pulled tight. The English navy calls this process "frapping."[21]

Luke gives us the names of the officers on board Paul's ship (verse 11). The Roman centurion was in chief command of the ship. Then came the pilot and captain (cf. Williams' Tr.).[22]

Ancient ships as now had their own individual ensign. Thus the ship on which Paul took the final stage of his journey to Rome was called Castor and Pollux which means, "The Twin Brothers" (cf. Acts 28:11, Williams). Ancient ships were personified, and thus grew the custom of painting an eye on each side of the ship's bow. This custom has persisted down to modern times among Mediterranean ships. Luke evidently was referring to this custom when he wrote: "When the ship was caught and could not face the wind, we gave way to it" (Acts 27:15, A. R. V.). Literally translated it would be, "could not look the wind in the face."[23]

CHAPTER 28

Palestine Water Supply

W ELLS AND THEIR LOCA-
TION. In many cases wells have been depended upon for water
in Palestinian towns through the years. Often the well is
located outside the city walls, but sometimes the people are
fortunate to have the well inside their town. Archaeologists
have discovered at least two ancient cities in addition to
Jerusalem, that brought water inside their city through a tunnel. The city of Gezer had such a tunnel that led from within
the city to a water supply beneath. And the Canaanites at
Megiddo, rather than go outside their city for water, sunk a
shaft straight down to the level of the spring, and then dug
a tunnel horizontally until they reached it.[1]

Securing water for home use. We have already seen
(Chapter 8, pp. 88–90) that it is the duty of the women to go
to the well to get the family supply of water. This is carried
by them in pitchers of earthenware either upon their shoulder or head. If larger supplies of water are needed, then the
men carry such in sheepskin or goatskin "bottles."

Famous wells and fountains of Scripture. Wells were dug
by the early *patriarchs* in various places in the land of Canaan.

The town of Beersheba was named after an event that happened at the time Isaac's servants dug a well there. The name means "The Well of the Oath," commemorating the covenant made between Isaac and Abimelech, which followed soon after the trouble over possession of wells at Gerar (Genesis 26).

Jacob's well at Sychar was made famous by the incident of Jesus talking with the woman of Samaria there. There is nothing left at these wells that may be used for drawing water from a depth. Each woman who comes for water brings with her, in addition to the pitcher in which to carry the water, a hard leather portable bucket with a rope, in order to let it down to the level of the water.[2] The Samaritan woman had brought all this with her, but Jesus had no such equipment with him. Hence she said to him, after he had asked her for a drink: "You have no bucket, sir, and the well is deep" (John 4:11, Twentieth Century N. T.). In response to his request she drew from the well and gave him a drink.

It was water from a *Bethlehem well* for which David in the wilderness longed. To appreciate his desire, one needs to know what thirst in the wilderness means, and also be acquainted with the cool water of the Bethlehem wells and cisterns. In the hillsides around Bethlehem are terraced vineyards, and most of these have a rock-hewn cistern located in them, which collects rain water in the winter months and preserves this water in a delightfully cool condition in the hot summer months. The men of Bethlehem boast of their cool water. One man was given a drink, but expressed a longing for water out of his father's vineyard, saying that it was so cold that he couldn't drink an entire glassful without taking it away from his lips at least three times.[3] Thus David, stationed at the cave of Adullam, and living in the parched wilderness, and weary from fighting, said: "Oh that one would give me drink of the water of the well of Bethlehem, which is by the gate" (II Sam. 23:15). When three of his men risked their lives in fighting Philistines in order to secure for him some of this cool Bethlehem water, David "poured it out unto the Lord" (II Sam. 23:16). This was according to the ancient custom of a libation offering, or the pouring on the ground as an act of worship, wine, or oil, or milk, or honey, or water. Sometimes these drink offerings were poured by the Hebrews on the animal sacrificed to the Lord. In doing what he did, David was giving to the Lord the drink of water that had cost so much for the men to secure for him.[4]

Throughout the centuries the town of *Nazareth* has had but one main source for its water supply, a well or fountain that is located at the northwest extremity of the town. We may be fairly certain that Mary came here with her pitcher to draw water for her household use, and that here the boy Jesus often quenched his thirst.

One of the most important springs in Palestine is the one at *Jericho*. Its water comes from the Judean wilderness mountains located behind the town. This spring contributes to a pool of water adjoining the excavated mound of old Jericho, and this is now called "Elisha's Fountain." It is believed to be the waters healed by the prophet long ago (II Kings 2:21). Although the level of this water gets quite low in the hot weather, it seldom dries up entirely, and is a source of water for men, animals, and the oasis of banana, fig, and date palms of the vicinity.

CISTERNS

The word "well" to the average native of Palestine has meant "spring" or "fountain," but in the Bible account it often means "cistern." Actually the cistern has been a more common source of Palestine's water supply than has the well. To drink water out of the family cistern was the proverbial wish of every Jew, and such was the promise that King Sennacherib of Assyria used to try and tempt the Jews into making peace with him. He said to them: "Make an agreement with me by

Oriental Well or Cistern

a present, and come out to me, and then eat ye every man of his own vine, and every one of his fig tree, and drink ye every one the waters of his cistern" (II Kings 18:31; cf. Isa. 36:16). These family cisterns were often dug in the open courtyard of houses as was the case of "the man which had a well [cistern] in his court." At the time of year referred to this cistern was dry and so two men could easily be hidden therein (II Sam. 17:18–19). During the rainy season the rain water is conducted from the houseroofs to these cisterns by means of troughs. Usually the water is drawn up by means of a rope that runs over a wheel, and a bucket made of animal skins is fastened to the rope. Jeremiah used the picture of a cistern that leaked water, to illustrate one of his sermons: "For my people have committed two evils"; the prophet said of the Lord, "They have forsaken me the fountain of living waters, and hewed them out cisterns, broken cisterns, that can hold no water" (Jer. 2:13).

THE SOURCE OF JERUSALEM'S WATER

Pools of water in and around the city. Throughout most of its history, the Holy City has depended largely upon private cisterns which its inhabitants have maintained to catch rain water. The city itself has had through the years no living fountain or spring within its walls. The spring of Gihon now called "The Virgin's Fountain," is located in the Valley of Kidron just outside the old city of the Jebusites or the City of David. King Hezekiah constructed a conduit or tunnel from this spring through the rock underneath the city to a place in the Tyropean Valley, where a reservoir was constructed to receive the water (II Kings 20:20). This reservoir has gone by the name of *The Pool of Siloam.* This water project was undertaken mainly to give the city a water supply in time of siege. The pool has been an important source of water for Jerusalem through the centuries. Here the Arab women of the old city often come to wash their clothes, or their vegetables, or their children. And farther in the pool or mouth of the tunnel, they get their pitchers filled with the family supply of water. And at this pool also an occasional shepherd will come to wash his sheep.[5]

Other pools located in and around the city that have supplied water include the *Pool of Hezekiah,* located inside the walls and fed with water through an underground conduit from the Pool of Mamilla. This latter pool lies 2000 feet to the west of Jaffa Gate outside the walls, and is in the Valley of Hinnom and receives drainage water coming down that valley. The *Pool of the Sultan* lies just outside the Southwestern corner of the wall in this same valley. The *Pool of Bethesda* is to be found just inside the Eastern wall, between St. Stephen's Gate and the Northern wall of the temple enclosure. It was here that many sick ones bathed in Christ's time, believing its waters had healing properties. It was here Christ healed the impotent man (John 5).

Solomon's Pools and the Temple Area Reservoir. Two miles south of Bethelehem there are three reservoirs of water that have for centuries been called Solomon's Pools, because it is generally believed that he originally constructed them. Josephus indicated that it was probably Pontius Pilate who rebuilt and enlarged them. Water from these pools was brought to Jerusalem by means of a rock aqueduct and emptied into a great reservoir located under the temple area.[6] Even today water from this source is brought up to the surface at a point between the Dome of the Rock and the Mosque el-Aksa, by an animal skin bucket attached to a rope and running over a wheel. Water carriers using goatskin "bottles" come here to get their water and carry it to many parts of the old city of Jerusalem.[7]

During six months of the year, when there is no rain, water becomes scarce in many parts of Palestine, especially during the latter part of that season when one after another cistern has dried up, and permanent wells and ever-flowing sources must be depended upon for water. In such times the water carrier will go to a well, or reservoir, and then peddle his supply of water to those who need it. He may go down the streets of the city, or he may go into the marketplace. He will call out: "Ho, ye thirsty ones, come ye and drink." There have been times when a philanthropic person has paid the water carrier for all his supply of water and thus let him offer it free of charge to those who need it. Then he will call forth: "Ho, ye thirsty ones, come and drink today for nothing, for nothing!"[8] Such words remind us of the prophetic invitation of Isaiah: "Ho, every one that thirsteth, come ye to the waters, and he that hath no money; come ye, buy . . . without money and without price" (Isa. 55:1).

Water for modern Jerusalem. The portion of Palestine now included in the new nation of Israel has undergone a marvelous transformation in regard to the supply of water for irrigation purposes as well as for household use. Primitive customs are fast disappearing and modern customs are taking their place in the Jewish sections of the land. The Jewish part of Jerusalem has had a new supply of water coming thirty miles from ancient Antipatris or Ras el Ein, located in the Plain of Sharon. Water coming from copious springs located there is pumped by relay pumping stations through a large pipeline up to the crest of the hills where the Holy City stands. The Jerusalem under the control of Israel has become very much westernized, with water piped to the houses. But in much of the ancient or Arab portion of Jerusalem, one still sees women carrying water pitchers on their head or shoulder, and men carrying goatskin "bottles" of water, very much like it was done by the ancient Hebrews. And numerous cisterns still conserve rain water.

CHAPTER 29

Raids and Blood Avenging

RAIDS

Practice among Arab Desert tribes. When there is no strong ruler among the desert tribes of Arabs, who is able to keep peace between the tribes, then some of the tribes may revert to the old pastime of raiding another tribe. They will select a tribe that is well supplied with cattle and goods, and will send out scouts to familiarize themselves with the tribe they wish to raid. They will organize their forces and plan to arrive there on a set night and usually in the dark of the moon. They will come up in stealth. One of the men or boys will approach the tents in order to attract the attention of the dogs, and then this young man will run in a different direction in order to attract the dogs away from the tents. When the place is sufficiently cleared of the dogs, then the men will rush in from different directions, untie the camels, drive off the sheep and cattle, and steal all the valuable property they can, to take home to their tents and give to their sheik. This will be done amid the screaming of the women. The men who oppose them are overcome. But the raiders are careful not to harm the women, and they are careful not to shed blood. The Mohammedan religion permits raids, but does not allow lives to be lost in the process. If blood is shed then a "blood feud" is started, and this is a very serious matter, for they often run for generations. The tribe will endeavor to kill as many as were killed in the raid.[1]

Practice in Old Testament days. In the book of Judges, bands of desert people called "the Children of the East," were a constant menace to the Israelites. When these pastoral encampments neared the borders of agriculture, a raid would be planned against the harvest of Israel, or any of their flocks, herds, or other valuable goods. Scripture says of these people: "And so it was, when Israel had sown, that . . . the children of the east, even they came up against them; and they encamped against them, and destroyed the increase of the earth . . . and left no sustenance for Israel, neither sheep, nor ox, nor ass" (Judges 6:3, 4).[2] The tent-dwelling robbers were known in the days of Job, for he says of them: "The tents of robbers prosper" (Job 12:6, A. R. V.). The prophet Obadiah tells of robbers stealing by night. "If thieves came to thee, if robbers by night . . . would they not have stolen till they had enough?" (Obadiah 5). These robbers of ancient times are in many ways similar to the Arab raiders of modern times. The latter illustrate for us methods used by the former.

BLOOD AVENGING

Ancient character of this custom. The shedding of blood during a raid starts a blood feud which may continue for many years. The basis for this feud is a custom or law that is common among many Semitic people. The unit of society among these peoples is the tribe or clan. The members of any one tribe have a responsibility to punish anybody who wrongs a member of their clan. The blood of a murdered member of the tribe "crieth . . . from the ground" (Gen. 4:10), and the nearest male relative is especially duty bound to avenge the murder. In olden times, instead of the state executing a murderer, it became the duty of the kinsman to avenge the death of the relative. The law of Moses recognized this right of the kinsman, but it did protect one who killed a person by accident and not by purpose, and so provided the cities of refuge, where such a man might flee and receive justice. "These six cities shall be a refuge, both for the children of Israel, and for the stranger, and for the sojourner among them: that every one that killeth any person unawares may flee thither" (Num. 35:15). But these cities of refuge were no protection for a real murderer. He was turned over to the kinsman for vengeance. "The revenger of blood [i.e., the kinsman] himself shall slay the murderer: when he meeteth him, he shall slay him" (Num. 35:19).

Application of the principle to Bible times. The Bedouin tribes of Arabs today govern themselves according to the old customs and laws. The whole tribe shares with the kinsman in the responsibility to avenge the shedding of blood. These old regulations need to be known in order to have an understanding of what happened in the twenty-first chapter of Second Samuel. A famine came to the land of David three successive years, and when David inquired of the Lord for the cause of it, "The Lord answered, It is for Saul, and for his bloody house, because he slew the Gibeonites" (II Sam. 21:1). King Saul had broken the covenant Israel had made with the Gibeonites, and had cruelly murdered many of these people. As a tribe of people this band of men felt duty bound to avenge the crime of Saul, but had no opportunity to do so. According to the law of the kinsman, commonly accepted among them, since the guilty man was dead, certain of his descendants should pay the penalty for the crime. Thus the death of seven male descendants of Saul atoned for Saul's sin, as far as this tribe was concerned.[3]

CHAPTER 30

Slavery in Bible Times

SLAVERY UNDER THE LAW OF MOSES

SLAVERY AMONG THE HE-BREWS THEMSELVES. Hebrews could be "hired servants" of their brethren, but they were not allowed to be "bondservants" (Lev. 25:39, 40). Concerning the one thus hired out as a servant, the Lord said: "Thou shalt not rule over him with rigor; but shalt fear thy God" (Lev. 25:43). Such slavery was ordinarily brought about by poverty, i.e., because of debts a man could not meet (Lev. 25:39); or by theft, i.e., because of restitution a man could not pay (Exod. 22:2, 3). Such a Hebrew slave could be redeemed by relatives at any time (Lev. 25:48, 49). If not redeemed, he was set free after six years of service and was sent away with presents of cattle and fruit (Deut. 15:12–14). A Hebrew slave could choose out of love for his master not to be free in the seventh year, and thus become a lifelong servant of his master. The following custom was observed in such a case: "Then thou shalt take an aul, and thrust it through his ear unto the door, and he shall be thy servant for ever" (Deut. 15:17).[1]

Slavery with Hebrew masters and foreign slaves. Most of these slaves were those who were captured in wartime (See Num. 31:26 f. and Deut. 21:10). Some were bought in foreign slave markets (Lev. 25:44). And foreigners living in the land could become slaves for the same reasons Hebrews could, through poverty or theft. Such slaves were treated as the property of their masters (Lev. 25:45). There are indications, however, that some of them were freed under certain conditions, and some writers are of the opinion that they were freed under the law of Jubilee.[2]

Protection of the slaves. The Mosaic Code contains various regulations that protect the rights and privileges of slaves. For instance, a fugitive slave law was quite favorable to the slave and was designed to protect him from oppression (Deut. 23:15, 16). All the religious privileges enjoyed by free Israelites were assured to their slaves, including the rest of the Sabbath (Exod. 20:10), the right to attend the national festivals (Deut. 16:10, 11), and the right to attend the gathering of the people to hear the reading of the law (Deut. 31:10–13).[3]

Why the Mosaic Law permitted slavery instead of abolishing it. When the laws were given at Mt. Sinai, slavery was universal among the nations of the world. It was not practical to do away with it all at once. Rather, laws were given to prevent the worst abuses and evils of it from being present among the Jews. W. M. Taylor has this to say in regard to the relation of the law to slavery, divorce, etc.

> It is noticeable, however, that wherever things in themselves questionable are tolerated, because they were too deeply seated to be removed by an immediate prohibition, the legislation regarding them is of such a character as to mitigate the evils, and prepare the way for their ultimate repression.[4]

The wisdom of such a policy is seen in the actual influence of the Mosaic legislation upon slavery among the Jews. Due to this influence, slavery among the Jews themselves had virtually disappeared by the time of Christ and His disciples.[5]

SLAVERY UNDER ISRAEL'S ENEMIES

Many of the Jews experienced slavery under foreign rule in the time of the captivities. They became captives of war to the Phoenicians who sold them to the Greeks (Joel 3:4–6). The Philistines captured them and then delivered them up to Edom (Amos 1:6). When the Assyrians conquered Samaria, many of the Jews were taken away to the land of Assyria to serve as slaves of that people (II Kings 17:6). When Jerusalem was destroyed, the Babylonians carried away to Babylon many Hebrews to become their slaves in this foreign capital (II Chron. 36:20). At a later date, the Syrian merchants came into camp in order to secure Jewish slaves (1 Maccabees 3:41 in Apocrypha). And in the days of Rome's supremacy many Jews served as slaves of the empire. But slavery under Gentile dominion was indeed altogether different from slavery under the Mosaic Law. Masters were for the most part cruel and slaves were usually oppressed greatly.[6]

SLAVERY IN THE ROMAN EMPIRE

Character and extent of slavery. In the first century human life was indeed cheap, for it has been estimated that a half of the total population of the empire, or about sixty million people, were slaves. Some wealthy Romans possessed as many as twenty thousand slaves. Slave owners became very brutal, and the slaves themselves were without hope and many of them very corrupt.[7] For the most part these slaves were those conquered in war. Some of those captured were more educated than their captors. Thus it came about that sometimes Greek slaves became schoolteachers for the family of their masters.[8]

The Roman law and the slave. Under the Roman law the slave did not have the rights or protection such as he enjoyed under the Hebrew legislation. A master might have his slave crucified for almost any reason. Augustus Caesar had thirty thousand slaves crucified during his reign.[9] A slave who stole might be branded by his master on the face with the letters C. F., representing the words "Cave furem," meaning, "Beware the thief." And in the case of a runaway slave, if he were caught, his master might brand him, give him more than customary labor, or could have him put to death if he so desired. The law did allow that he could be reinstated with mercy, through the intercession of a special friend of the master.[10] The Apostle Paul was Philemon's friend who interceded on behalf of the runaway slave Onesimus. *The Epistle to Philemon* was Paul's plea to his friend on behalf of the converted slave. No doubt Philemon gave Onesimus his freedom after receiving Paul's letter.

Attitude of the Apostles toward slavery in the Roman Empire. They did not attempt to do away with the terrible evil immediately. This would have been a hopeless task, and such an attempt would have been doubtless crushed by the iron hand of Rome. Rather, they were satisfied to give forth Christian principles, and so preach the gospel of liberation from sin, that the result would be to do away with human slavery through the conquering power of Christ.[11] Paul's letter to Philemon has, no doubt, done more to overcome slavery than any other document ever written.

New Testament use of the word slave in relation to Christ. In view of the way slaves were so often treated in the first century, it is remarkable that the Apostles again and again called themselves the slaves of Christ. Paul refers to himself thus (Rom. 1:1 and Phil. 1:1, Williams). James, Peter, and Jude do the same thing (Jas. 1:1; II Pet. 1:1; Jude 1, Williams). To be the slave of Christ is to be God's freeman (I Cor. 7:22). Of course, some of those first century slaves were treated as friends to be trusted, and they really loved their masters and served them faithfully.[12] This is the picture of all true believers in relation to Christ. Christ is our Owner, and we are His willing and loving slaves.

CHAPTER 31

Greek Athletics and Roman Gladiatorial Shows

F OLLOWING THE VICTORIOUS
ARMY of Alexander the Great, the games and gymnastic sports
of the Greeks were introduced into Palestine, and a gym-
nasium was erected at Jerusalem. These athletic events de-
lighted the Gentiles, but were repugnant to the pious Jews,
because they were of a demoralizing character. Those who
took part in these contests did so with naked bodies.[1] Under
the rule of the Maccabees these spectacles came to an end,
but Herod the Great revived them, building a theater at
Jerusalem, and similar ones in other places. The Romans carried on many of the Greek athletic customs, but came to give
special prominence to their gladiatorial shows.[2]

THE GREEK OLYMPIC GAMES

Character of the Olympic Games. Although the four principal Grecian games were the Isthmian, the Nemean, the Py-
thian, and the Olympian Games, the latter were by far the
most celebrated. They were held every four years at Olympia
in honor of the god Zeus. The event began with special

294

presentation of offerings to various gods and heroes. Following this there were four heats of short races to determine a winner; then longer races were held; and then came a contest of a five-fold nature including leaping, racing, quoits, spear-throwing, and wrestling; then there was chariot-racing, boxing, running in armor, and contests between heralds and trumpeters.[3]

Preparation for the Olympian Games. Contestants were under very rigid rules, which began with a prescribed diet for their meals at home, and for thirty days before the events began they resided at one place where they were under constant supervision. They had to agree to refrain from dainties, to exercise their bodies regularly, and to obey all of the rules of the games when the events took place.[4] The Apostle Paul referred to this self-discipline when he wrote to the Corinthians: "And every man that striveth in the games exerciseth self-control in all things" (I Cor. 9:25, A. R. V.). And to young Timothy he said, "No contestant in the game is crowned unless he competes according to the rules" (II Tim. 2:5, Williams).

Prizes for winning in the games. When an athletic event was completed, a herald proclaimed aloud the name of the victor and the city from which he came. He was presented with a palm branch by the judges, and the prizes were given out on the last day of the games. It came to be customary to give the winners a wreath made from the leaves of what was considered to be the sacred wild olive tree.[5] Paul refers to the incorruptible nature of the Christian's reward-crown in contrast to the perishable character of the prize in the Greek games. "Now they do it to obtain a corruptible crown; but we an incorruptible" (I Cor. 9:25). Peter had the same thought in mind when he wrote: "Ye shall receive a crown of glory that fadeth not away" (I Pet. 5:4).

Allusions to races in the Epistles. Paul compares himself to an Olympian racer when he writes: "I press toward the mark for the prize of the high calling of God in Christ Jesus" (Phil. 3:14). And as his valedictory, he declares: "I have run my race" (II Tim. 4:7, Williams). The writer to the Hebrews sees the Christian's race as being run with endurance before a great crowd of spectators: "Therefore, as we have so vast a crowd of spectators in the grandstands, let us throw off every impediment and the sin that easily entangles our feet, and run with endurance the race for which we are entered" (Heb. 12:1, Williams).

Allusions to wrestling and boxing in the Epistles. In writing about the Christian's contest with the powers of Satan, Paul likens it to a wrestling match, such as was part of the activity of a Greek Olympian festival. The contest was between two men each of whom tried to throw the other man, and when one succeeded in first throwing down, and then holding down his opponent with his hand upon his neck, he was declared to be the winner.[6] When Paul wrote to the Romans: "Strive together with me in your prayers" (Rom. 15:30), he was wanting them to put the same energy into their prayers as a wrestler would put into his efforts to win his contest. (Cf. Williams and Weymouth translations of this verse.) In writing to the Corinthians Paul clearly refers to boxing. He says: "So fight I, not as one that beateth the air: but I keep under my body, and bring it into subjection" (I Cor. 9:26–27). He is thinking of keeping his body under control lest if he fails to do so he be disqualified to be an effective Christian worker.

Allusions to various athletic ideas in the New Testament. The Apostle Paul was fond of making use of athletics to illustrate truth. To the Philippians he spoke of "striving together for the faith of the gospel" (Phil. 1:27). The words *striving together* actually mean "acting as athletes in concert."[7] In the language of modern athletics, he was thinking of the importance of "team spirit" in church work. And when Paul wanted to give a gentle rebuke to two women at Philippi who were not of the same mind, he also complimented them by referring to them as "those women which labored with me in the gospel" (Phil. 4:3). The reference here again is to athletics. "These women were spiritual athletes."[8] He was saying that they had worked with him like young men labor together to win an athletic contest. When Jude urged his readers to "earnestly contend for the faith which was once for all delivered unto the saints" (Jude 3, A. R. V.), he was using "another athletic word."[9]

THE ROMAN GLADIATORIAL SHOWS

One of the chief forms of amusement among the Romans of the early Christian era was to condemn criminals, and especially Christians, to fight with lions, bears, elephants, or tigers in the amphitheaters of the empire, before huge crowds of spectators. The crowds would urge on the beast by throwing darts or by shouting in a mad spirit, and then watch the poor victim torn to pieces by the animal.[10] Paul referred to this practice when he said, "If after the manner of men I have fought with beasts at Ephesus" (I Cor. 15:32). It is believed, however, that Paul was comparing his bitter experience at Ephesus (Acts 19), with such a contest in the amphitheater, because he was himself a Roman citizen, and the Romans would not allow a citizen to be subjected to a degradation such as fighting with beasts.[11] The writer to the Hebrews compares the experiences of his hearers to what happened in the arena. "In consequence of the taunts and injuries heaped upon you, you became a public spectacle" (Heb. 10:33, Twentieth Century N. T.).

The Romans had a custom in the arena to which Paul refers. Often they allowed the men who fought with beasts in the morning, to have armor and equipment with which to fight the animals. But as a last event that took place about noon, men who were naked and without any armor or defense were brought in, and the animals were turned loose upon them.[12] Thus in telling of the sufferings of apostles, Paul said: "For I think that God hath set forth us the apostles last, as it were appointed to death: for we are made a spectacle unto the world, and to angels, and to men" (I Cor. 4:9).

Reference Notes

Chapter 1

1. W. M. Thomson, *The Land and the Book*, Vol. I, p. 562.
2. John D. Whiting, "Bedouin Life in Bible Lands," *The National Geographic Magazine*, January, 1937, pp. 64, 65. See also pp. 68–69 for photographs of goat's hair tents.
3. *Ibid.*, pp. 64, 65.
4. George H. Scherer, *The Eastern Color of the Bible*, pp. 54, 55.
5. Whiting, *op. cit.*, p. 67.
6. Selah Merrill, *East of the Jordan*, pp. 469, 470.
7. Edwin W. Rice, *Orientalisms in Bible Lands*, p. 241.
8. *Ibid.*, pp. 241, 242.
9. Scherer, *op. cit.*, pp. 54, 55.
10. Rice, *op. cit.*, pp. 245, 246; Scherer, *op. cit.*, pp. 55, 56.
11. Information received during personal interview with Mr. G. Eric Matson, photographer, and long time resident of Palestine.
12. Whiting, *op. cit.*, p. 67.
13. Barbara M. Bowen, *Through Bowen Museum with Bible in Hand*, p. 18. (Grand Rapids: William B. Eerdmans Publishing Co., 1946.)
14. Merrill, *op. cit.*, pp. 470, 471.
15. George M. Mackie, *Bible Manners and Customs*, pp. 89, 90.

Chapter 2

1. W. M. Thomson, *The Land and the Book*, Vol. I, pp. 98, 99.
2. *Ibid.*, Vol. II, p. 634.
3. Max Radin, *The Life of People in Biblical Times*, pp. 175, 176.
4. Abraham M. Rihbany, *The Syrian Christ*, p. 243.
5. *Ibid.*, p. 241.
6. George A. Barton, *Archaeology and the Bible*, p. 126.
7. "House," *The People's Bible Encyclopedia*, Charles R. Barnes, ed., p. 505.
8. Barton, *op. cit.*, p. 126.
9. E. P. Barrows, *Sacred Geography and Antiquities*, p. 389, also Edwin W. Rice, *Orientalisms in Bible Lands*, p. 249.

10. George M. Mackie, *Bible Manners and Customs*, p. 92.
11. Col. Wilson, *Picturesque Palestine, Sinai, and Egypt*, Vol. I, p. 300.
12. James M. Freeman, *Handbook of Bible Manners and Customs*, p. 240.
13. *Ibid.*, p. 212.
14. Barton, *op. cit.*, p. 126.
15. Freeman, *op. cit.*, p. 123; also Mackie, *op. cit.*, p. 95.
16. Carl F. Keil, *Manual of Biblical Archaelogy*, Vol. II, p. 106.
17. G. Robinson Lees, *Village Life in Palestine*, pp. 89, 90.
18. Edmond Stapfer, *Palestine in the Time of Christ*, pp. 179, 180; also James Neil, *Pictured Palestine*, p. 123.
19. Rihbany, *The Syrian Christ*, p. 216.
20. See "Candle," *The People's Bible Encyclopedia*, p. 183.
21. G. E. Wright, "Lamps, Politics, and the Jewish Religion," *The Biblical Archaeologist*, May, 1939, pp. 22–24; also Elisabeth Fletcher, "Archaeology Comes Down to Earth," *Christian Life*, December, 1950, p. 14.
22. George A. Barton, *Archaeology and the Bible*, p. 151.
23. Stapfer, *op. cit.*, p. 180.
24. Thomson, *op. cit.*, Vol. III, pp. 472, 473.
25. Rihbany, *op. cit.*, pp. 153, 154.
26. Lees, *op. cit.*, pp. 88, 89.
27. *Ibid.*, p. 103.
28. *Loc. cit.*
29. Freeman, *op. cit.*, p. 341.
30. Information received by consultation with Dr. G. Frederick Owen, and Mr. G. Eric Matson, both of whom have had prolonged residence in Palestine.
31. Young's Bible Translation; also see translation of Carl F. Keil, *The Twelve Minor Prophets*, Vol. I, p. 155. (Edinburgh: T. & T. Clark, 1880.)
32. Concerning early practice, see Thomas Upham, *Jahn's Biblical Archaeology*, pp. 147–148. Concerning later practice, see II Macc. 10:3.
33. Franz Delitzsch, *Biblical Commentary on the Prophecy of Isaiah*, Vol. II, p. 257. (Edinburgh, T. & T. Clark, 1890.)
34. Thomson, *op. cit.*, Vol. III, pp. 54, 55.
35. Freeman, *op. cit.*, p. 118.
36. *Ibid.*, p. 258.
37. Thomson, *op. cit.*, Vol. III, p. 56.
38. Rihbany, *op. cit.*, pp. 273, 274.
39. Thomson, *op. cit.*, Vol. III, p. 57.
40. Alfred Edersheim, *Sketches of Jewish Social Life in the Days of Christ*, pp. 93, 94.
41. John D. Whiting, "Village Life in the Holy Land," *The National Geographic Magazine*, March, 1914, pp. 249–253.
42. *Ibid.*, p. 251. See also photograph, p. 310.
43. *Loc. cit.*
44. *Ibid.*, p. 253.

CHAPTER 3

1. George M. Mackie, *Bible Manners and Customs*, p. 90.
2. *Ibid.*, pp. 90, 91.

3. E. P. Barrows, *Sacred Geography and Antiquities*, p. 384.
4. James M. Freeman, *Handbook of Bible Manners and Customs*, p. 390.
5. Barrows, *op. cit.*, p. 385.
6. Freeman, *op. cit.*, p. 198.
7. *Loc. cit.*
8. Barrows, *op. cit.*, p. 386.
9. Freeman, *op. cit.*, p. 146.
10. *Ibid.*, p. 144.
11. Edmond Stapfer, *Palestine in the Time of Christ*, p. 178.
12. Barrows, *op. cit.*, pp. 384, 385.
13. Edwin W. Rice, *Orientalisms in Bible Lands*, p. 251.
14. W. M. Thomson, *The Land and the Book*, Vol. III, pp. 413, 414.
15. Barrows, *op. cit.*, p. 385.
16. Rice, *op. cit.*, p. 251.
17. Milton B. Lindberg, *A Guest in a Palestinian Home* (pamphlet), pp. 3, 4.
18. Mackie, *op. cit.*, pp. 92, 93.
19. Thomson, *op. cit.*, Vol. I, p. 562.
20. *Ibid.*, Vol. II, pp. 433, 434.
21. "Tiling," *The People's Bible Encyclopedia*, Charles R. Barnes, ed., p. 1107.
22. Alfred Edersheim, *The Life and Times of Jesus the Messiah*, Vol. I, p. 503.
23. Barrows, *op. cit.*, p. 394.

CHAPTER 4

1. W. M. Thomson, *The Land and the Book*, Vol. I, p. 98.
2. Edwin W. Rice, *Orientalisms in Bible Lands*, p. 94.
3. James Freeman, *Handbook of Bible Manners and Customs*, pp. 128, 129.
4. *Ibid.*, p. 50.
5. Abraham Rihbany, *The Syrian Christ*, pp. 193, 194.
6. *Ibid.*, pp. 196–198.
7. James Neil, *Pictured Palestine*, p. 78; cf. also Anis C. Haddad, *Palestine Speaks*, pp. 71, 72.
8. Rice, *op. cit.*, p. 96.
9. Thomson, *op. cit.*, Vol. II, pp. 181, 182.
10. From class notes in course: "Manners and Customs of Bible Lands," Pasadena College, June, 1950, taught by Dr. G. Frederick Owen.
11. George M. Mackie, *Bible Manners and Customs*, p. 99.
12. Freeman, *op. cit.*, p. 89.
13. *Loc. cit.*
14. Mackie, *op. cit.*, p. 99.
15. Rihbany, *op. cit.*, pp. 200, 202.
16. Mackie, *op. cit.*, p. 72.
17. *Loc. cit.*
18. Thomson, *op. cit.*, Vol. I, p. 252.
19. "Pulse," *The People's Bible Encyclopedia*, Charles R. Barnes, ed., p. 1149.
20. "Milk," *ibid.*, p. 724.

21. From class notes in course: "Manners and Customs of Bible Lands," Pasadena College, June, 1950, taught by Dr. G. Frederick Owen.
22. "Butter," *The People's Bible Encyclopedia*, p. 169.
23. Thomson, *op. cit.*, Vol. II, pp. 456, 457.
24. *Loc. cit.*
25. From class notes in course: "Manners and Customs of Bible Lands," Pasadena College, June, 1950, taught by Dr. G. Frederick Owen.
26. Thomas Upham, *Jahn's Biblical Archaeology*, p. 151.
27. Edmond Stapfer, *Palestine in the Time of Christ*, pp. 185, 186.
28. "Food—Preparation of," *The People's Bible Encyclopedia*, pp. 378–380.
29. Upham, *op. cit.*, p. 151.
30. W. F. Albright, *The Archaeology of Palestine*, p. 217.
31. E. P. Barrows, *Sacred Geography and Antiquities*, p. 366.
32. Thomson, *op. cit.*, Vol. II, p. 259.
33. Mackie, *op. cit.*, p. 45.
34. Thomson, *op. cit.*, Vol. I, pp. 284–286.

CHAPTER 5

1. Edwin W. Rice, *Orientalisms in Bible Lands*, p. 101.
2. Edwin C. Bissell, *Biblical Antiquities*, p. 81.
3. Abraham Rihbany, *The Syrian Christ*, p. 225.
4. Selah Merrill, *East of the Jordan*, pp. 480, 481.
5. Francis Brown, S. R. Driver, and Charles A. Briggs, *A Hebrew and English Lexicon of the Old Testament*, p. 1020. (New York: Houghton Mifflin Company, 1906).
6. "Table," *The People's Bible Encyclopedia*, Charles R. Barnes, ed., p. 1078.
7. W. M. Thomson, *The Land and the Book*, Vol. III, p. 75.
8. E. P. Barrows, *Sacred Geography and Antiquities*, p. 413.
9. Thomas Upham, *Jahn's Biblical Archaeology*, p. 156.
10. Thomson, *op. cit.*, Vol. III, p. 75.
11. Rice, *op. cit.*, p. 102.
12. Alfred Edersheim, *The Life and Times of Jesus the Messiah*, Vol. I, p. 684.
13. Edmond Stapfer, *Palestine in the Time of Christ*, p. 184.
14. Merrill, *op. cit.*, pp. 480, 481.
15. Rice, *op. cit.*, p. 103.
16. Bissell, *op. cit.*, p. 80.
17. Thomson, *op. cit.*, Vol. III, p. 78.

CHAPTER 6

1. James M. Freeman, *Handbook of Bible Manners and Customs*, p. 363.
2. Abraham Rihbany, *The Syrian Christ*, pp. 208–210.
3. E. P. Barrows, *Sacred Geography and Antiquities*, p. 416.
4. Freeman, *op. cit.*, pp. 210, 211.
5. Barrows, *op. cit.*, pp. 413, 414.

6. Information received by personal consultation with Dr. G. Frederick Owen.
7. Milton Lindberg, *A Guest in a Palestinian Home,* a pamphlet, p. 6.
8. Carl F. Keil, *Manual of Biblical Archaeology,* Vol. II, p. 282.
9. See Rihbany, *op. cit.,* pp. 60, 61.
10. "Sop," *The People's Bible Encyclopedia,* Charles R. Barnes, ed., p. 1047.
11. Anis C. Haddad, *Palestine Speaks,* p. 74 (Anderson, Ind.: The Warner Press, 1936).
12. Rihbany, *op. cit.,* p. 69.

CHAPTER 7

1. James M. Freeman, *Handbook of Bible Manners and Customs,* p. 214.
2. H. Clay Trumbull, *Studies in Oriental Social Life,* p. 97.
3. Edwin W. Rice, *Orientalisms in Bible Lands,* p. 82.
4. Trumbull, *op. cit.,* pp. 75, 77.
5. Joseph H. Thayer, *A Greek-English Lexicon of the New Testament,* p. 654. (New York: American Book Company, 1889.)
6. Rice, *op. cit.,* p. 82.
7. Trumbull, *op. cit.,* p. 115.
8. Selah Merrill, *East of the Jordan,* pp. 480, 481.
9. John D. Whiting, "Village Life in the Holy Land," *The National Geographic Magazine,* March, 1914, pp. 253–257. This article is illustrated with numerous photographs showing manners and customs of the Palestinian Arabs.
10. Rice, *op. cit.,* p. 253.
11. George M. Mackie, *Bible Manners and Customs,* pp. 93, 94.
12. James Neil, *Pictured Palestine,* pp. 64, 65.
13. *Ibid.,* pp. 65–67.
14. John D. Whiting, "Bedouin Life in Bible Lands," *The National Geographic Magazine,* January, 1937, p. 72.
15. Neil, *op. cit.,* p. 68.
16. Freeman, *op. cit.,* p. 36.
17. W. M. Thomson, *The Land and the Book,* Vol. III, p. 85.
18. Rice, *op. cit.,* p. 88.
19. Freeman, *op. cit.,* pp. 219, 220.
20. Trumbull, *op. cit.,* pp. 106, 108, 112.
21. *Ibid.,* p. 108.
22. Abraham M. Rihbany, *The Syrian Christ,* p. 191.
23. *Ibid.,* pp. 191, 192.
24. Trumbull, *op. cit.,* pp. 110, 111.
25. Milton B. Lindberg, *A Guest in a Palestinian Home,* a pamphlet, pp. 6, 7.
26. Mackie, *op. cit.,* p. 93.
27. Trumbull, *op. cit.,* p. 110.
28. Freeman, *op. cit.,* p. 223.
29. George H. Scherer, *The Eastern Color of the Bible,* p. 66.
30. Cf. Rihbany, *op. cit.,* pp. 218, 219.
31. John D. Whiting, "Bedouin Life in Bible Lands," *The National Geographic Magazine,* January, 1937, p. 72.
32. Rihbany, *op. cit.,* p. 221.

CHAPTER 8

1. James M. Freeman, *Handbook of Bible Manners and Customs*, p. 22.
2. Anis C. Haddad, *Palestine Speaks*, pp. 54, 55.
3. *Ibid.*, p. 56.
4. Anis C. Haddad, *Palestine Speaks*, p. 56 (Anderson, Ind.: The Warner Press, 1936).
5. W. M. Thomson, *The Land and the Book,* Vol. I, p. 108.
6. Edwin W. Rice, *Orientalisms in Bible Lands*, p. 101.
7. John A. Broadus, *Commentary on the Gospel of Matthew* (vol. 1, *An American Commentary on the New Testament*), p. 446. (Philadelphia: American Baptist Publication Society, 1886.)
8. Flavius Josephus, *Antiquities*, (Vol. I, Complete Works), p. 331.
9. Broadus, *loc. cit.*
10. Broadus, *loc. cit.*
11. Harold B. Hunting, *Hebrew Life and Times*, pp. 17–19.
12. Abraham M. Rihbany, *The Syrian Christ*, pp. 360, 361.
13. Information received during personal interview with Mr. G. Eric Matson, photographer, and long time resident of Palestine.
14. Alexander Maclaren, *The Psalms* (*The Expositor's Bible*), Vol. II, p. 130. (New York: George H. Doran Company, 1892.)
15. Thomson, *op. cit.*, Vol. I, p. 130.
16. John D. Whiting, "Bedouin Life in Bible Lands," *The National Geographic Magazine*, January, 1937, pp. 61–63.
17. From class notes in course: "Manners and Customs of Bible Lands," Pasadena College, June, 1950, taught by Dr. G. Frederick Owen.
18. James Neil, *Pictured Palestine*, pp. 84–88.
19. Rihbany, *op. cit.*, p. 117.
20. *Ibid.*, pp. 115–118.
21. *Ibid.* pp. 118, 119.
22. Neil, *op. cit.*, pp. 90, 91.
23. Freeman, *op. cit.*, pp. 26–29.
24. See Thomson, *op. cit.*, Vol. I, p. 261.
25. A. Goodrich-Freer, *Things Seen in Palestine*, p. 72.
26. Neil, *op. cit.*, p. 155.

CHAPTER 9

1. James Neil, *Pictured Palestine*, pp. 5, 6.
2. E. P. Barrows, *Sacred Geography and Antiquities*, pp. 396, 397.
3. *Ibid.*, p. 397.
4. Edmond Stapfer, *Palestine in the Time of Christ*, pp. 191, 192.
5. Barrows, *op. cit.*, p. 397.
6. "Outer Tunic," *The People's Bible Encyclopedia*, Charles R. Barnes, ed., pp. 281–282. See also Barrows, *op. cit.*, pp. 398, 399.
7. "The Girdle," *loc. cit.* (Encyclopedia).
8. Stapfer, *op. cit.*, p. 192.
9. Anis C. Haddad, *Palestine Speaks*, pp. 105, 106 (Anderson, Ind.: The Warner Press, 1936).

10. *Ibid.*, pp. 103, 104.
11. *Ibid.*, p. 108.
12. John A. Broadus, *Commentary on the Gospel of Matthew* (vol. 1, *An American Commentary on the New Testament*), p. 120. (Philadelphia: American Baptist Publication Society, 1886.)
13. Stapfer, *op. cit.*, pp. 192, 193.
14. *Ibid.*, p. 198.
15. *Ibid.*, pp. 198, 199.
16. James M. Freeman, *Handbook of Bible Manners and Customs*, pp. 345 and 442.
17. John D. Whiting, "Bedouin Life in Bible Lands," *The National Geographic Magazine*, January, 1937, p. 79.
18. Max Radin, *The Life of the People in Biblical Times*, p. 131 (Philadelphia: The Jewish Publication Society of America, 1929).
19. Thomas Upham, *Jahn's Biblical Archaeology*, p. 141.
20. Stapfer, *op. cit.*, p. 193.
21. John D. Whiting, "Village Life in the Holy Land," *The National Geographic Magazine*, March, 1914, pp. 262–264.
22. Stapfer, *op. cit.*, p. 199.
23. George M. Mackie, *Bible Manners and Customs*, pp. 69–71.
24. Stapfer, *op. cit.*, p. 199, 200.
25. *Loc. cit.*
26. *Ibid.*, pp. 200, 201.

CHAPTER 10

1. Edwin W. Rice, *Orientalisms in Bible Lands*, pp. 12, 13.
2. Thomas Upham, *Jahn's Biblical Archaeology*, pp. 176, 177.
3. H. Clay Trumbull, *Studies in Oriental Social Life*, pp. 249, 250.
4. W. M. Thomson, in early edition of *The Land and the Book*, quoted and paraphrased by E. P. Barrows in, *Sacred Geography and Antiquities*, p. 438.
5. Trumbull, *op. cit.*, pp. 250–252.
6. W. M. Thomson, *The Land and the Book*, Vol. II, pp. 12, 13.

CHAPTER 11

1. Carl F. Keil, *Manual of Biblical Archaeology*, Vol. II, p. 175.
2. From class notes in course: "Manners and Customs of Bible Lands," Pasadena College, June 1950, taught by Dr. G. Frederick Owen.
3. Elihu Grant, *The People of Palestine*, pp. 64, 65.
4. James Neil, *Pictured Palestine*, p. 83.
5. Edmond Stapfer, *Palestine in the Time of Christ*, p. 140.
6. *Ibid.*, pp. 140, 141.
7. Edwin W. Rice, *Orientalisms in Bible Lands*, p. 279.
8. Meanings given under each separate name in, *The People's Bible Encyclopedia*.
9. Grant, *op. cit.*, p. 60.
10. James M. Freeman, *Handbook of Bible Manners and Customs*, p. 430.
11. George M. Mackie, *Bible Manners and Customs*, pp. 120, 121.
12. Kiel, *op. cit.*, Vol. II, p. 176.

CHAPTER 12

1. Sir Leonard Woolley, *Abraham; Recent Discoveries and Hebrew Origins*, pp. 101–103. (New York: Charles Scribner's Sons, 1936.)
2. Barbara Bowen, *The Bible Lives Today*, pp. 31, 32.
3. William M. Taylor, *Moses the Law-Giver*, pp. 24–28. (New York: George H. Doran Company, 1907.)
4. *Ibid.*, pp. 266, 267.
5. William G. Blaikie, *A Manual of Bible History*, p. 224. (London: T. Nelson and Sons, 1912). See also "Schools of the Prophets," *The People's Bible Encyclopedia*, Charles R. Barnes, ed., p. 983.
6. Alfred Edersheim, *The Life and Times of Jesus the Messiah*, Vol. I, p. 231.
7. *Ibid.*, pp. 230–234.
8. A. T. Robertson, *Epochs in the Life of Paul*, pp. 16–18. (New York: Charles Scribner's Sons, 1909.)
9. *Loc. cit.*
10. Camden M. Cobern, *The New Archaeological Discoveries and Their Bearing on The New Testament*, pp. 639, 640.
11. *Ibid.*, p. 123.
12. *Ibid.*, pp. 473, 474.

CHAPTER 13

1. Thomas Hartwell Horne, *An Introduction to the Critical Study and Knowledge of the Holy Scriptures*, (Philadelphia: Desilver, Thomas & Co., 1836) Vol. II, p. 163.
2. Barbara M. Bowen, *The Bible Lives Today*, p. 70.
3. Sir Leonard Woolley, *Abraham; Recent Discoveries and Hebrew Origins*, pp. 164, 165. (New York: Charles Scribner's Sons, 1936.)
4. *Loc. cit.*
5. Theodore S. Soares, *The Social Institutions and Ideals of the Bible*, p. 60.
6. *Ibid.*, pp. 61, 62.
7. Abraham M. Rihbany, *The Syrian Christ*, pp. 49–51.
8. Edmond Stapfer, *Palestine in the Time of Christ*, pp. 386–388; also 143.
9. *Ibid.*, p. 389.
10. See "Special Dress of the Pharisees," Ch. IX, p. 101 f.
11. Kenneth S. Wuest, *First Peter in the Greek New Testament*, pp. 115, 116. (Grand Rapids: Wm. B. Eerdmans Publishing Company, 1942.)
12. Joseph P. Free, *Archaeology and Bible History*, p. 335.
13. Archibald Thomas Robertson, *Paul and the Intellectuals*, pp. 207, 208. (Garden City: Doubleday, Doran and Company, 1928.)

CHAPTER 14

1. Theodore S. Soares, *The Social Institutions and Ideals of the Bible*, pp. 42, 43.
2. *Ibid.*, pp. 43, 44.
3. H. Clay Trumbull, *Studies in Oriental Social Life*, pp. 37, 38.

4. Soares, *op. cit.*, pp. 44, 45.
5. Rev. Khodadad E. Keith, *The Social Life of a Jew in the Time of Christ*, p. 55.
6. Trumbull, *op. cit.*, pp. 9, 10.
7. *Ibid.*, p. 14.
8. *Ibid.*, pp. 17–20.
9. Keith, *op. cit.*, p. 58.
10. *Loc. cit.*
11. H. Clay Trumbull, *Studies in Oriental Social Life*, pp. 37, 38.
12. Keith, *op. cit.*, pp. 58, 59.
13. Edmond Stapfer, *Palestine in the Time of Christ*, pp. 159, 160.
14. *Ibid.*, p. 161.
15. *Ibid.*, p. 162.
16. *Ibid.*, p. 160.
17. Rev. Daniel March, *Home Life in the Bible*, p. 465.
18. *Ibid.*, pp. 465, 466.
19. Stapfer, *op. cit.*, p. 163.
20. John A. Broadus, *Commentary on the Gospel of Matthew* (Vol. I, An American Commentary on the New Testament), p. 498. (Philadelphia: American Baptist Publication Society, 1886.)
21. Alfred Edersheim, *The Life and Times of Jesus the Messiah*, Vol. II, p. 455.
22. Stapfer, *op. cit.*, p. 164.
23. *Ibid.*, p. 163.
24. *Ibid.*, p. 164.
25. Thomas Hartwell Horne, *An Introduction to the Critical Study of the Holy Scriptures*, Vol. II, p. 162.
26. Stapfer, *op. cit.*, pp. 164, 165.
27. *Ibid.*, p. 165.

CHAPTER 15

1. James M. Freeman, *Handbook of Bible Manners and Customs*, p. 110.
2. C. H. Spurgeon, *The Treasury of David*, Vol. II, p. 52. (New York: Funk & Wagnalls Company, 1881.)
3. Freeman, *op. cit.*, p. 21.
4. Elihu Grant, *The People of Palestine*, p. 66.
5. Freeman, *op. cit.*, pp. 71, 72.

CHAPTER 16

1. "Treatment of Disease," *The People's Bible Encyclopedia*, pp. 271, 272.
2. Edmond Stapfer, *Palestine in the Time of Christ*, pp. 251, 252.
3. *Ibid.*, pp. 256, 257.
4. H. Clay Trumbull, *Studies in Oriental Social Life*, pp. 295–298.
5. *Ibid.*, p. 304.
6. *Ibid.*, pp. 308–309.

CHAPTER 17

1. George M. Mackie, *Bible Manners and Customs,* p. 126.
2. H. Clay Trumbull, *Studies in Oriental Social Life,* pp. 144, 145.
3. *Ibid.,* p. 154.
4. *Ibid.,* p. 155.
5. Edwin W. Rice, *Orientalisms in Bible Lands,* p. 121.
6. Trumbull, *op. cit.,* pp. 177, 178.
7. G. Robinson Lees, *Village Life in Palestine,* p. 130.
8. "Grave—Hebrew," *The People's Bible Encyclopedia,* Charles R. Barnes, ed., pp. 435, 436.
9. C. Von Orelli, *The Prophecies of Jeremiah,* p. 134. (Edinburgh: T. & T. Clark, 1889.)

CHAPTER 18

1. "Sheep," *The People's Bible Encyclopedia,* Charles R. Barnes, ed., pp. 63, 64.
2. John D. Whiting, "Among the Bethlehem Shepherds," *The National Geographic Magazine,* December, 1926, p. 729. This article has numerous photographs accompanying it that illustrate Bible-land shepherd life.
3. *Loc. cit.*
4. G. Robinson Lees, *Village Life in Palestine,* p. 164.
5. Cf. George M. Mackie, *Bible Manners and Customs,* p. 31.
6. James Neil, *Everyday Life in the Holy Land,* pp. 33, 34.
7. See "Scepter," *The People's Bible Encyclopedia,* p. 981.
8. Mackie, *op. cit.,* p. 31.
9. "The Sling," *"The People's Bible Encyclopedia,"* p. 85.
10. Mackie, *op. cit.,* p. 33.
11. See Whiting, *op. cit.,* p. 730.
12. *Ibid.,* pp. 736–746.
13. W. M. Thomson, *The Land and the Book,* Vol. II, p. 595.
14. J. G. Wood, *Bible Animals,* pp. 149, 150.
15. Cf. Abraham Rihbany's, *The Syrian Christ,* pp. 295, 296. Also Thomson, *op. cit.,* Vol. II, p. 593.
16. Thomson, *op. cit.,* Vol. I, p. 313.
17. James Neil, *Pictured Palestine,* pp. 248, 249; also Thomson, *op. cit.,* Vol. II, p. 591.
18. Lees, *op. cit.,* p. 170.
19. *Ibid.,* pp. 170–173.
20. Rihbany, *op. cit.,* p. 303.
21. Thomson, *op. cit.,* Vol. II, p. 593; also Wood, *op. cit.,* p. 158.
22. Rihbany, *op. cit.,* p. 299.
23. *Ibid.,* pp. 299, 300.
24. *Ibid.,* pp. 301, 302.
25. Thomson, *op. cit.,* Vol. II, p. 595.
26. Cunningham Geikie, *The Holy Land and the Bible,* Vol. I, p. 222.
27. Mackie, *op. cit.,* p. 35.
28. H. R. P. Dickson, *The Arab of the Desert,* pp. 403, 404.

29. Geikie, *op. cit.*, Vol. I, p. 219.
30. Thomson, *op. cit.*, Vol. III, pp. 25, 26.
31. Geikie, *op. cit.*, Vol. I, p. 223.
32. Whiting, *op. cit.*, p. 753.
33. H. B. Tristram, *The Land of Israel*, p. 638.
34. Whiting, *op. cit.*, p. 745.
35. Rihbany, *op. cit.*, pp. 307, 308.
36. Geikie, *op. cit.*, Vol. I, p. 228.
37. Mackie, *op. cit.*, p. 36.
38. Wood, *op. cit.*, p. 172.
39. *Ibid.*, pp. 163, 164.
40. *Ibid.*, pp. 177, 178.
41. *Ibid.*, pp. 172, 173.
42. *Ibid.*, pp. 174, 175.
43. Geikie, *op. cit.*, Vol. I, p. 232.
44. Geikie, *op. cit.*, Vol. I, pp. 224, 225; also Edwin W. Rice, *Orientalisms in Bible Lands*, p. 167.
45. John A. Broadus, *Commentary on the Gospel of Matthew* (Vol. I, *An American Commentary on the New Testament*), p. 509, footnote 1. (Philadelphia: American Baptist Publication Society, 1886.)
46. Wood, *op. cit.*, pp. 189, 190.
47. Geikie, *op. cit.*, Vol. II, pp. 130, 131.

CHAPTER 19

1. W. M. Thomson, *The Land and the Book*, Vol. II, p. 549.
2. A. C. Haddad, *Palestine Speaks*, pp. 18, 19.
3. Abraham Rihbany, *The Syrian Christ*, p. 287.
4. Edwin W. Rice, *Orientalisms in Bible Lands*, p. 135.
5. Cf. E. P. Barrows, *Sacred Geography and Antiquities*, p. 342.
6. *Loc. cit.*
7. Samuel Schor, *Palestine and the Bible*, p. 8.
8. James Neil, *Pictured Palestine*, pp. 261, 262.
9. Schor, *loc. cit.*
10. G. Robinson Lees, *Village Life in Palestine*, p. 141.
11. Schor, *op. cit.*, p. 6.
12. Barrows, *op. cit.*, pp. 342, 343.
13. Rice, *op. cit.*, p. 135.
14. George M. Mackie, *Bible Manners and Customs*, p. 39.
15. See Brown, Driver, and Briggs, *Hebrew and English Lexicon of the Old Testament*, p. 281. (New York: Houghton Mifflin Company, 1906.)
16. Cf. George A. Barton, *Archaeology and the Bible*, p. 132.
17. Richard C. Trench, *Notes on the Parables of our Lord*, pp. 60, 61.
18. Rihbany, *op. cit.*, pp. 289–290.
19. Mackie, *op. cit.*, p. 40.
20. Trench, *op. cit.*, p. 59.
21. Thomson, *op. cit.*, Vol. II, pp. 395, 396.
22. *Ibid.*, pp. 292, 293.

23. C. H. Toy, *International Critical Commentary: Proverbs,* pp. 534, 535. (New York: Charles Scribner's Sons, 1899.)
24. Upham, *Jahn's Biblical Archaeology,* pp. 26–28. See also illustrated article by John D. Whiting, "Jerusalem's Locust Plague," in the *National Geographic Magazine,* December, 1915, pp. 511–550.
25. C. F. Keil, *Commentary on Minor Prophets,* Vol. I, p. 180. (Edinburgh: T. & T. Clark, 1880.)
26. Lees, *op. cit.,* p. 144.
27. *Loc. cit.*
28. Neil, *op. cit.,* pp. 263, 264.
29. Rihbany, *op. cit.,* pp. 290, 291.
30. Lees, *op. cit.,* p. 146.
31. Barton, *op. cit.,* p. 135.
32. Thomson, *op. cit.,* Vol. I, pp. 162, 163.
33. "Ass," *The People's Bible Encyclopedia,* p. 53.
34. Thomson, *op. cit.,* Vol. I, p. 151.
35. See "Harvest," *The People's Bible Encyclopedia,"* p. 28.
36. Rihbany, *op. cit.,* pp. 377, 378.
37. "Harvest," *Encyclopedia: loc. cit.*
38. Neil, *op. cit.,* p. 273.
39. *Ibid.,* pp. 273, 274.
40. *Ibid.,* p. 270.
41. "Harvest," *Encyclopedia: loc. cit.*
42. Rice, *op. cit.,* p. 143.
43. *Ibid.,* p. 142.
43A. Thomas A. Lambie, *A Bruised Reed,* pp. 126, 127.
44. Lees, *op. cit.,* pp. 156–159.
45. Mackie, *op. cit.,* p. 98.
46. Barton, *op. cit.,* p. 134.

CHAPTER 20

1. George M. Mackie, *Bible Manners and Customs,* p. 43.
2. Edwin W. Rice, *Orientalisms in Bible Lands,* p. 152.
3. E. P. Barrows, *Sacred Geography and Antiquities,* p. 340.
4. Edwin C. Bissell, *Biblical Antiquities,* p. 126.
5. "Vineyard," *The People's Bible Encyclopedia,* Charles R. Barnes, ed., p. 1166.
6. For discussion of vineyard-booths and towers see: Bissell, *op. cit.,* pp. 12–13; Rice, *op. cit.,* pp. 152, 153.
7. Mackie, *op. cit.,* p. 44.
8. Rice, *op. cit.,* pp. 151, 152.
9. Mackie, *op. cit.,* pp. 45–47.
10. G. Robinson Lees, *Village Life in Palestine,* p. 147.
11. See Rice, *op. cit.,* p. 154; also "grape-honey," *The People's Bible Encyclopedia,* p. 500.
12. Mackie, *op. cit.,* pp. 45, 46.
13. Rice, *op. cit.,* p. 152.

CHAPTER 21

1. George M. Mackie, *Bible Manners and Customs*, p. 49.
2. W. M. Thomson, *The Land and the Book*, Vol. III, p. 34.
3. E. P. Barrows, *Sacred Geography and Antiquities*, p. 356.
4. Edwin W. Rice, *Orientalisms in Bible Lands*, pp. 148, 149.
5. Mackie, *op. cit.*, p. 50.
6. John D. Whiting, "Village Life in the Holy Land," *The National Geographic Magazine*, March, 1914, p. 291.
7. Mackie, *op. cit.*, p. 50.
8. George A. Barton, *Archaeology and the Bible*, p. 137.
9. Barrows, *op. cit.*, p. 357.
10. *Loc. cit.*
11. Mackie, *op. cit.*, p. 51.
12. *Loc. cit.*
13. *Ibid.*, pp. 52–53.

CHAPTER 22

1. George M. Mackie, *Bible Manners and Customs*, p. 78.
2. Albert E Bailey, *Daily Life in Bible Times*, p. 188.
3. James Freeman, *Handbook of Bible Manners and Customs*, p. 286.
4. Cunningham Geikie, *The Holy Land and the Bible*, Vol. II, p. 49.
5. W. M. Thomson, *The Land and the Book*, Vol. I, pp. 35, 36.
6. Mackie, *op. cit.*, p. 80.
7. Cf. Geikie, *op. cit.*, Vol. II, p. 50.
8. Thomson, *op. cit.*, Vol. I, p. 37.
9. See Miller, *Encyclopedia of Bible Life*, p. 136.
10. See Geikie, *op. cit.*, Vol. II, p. 274.
11. "Ax," *The People's Bible Encyclopedia*, Charles R. Barnes, ed., p. 106.
12. George A. Barton, *Archaeology and the Bible*, p. 152.
13. *Ibid.*, p. 153.
14. *Ibid.*, p. 152.
15. John A. Broadus, *Commentary on the Gospel of Matthew*, (Vol. I, *An American Commentary on the New Testament*), p. 310. (Philadelphia: American Baptist Publication Society, 1886.)
16. Mackie, *op. cit.*, p. 66.
17. Edwin W. Rice, *Orientalisms in Bible Lands*, pp. 211, 212.
18. J. G. Wood, *Bible Animals*, pp. 434, 435.
19. Rice, *op. cit.*, pp. 188, 189.
20. See "Hunting—nets," *The People's Bible Encyclopedia*, p. 787.
21. See "Snare," *ibid.*, p. 1040.
22. Geikie, *op. cit.*, Vol. II, p. 370.
23. John Calkin, *Historical Geography of Bible Lands*, p. 51. (Philadelphia: Westminster Press: 1928.)
24. A. C. Haddad, *Palestine Speaks*, p. 168.
25. Barton, *op. cit.*, p. 154. See illustration: Figure 156. (Barton)
26. See picture, *The People's Bible Encyclopedia*, p. 374.

27. "Fishing," *loc. cit.*
28. Rice, *op. cit.*, pp. 185, 186.
29. Haddad, *op. cit.*, pp. 169, 170.
30. Thomson, *op. cit.*, Vol. II, p. 349.
31 Haddad, *op. cit.*, pp. 170, 171.
32. *Loc. cit.*
33. Mackie, *op. cit.*, p. 63.
34. *Ibid.*, pp. 64, 65.
35. Rice, *op. cit.*, p. 208.
36. George Adam Smith, *The Historical Geography of the Holy Land*, pp. 158, 206. (New York & London: Hodder and Stoughton, 1894.)
37. Mackie, *op. cit.*, p. 68.
38. Nelson Glueck, "On the Trail of King Solomon's Mines," *The National Geographic Magazine*, February, 1944, pp. 237–242.
39. Cf. Kenneth S. Wuest, *First Peter in the Greek New Testament*, p. 27. (Grand Rapids: Wm. B. Eerdmans Publishing Company, 1942.)
40. Haddad, *op. cit.*, pp. 149–151.
41. *Ibid.*, p. 153.
42. Conybeare and Howson, *The Life and Epistles of Saint Paul*, p. 255. (Cincinnati: National Publishing Co., 1869.)
43. A. T. Robertson, *Types of Preachers in the New Testament*, p. 60. (New York: George H. Doran Company, 1922.)
44. Alfred Edersheim, *Sketches of Jewish Social Life*, p. 89.
45. G. Robinson Lees, *Village Life in Palestine*, p. 180; Abraham Rihbany, *The Syrian Christ*, p. 259.
46. Lees, *op. cit.*, p. 188; Rice, *op. cit.*, p. 233.
47. Rice, *op. cit.*, p. 234
48. Haddad, *op. cit.*, pp. 50, 51.
49. Rihbany, *op. cit.*, p. 267.
50. Mackie, *op. cit.*, p. 83; Haddad, *op. cit.*, p. 163.
51. Edwin C. Bissell, *Biblical Antiquities*, p. 179; "Money changer," *The People's Bible Encyclopedia*, pp. 753, 754.
52. John A. Broadus, *Commentary on the Gospel of Matthew* (Vol. I, *An American Commentary on the New Testament*), pp. 505, 506. (Philadelphia: American Baptist Publication Society, 1886.)
53. Mackie, *op. cit.*, pp. 82, 83.
54. See A. T. Robertson, *op. cit.*, pp. 193–195.
55. Mackie, *op. cit.*, pp. 150–154.
56. Barbara M. Bowen, *The Bible Lives Today*, p. 48.
57. Camden M. Cobern, *The New Archaeological Discoveries and Their Bearing Upon the New Testament*, p. 377.

CHAPTER 23

1. For information about these discoveries at Ur, see: C. Leonard Woolley, *Ur of the Chaldees*, pp. 65–66. For photograph of this beautiful gold lyre, see: M. E. L. Mallowan, "New Light on Ancient Ur," *The National Geographic Magazine*, January, 1930, p. 114.
2. Miller, *Encyclopedia of Bible Life*, p. 289.

3. William M. Taylor, *Moses the Law-Giver*, p. 28. (New York: George H. Doran Company, 1907.)

4. Thomas Hartwell Horne, *An Introduction to the Critical Study and Knowledge of the Holy Scriptures*, Vol. II, p. 183.

5. E. P. Barrows, *Sacred Geography and Antiquities*, p. 459.

6. *Ibid.*, p. 458.

7. Miller, *op. cit.*, p. 285.

8. Horne, *op. cit.*, pp. 183, 184.

9. See Miller, *op. cit.*, p. 293.

10. John A. Broadus, *Commentary on the Gospel of Mark*, p. 118. (Philadelphia: American Baptist Publication Society, 1905.)

11. For arrangement and character of this hymn, see: Westcott, *The Epistle to the Ephesians*, p. 4 f. (New York: The Macmillan Company, 1906.)

CHAPTER 24

1. See Edwin C. Bissell, *Biblical Antiquities*, p. 31.

2. James M. Freeman, *Handbook of Bible Manners and Customs*, pp. 187, 188.

3. Bissell, *op. cit.*, p. 32.

4. Freeman, *op. cit.*, p. 20.

5. E. P. Barrows, *Sacred Geography and Antiquities*, p. 499. See also, "Gate," *The People's Bible Encyclopedia*, pp. 297, 298.

6. See Bissell, *op. cit.*, pp. 32–34.

7. See Abraham Rihbany, *The Syrian Christ*, pp. 263, 264.

8. G. Robinson Lees, *Village Life in Palestine*, pp. 184–187. For photograph of "porter" carrying burden in modern times, see article by Major Edward Keith-Roach, "The Pageant of Jerusalem," *The National Geographic Magazine*, December, 1927, p. 646.

9. Rihbany, *op. cit.*, p. 264.

10. Lees, *op. cit.*, p. 196.

11. *Ibid.*, p. 193.

12. "Beggar," *The People's Bible Encyclopedia*, p. 131.

13. Edwin W. Rice, *Orientalisms in Bible Lands*, pp. 248, 249.

CHAPTER 25

1. A. C. Haddad, *Palestine Speaks*, p. 11.

2. G. Robinson Lees, *Village Life in Palestine*, pp. 137, 138.

3. *Ibid.*, p. 138.

4. James M. Freeman, *Handbook of Bible Manners and Customs*, pp. 287, 288.

5. A. Forder, *'Ventures Among the Arabs*, pp. 274, 275.

6. W. M. Thomson, *The Land and the Book*, Vol. II, pp. 640, 641.

7. For information on the "Kinsman-Redeemer," see: J. Vernon McGee, *Ruth, the Romance of Redemption*, pp. 110–123. (Grand Rapids: Zondervan Publishing House, 1943.)

CHAPTER 26

1. Because some scholars have not discovered what they deem to be certain evidence of the domestication of the camel earlier than the end of the twelfth century B.C., therefore they suggest the possibility that references to the camel in Genesis and Exodus are anachronistic. But in the face of at least some early references to the camel outside the Bible, such a line of reasoning is indecisive. For answer to these critical views, see Joseph P. Free, *Archaeology and Bible History*, pp. 170–171.
2. J. G. Wood, *Bible Animals*, pp. 218–229.
3. H. R. P. Dickson, *The Arab of the Desert*, pp. 413, 414.
4. Wood, *op. cit.*, pp. 237, 238.
5. *Ibid.*, p. 239.
6. E. P. Barrows, *Sacred Geography and Antiquities*, p. 370.
7. Wood, *op. cit.*, pp 223, 224.
8. Dickson, *op. cit.*, pp. 416, 417.
9. Wood, *op. cit.*, p. 228.
10. W. M. Thomson, *The Land and the Book*, Vol. III, p. 550.
11. Wood, *op. cit.*, pp. 228, 229.
12. *Ibid.*, p. 222.
13. A. Forder, *'Ventures Among the Arabs*, pp. 174, 175.
14. Cunningham Geikie, *The Holy Land and the Bible*, Vol. I, p. 17.
15. Albert E. Bailey, *Daily Life in Bible Times*, p. 158.
16. Wood, *op. cit.*, pp. 229, 230.
17. *Ibid.*, pp. 218, 241.
18. A. T. Robertson, *Luke the Historian in the Light of Research*, p. 95.
19. John A. Broadus, *Commentary on the Gospel of Matthew*, p. 473. (Philadelphia: American Baptist Publication Society, 1886.)
20. "Ass," *The People's Bible Encyclopedia*, p. 53.
21. Wood, *op. cit.*, p. 275.
22. Edwin C. Bissell, *Biblical Antiquities*, p. 117.
23. Wood, *op. cit.*, pp. 264–267.
24. Bissell, *op. cit.*, p. 117.
25. *Ibid.*, p. 118.
26. Wood, *op. cit.*, pp. 271, 272; Bissell, *op. cit.*, p. 118.
27. Wood, *ibid*, p. 291.
28. The word "mules" as translated in the A. V. of Gen. 36:24, is rendered "hot springs" in the A. R. V.
29. Wood, *op. cit.*, pp. 285–289.
30. *Ibid.*, p. 250.
31. Cf. George L. Robinson, *The Bearing of Archaeology on the Old Testament*, pp. 179, 180.
32. Wood, *op. cit.*, p. 257.
33. *Ibid.*, p. 257, 258.
34. *Ibid.*, pp. 101–110.
35. From class notes in course: "Manners and Customs of Bible Lands," Pasadena College, June, 1950, taught by Dr. G. Frederick Owen.
36. W. M. Thomson, *The Land and the Book*, Vol. II, p. 205.
37. Amos 5:22, translation of C. F. Keil in, *The Twelve Minor Prophets*, Vol. I, p. 288. (Edinburgh: T. & T. Clark, 1880.)
38. Miller, *Encyclopedia of Bible Life*, p. 36.

Chapter 27

1. George M. Mackie, *Bible Manners and Customs*, p. 146.
2. Cf. Abraham M. Ribhany, *The Syrian Christ*, pp. 247–249.
3. Mackie, *op. cit.*, pp. 147, 148.
4. Edwin W. Rice, *Orientalisms in Bible Lands*, p. 198.
5. "Day's Journey," and "Sabbath Day's Journey," *The People's Bible Encyclopedia*, p. 711.
6. "Inn," *ibid.*, p. 529.
7. See Rice, *op. cit.*, pp. 90–91; E. P. Barrows, *Sacred Geography and Antiquities*, p. 466; "Inn," *Encyclopedia*, pp. 529–530.
8. For detailed examples of such salutations see: Rihbany, *op. cit.*, pp. 255–256; or Mackie, *op. cit.*, pp. 149, 150.
9. A. T. Robertson, *Luke the Historian in the Light of Research*, pp. 207–208.
10. Barrows, *op. cit.*, p. 464.
11. Miller, *Encyclopedia of Bible Life*, p. 374; "Paul's Sea Way."
12. *Ibid.*, pp. 372–374; also Robertson, *op. cit.*, p. 207.
13. Thomas H. Horne, *An Introduction to the Critical Study and Knowledge of the Holy Scriptures*, Vol. II, pp. 187, 188.
14. Barrows, *op. cit.*, p. 464.
15. Robertson, *op. cit.*, pp. 206, 207.
16. Camden Cobern, *The New Archaeological Discoveries and Their Bearing Upon the New Testament*, p. 557.
17. Lieutenant Edwin Smith, "The Last Voyage and Shipwreck of Saint Paul," *The Homiletic Review*, August, 1919, pp. 101 f.
18. *Ibid.*, pp. 102, 103.
19. "Ship—Steering," *The People's Bible Encyclopedia*, p. 1024.
20. Robertson, *op. cit.*, p. 214.
21. "Ship—Undergirders," *Encyclopedia*, *loc. cit.*
22. For comment about names of these officers see: Robertson, *op. cit.*, p. 210.
23. "Ship—Construction and Equipment," *Encyclopedia*, *loc. cit.*

Chapter 28

1. For details about the water system of these two cities, see Miller, *Encyclopedia of Bible Life*, pp. 428, 429.
2. James Neil, *Pictured Palestine*, p. 155.
3. John D. Whiting, "Bethlehem and the Christmas Story," *The National Geographic Magazine*, December, 1929, pp. 730, 731.
4. See "Libation," *The People's Bible Encyclopedia*, p. 647.
5. For photograph of this pool, showing some of these actions, see article by Maynard Owen Williams, "Home to the Holy Land," *The National Geographic Magazine*, December, 1950, p. 722.
6. Major Edward Keith-Roach, "The Pageant of Jerusalem," *The National Geographic Magazine*, December, 1927, pp. 665–667. For further details regarding Solomon's Pools, see G. Frederick Owen, *Abraham to Allenby*, p. 320, ch. VII, reference note 2.

7. For picture showing men filling these "bottles" with water from this source, see article by Keith-Roach, p. 669.
8. Samuel Schor, *Palestine and the Bible,* pp. 49, 50.

CHAPTER 29

1. See H. R. P. Dickson, *The Arab of the Desert,* chapter on "Raids."
2. Cp. Mackie, *Bible Manners and Customs,* p. 28.
3. See "Kinsman—Blood Avenger," *The People's Bible Encyclopedia,* pp. 621, 622.

CHAPTER 30

1. "Service—Hebrew," *The People's Bible Encyclopedia,* pp. 1003, 1004.
2. William M. Taylor, *Moses the Law-Giver,* p. 260. (New York: George H. Doran Company, 1907.)
3. E. P. Barrows, *Sacred Geography and Antiquities,* p. 431.
4. Taylor, *op. cit.,* p. 258.
5. *Ibid.,* p. 261.
6. Barrows, *op. cit.,* p. 434.
7. Frank E. Gaebelein, *Philemon the Gospel of Emancipation,* p. 17. (New York City: Our Hope Publications, 1939.)
8. A. T. Robertson, *Epochs in the Life of Paul,* p. 278. (New York: Charles Scribner's Sons, 1909.)
9. Camden Cobern, *The New Archaeological Discoveries and Their Bearing Upon the New Testament,* p. 595.
10. Gaebelein, *op. cit.,* pp. 18, 19.
11. Cp. Taylor, *op. cit.,* p. 261.
12. Cobern, *loc. cit.*

CHAPTER 31

1. See G. Frederick Owen, *Abraham to Allenby,* ch. XIII, "The Clash Between Judaism and Hellenism," especially pp. 115, 116.
2. Thomas H. Horne, *An Introduction to the Critical Study and Knowledge of the Holy Scriptures,* Vol. II, p. 190.
3. "Games—Grecian," *The People's Bible Encyclopedia,* pp. 394, 395.
4. Horne, *op. cit.,* Vol. II, p. 192.
5. *Encyclopedia, ibid.,* p. 395.
6. H. S. Miller, *The Book of Ephesians,* p. 222. (Harrisburg: The Evangelical Press, 1931.)
7. A. T. Robertson, *Paul's Joy in Christ,* p. 106, footnote 1. (New York: Fleming H. Revell Company, 1917.)
8. *Ibid.,* p. 230.
9. *Ibid.,* p. 106, footnote 2.
10. Horne, *op. cit.,* Vol. II, p. 191.
11. *Loc. cit.*
12. *Loc. cit.*

Bibliography

Albright, W. F., *The Archaeology of Palestine*, Harmondsworth, Middlesex: Penguin Books, 1949.

Bailey, Albert E., *Daily Life in Bible Times*, New York: Charles Scribner's Sons, 1943.

Barnes, Charles Randall, editor, *The People's Bible Encyclopedia*, Chicago: The People's Publication Society, 1913.

Barrows, E. P., *Sacred Geography and Antiquities*, New York: American Tract Society, 1875.

Barton, George A., *Archaeology and the Bible*, Philadelphia: American Sunday School Union, 3rd ed., 1920.

Bissell, Edwin Cone, *Biblical Antiquities*, Philadelphia: The American Sunday School Union, 1888.

Bowen, Barbara M., *Modern Spies in the Land of Israel*, Grand Rapids: William B. Eerdmans Publishing Company, 1940.

——, *Strange Scriptures that Perplex the Western Mind*, Grand Rapids: William B. Eerdmans Publishing Company.

——, *The Bible Lives Today*, Grand Rapids: William B. Eerdmans Publishing Company, 1942.

Budden, Charles W., and Edward Hastings, *The Local Colour of the Bible*, 3 volumes, Edinburgh: T. & T. Clark, 1923.

Cobern, Camden M., *The New Archeological Discoveries and Their Bearing Upon The New Testament*, New York: Funk & Wagnalls Company, 5th ed., 1921.

Dalman, Gustaf. *Sacred Sites and Ways, Studies in the Topography of the Gospels*, New York: Macmillan Company, 1935.

Dickson, H. R. P.. *The Arab of the Desert*, London: George Allen & Unwin Ltd., 1949.

Edersheim, Alfred. *Sketches of Jewish Social Life in the Days of Christ*. New York: Hodder & Stoughton Co., n. d.

——. *The Life and Times of Jesus the Messiah*, 2 volumes, New York: Longmans, Green, and Co., 1899.

317

Forder, Archibald, *Ventures Among the Arabs,* New York: Gospel Publishing House, 1909.

Free, Joseph P., *Archaeology and Bible History,* Wheaton: Van Kampen Press, 1950.

Freeman, Rev. James M., *Hand-book of Bible Manners and Customs,* New York: Nelson & Phillips, 1874.

Geikie, Cunningham, *The Holy Land and the Bible,* 2 volumes, New York: James Pott & Co., 1888.

Goodrich-Freer, A., *Things Seen in Palestine,* London: Seeley, Service & Co., Ltd., n. d.

Grant, Elihu, *The Orient in Bible Times,* Philadelphia & London: J. B. Lippincott Company, 1920.

——, *The People of Palestine,* Philadelphia: J. B. Lippincott Co., 1921.

Haddad, Anis Charles, *Palestine Speaks,* Anderson: The Warner Press, 1936.

Horne, Thomas Hartwell, *An Introduction to the Critical Study and Knowledge of the Holy Scriptures,* Volume II, Philadelphia: Desilver, Thomas, and Co., 1836.

Hunting, Harold B., *Hebrew Life and Times,* New York: The Abingdon Press, 1921.

Josephus, Flavius, *Antiquities,* Vol. I, *Complete Works of Josephus,* New York: Bigelow, Brown and Co., n. d.

Keil, Carl Friedrich, *Manual of Biblical Archaeology,* Vol. II, trans. from German by Peter Christie and Alex Cusin, Edinburgh: T. & T. Clark, 1888.

Keith, Rev. Khodadad E., *The Social Life of a Jew in the Time of Christ,* Liverpool: J. A. Thompson & Co., Limited, 3rd ed., revised, 1929.

Klinck, Arthur W., *Home Life in Bible Times,* St. Louis: Concordia Publishing House, 1947.

Lambie, Thomas A., *A Bruised Reed,* New York: Loizeaux Brothers, 1952.

Lees, G. Robinson, *Village Life in Palestine,* London: Longmans, Green, and Co., 1907.

Levison, Rev. N., *The Jewish Background of Christianity,* Edinburgh: T. & T. Clark, 1932.

Lindberg, Milton B., *A Guest in a Palestinian Home,* a pamphlet published by the author, superintendent of Chicago Hebrew Mission, 2nd ed., 1934.

Mackie, George M., *Bible Manners and Customs,* New York: Fleming H. Revell Co., n. d.

March, Rev. Daniel, *Home Life in the Bible,* Philadelphia: Ziegler & McCurdy, 1873.

Merrill, Selah, *East of the Jordan,* New York: Charles Scribner's Sons, 1881.

Miller, Madeleine S., *Footprints in Palestine,* New York: Fleming H. Revell Company, 1936.

Miller, Madeleine S., and J. Lane, *Encyclopedia of Bible Life,* New York: Harper and Brothers, 1944.

Neil, James, *Everyday Life in the Holy Land,* London, New York, Toronto, and Melbourne: Cassell and Company, Limited, 1913.

——, *Pictured Palestine,* New York: Anson D. F. Randolph and Company, n. d.

Orr, James, editor, *The International Standard Bible Encyclopedia,* Grand Rapids: William B. Eerdmans Publishing Company.

Owen, G. Frederick, *Abraham to Allenby,* Grand Rapids: William B. Eerdmans Publishing Company, 1939.

Radin, Max, *The Life of the People in Biblical Times,* Philadelphia: The Jewish Publication Society of America, 1929.

Ramsay, W. M., *The Bearing of Recent Discoveries on the Trustworthiness of the New Testament,* Grand Rapids, Baker Book House.

——, *The Letters to the Seven Churches of Asia,* New York: George H. Doran Company.

Rice, Edwin Wilbur, *Orientalisms in Bible Lands,* Philadelphia: The American Sunday School Union, 1910.

Rihbany, Abraham Mitrie, *The Syrian Christ,* Boston, Houghton Mifflin Company, 1916.

Robertson, A. T., *Luke the Historian in the Light of Research,* New York: Charles Scribner's Sons, 1920.

Robinson, George Livingstone, *The Bearing of Archaeology on the Old Testament,* New York: American Tract Society, 1941.

Scherer, George H., *The Eastern Color of the Bible,* New York: Fleming H. Revell Co., n. d.

Schor, Rev. Samuel, *Palestine and the Bible,* London: London Society for Promoting Christianity Amongst the Jews, n.d.

Schurer, Emil, *A History of the Jewish People in the Time of Jesus Christ,* 2 volumes, Edinburgh: T. & T. Clark, 1901.

Soares, Theodore S., *The Social Institutions and Ideals of the Bible,* New York: The Abingdon Press, 1915.

Stapfer, Edmond, *Palestine in the Time of Christ,* trans. from French by Annie H. Holmden, New York: A. C. Armstrong and Son, 1885.

Thomson, William M., *The Land and the Book,* 3 volumes, New York: Harper and Brothers, 1880.

Tristram, H. B., *Eastern Customs in Bible Lands,* New York: Hodder & Stoughton Co.

——, *The Land of Israel: A Journal of Travels in Palestine,* London: Society for Promoting Christian Knowledge, 1866.

Trumbull, H. Clay, *Studies in Oriental Social Life,* Philadelphia: The Sunday School Times Co., 1894.

——, *The Blood Covenant,* Philadelphia, John D. Wattles & Co., 1898.

Upham, Thomas C., *Jahn's Biblical Archaeology,* trans. from Latin, New York: Newman & Ivison, 1853.

Waddy, Stacy, *Homes of the Psalms,* London: Society for Promoting Christian Knowledge, 1928.

Whiting, John D., "Among the Bethlehem Shepherds," *The National Geographic Magazine,* December, 1926, pp. 729–753.

——, "Bedouin Life in Bible Lands," *The National Geographic Magazine,* January, 1937, pp. 59–84.

——, "Bethlehem and the Christmas Story," *The National Geographic Magazine,* December, 1929, pp. 699–735.

——, "Jerusalem's Locust Plague," *The National Geographic Magazine,* December, 1915, pp. 511–550.

——, "Village Life in the Holy Land," *The National Geographic Magazine,* March, 1914, pp. 249–296.

Wilson, Col., *Picturesque Palestine Sinai and Egypt,* New York: D. Appleton and Co., 1881.

Wood, Rev. J. G., *Bible Animals,* New York: Charles Scribner and Co., 1870.

Wright, G. E., "Lamps, Politics, and the Jewish Religion," *The Biblical Archaeologist* (published by American School of Oriental Research), May, 1939, pp. 22–24.

General Index

Abraham and tent life, 13; schools when a boy, 112
Altar, 118–119
Amphitheater, Roman, 297–298
Angling, 214
Animals, domestic, 251–269
Animals, wild, 212–213
Anvil, 219
Apparel, *see* Dress
Arabian horses, 263
Arabs as custodians of Bible manners and customs, 7–8
Arena, Roman, 297–298
Ass, 258–261
Athletics, Greek, 294–297
Avenging, blood, 288–289

Babies, birth of, 107–111; care of, 108–109
Bagpipe, 234
Baking bread, 46–48
Baking pottery, 205–206
Bankers, 225
Banquets, entertainment at, 65–66; food at, 65–66; places of honor at, 64–65; special occasions, 61–68; wedding, 134
Barley, growing of, 173; harvest of, 178; bread of, 45–46
Barns, 186
Barrels, 186
Bathing in courtyard, 38
Bathsheba, 38
Bedouin Arabs, 7–8
Beds, 26–27, 40, 42
Beggars, 245
Belladin Arabs, 7–8
Bellows, 219

Bethlehem house and manger, 33–34
Bethlehem, women, dress of, 99–100
Betrothal, 129–130
Bible in Jewish home, 115, 121–122
Birds, as food, 51; eating grain, 174–175
Birth of children, 107–111
Blacksmith, 218–219
Blood-avenging, 288–289
Booth, 190–191
Bowing, 72–73
Boxing contests, 296
Boy babies, preference for, 107–108
Bread, 44–48; baking of, 46–48; breaking of, 45; forms of loaves, 46; kinds of, 45; sacredness of, 44; the principal food, 44
Bride, 130–134
Bridegroom, 130–134
Bucket, 90
Burial of bodies, 144–145
Burying of valuables, 249
Business dealings, 221–224; place of, 221
Butter, 50
Buttermilk, 51
Buying and selling, 221–224

Calf, fatted, 167, 268–269
Camel, 251–258; caravans, 256–257; furniture, 254–255; ornaments, 255; products, 257; saddle, 254
Candle, 27
Caravan, 256–257
Caravansary, 273–274
Carpenter, 207–209
Cattle, 267–269

Caves, burial in, 144–145; sheepfold in, 154
Ceramic quarters, 203
Chair, 57–58
Chariots, 264–267
Cheese, 51
Children, birth of, 107–111; naming of, 110–111; playing of, 235, 244; respect for parents, 104–106; training of, 111
Chimney, 31
Christ, birth of, 33–34; as a boy in Jerusalem, 120–121; as a pupil in synagogue school, 115; as a carpenter at Nazareth, 207–209; dress of, 101–102; eating with disciples at Last Supper, 66–68
Church in home, 123
Churning of milk, 50
Circumcision, 109
Cisterns, 36–37; 282–283
Clay and potter, 203–207
Clothes, making of, 83–84; washing of, 84–85
Coins, 223
Comfort, 143
Compelling guests to attend a feast, 62
Conversation, daily, 86–88
Cooking arrangements, in tent, 17; in house, 30–31
Copper smelting, 219
Coppersmith, 219
Cornerstone, 217
Courthouse, 240–241
Court of justice, 240–241; 244–245
Courtyard, 36–38
Covenants, 76–79
Cows, 267–269
Cymbals, 234

Dairy products, 49–51
Dancing, 66, 236
Darkness, outer, 62–63
David, King, contribution to music, 232–233; use of chariots, 265; use of horses, 265; use of mules, 262
Death, 142–146
Deeds, property, 247–248
Dishes, 58
Divorce, 125, 128
Dogs, 156, 269
Donkey, 258–261
Door, of one-room house, 25–26; of house of more than one room, 38
Dowry, marriage, 127–129
Dress of men and women, 91–102

Dung, see Fertilizer
Dyers, 220

Early rain, see Rain
Early rising, 80
Eating, dipping in dish, 66–67; giving of sop, 66–67; position while, 56, 63–64; time of, 82–83; use of hand in, 59
Education of youth, 112–117
Eggs, 52
Egypt, schools in, 113; ships of, 276
Encampment, tent, 15
Engagement to marry, 126–130
Esau and lentils, 48–49
Exaggerated expressions, 87–88

Family pilgrimages, 120–121
Farmer, 169–186; law of hospitality, 179
Father, position of, 103–104
Fat-tailed sheep, 147
Fatted calf, 167; 268–269
Feast, wedding, 134. See also Banquet
Feet washing, 75
Fellahin Arabs, 7–8
Fertilizer, 30, 173, 192, 201
Figs, 54, 200–202
Fig tree, 200–202
Figurative language, 87–88
Fire, in courtyard, 37–38; in grain fields, 176; kindling a, 31
Fire-place, 30–31
Fish, 51; 213–217
Fishermen, 213–217
Flax, smoking, 28–29
Floor of house, 22
Flute, 151, 234–235
Foods and their preparation, 43–54
Fork in eating, 59
Fortifications, 238
Foundations, 217
Fountains, 280–282
Fowl, 211
Friendship, pledge of, 76–77
Fruit, 53–54, 187–195, 200–202
Funerals, 144–145, 235–236
Furnishings, of tent, 16–17; of one-room house, 26; of house of more than one room, 42

Games, Olympic, 294–297
Gates, of city, 239–241; of house, 38
Gathering place, 240, 242
Girdle, 93
Gladiatorial shows, 297–298

Goad, 171
Goats, 85, 165–168; hair of used, 168; meat of, 167; separation from sheep, 166–167; use of for sacrifice, 168; use of for skins, 14–15, 168
Goldsmith, 219–220
Grace at meals, 58–59
Grafting olive trees, 197
Grain, cutting of, 180; grinding of, 81–82, 260; parched used, 44; planting of, 169–175; raw eaten, 43; sifting of, 185–186; storing of, 186; thieves of, 177–178; threshing of, 181–184; transporting of, 181; winnowing of, 184
Grapes, 54, 187–195
Graves, 144–145
Greek, Olympic games, 294–297; erection of gymnasiums, 294
Greetings, 73–74, 79, 274
Grinding of grain, 81–82; 260
Guest chamber, 272
Guests, kinds of, 70; where entertained, 71–72; how entertained, 72–77; made lord of house, 77; protected from enemies, 78; departure of, 79

Hair, care of, 96
Hammer, 209
Hand, use of in eating, 59
Harps, 229–230, 232–234, 237
Harvest home, 136–137
Harvesting, figs, 200; grain, 180–186; grapes, 193–194; olives, 198
Headdress, 96
Healing of sickness, 138–141; see also Physician
Health and sickness, 138–139
Hearth, tent, 17
Hedges, 189
Hireling, 159
Home, Bible in, 121–122; religion in, 118–123
Honey, 52–53
Honor, places of at banquets, 64–65
Horn, ram's, 164–165
Horses, 263–267
Hospitality, abuse of, 78; Christian, 122–123; Oriental, 69–79
Hotel, 272–274
House, dedication of, 135
Houses, of one room, 20–34; of more than one room, 35–42
Hunters, 210–214
Hyperbole, use of, 88

Infant child, care of, 108–109
Inheritances, 250
Inn, 272–274
Inner garment, 91–92
Inn keeper, 272–274
Invitations to banquets, 61–62
Isaac and tent life, 13
Ishmael and tent encampments, 15, as a hunter, 210

Jacob and tent life, 13
Jerusalem water supply, 284–286
Jesus, see Christ
Jewelry, 100–101
Jews, customs of in Bible times, 8, 28, 43, 56, 59, 64, 83, 96, 101, 106, 107, 109, 110, 116, 121–122, 224, 282, 286
Jubilee, year of, 245, 291

Keys of house, 38–39
Khan, 273–274
Kindling a flame, 31
Kinsman-avenger, 288–289
Kinsman-redeemer, 250
Kissing, 74
Knife in eating, 59

Laborers, hiring, 244
Lambs, baby, 160–161
Lamentation, 142–143
Lamps, in house, 27–30; in tent, 17
Land allotting, 246–247
Land marks, 247
Latter rain, see Rain
Lentils, 48–49
Lighting of house, 27–30; of tent, 17
Light, significance of, 29–30
Locusts, 176–177
Lord of house, guest made, 77
Lost, inheritances, 250; sheep, 162–163
Love, after marriage, 126–127; before marriage, 126–127
Lyres, 229–230; 232, 234

Manger, Bethlehem, 33–34
Mantle, outer garment, 94–96
Market place, 242–245
Marriage, 124–134
Marring the vessel, 205
Mary and Joseph at Bethlehem, 33–34, 272
Masons, 217–218
Mattock, 173
Meals, customs at, 55–60; eaten in

courtyard, 38; grace at, 58–59; time of, 82–83
Measuring, distances, 271–272; grain, 223; land, 246; line, 208; reed, 218
Meat, 51–52
Meeting place, 240
Merchants, 221–224
Metal workers, 218–220
Mid-day siesta, 85–86
Milk, 49–50, 164, 167
Money, 222–223
Money-changers, 224–225
Moses, schools when young man, 113
Mother, position of, 104–106
Mourners, professional, 143
Mourning expressions, 145–146
Mourning feast, 145
Mules, 262–263
Music, 229–237
Musical instruments, 229–237

Nails, 209
Naming of children, 110–111
Nets, fishing, 215–216
Nomad Arabs, 7–8

Ocean travel, 274–279
Oil, olive, 53–54, 198–200
Olives, as food, 53, 198; harvesting of, 198; oil, 53; 198–200; press, 198–199; trees, 196–197
Olympic games, 294–297
Organ, 234
Ornamentation, 100–101
Ostraca, 207
Outer garment, 94–96
Ovens, 46–48
Oxen, 171, 183, 267–269

Pack animals, 258
Parental position in home, 103–106
Paul, Apostle, schools of his day, 115–117; reference to athletics, 295–297; reference to gladiatorial shows, 297; reference to hospitality, 122–123
Payment for goods, 222–223
Pharisees, complaint about washing of hands, 56; dress of, 101
Phoenician ships, 276–278
Physicians, 139–140, 227–228
Pick ax, 173
Pilgrimages, family, 120–121
Pipe, musical, 234
Pitcher for water, 89–90
Pitfalls, 211
Pledge of friendship, 76–77

Plough, 170–172, 209
Ploughing, 170–172, 259
Plumb-line, 217–218
Polygamy, 124–125
Pomegranates, 54
Pools of water, 284, 285
Porch, 39
Porter, 39, 243
Posture while eating, 63–64
Potter, 203–207
Prizes in games, 295
Procession, wedding, 131–133
Proclamation, public, 32–33
Property, 246–250
Prophets, school of, 114–115
Pruning grapevines, 192–193
Psaltery, 234
Publicans, 225–226

Races, 295–296
Rachel, and stolen teraphim, 119–120
Raids, 287–288
Rain in Palestine, 169–170, 178–179
Raisins, 54, 193–194
Ram's horn, 164–165
Reclining at meals, 63–64
Recording of deeds, 247–248
Redemption of inheritances, 250
Religion in home, 118–123
Religious education, 120
Rising early, 80
Robe, 92–93
Rod, shepherd's, 149
Roman, gladiatorial shows, 297–298; schools, 116–117; ships, 276, 279; slavery, 292–293
Roof of house, how made, 23; letting man through, 41–42; uses of, 32–33
Rooms of house, arrangement of, 35–36

Saddle, camel, 254; donkey, 261; horse, 263; mule, 262
Salutations, 73–74, 79, 274
Sandals, 97
Scepter, king's, 149
Schools, at Ur, 112–113; in Egypt, 113; under Law of Moses, 113–114; of prophets, 114–115; of synagogue, 115; rabbinical, 115–116; Roman, 116–117
Scrip, shepherd's, 149
Sea travel, 274–279
Selling, 221–224
Separating sheep and goats, 155
Sheep, 147–165; finding lost, 162–163; gathering, 155–156; guiding,

157; meat of, 163–164; milk from, 164; naming, 157; playing with, 158; products of, 163–165; protection of, 161–162; sacrificial use of, 163–164; shearing feast, 137; sickness among, 161; skins of, 163; watching of, 161
Sheep-fold, 153–155
Shepherd life, 147–168
Shipping, nations, 276–277; routes, 276
Ships, Oriental, 276–279
Shirt, 91–92
Shoals of fish, 216
Shoes, Oriental, 97; removing of, 74–75
Shofar, Jewish, 165
Sickness, 138–141
Sifting grain, 185–186
Signet ring, 100
Silversmith, 219–220
Slavery, 290–293
Sleeping arrangements, 26–27, 32
Sling, shepherd's, 150–151
Smoking flax, 28–29
Snares, 212
Solomon, King, copper refineries, 219; use of horses, 265; meat at table, 51; Pools of, 284–285; ships of, 276–277; stables of, 265
Songs of Bible, 234, 236
Sop, giving of at meals, 66–67
Sorrow in Orient, 143
Sowing seed, 173–175
Spoon, bread, 48–49, 59
Springs of water, 280–282
Staff, shepherd's, 149–150
Stones, in house walls, 22, 217; in vineyard, 189–190
Storage, of grain, 186; roof as place of, 32
Stove, 30–31
Streets, 242
Suppers, special, 61–68
Surgeons, 227–228

Table, 56–57
Tanners, 220
Tares, 175–176
Taxgatherers, 225–226
Team spirit, 296
Tent dwellings, 13–18
Tent encampments, 15
Tent life, 18
Tent-makers, 221
Teraphim, 119–120
Terraces, vineyard, 189
Thanksgiving, 58–59

Threshing-floor, 181
Threshing grain, 181–184
Timbrels, 229–230
Tombs, 144–145
Tower, city, 241; vineyard, 190–191
Transfer of property, 247–248
Transportation, 251–252; 260; 270–279
Traveling, 270–279
Treasure, buried, 249
Trumpet, 165, 236
Tunic, inner garment, 91–92
Turban, 96, 101–102

Upper room, 40–41
Ur of Chaldees, musical instruments found at, 229; schools at, 112; tablet about teraphim found near, 119

Valuables, burying, 249
Vegetables, 48–49
Veil of women, 98–100
Venison, 210
Vessel, marring the, 205
Vines, pruning the, 192–193
Vineyards, 187–195

Wail, death, 142
Walls, of city, 238–239; of house, 22–24
Warfare, ancient, 238, 241, 264–267
Washing, of clothes, 84–85; of feet, 75; of hands, 55–56, 60
Water supply of Palestine, 280–286
Water, women going for, 88–90, 280
Weaning feast, 136
Weaving of cloth, 83–84
Wedding, 130–134; feast, 134; procession, 131–133, 235
Wells, 280–282
Wheat, bread of, 45–46; growing of, 173; harvest of, 178
Wheels of potter, 203–205
Wild animals, 212–213
Windows, 25
Wine, 65–66, 194
Winepress, 194
Winnowing grain, 184
Women, dress of, 97–100; going for water, 88–90, 280; position of in Orient, 104–106
Wool, 163
Worship, 33
Wrestling, 296

Yoke, 170–171, 209
Youth, education of, 112–117

Scriptural Index

GENESIS

1:28	107	24:15	89
4:10	288	24:17–18	76
4:20	13	24:20	253
4:20–21	103	24:22	100
4:21	229	24:32	75
4:22	218	24:33	77, 127
9:27	13	24:58	126
10:9	210	24:59, 61	129
11:8	200	24:60	131
12:4	99	24:64	251
12:8	13	24:64–65	99
12:16	251	24:67	126
12:18	118	25	104
13:16	107	25:16	15
14:23	97	25:23–26	88
16	113	25:27	210
16:6	105	25:33–34	48
17:10	109	26	281
18:1	86	26:12	174, 175
18:1–10	71	26:17	13
18:2–3	73	26:30	76
18:2–7	69	26:31	79
18:4	75	26:34–35	126
18:7	51	27	104
18:8	50	27:3	210
18:10–15	16	27:27	74
18:16	79	29:1–3	155
19:1	240	29:8–10	153
19:2	75, 77	29:10–18	126
21:8	136	29:18	128
21:20	210	30	113, 124
22:3	80, 258, 260	30:1	107
22:17	241	30:36	271
23:7, 12	73	30:43	251
23:16	223	31:15	128
23:17	248	31:19	119
24:11	89, 254	31:23	271

31:27 230
31:30 119
31:33 16
31:34 .... 17, 255
31:40 161
31:53–54 79
32 105
32:15 .... 49, 257
33:4 74
33:8–20 118
33:18 13
35:2 119
35:3 118
35:4 100
35:8 145
37:3 92
37:7 181
37:25 44
37:25, 28 251
37:34 15
38:18 100
41:43 264
42:26–27 .... 181, 259
42:27 272
43:1 194
43:21 .... 223, 272
43:24 75
43:31–32 44
43:33 58
45:8 103
45:15 74
48:10 74
49:10 108
49:13 276
49:31 145
50:13 145

EXODUS

2:15–21 85
2:16 128
2:20 44
3:5 75
3:8 .... 49, 52
3:9, 16 101
4:20 201
4:24 272
4:27 74
9:32 173
12 164
12:26 114
12:30 142
13:5 .... 49, 52
14:9 264
15 234
15:20 230
15:26 138
20:10 291

20:12 103
21:6 209
21:19 227
22:2–3 290
22:6 176
22:26–27 95
23:16 .... 136, 137
23:29 210
26:7 168
29:22 147
30:13–15 224
32:2 100
34:4 80
34:21 137
34:23–24 120
35:33 168

LEVITICUS

1:5 268
1:10 168
2:1 199
2:4 47
2:5 54
3:5 f 164
3:9 147
8:12 200
11:4 257
12 110
16:22 168
17:13 210
19:19 262
20:10 125
20:14 125
23:14 43
23:22 179
23:39–43 137
25:3 174
25:8–9 231
25:9 165
25:29 238
25:31 238
25:39–40 290
25:43 290
25:44 .... 290, 291
25:48 290
27:32 149

NUMBERS

1:52 13
8:8 200
10:2 230
10:9 231
11:5 .... 49, 213
11:32 211
13:23 .... 54, 189
15:37–38 101
19:2 172

21:7	139
21:17–18	234
22:22	125
23:33	86
24:2	13, 125
24:17	108
29:1	165
31:26 f	290
35:15	289
35:19	289

DEUTERONOMY

4:9	120
6:4–9	122
6:6–9	114
6:11	196
8:8	54, 196
8:9	219
8:10	59
11:13–21	122
15:12–14	290
15:17	209, 290
16:10–11	291
16:18	241
17:16	264
17:17	124
19:5	208
19:14	247
20:1	264
20:5	134
20:7	130
21:10	290
21:18–21	104
22:5	97
22:8	23
22:10	172, 259
22:12	101
23:15–16	291
23:18	269
23:19–20	225
23:24	193
23:25	43, 179
24:1	125
24:20	198
25:4	183, 268
28:4	107
28:8	186
28:60–61	139
31:10–13	291
32	234
32:13	53, 197
32:14	49, 50, 268

JOSHUA

2:6	32
2:19	242
5:6	49, 52

6:4	165
9:14	77
11:6, 9	265
15:45	238
17:11	238

JUDGES

1:14	260
1:15	129
3:24	83
3:31	171
4:3	265
4:12	15
4:19	50
4:46	241
5	234
5:10	260
5:25	50
6:3	178
6:3–4	288
6:5	176
6:11	182
6:19	51, 58, 167
6:19–20	52
7:12	176
7:13	45
8:21	255
8:32	145
9:27	193
10:3	260
14:2	127
14:8–9	52
14:12–18	134
14:17	134
16:21	82, 260
19:5–10	79

RUTH

1:20	111
2	179
2:4	86
2:14	60
2:17	182
3:2	184
3:3	199
3:15	96
4:1	240
4:7–8	250
4:11	134
4:14	87

I SAMUEL

1:1–6	124
1:3	121
1:6	107
1:12	99
1.23	136

2 234
2:8 245
2:15 52
2:19 93
6:7 268
9:11 89
9:26 .... 32, 72
10:5 231
13:19 218
13:20 170
14:14 172
14:25–27 52
16:1 165
16:11 148
16:13 200
16:18 232
16:20 259
17:17 .... 44, 46
17:18 51
17:34–36 149
17:34–37 162
17:40 149
17:40–49 150
18:6 231
18:20 127
18:25 128
19:18–21 114
20:5, 18 58
20:41 74
23:7 239
24:3 .... 86, 154
24:4 93
25:1 145
25:4 .... 75, 137
25:13 93
25:18 ...... 44, 54, 193, 202, 259
25:23 260
25:29 151
25:36 137
27:9 252
28:14 93
28:22–25 44
28:24 269
30:12 .... 54, 202

II SAMUEL
3:31 .... 15, 143
4:5 86
6:14 66
7:28 48
8:3–4 265
10:4–5 96
11:2 38
11:11 13
13:18 92
13:23 f 137
13:29 262

14:25–26 96
15:1 266
16:1 .... 54, 194
17:18–19 .... 36, 283
17:28 44
17:29 51
18:11 93
18:24 240
18:33 143
21:1 289
23:6–7 30
23:15 281
23:16 282

I KINGS
1:33 262
1:34 200
1:39 165
1:44 f 262
2:10 145
2:19 106
4:23 .... 51, 210
4:25 202
4:26 265
4:28 264
5:11 199
6:23, 31, 33 200
7:9 22
7:45 219
8:63 147
9:27–28 277
10:24–25 262
10:28–29 .... 264, 265
12:16 14
12:18 266
17:8 19
17:10 31
17:12 53
17:12, 14, 16 186
17:16 53
18:5 263
18:33 186
18:44 266
19:6 46
19:16 199
19:19 .... 173, 268
20:35 114
21:27 15
22:35 266
22:48 277

II KINGS
1:2 40
1:8 93
2:3 114
2:5 114
2:7 115

2:8, 13 94
2:21 282
2:23 96
3:11 55
3:15 232
4:10 .... 40, 72
4:12–13 99
4:22 43
4:24 261
4:29 93
4:38 56
4:38–44 115
4:39 49
6:5 208
8:9 255
10:1–5 111
11:1 109
17:6 292
18:31 283
19:1 15
19:26 23
20 139
20:7 202
20:20 284
21:13 218
23:6 145
23:12 40
24:12 106

I CHRONICLES

4:23 203
4:39 152
12:40 .... 54, 193, 202, 255
16:42 233
23:5 233
25:6–7 233

II CHRONICLES

1:14 265
2:10 199
6:28–30 139
8:5 239
9:24 262
9:25 265
16:12 139
16:12–13 228
23:13 231
26:15 241
29:26 233
32:6 240
36:20 292

NEHEMIAH

3:8 219
8:1 242

ESTHER

2:21 240
5:8 61
6:14 61

JOB

1:3 251
1:5 80
1:20 93
3:20–21 249
4:19 22
9:30 85
12:6 288
13:4 .... 139, 227
15:33 197
18:6 29
24:16 24
29:14 96
29:23 169
30:1 .... 156, 269
31:17 69
39:15 183
41:7 214
41:24 82
41:28–29 212
42:12 .... 147, 251

PSALMS

1:4 187
2:9 206
16:5–6 247
18 232
18:28 29
18:39 93
18:42 242
19:10 53
23 232
23:2 153
23:3 .... 157, 158
23:4 149
23:5 .... 75, 78, 161
32:9 .... 263, 264
37:25 245
41:9 78
45:14–15 133
51 232
51:2 84
52:8 .... 36, 197
57 232
59:6 269
61:3 21
65:10 169
68:17 267
69:12 240
78:55 246
79:13 152

80:12–13	189	31:26		105
81:16	52	31:28		105
84:1–10	19			
92:13	36	**ECCLESIASTES**		
104:3	267	7:6		30
107:4–7	271	12:6		206
107:16	239			
107:17–21	139	**CANTICLES**		
107:23	276	1:5		14
107:25–30	275	1:7		166
109:10	245	2:11–13		201
115–118	236	2:13		192
118:12	30	2:14		211
118:19	241	2:15		189
118:22	217	4:2		163
119:83	31	4:11		53
119:105	131	4:13		54
119:136	146	5:1		53
119:176	158	5:3		91
124:7	212	5:4		39
126:5–6	178	5:11		96
127:3	86	6:11		54
128:3	107, 197	7:2		181
129:6	23	7:12		54
129:7	181	8:2		54
131:2	136	8:6		100
137:1–5	235			
144:12	130	**ISAIAH**		
		1:8		49, 190
PROVERBS		1:18		163
1:8	111	2:4		170
1:21	240	3:18		101
2:3–5	249	3:19		100
3:10	186	3:20		101
6:20	111	3:21		101
7:6	25	3:23		96
7:8	242	4:6		21
10:26	31	5:1		188
15:17	267	5:1–2		187
16:24	53	5:2		190, 194
18:19	25	5:10		172
19:13	24	5:12		231
20:4	169	5:24		184
20:14	222	5:28		263
24:13–14	53	6:10		193
24:30–31	192	7:25		173
25:20	85	9:3		136
25:25	257	9:8–10		22
26:3	264	9:10		25
27:15	24	9:18		30
27:27	49, 167	10:6		242
30:27	177	10:7		30
30:31	166	10:15		209
30:33	50	11:5		93
31:1	111	14:9		166
31:11	105	17:6		198
31:19	84	18:1–2		276

19:8 214
20:2–4 92
21:13 256
22:1 32
22:2 38
24:8 234
28:9 49
28:25 173
28:27–28 183
28:28 263
30:6 255
30:14 207
31:1 266
32:20 259
33:12 30
36:16 283
38:12 16
40:11 .... 152, 161
41:7 219
41:15 183
41:25 203
42:3 28
43:2 160
44:12 219
44:13 208
45:1 239
49:14 158
50:11 31
51:20 211
52:12 157
53:6 158
54:2 18
54:4 52
55:1 285
58:11 271
61:10 130
63:3–6 194
65:5 31
66:15 267
66:20 263

JEREMIAH

2:13 283
2:22 85
2:23 257
2:32 131
4:5 165
6:9 193
6:29 219
7:34 133
8:20 179
8:22 139
9:1 146
9:17–18 143
10:4 209
11:5 .... 49, 52
11:16 197

13:1 93
14:4 169
15:7 184
16:7 145
17:19 240
17:25 266
18:4 205
18:6 205
19:11 206
22:18 143
24:1–2 202
25:10 81
28:13 170
31:4 66
32:9–12 248
37:21 .... 48, 221
48:33 194
49:19 213
50:8 166
50:16 180

LAMENTATIONS

4:2 89
4:4 45
5:13 82

EZEKIEL

4:9 .... 48, 173
4:15 30
16:4 109
16:8 129
16:11–12 131
16:13 .... 54, 199
19:3 211
20:37 149
27:17 .... 194, 199
34:12–13 156
34:14 154
40:3 218

DANIEL

1:12 49
3:5 234
3:21 95
7:23 183
8:5 166
9:3 15

HOSEA

7:4 48
9:10 200
12:1 199
13:3 31
14:6 197

JOEL

1:4 177
1:10 200

1:18 268
2:2, 3, 5, 6, 9 177
3:4–6 292
3:10 170
3:13 180
3:23 178

AMOS
1:6 292
2:6 97
3:12 162
4:2 214
5:15 241
5:16 143
5:22 269
6:4 64
6:4–6 66
7:8 218
7:17 246

OBADIAH
1:5 288
1:7 78

JONAH
1 .... 276, 277, 278
1:13 277
3:5 15
4:6–10 49

MICAH
1:8 .... 92, 143
4:3 170
4:3–4 202
4:13 263
6:15 199
7:14 .... 149, 152

NAHUM
1:10 30
3:12 200
3:14 206
3:17 177

ZEPHANIAH
1:5 33

ZECHARIAH
9:9 261
10:3 166

MALACHI
2:14–16 125
3:2 85
4:1 48
4:2 268

THE APOCRYPHA

ECCLESIASTICUS
38:29–30 205

I MACCABEES
3:41 292

II MACCABEES
7:27 136

MATTHEW
1:18 130
2:13–15 261
3:4 .... 53, 93, 148, 257
3:7–9 87
3:12 .... 184, 186
5:15 28
5:16 30
5:28 99
5:29–30 88
5:31–32 125
5:40 95
6:7 122
6:11 44
6:19 24
6:30 30
7:3 88
8:11 64
8:12 63
9:11 226
9:15 134
9:23 235
10:10 92
10:27 33
10:42 203
11:16–17 244
11:19 226
11:28 244
11:30 170
12:1 .... 48, 174
12:27 140
13:3–4 174
13:3–8 174
13:5–6 175
13:25 175
13:44 249
13:47–48 215
14:6 66
14:27 39
15:1–2 56
15:3–6 116
15:27 269
15:32 271
15:36 59

16:17	110
17:27	214
18:6	260
18:26	73
19:24	88, 258
19:26	258
20:1–3	190
20:3–4	244
21:31	226
21:33	187, 189
21:33–34	195
22:2–3	61
22:4	83
22:12	134
22:13	63
23:5	101
23:6	65
23:24	88, 258
24:17	33
24:32	201
24:43	24
25:1	199
25:1–13	132
25:27	225
25:30	63
25:32–33	167
26:17–29	164
26:23	58, 60
26:26	45
26:69	36
26:71	39

MARK

1:7	98
1:13	213
1:16–17	215
1:32–34	141
1:35	80
2:4	41
2:23	43, 174
4:3–8	174
4:4	175
5:26	140, 227, 228
5:38	143
6:3	207
6:8	93
6:13	200
6:50	39
7:1–5	56
9:41	76
10:25	258
10:35–37	65
10:46	245
11:13	201
12:38	242
13:15	33
13:28	201

14:12–16	40
14:13	90
14:14	272
14:18–20	66
14:20	58
14:26	236
14:68	39

LUKE

1:25	107
1:46–55	236
1:67–79	236
2:7	272
2:8	161
2:12	109
2:14	236
2:21	109, 110
2:41–42	121
2:44	121, 271
2:49	121
3:11	92
3:12–13	226
3:17	184
5:5	216
5:19	41
5:27	226
6:1	43, 174
6:1–2	179
6:29	95
6:38	96, 224
6:48	217
7:11–17	145
7:32	235
7:36	62
7:38	64
7:45	74
7:46	75
8:5–8	174
8:27	144
9:62	172
10:4	274
10:5–6	74
10:34–35	273
11:5–7	27
11:7	26
11:11	51
11:12	52
11:46	244
12:3	33
12:18	186
12:28	30
12:35	93
13:1–9	173
13:6–9	201
14:8–10	65
14:12	83
14:16–17	62

14:23 62
14:28–30 191
15 29
15:6 163
15:8–9 128
15:8-10 99
15:11–32 105
15:20 74
15:22 100
15:23 269
15:24–25 66
15:25 236
15:29 167
16:5–7 223
16:19–20 245
16:22 64
17:31 33
18:25 258
19:8 226
19:23 225
21:38 80
22:7–13 40
22:11 272
22:31 186
23:48 143
24:30, 41, 43 79
24:41–43 53

JOHN
1:29 168
2:1–11 134
2:8–9 134
3:19 26
3:29 127
4:11 281
5 284
5:1–4 141
6:9 46
6:11 58
6:20 39
6:35 45
9:2 140
10:1–3 155
10:3 157
10:4 157
10:4–5 155
10:10 162
10:11 162
10:12 159
10:13 159
10:14 159
11:16 110
11:33 143
11:39 144
11:44 144
12:15 261
13:4–5 75

13:18 78
13:23–25 64
13:25–26 67
13:26 60
15:1–3 192
18:18 ....31, 37
19:23 92
19:40 144
21:4–6 217
21:7 92
21:9 31
21:12 83
21:12–13 79

ACTS
1:12 .... 271, 272
1:13 40
3:2 245
7:22 113
8:4 122
8:28 f 266
9:36–41 41
9:37 40
9:43 220
10:9 33
10:25 73
12:8 97
12:12 123
12:13 38
12:13–14 39
16:14 220
16:15 62
16:19 245
16:40 123
17:17 243
18:1–3 .... 123, 221
19 297
19:9 117
19:24 219
20:7 45
20:8 40
20:37 74
21:1–8 276
21:10–11 87
22:3 116
26:14 171
27 .... 277, 278
27:12 275
27:15, 17 f 270
27:40 278
28 278
28:11 279

ROMANS
1:1 293
9:20–21 205
11:24 198

12:13 .... 70, 123
12:15 146
15:20 217
15:30 296
16:5 123

I CORINTHIANS

4:9 298
7:22 293
9:9 183
9:25 295
9:26–27 296
15:32 297
16:9 123

II CORINTHIANS

6:14 172
11:26–27 270

GALATIANS

3:24 116
6:2 244

EPHESIANS

1:3–14 236
6:1 104
6:14 93

PHILIPPIANS

1:1 293
1:27 296
3:14 296
4:3 297

COLOSSIANS

3:20 104
4:14 228

I TIMOTHY

2:9 100
3:2 123
3:16 236
5:10 75
5:18 183

II TIMOTHY

1:5 111
2:5 295
2:15 221
3:15 101
4:7 296

PHILEMON

1 293
1:2 f 123

HEBREWS

10:33 297
11:9 18
11:13 18
11:37 163
12:1 296
13:2 70
13:5 158

JAMES

1:1 293
3:4 278
4:15 86
5:14 200

I PETER

1:7 219
3:3 100
4:9 123
5:4 295

II PETER

1:1 293

I JOHN

2:27 200

JUDE

1:1 293
1:3 297

REVELATION

2:17 70
2:27 206
3:8 26
3:9 73
3:20 .... 26, 39
5:9–10 236
6:12 14
9:9 266
14:2–3 237
15:3–4 236
18:22 236
19:10 73
19:11, 14 267
19:13, 15 194
21:1 275
21:2 131
21:21 242
21:25 241
22:15 269